ROYAL HISTORICAL SOCIETY
STUDIES IN HISTORY

New Series

THE PRACTICE OF PENANCE
900–1050

Studies in History New Series

Editorial Board

Professor Martin Daunton (*Convenor*)
Professor David Eastwood
Dr Steven Gunn
Professor Colin Jones
Professor Peter Mandler
Dr Simon Walker
Professor Kathleen Burk (*Honorary Treasurer*)

FOR JAN AND BERNARD

Miniature from the Fulda Sacramentary (c. 980) illustrating the 'ordo for giving penance in the usual way on Ash Wednesday' (Niedersächsische Staats- und Universitätsbibliothek, Göttingen, Cod. theol. 231, fo. 187r). Reproduced by courtesy of the Neidersächsische Staats- und Universitätsbibliothek, Göttingen.

THE PRACTICE OF PENANCE
900–1050

Sarah Hamilton

THE ROYAL HISTORICAL SOCIETY
THE BOYDELL PRESS

© Sarah Hamilton 2001

All rights reserved. Except as permitted under current legislation
no part of this work may be photocopied, stored in a retrieval system,
published, performed in public, adapted, broadcast,
transmitted, recorded or reproduced in any form or by any means,
without the prior permission of the copyright owner

The right of Sarah Hamilton to be identified as
the author of this work has been asserted in accordance with
sections 77 and 78 of the Copyright, Designs and Patents Act 1988

First published 2001
The Royal Historical Society, London
in association with
The Boydell Press, Woodbridge
Reprinted in paperback and transferred to digital printing 2011
The Boydell Press, Woodbridge

ISBN 97 0 86193 250 4 hardback
ISBN 978 1 84383 638 4 paperback

The Boydell Press is an imprint of Boydell & Brewer Ltd
PO Box 9, Woodbridge, Suffolk IP12 3DF, UK
and of Boydell & Brewer Inc,
668 Mt Hope Avenue, Rochester, NY 14620, USA
website: www.boydellandbrewer.com

A CIP catalogue record for this book is available
from the British Library

Library of Congress Catalog Card Number 00–069688

This publication is printed on acid-free paper

Contents

	Page
Acknowledgements	ix
Abbreviations	xi
Introduction	1
1 The church law of penance: the evidence of the collections	25
2 Education and communication: councils, synodal sermons and capitularies	51
3 Penance and the regular life	77
4 The penitential liturgy: unity or diversity?	104
5 The penitential liturgy: regional diversity	136
6 Penance and the wider world	173
Afterword	207

Appendices

1. The distribution of the Romano-German pontifical	211
2. Penitential rites outside the Romano-German pontifical tradition	224
Bibliography	239
Index	269

Publication of this volume was aided by a grant from the Scouloudi Foundation, in association with the Institute of Historical Research.

Acknowledgements

It is a pleasure to acknowledge the help that I have received in writing this book. Most of the research was financed with the help of a British Academy doctoral studentship, a Scouloudi Fellowship from the Institute of Historical Research and a Three-Month Award from the British School at Rome; the text was finished whilst I held a British Academy postdoctoral research fellowship. It was completed with the assistance of the staff of the following libraries: the Warburg Institute; the University of London Library; the Institute of Historical Research; King's College London; the British Library; Cambridge University Library; Corpus Christi College, Cambridge; the Bodleian Library; the University Library of Glasgow; the John Rylands Library; the Biblioteca Apostolica Vaticana; the Biblioteca Vallicelliana; the Bibliothèque nationale; the Staatsbibliothek, Bamberg; the Preussischer Staatsbibliothek, Berlin; the Bayerische Staatsbibliothek, Munich; the Diözesan- und Dombibliothek, Cologne; and the Herzog-August-Bibliothek, Wolfenbüttel. The jacket/frontispiece illustration is reproduced by kind permission of the Niedersächsische Staats- und Universitätsbibliothek, Göttingen. Chapters 5 and 6 benefited immeasurably from the constructive criticism of those who heard parts of earlier versions at the early medieval seminar at the Institute of Historical Research, at the Leeds international medieval congress, at the Ecclesiastical History Society conferences and at the medieval seminars at the universities of Glasgow, Edinburgh and St Andrews. Thanks are also due to Rob Meens, Mayke de Jong and Rob Bartlett who provided me with advance copies of their research. Diana Webb and Marty Claussen provided valuable information. Rosamond McKitterick and David d'Avray examined the doctoral thesis on which this book is based, and their observations and advice on that occasion helped me immeasurably in turning the thesis into the book. Tim Reuter read a draft of the whole text and offered pertinent and detailed criticisms. The comments of Simon Walker proved invaluable. Anne Duggan co-supervised my thesis and it owes much to her attention to detail and guidance on the problems of canon law. My debt to my other supervisor, Jinty Nelson, is perhaps more obvious; her scholarship and friendship have been a source of inspiration and comfort over the years, and her comments on a draft of the introduction helped me to finish what seemed to be an impossible task. Whatever faults remain are, of course, my own. That it was finished owes a great deal to the friendship of Carol Davidson-Cragoe, Alice Hamilton, Anke

Holdenried, Stephen Lee and Michelle Lucey-Roper. My greatest debt, however, is to my parents, Jan and Bernard, without whose intellectual, emotional and material support this book would not have been written.

Sarah Hamilton
Exeter

Abbreviations

BAV	Biblioteca Apostolica Vaticana
BL	British Library
BN	Bibliothèque nationale
Bussbücher I	Die Bussbücher und die Bussdisciplin der Kirche, ed. H. J. Schmitz, Mainz 1883
Bussbücher II	Die Bussbücher und das kanonische Bussverfahren, ed. H. J. Schmitz, Düsseldorf 1898
CCCM	Corpus Christianorum Continuatio Mediaevalis
CCEL	Corpus Scriptorum Ecclesiasticorum Latinorum
CCM	Corpus consuetudinum monasticarum cura pontificii Athenaei sancti Anselmi de urbe praesidiisque instituti Herwegeniani, ed. K. Hallinger, Siegburg 1963–
CCSL	Corpus Christianorum Series Latina
Chrodegang I	S. Chrodegangi Metensis episcopi (742–66): regula canonicorum aus dem Leidener Codex Vossianus Latinus 94 mit Umschrift der Tironischen Noten, ed. W. Schmitz, Hanover 1889
Chrodegang II	Chrodegang of Metz, Regula canonicorum, PL lxxxix. 1057–95
CLLA	K. Gamber, Codices liturgici latini antiquiores, 2nd edn, Oxford 1968
CP	Cracow pontifical (Pontificale Cracoviense saeculi xi): Cracow, Jagellionian Library, MS. 2057, ed. Z. Obertynski (HBS c, 1967–71)
DA	Deutsches Archiv für Erforschung des Mittelalters namens der Monumenta Germaniae Historica
Das Dekret	H. Hoffmann and R. Pokorny, Das Dekret des Bischofs Burchard von Worms: Textstufen–frühe Verbreitung–Vorlagen (MGH, Hilfsmittel xii, 1991)
DTC	Dictionnaire de théologie catholique, Paris 1930–46
EHR	English Historical Review
EME	Early Medieval Europe
HBS	Henry Bradshaw Society
HCC	P. Fournier and G. Le Bras, Histoire des collections canoniques en occident, Paris 1931
JEH	Journal of Ecclesiastical History
LMA	Lexikon des Mittelalters, Munich–Zurich, 1980–99
Mansi, Concilia	J. D. Mansi, Sacrorum conciliorum nova et amplissima collectio, Venice 1759–98, repr. Graz 1960

MGH	Monumenta Germaniae Historica
MGH, *Capit. Ep. I*	MGH, *Capitula episcoporum*, I, ed. P. Brommer, Hanover 1984
MGH, *Capit. Ep. II*	MGH, *Capitula episcoporum*, II, ed. R. Pokorny and M. Stratmann, Hanover 1995
MGH, *Capit. Ep. III*	MGH, *Capitula episcoporum*, III, ed. R. Pokorny, Hanover 1995
MGH, *Capitularia II*	*Capitularia regum francorum*, II, ed. A. Boretius and V. Krause (MGH Legum ii/2, Hanover 1897)
MGH, *Concilia II*	*Concilia aevi Karolini*, I, ed. A. Werminghoff (MGH, Legum iii, Hanover–Leipzig 1906)
MGH, *Concilia III*	*Concilia aevi Karolini*, II: 843–59, ed. W. Hartmann (MGH, Hanover 1984)
MGH, *Concilia VI*	*Concilia aevi Saxonici*, I: 916–60, ed. E.-D. Hehl and H. Fuhrmann (MGH, Hanover 1987)
MGH, *Constitutiones I*	MGH, *Constitutiones et acta publica imperatorum et regum*, I: 911–1197, ed. L. Weiland (MGH, Legum iv/1, Hanover 1893)
MGH, *Ordines de celebrando concilio*	MGH, *Ordines de celebrando concilio*, ed. H. Schneider, Hanover 1996
MGH, Schriften	Schriften der MGH
MGH, SRG	MGH, Scriptores rerum Germanicarum in usum scholarum separatim editi
MGH, SRG n.s.	MGH, Scriptores rerum Germanicarum nova series
MGH, SS	MGH, Scriptores
Miscellanea	Miscellanea del centro di studi medioevali, Milan
OR	*Ordines romani du haut moyen âge*, ed. M. Andrieu, Louvain 1931–61
PG	*Patrologiae Graeca cursus completus, series graeca*, ed. J.-P. Migne, Paris 1857–66
PL	*Patrologiae cursus completus, series latina*, ed. J.-P. Migne, Paris 1844–64
PRG	*Pontifical romano-germanique du Xe siècle*, ed. C. Vogel and R. Elze (SeT, ccvi, ccvii, cclxix, 1963, 1972)
Rather, *Synodica*	*Die Briefe des Bischofs Rather von Verona*, ed. F. Weigle (MGH, Die Briefe der deutschen Kaiserzeit i, Weimar 1949), no. xxv, pp. 124–37
RB	*Règle de Saint Benoît*, ed. A. de Vogüe with J. Neufville (SC clxxxi–lxxxvi, 1972)
Rev. Bén.	*Revue Bénédictine*
SC	Sources Chrétiennes
SCH	Studies in Church History
SeT	Studi e Testi, Vatican City
Settimane	Settimane di studio del centro italiano di studi sull'alto medioevo, Spoleto

SF	*Sacramentarium Fuldense saeculi X: Cod. theol. 231 der K. Universitätsbibliothek zu Göttingen*, ed. G. Richter and A. Schönfelder, Fulda 1912 (repr. HBS ci, 1972–7)
SGR	*Sacramentaire Grégorien: ses principales formes d'après les plus anciens manuscrits*, ed. J. Deshusses (Spicilegium Friburgense xvi, xxiv, xxxviii, 1971, 1979, 1982)
SM	*Studi medievali*
TRHS	*Transactions of the Royal Historical Society*
Typologie	*Typologie des sources du moyen âge occidental*, Turnhout
VMA	'Vita Mathildis reginae antiquior', in *Die Lebensbeschreibungen der Königen Mathilde*, ed. B. Schütte (MGH, SRG lxvi, 1994)
VMP	'Vita Mathildis reginae posterior', in *Die Lebensbeschreibungen der Königen Mathilde*, ed. B. Schütte (MGH, SRG lxvi, 1994)
VN	βιοσ και πολιτεια του 'οσιου πατρος 'ημων Νειλου του Νεου [Life of Nilus of Grottaferrata], ed. G. Giovanelli, Grottaferrata 1972
ZRG Kan. Abt.	*Zeitschrift der Savigny-Stiftung für Rechtsgeschichte: Kanonistische Abteilung* (volume numbers given are those for *Kanonistische Abteilung*)

Introduction

In April 999 Arduin of Ivrea, a leading Italian nobleman and future contender for the kingdom of Italy, appeared before a church council in Rome, presided over by the Emperor Otto III and his newly consecrated pope, Silvester II. Arduin publicly confessed his guilt for the murder of Bishop Peter of Vercelli in 997, and the council awarded him the penance which would have been given to him if he had confessed secretly: he should put down his arms, eat no meat, kiss no man nor woman, wear no linen clothes, never remain more than two nights in one place unless he was sick, and not take communion until his deathbed. Nor should he take action against those who had sworn against him. He was excommunicated, becoming in effect an itinerant pilgrim exiled from society; alternatively, he could become a monk.[1] His sentence was accompanied by an imperial grant of his property and that of his accomplices to the church of Vercelli.[2] The case against Arduin was brought by one of Otto III's advisers, Leo, bishop of Vercelli, but there was a tradition of hostility between Arduin and his family and the Ottonians as well as with the see of Vercelli.[3] Arduin himself was proclaimed king of Italy in 1002 on Otto III's death. Although effectively removed from office by King Henry II of Germany's expedition to Italy in 1004, he was not finally dealt with until Henry's second Italian expedition in 1014.[4] If Arduin performed his prescribed penance at all, it was not for life.

Though mostly ignored by historians of penance, this case has been noted by one historian of early medieval Italian justice as an illustration of how penance could be administered as a judicial penalty by Church and Emperor acting together against a common enemy.[5] For by c. 1000 penance had a long history as a political punishment administered by rulers as well as bishops: exile to a monastery for political enemies had been practised since the

---

[1] MGH, *Constitutiones I*, no. xxv, p. 53; F. Bougard, *La Justice dans le royaume d'Italie de la fin du VIIIe siècle au début du XIe siècle*, Rome 1995, 239, 412: no. 108.
[2] MGH, *Diplomatum regum et imperatorum Germaniae*, II/i: *Ottonis III. Diplomata*, ed. T. Sickel, Hanover 1893, nos cccxxiii (7 May 999), ccclxxxiii (7 Nov. 1000), pp. 748–51, 811–12.
[3] G. Sergi, 'Movimento signorile e affermazione ecclesiastica nel contesto distrettuale di Pombia e Novara fra X e XI secolo', SM 3rd ser. xvi (1975), 153–206; L. Fasola, 'Arduin von Ivrea', in LMA i. 915–16; G. Wolf, 'Der sogenannte "Gegenkönig" Arduin von Ivrea (ca. 955–1015)', *Archiv für Diplomatik: Schriftsgeschichte Siegel- und Wappenkunde* xxxix (1993), 19–34 at pp. 23–5.
[4] S. Hirsch and H. Bresslau, *Jahrbücher des deutschen Reichs unter Heinrichs II.*, Leipzig 1862, 1875, i. 302–14.
[5] Bougard, *La Justice*, 235–43.

seventh century.[6] Further, early medieval bishops, not only in Italy but elsewhere, were important administrators of local authority, and penance with its accompanying penalties was one of the more useful weapons in their armoury.[7] For the effects of the practice of penance were never confined to the spiritual realm, as Arduin's case demonstrates, because penitential practice was a reflection of the symbiotic relationship between the spiritual and secular worlds. Arduin's subsequent political career demonstrates not only the fragility of both the ecclesiastical and imperial authorities in failing successfully to impose a penitential life sentence but also draws attention to the problems posed by most sources for penitential practice: they are prescriptive, representing the clergy's aspirations, not reality. Arduin's penance therefore identifies some of the principal themes of this book: the role of penance in the clergy's relationship both with the laity and each other; the problems of the aspirational nature of the sources for penance and how these may be overcome; and, most important, what was involved in the practice of penance itself during the earlier Middle Ages.

The tripartite model for the history of medieval penance

The Latin word for penance, *poenitentia*, denotes the process by which Christians sought to atone for their sins through confession, through penitential acts which demonstrated their repentance, and through good works, in order to ensure their salvation at the Last Judgement.[8] Penance was a preventive act, designed to protect Christians from the consequences of their sinful mortal life in their immortal life.

Arduin was told that although he had confessed his sin publicly the synod had awarded him the same penance as it would had he confessed secretly.[9]

---

[6] M. de Jong, 'Power and humility in Carolingian society: the public penance of Louis the Pious', EME i (1992), 29–52 at pp. 43–7, and 'What was public about public penance? *paenitentia publica* and justice in the Carolingian world', in *La giustizia nel'alto medioevo*, ii (Settimane xliii, 1996), 863–902 at pp. 877–87.
[7] H. Platelle, 'La Violence et ses remèdes en Flandre au XIe siècle', in *Sacris Erudiri: Jaarboek voor Godsdienstwetenschappen* xx (1971), 101–73; W. Hartmann, 'I vescovo com giudice', *Rivista di storia della chiesa in Italia* xl (1986), 320–41; J. Chelini, *L'Aube de moyen âge: naissance de la chrétienté occidentale: la vie religieuse des laïcs dans l'Europe carolingienne (750–900)*, Paris 1991, 360–441; Bougard, *La Justice*, 236–43. For the argument that penitentials were used only by bishops rather than at a lower level by priests see F. Kerff, 'Libri paenitentiales und kirchliche Strafgerichtsbarkeit bis zum Decretum Gratiani: ein Diskussionsvorschlag', *ZRG Kan. Abt.* lxxv (1989), 23–57. It is rebutted by Rob Meens in 'The frequency and nature of early medieval penance', in P. Biller and A. J. Minnis (eds), *Handling sin: confession in the Middle Ages*, Woodbridge 1998, 35–61. Both sides of this argument are more fully evaluated in ch. 1.
[8] On the etymology of *poenitentia*, and its relationship to the Greek *metanoia* of the New Testament see É. Amann, 'Pénitence–Repentir', in *DTC* xii/1, 722–3.
[9] 'Ideoque quia publice confessus est, eandem poenitenciam vult ei sancta synodus imponere quae ei daretur, si secreto confiteretur, manu sua episcopum interfecisse': MGH,

This distinction between public and secret penance is one found in very few sources from the early ninth century onwards: the bipartite system of penance is, however, one found in most works of modern scholarship.[10] It is fundamental to the current historiographical orthodoxy which divides the development of early medieval penance into three stages.

According to stage one of this model, the early medieval world inherited the practice of canonical penance from late antiquity. At the beginning of Lent the bishop imposed penance in a public ritual: sinners confessed their sins, were enrolled in a group of penitents and dressed in sackcloth (*cilicium*) before being expelled from the church to perform penance. On Maundy Thursday the penitents were readmitted and reconciled in a similarly public ritual. But even after being reconciled the penitent remained unable to marry or hold public or sacerdotal office, and late antique penance could be performed only once in a lifetime.[11] This rite was designed to maintain the purity of the early church community through exclusion of those who had violated ecclesiastical precepts and also to deter others from committing similar offences. Public shame was thus integral to penance. However, the fact that penance could not be repeated and that it entailed such enormous penalties deterred people from seeking it before their deathbeds. It is thought to have been less and less used in the sixth and seventh centuries. Consequently the practice of 'secret' or tariff penance, often termed in modern scholarship private penance, developed to meet the need, posed by the decline of canonical penance, for atonement and restitution after sin. Seemingly originating in monastic practice, the penitent confessed his (or her) sin to his confessor priest, who then prescribed the form that his penance should take according to the tariff prescribed in the penitentials.[12] Whether the

---

Constitutiones I, no. xxv, p. 53. A similar distinction was made by Bishop Fulbert of Chartres in a letter to Bishop Radulf of Senlis (1018x1020) about Radulf's request to stand trial for his involvement in the murder of Evrardus rather than expiate it through secret satisfaction: *Letters and poems of Fulbert of Chartres*, ed. F. Behrends, Oxford 1976, no. xxxii, pp. 58–60. This case has been studied by E. Peters, 'The death of the subdean: ecclesiastical order and disorder in eleventh-century Francia', in B. S. Bachrach and D. Nicholas (eds), *Law, custom and the social fabric in medieval Europe: essays in honour of Bryce Lyon*, Kalamazoo, Michigan 1992, 51–71.

[10] It was articulated most clearly by Cyrille Vogel, *Le Pécheur et la pénitence au moyen âge*, Paris 1969, 24–33, 36. See also his *Les 'Libri paenitentiales'* (Typologie xxvi, 1978), rev. A. J. Frantzen 1985, 39–43. This division predates Vogel, however, and can be found in B. Poschmann, *Die abendländische Kirchenbusse im frühen Mittelalter*, Breslau 1930, and *Penance and the anointing of the sick*, Freiburg–London 1964 (English trans. by F. Courtney of *Busse und letzte Ölung*, Freiburg-im-Breisgau 1951), and also in É. Amann, 'Pénitence–sacrement: la pénitence privée: son organisation, premières spéculations a son sujet', in *DTC* xii/1, 845–948.

[11] For further details on this interpretation of public penance in late antiquity see B. Poschmann, *Die abendländische Kirchenbusse in Ausgang des christlichen Altertums*, Munich 1928, and *Penance*, 81–121; É. Amann, 'Pénitence–sacrement: la pénitence primitive', in *DTC* xii/1, 749–845; C. Vogel, *Le Pécheur et la pénitence dans l'église ancienne*, Paris 1966.

[12] Singular penitents are referred to as male throughout following the conventions of the

penitent received immediate absolution at the same time as confession or whether he had to wait to be absolved and reconciled with the Church until after he had performed his penance is a problem as yet unresolved, and seems to vary from source to source, penitential to penitential.[13] Although this process may not have been secret in a modern sense – it is difficult to conceal a penitential fast, for example, whether you live in a big house or in a village – the penitent was not identified as such in a formal public ritual, and public shame was not an essential element of the process. Instead the focus appeared to be on the individual's relationship with God rather than his or her role within the wider community.[14] Unlike 'canonical' penance, this process could be repeated as often as required by the penitent's lifestyle. Last but not least, secret penance could be administered by a priest rather than a bishop. It used to be thought that the practice of secret penance originated in sixth-century Irish monasticism, and was spread to England and the continent by missionary monks in the seventh century, but recent work has demonstrated that secret penance was not a specifically insular invention but rather that late sixth-century Frankish aristocrats supported the Irish missionary Columbanus precisely because the practice of secret penance had already evolved independently on the continent during the sixth century.[15]

Stage two of this traditional model occurs in the later eighth and ninth centuries, when the Carolingian reforming bishops raised the profile of penance as part of their attempts to reform the Frankish Church, and encourage participation within the Christian life by those living within the Frankish kingdoms.[16] In so doing they sought to promote the practice of two separate forms of penance, public and private, the so-called Carolingian

---

texts of the period; the Latin male gender included feminine and neuter genders as appropriate. Penance was, of course, conceived of as having a universal application.

[13] Current orthodoxy suggests that reconciliation was introduced into the rite for secret penance in the ninth century: J. A. Jungmann, *Die lateinischen Bussriten in ihrer geschichtlichen Entwicklung*, Innsbruck 1932, 267; J. Dallen, 'The absence of a ritual of reconciliation in Celtic penance', in A. W. Sadler (ed.), *The journey of western spirituality*, Chico 1981, 79–106. Reconciliation did not become a certain part of a one-stage rite until much later; for a date c. 1000 see Jungmann, *Bussriten*, 191–5; Poschmann, *Penance*, 145. For doubts about the evidence adduced by these two historians for this date see R. Kottje, 'Busspraxis und Bussritus', in *Segni e riti nella chiesa altomedievale occidentale* (Settimane xxxiii, 1987), 369–95 at p. 391, who argues that evidence for a one-stage ritual is present in the penitentials from at least the ninth century if not earlier.

[14] K. Dooley, 'From penance to confession: the Celtic contribution', *Bijdragen: Tijdschrift voor filosofie en theologie* xliii (1982), 390–411.

[15] For the argument that it may have also been an indigenous continental development see ibid. and for an excellent summary of the older view of insular beginnings interspersed with pointers towards private penance's continental origins see A. J. Frantzen, *The literature of penance in Anglo-Saxon England*, New Brunswick, NJ 1983, 5–7, 19–60. On the indigenous Frankish developments preceding Columbanus' mission see I. Wood, 'The *Vita Columbani* and Merovingian hagiography', *Peritia* i (1982), 63–80 at pp. 72–4.

[16] On the Carolingian reforms in general see R. McKitterick, *The Frankish Church and the Carolingian reforms, 789–895*, London 1977.

dichotomy identified by Cyrille Vogel: public sins merit public penance, hidden sins hidden penance.[17] This dichotomy emerged at the end of the eighth century and was popularised in legal texts – councils, capitularies, penitentials – from the early ninth century onwards. It was repeated in the tenth century at the Council of Trier (927).[18] But in both the Carolingian and post-Carolingian period, as this study will show, the dichotomy was mostly confined to legal texts: the authors of liturgical and narrative texts, as we shall see, usually preferred to take refuge in the ambiguity of an unadorned *poenitentia*.[19] The Carolingian bishops encouraged both forms of penance. In episcopal *capitula* and conciliar canons we see a concerted attempt on the bishops' part to promote the widespread practice of regular penance together with regular communion by the laity: Theodulf of Orléans, in his first capitulary (c. 800), encouraged the laity to confess their sins at the beginning of Lent as part of their preparations for Easter.[20] An early ninth-century Bavarian council ordained that Christians should prepare for regular communion (every three or four weeks) through confession, penance and sexual abstinence.[21] The bishops also promoted the practice of penance through

---

[17] For a summary of the view that the concurrent existence of two forms of penitential practice was peculiar to the Carolingians and had not occurred before see Kottje, 'Busspraxis', 369–71. For the identification of the dichotomy see Vogel, *Le Pécheur au moyen âge*, 24–7. It is found in one of the reform councils, that of the Council of Reims (813): 'Ut discretio servanda sit inter paenitentes qui publice et qui absconce paenitere debent': c. xxxi, MGH, *Concilia II*, i. 256. But there is earlier evidence for this distinction in the *Paenitentiale Remense* (c. 800), IV, cc. 50–1: 'Si publice peccaverint, publice peniteant. Si occulte peccaverint, occulte peniteant': *Das Poenitentiale Remense und der sogen.: excarpsus Cummeani: Überlieferung, Quellen und Entwicklung zweiter kontinentaler Bussbücher aus der 1. Hälfte des 8. Jahrhunderts*, ed. F. Asbach, Regensburg 1975, 30. It is made more explicit in Theodulf of Orléans's second capitulary, 'quod autem supra diximus de his agatur, qui publice ad confessionem venerint et publice paenitentiam egerint. Quod si occulte actum est et occulte ad sacerdotem venerint et puram confessionem fecerint, occulte poenitere debent': c.vii.8, MGH, *Capit. Ep. I*, 166–7. This capitulary has been variously dated to c. 802 (MGH, *Capit. Ep. I*, 142–5) or more recently to c. 850 (MGH, *Capit. Ep. III*, 91 n. 70). For these pre-813 citations of the dichotomy see de Jong, 'What was public', 867–8.
[18] c. xv, MGH, *Concilia VI*, 84. This canon was derived from the ninth-century episcopal capitulary of Radulf of Bourges.
[19] There are of course exceptions to this rule, the major one being the *ordo agentibus publicam paenitentiam* which first appeared in the Gelasian Sacramentary, the oldest manuscript of which (Vatican, BAV, MS Vat. lat. 316) dates from Frankia c. 750 and was repeated in later sacramentaries, for example the Fulda Sacramentary (c. 975x980), no. 56: *SF*, 46. But the *ordo* in the Roman-German pontifical (c. 950) is not as specific; it forms parts of the *ordo* for the beginning of Lent and the divine office for Maundy Thursday: *PRG* ii. 14, 59.
[20] c. 36, MGH, *Capit. Ep. I*, 133–4. On the general connection between communion and confession see J. Avril, 'Remarques sur un aspect de la vie paroissale: la pratique de la confession et de la communion du Xe au XIVe siècle', in *L'Encadrement religieux des fidèles au moyen-âge et jusqu'au Concile de Trente: la paroisse – le clergé – la pastorale – la dévotion: actes du 109e congrès national des sociétés savantes, Dijon 1984: section d'histoire médiévale et de philologie*, i, Paris 1985, 345–63 at pp. 349–50. For a refinement of Avril's work see Meens, 'Frequency', 37–8.
[21] Capitula Bavarica, c. vi, MGH, *Capit. Ep. III*, 196.

ensuring the widespread composition and copying of penitentials for its administration. The decrees of the Council of Châlon (813) which legislated against the 'texts called penitentials whose errors are certain and whose authors uncertain', and the Council of Paris (829) which condemned erroneous penitential *libelli* to be burnt, seem to have been aimed at ensuring that only texts authorised by the bishops continued in circulation.[22]

The inclusion of a rite for the administration of penance, placed before the list of penitential tariffs, also became common in the ninth century and suggests an attempt to make the penitentials more usable.[23] At the same time the Carolingian bishops revived, as they thought, or reinvented, as it seems to modern historians, the late antique ritual for 'canonical' penance as public penance.[24] Drawing on Visigothic legislation from the seventh century, *paenitentia publica*, as it was sometimes referred to, as defined by the bishops, followed the basic procedure outlined for 'canonical' penance, and remained an episcopal prerogative. The consequences for those undergoing public penance were severe according to the prescriptions of several ninth-century councils: they should not assume the belt of knighthood, *cingulum militare*, nor marry, nor fulfil any public office; they should eat no meat and must travel everywhere on foot.[25] Whether the consequences of public penance – abstinence from sex, war and public office – had to last a lifetime or merely for the period of the penance varies from source to source, but all envisaged a loss in status for any individual of high standing.[26] Loss of status helps to explain the notoriety of the most famous case of public penance in the early medieval period, that of Louis the Pious, who was, according to the Annals of Saint-Bertin, accused of many crimes in the assembly which met at Compiègne in the autumn of 833 by his son Lothar acting in league with various bishops, led by Ebo, archbishop of Rheims. Here, the emperor, who

---

[22] Allen Frantzen demonstrated that the Frankish bishops sought to regulate rather than abolish the use of penitentials: 'The significance of the Frankish penitentials', *JEH* xxx (1979), 409–21, against the view of R. Pierce [McKitterick], 'The "Frankish" penitentials', in D. Baker (ed.), *The materials, sources and methods of ecclesiastical history* (SCH xi, 1975), 31–9, that the bishops sought to eradicate the use of the penitentials.

[23] Frantzen, *Literature*, 105–6. One of the earliest texts to include an *ordo confessionis* was the penitential compiled by Halitgar of Cambrai, c. 830, *Bussbücher* II, 290–300.

[24] Mayke de Jong's work on public penance in the ninth century demonstrates how largely it was a creation of ninth-century bishops: 'Power and humility', and 'What was public'.

[25] The Council of Mainz (847) decreed that a parricide should not assume the *miliciae cingulum* nor marry: c. xx, no. xiv, MGH, *Concilia* III, 171; the Synod of Pavia (850) that anyone subject to public penance should not use his sword-belt nor administer any sort of public office: ibid. 225–6; the Council of Worms (868) in c. xxvi that anyone guilty of killing a priest should eat no meat, nor take up arms or travel on horseback: Mansi, *Concilia* xv. 874. These examples are all cited by Karl Leyser in 'Early medieval canon law and the beginnings of knighthood', in L. Fenske, W. Rösener and T. Zotz (eds), *Institutionen, Kultur und Gesellschaft im Mittelalter: Festschrift für Josef Fleckenstein zu seinem 65. Geburtstag*, Sigmaringen 1984, 549–66 at pp. 555–7 (repr. in his *Communications and power in medieval Europe*, I: *The Carolingian and Ottonian centuries*, ed. T. Reuter, London 1994, 51–71).

[26] Ibid. 555–62; de Jong, 'Power and humility', 33–4.

had previously been captured and imprisoned by Lothar, was forced 'to put down his weapons and change his dress' and exiled, as a penitent, to a monastery; he had effectively been deposed from rulership over the Franks. Louis was subsequently rescued by his younger son, Louis the German, after a change in the political alliances which had led to his capture and forced penance; he regained his throne in 834.[27] But, as Mayke de Jong has suggested in her study of the case, for all concerned Louis's enforced penance was a 'bridge too far': the consequences of a royal penance for the *regnum* were too extreme.[28] These pieces of evidence suggest that public penance was not intended to be universal but rather aimed at those of superior rank within the Carolingian world. It was a procedure supposedly reserved for particularly heinous and notorious sins, *scandala*, such as the murder of kinsfolk or bishops, as in Arduin's case, which were thus atoned for in a public manner.[29] Similar crimes, as long as they had not attracted public attention, could be atoned for through secret penance, according to the alleged Carolingian dichotomy. The significance of the Carolingian period in the history of the development of penance is a subject to which we shall return.

The twelfth and thirteenth centuries provide the backdrop to stage three of the historiographical model. This was the period which led up to and followed on from the *omnes utriusque* decree of the Fourth Lateran Council of 1215, enjoining annual confession on all Christians.[30] This decree heralded a vast expansion in the numbers following the practice hitherto known as secret penance which is seen as evolving at this time into one more akin to late medieval confession. This change is supposedly accompanied by a shift from the early medieval emphasis on the external performance of penance, the penitential tariff, as necessary for reconciliation with the Almighty, to more emphasis being placed on the contrition felt by the individual.[31] At about the same time, c. 1200, a tripartite system is seen as coming into place: solemn penance (the heir of public penance), penitential pilgrimage (allegedly an innovation) and private penance (the heir of secret penance).[32]

---

[27] *Annales de Saint-Bertin*, ed. F. Grat, J. Vielliard and S. Clémencet, intro. L. Levillain, Paris 1964, a. 833, pp. 8–12.
[28] 'It seems as if Louis's public penance in 833 had been one bridge too far – for all parties involved': de Jong, 'Power and humility', 52.
[29] Ibid. 34.
[30] c. 21, *Decrees of the ecumenical councils*, I: *Nicea to Lateran V*, ed. N. P. Tanner, London–Washington, DC 1990, 245. In modern scholarship the importance of the twelfth century as a period of change in the history of penance was first highlighted by K. Müller, 'Der Umschwung in der Lehre von der Busse während des 12. Jahrhunderts', in *Theologische Abhandlungen: Carol von Weizsäcker zu seinem siebsigsten Geburtstage 11 December 1892*, Freiburg 1892, 289–320.
[31] P. Anciaux, *La Théologie du sacrement de pénitence au XIIe siècle*, Louvain 1949, 7–55; Vogel, *Le Pécheur au moyen âge*, 27–36.
[32] For the dating of the appearance of this tripartite system to c. 1200 see ibid. 33–6. Mary Mansfield's research demonstrates that the tripartite system is, however, largely a scholastic

Public and private penance: a useful distinction?

All three stages of this model are constructed largely from the evidence of prescriptive legal sources – collections of canon law, conciliar decrees and episcopal capitularies. It is, however, much easier to simplify penance into a bipartite practice of either secret or public penance in the abstract than it is in reality: those present at the Council of Rome in 999 were aware of the distinction between public and secret, yet they viewed the sentence they imposed on Arduin, which seems to have all the elements one would expect of a public penance – abstinence from war, marriage and home – as a secret one. They were interchangeable parts of a single process. Recent work has also highlighted the gap between the distinction made in the legal sources and evidence found in narrative sources for more mixed forms of penitential practice, combining elements from both public and secret penance. For instance, in the mid eleventh century Ekkehard of St Gall tells a story of a couple c. 830 whose penance for the sin of having sexual relations in Lent followed most of the outward forms of public penance but was performed before their parish priest.[33] Historians in other spheres have recently challenged the assumption that the distinction between public and private was a familiar one in the early Middle Ages. This assumption is characterised by Georges Duby's statement that the distinction between the public world, 'that which is open to the community, and subject to the authority of its magistrates – and the private' is a 'commonsensical' one which needs no further discussion.[34] But the distinction is not a timeless one – in other words it has to be contextualised in time and place.[35] Roman law distinguished between public and private law: in theory public law pertained to the state,

---

invention with little reflection in practice: *The humiliation of sinners: public penance in thirteenth-century France*, Ithaca–London 1995.

[33] *Ekkehard IV, Casus Sancti Galli*, ed. H. F. Haefele, Darmstadt 1980, 70–2. For a detailed consideration of this case see M. de Jong, 'Pollution, penance and sanctity: Ekkehard's *Life* of Iso of St Gall', in J. Hill and M. Swan (eds), *The community, the family and the saint: patterns of power in early medieval Europe*, Turnhout 1998, 145–58. It is also cited in Meens, 'Frequency', 48–9, and the example is discussed by Kottje in 'Busspraxis', 393–4. This case is considered further in ch. 6.

[34] 'Introduction: private power, public power', in P. Ariès and G. Duby (eds), *A history of private life*, II: *Revelations of the medieval world*, Cambridge, Mass.–London 1988 (trans. by A. Goldhammer of *Histoire de la vie privée*, II: *De l'Europe féodale à la Renaissance*, Paris 1985), 3–31.

[35] On the problems arising from historians seeking to impose modern distinctions of public and private onto the early Middle Ages see J. L. Nelson's criticisms of the first volume of Duby's series, *Histoire de la vie privée*, to be translated: 'The problematic in the private', *Social History* xv (1990), 355–64. In her work on early medieval queenship Pauline Stafford has also shown the failure of these modern distinctions when applied to the early medieval evidence: *Queens, concubines and dowagers: the king's wife in the early Middle Ages*, London–Washington, DC 1998 (repr. of 1983 edn).

private law to the individual, but this distinction was not made consistently or very often.³⁶ Further, the term *res publica* also carried with it heavy moral connotations; therefore public penance probably pertained to *scandala* which offended the whole community – the common weal – and hence were more likely to involve people of high status whilst secret penance was reserved for cases of individual conscience.³⁷ The doubts cast about the possibility of drawing a clear distinction between public and private in other spheres of medieval life help to reinforce those already raised with reference to the practice of penance.

Medieval penance: a historiographical survey

But before looking at the implications of this work, we need to consider how and why the three-stage model for the history of medieval penance with its bipartite framework of secret and public penance came to be erected. Only by understanding the paths which the historiography of penance has followed, can we identify any omissions in or problems posed by the work to date.

The historiography of medieval penance has been very partisan. Both sides are characterised by a teleological approach which has been preoccupied with seeking the origins of later medieval practice in the early Church. The dominant model thus presented the history of penance in terms of a decline in the use of public penance from late antiquity onwards, albeit with a brief resurgence under the Carolingians, followed by the inexorable rise and eventual dominance of secret penance. The origins of this approach lie in the sixteenth century: a key issue in the Reformation was Protestant criticism of the medieval penitential system as an ecclesiastical institution not founded in the Bible but invented by the Church. Catholics responded to this critique by defending the apostolic origins of penance.³⁸ In particular attention focused on what was by then the most important penitential practice – auricular confession and its accompanying indulgences. Although most debate focused on biblical evidence and contemporary practice, Protestant historians also attacked Catholic doctrine: the Centuriators, a group of Lutheran historians based in Magdeburg, remembered now because they were some of the earliest scholars to divide their account into centuries, were the first group of Reformation scholars to attempt to compile a history of the

---

[36] 'Huius studii duae sunt positiones, publicum et privatum. Publicum ius est, quod ad statum rei Romanae spectat, privatum ius est, quod ad singulorum utilitatem pertinet': *The Institutes of Justinian: text, translation and commentary*, ed. J. A. C. Thomas, Leiden–Amsterdam–Oxford 1975, I.i.3, p. 3. On the failure of Roman law to distinguish often or clearly between the two see S. Reynolds, *Fiefs and vassals: the medieval evidence reinterpreted*, Oxford 1994, 25–6 and passim.

[37] de Jong, 'Power and humility', 36–9, and 'What was public', 893–901.

[38] On the confessional nature of much of the historiography of penance see A. Murray, 'Confession before 1215', *TRHS* 6th ser. iii (1993), 51–81 at pp. 52–4.

Church from its foundations in which they argued for the corruption and thus decline of the Church under the papacy.[39] Penance played a key part in their argument; thus in their volume on the eleventh century the Centuriators had a section on the power of the keys, that is the authority granted by Christ to Peter and thence to the priesthood to absolve sinners and thus allow them entry into heaven, as part of their attempt to show how papal monopoly of this power was a medieval invention. Jean Morin (1591–1659), a Catholic convert from the Huguenots, published the first major history of penance in 1651.[40] He had done a lot of research on medieval liturgical manuscripts and argued that contemporary auricular confession was a development of the later medieval period. His work was not influential, probably because he managed to please neither side. In the eighteenth century the French Catholic Edmond Martène published several rites, for both secret and public penance, as part of his great edition of medieval liturgies from manuscripts in French libraries, but he was not primarily interested in penance.[41]

Modern debates began with publication in 1896 of a history of auricular confession by the American Protestant historian Henry Charles Lea. Lea claimed that he had not consulted any Protestant writers because he wanted his book to be wholly impartial. But it bears a strong confessional taint: he argued that confession was a new practice introduced by Pope Innocent III in 1215, when the Fourth Lateran Council ordained that all Christians should make their confession once a year. The purpose of this innovation was, in his view, to enable the Church to control the laity.[42] The Catholic riposte came in the first half of the twentieth century: in England with Oscar Watkins's demonstration that confession originated in secret penance and was thus well-established long before 1215; in Germany with Bernhard Poschmann's argument that confession had developed its late medieval form by 1100. Josef Jungmann in Austria and É. Amann in France, also both Catholic historians, made a similar case for confession's long history and consequently legitimate origins.[43] Scrupulously, these historians did not ignore public penance, which they rightly pointed out was relatively seldom documented before the

---

39 M. Flacius Illyricus and others, *Historia integram ecclesiae Christi: undecima centuria*, Basle 1567, cols 171–3, 264–70. See also idem, *Decima centuria*, Basle 1567, cols 193–4. On the work of the Centuriators see D. Hay, *Annalists and historians: western historiography from the VIIIth to the XVIIIth century*, London 1977, 123–5.
40 J. Morin, *Commentarius historicus de disciplina in administratione sacramenti poenitentiae tredecim primis seculis in ecclesia occidentali, et hucusque in orientali observata, in decem libros distinctus*, Paris 1651. On Morin's work see Mansfield, *Humiliation*, 5–6.
41 E. Martène, *De antiquis ecclesiae ritibus libri*, 2nd edn, Antwerp 1736–8. On the manuscripts used by Martène see A.-G. Martimort, *La Documentation liturgique de Dom Edmond Martène: études codicologiques* (SeT cclxxix, 1978).
42 H. C. Lea, *A history of auricular confession and indulgences in the Latin Church*, London 1896. For Lea's methods see E. S. Bradley, *Henry Charles Lea: a biography*, Philadelphia 1931.
43 O. D. Watkins, *A history of penance*, London 1920; Poschmann, *Kirchenbusse in Ausgang des christlichen Altertums*, *Abendländische Kirchenbusse*, and *Penance*; Jungmann, *Bussriten*; Amann, 'La Pénitence primitive', and 'La Pénitence privée'.

Carolingian period, and was much better documented afterwards, but they tended to concentrate on secret penance.

Writing in the thirty years between 1952 and 1982, the Catholic historian Cyrille Vogel (1919–82) is one of the few historians to have studied all forms of penance in the early medieval period, and also the only one to have considered the tenth and eleventh centuries separately.[44] Working from a variety of liturgical, canonical and narrative sources, he saw the period 900–1050 as essentially one of post-Carolingian continuity. Like historians before him, he saw the Carolingian reforms as fundamental in the development of medieval penance. He identified the Carolingian dichotomy, the bipartite system of public and secret penance set up in the reform councils of 813, which continued, he thought, throughout the tenth and eleventh centuries. Change came only in c. 1200 with a tripartite system of solemn penance, penitential pilgrimage and private penance.[45] Vogel mapped his findings on to two pre-existing (and well-worn) historiographical models: first the Poschmann model of continuity between early medieval secret confession and late medieval confession; second the model of change in the twelfth century identified by Paul Anciaux and M.-D. Chenu.[46] Vogel argued for a twelfth-century shift of emphasis from the tariff, or penitential sentence, that is the performance of some external act to atone for sin, to the penitent's inner contrition.[47] This shift is supposedly one which corresponds to an over-riding concern with pastoral care rather than punishment. It further corresponds to the development of a one-stop procedure in which the penitent is both given his penance and reconciled, for what is now important in the rite is not the performance of penance but an internal change of heart. Vogel highlighted the importance of a change in mentalities for a change in

---

[44] Vogel's bibliography is very extensive. In addition to the articles collected in *En Rémission des péchés: recherches sur les systèmes pénitentiels dans l'église latine*, ed. A. Faivre, Aldershot 1994, see his *Le Pécheur et la pénitence dans l'église ancienne, Le Pécheur au moyen âge*, and *'Libri paenitentiales'*. He also coedited the Romano-German pontifical which made him aware than most historians of his time of the importance of the liturgical evidence: PRG. His specific article on penance in the tenth and eleventh centuries is 'Les Rites de la pénitence publique aux Xe et XI siècles', in P. Gallais and Y.-J. Riou (eds), *Mélanges René Crozet*, Poitiers 1966, i. 137–44 (repr. in *En Rémission*, no. viii).

[45] Idem, *Le Pécheur au moyen âge*, 24–36.

[46] Anciaux in *Théologie* relied on canonical and theological works from the second half of the eleventh century as an introduction to his study of the theology of penance in the twelfth century. See also the work of M.-D. Chenu, *Nature, man and society in the twelfth century: essays on new theological perspectives in the Latin west*, trans. J. Taylor and L. K. Little, Chicago–London 1968.

[47] Vogel, *Le Pécheur au moyen âge*, 31. Vogel was not the only Catholic historian to argue for such a change. P.-M. Gy, whose work is mostly based on the penitential liturgy, reached similar conclusions in 'Histoire liturgique du sacrement de pénitence', *La Maison Dieu* lvi (1958), 5–21, and 'Les Bases de la pénitence moderne', ibid. cxvii (1974), 63–85. Both men were influenced by the discussions surrounding the Second Vatican Council; they thus sought to ensure that reform of the penitential liturgy was placed on a sound historical basis.

secret penitential practice: self-awareness is, supposedly, one of the novelties of the twelfth-century renaissance.[48]

Scholarship on penance in the second half of the twentieth century, though less overtly confessional than earlier work, has been shaped by this weighty Catholic historiography. The search for the origins of confession partly explains why scholars still concentrate mainly on secret penance and confession in the early medieval period, rather than on public penance. One prominent strand of research has been concerned to establish how and when the penitential practice of tariff or secret penance originated, and how it was disseminated and administered, and has sought the answers in the manuscripts of the penitentials themselves. This has necessitated painstaking research into the manuscript history of particular texts.[49] Allen Frantzen's careful study, for example, traces the history of penance in Anglo-Saxon England, showing how penitentials were exported to the continent in the eighth century, modified there in the ninth, and re-imported in their modified form in the tenth century as part of the late Anglo-Saxon Church's own reform movement.[50] Frantzen's work typifies the importance attributed by historians of penitentials to the Carolingian reforms.[51] Carolingian episcopal efforts to regulate and promote penance constitute a theme taken up by one of the few historians to highlight the continuing importance of public penance in the early Middle Ages. Mayke De Jong's work on public penance in the earlier period, approximately 500–900, has shown that it was an important instrument not only for episcopal but also for royal justice. Her research

---

[48] For the idea that self-consciousness only emerged in the twelfth century see C. Morris, *The discovery of the individual, 1050–1200*, London 1972, and as a corrective C. Walker Bynum, 'Did the twelfth century discover the individual?', in her *Jesus as mother: studies in the spirituality of the high Middle Ages*, Berkeley 1982, 85–109. See also J. F. Benton, 'Consciousness of self and perceptions of individuality', in G. Constable and R. L. Benson (eds), *Renaissance and renewal in the twelfth century*, Oxford 1982, 263–95.

[49] Problematic nineteenth-century editions and concerns over the dating of many texts have led to the recognition that it was not possible to answer these wider questions without more detailed work on the manuscript and textual history of the penitentials. Work has thus begun on reassessing the textual history of the penitentials: R. Kottje, *Die Bussbücher Halitgars von Cambrai und des Hrabanus Maurus*, Berlin–New York 1980; G. Hägele, *Das Paenitentiale Vallicellianum, I: Ein oberitalienischer Zweig der frühmittelalterlichen kontinentalen Bussbücher: Überlieferung, Verbreitung und Quellen*, Sigmaringen 1984; L. Körntgen, 'Ein italienisches Bussbuch und seine fränkischen Quellen: das anonyme Paenitentiale der Handschrift Vatikan Archiv. S. Pietro H. 58', in H. Mordek (ed.), *Aus Archiven und Bibliotheken: Festschrift für Raymund Kottje zum 65. Geburtstag*, Frankfurt 1992, 189–205, and *Studien zu den Quellen der frühmittelalterlichen Bussbücher*, Sigmaringen 1993; *Paenitentialia Franciae, Italiae et Hispaniae saeculi VIII–XI, I: Paenitentialia minora Franciae et Italiae saeculi VIII–IX*, ed. R. Kottje with L. Körntgen and U. Spengler-Reffgen (CCSL clvi, 1994); II: *Paenitentialia Hispaniae*, ed. F. Bezler with L. Körntgen (CCSL clviA, 1998).

[50] Frantzen, *Literature*.

[51] For example, see the work of Kottje, *Bussbücher*; R. Meens, *Het tripartite boeteboek: overlevering en betekenis van vroegmiddeleeuwse biechtvoorschriften (met editie en vertaling van vier tripartita)*, Hilversum 1994; Körntgen, *Studien zu den Quellen*.

was mainly on conciliar, penitential and a very small number of highly tendentious narrative sources; on this basis public penance seems to have been restricted to the highest ranks of Carolingian society.[52] But Mary Mansfield, using not only the conventional sources of conciliar prescriptions and theological debate but also the evidence of a large number of liturgical manuscripts, was able to show that public penance remained a thriving practice after 1215 with a much wider application than in the ninth century.[53] Further, using the evidence of scholastic theologians, synodal statutes, episcopal registers and confession manuals, as well as chronicles, Mansfield showed that the practice of public penance was much more varied than that prescribed in the liturgy. Her methodological breakthrough was not just to use liturgical material but to reflect back on that material using a whole range of other evidence: a two-way critical process in which she placed the liturgy in its intellectual and social contexts, and at the same time viewed the prescriptive, narrative and documentary sources through the liturgical evidence. Her work therefore has some useful lessons for early medievalists. She was also able to put Vogel's model for the establishment of a new tripartite model of solemn penance, penitential pilgrimage and private penance c. 1200 in context; it was conceived by scholastic theologians in the late twelfth century and is therefore, as she showed, irrelevant to the chronology of change in penitential practice.[54] Indeed, Arduin's sentence to permanent penitential pilgrimage demonstrates that all three forms, public, secret and pilgrimage, were already established by 999.

Current problems and suggested solutions

As this survey of the historiography demonstrates, modern scholars have on the whole retained the model of a three-stage periodisation for penance: the sixth and seventh centuries when secret or tariff penance originated;[55] the later eighth and ninth centuries when the Carolingian reformers saw to the promotion of tariff penance while at the same time reviving public penance;[56] and the twelfth and thirteenth centuries, the age of the 'medieval reformation', when there was the promotion of annual confession, as outlined in the *omnes utriusque* decree.[57] But this periodisation has proved a

---

52 de Jong, 'Power and humility', and 'What was public'.
53 Mansfield, *Humiliation*.
54 Ibid. 21–34.
55 This model was most clearly articulated in the works of Bernhard Poschmann; its continuing influence for the early period may be seen in the articles by Dooley, 'From penance to confession', and Wood, 'The *Vita Columbani*'.
56 On tariff penance see, for example, Kottje, *Bussbücher*, and 'Busspraxis', and Körntgen, *Studien zu den Quellen*. On public penance see de Jong, 'Power and humility', and 'What was public'.
57 The term is taken from B. Bolton, *The medieval reformation*, London 1983. On the continuing importance of the twelfth century as leading to the development of confession see

mixed blessing. Artificial chronological divisions, constructed for the convenience of undergraduates and general readers, have become prisons for the historians themselves. Thus in the historiography of penance, as of other topics, there has been a notable lack of communication between specialists of different periods. Rob Meens has argued that some form of individual penance was regularly practised by the laity in the eighth and ninth centuries.[58] Historians of the twelfth and thirteenth centuries have argued for the individualisation of penance in their period,[59] whilst fourteenth- and fifteenth-century historians have stressed instead the communal aspect of penitential practice.[60]

A blockage currently exists for anyone trying to marry the historiography of the earlier period with that of the central Middle Ages.[61] Alexander Murray's 1993 article on confession before 1215 uses the model of twelfth-century change to argue that it cannot easily be done.[62] According to Murray, the hypothesis that confession was widespread in the early medieval period rests on prescriptive evidence which represents clerical aspirations, not reality. Further, using only such prescriptive evidence, Murray suggested that early medieval *poenitentia* – interpreted by him as referring only to secret penance – was used primarily as an instrument for ecclesiastical, specifically episcopal, control.[63] In an effort to move from ideal to reality and to substantiate his claims for the chronology of change, Murray selected a group of miracle accounts including stories about lay confession, arguing that for a miracle to be accepted by a contemporary audience, it had to be set in

Murray, 'Confession', and, with the exception of Meens, 'Frequency', the essays in Biller and Minnis, *Handling sin*.
[58] Meens, 'Frequency'. See also P. J. Payer, 'The humanity of the penitentials and the continuity of the penitential tradition', *Mediaeval Studies* xlvi (1984), 340–54, who emphasises the importance of contrition and personal piety in early medieval penitential practice, as outlined in the penitentials.
[59] Murray, 'Confession', and 'Counselling in medieval confession', in Biller and Minnis, *Handling sin*, 63–77; J. Baldwin, 'From the ordeal to confession', ibid. 191–209.
[60] J. Bossy, 'The social history of confession in the age of Reformation', *TRHS* 5th ser. xxv (1975), 21–38, and *Christianity in the west, 1400–1700*, Oxford 1985, 35–56; T. Tentler, *Sin and confession on the eve of the Reformation*, Princeton, NJ 1977.
[61] This is demonstrated very clearly by the set of papers in Biller and Minnis, *Handling sin*, which concentrate on the period c. 1200–c. 1400. Although in 'Frequency' Meens engages with Murray's arguments, there is no evidence (except in Biller's introduction to the volume) in the other papers that scholars of the later period have engaged with Meens's work. This partly reflects the fact that Meens's paper was not delivered at the conference at which most of the other papers in the volume were given but there is more to it than this: it illustrates a more general failing in the historiography of the Middle Ages as a whole.
[62] Murray, 'Confession'.
[63] Ibid. 59–61. Murray thus draws on the work of Kerff, '*Libri paenitentiales*'. Meens disagrees with Murray on this point, citing manuscript evidence to argue that penitentials were often used in a pastoral rather than legal context: 'Frequency'. While he is able to demonstrate the use of penitentials by the rural clergy in some areas in the ninth century, he cannot show that this practice was widespread nor that it continued into the tenth century. For further consideration of this issue see chapter 1.

circumstances which appeared 'real'. He identified tales about lay confession as appearing only in sources associated with a pastoral mission: the ninth-century miracle book of Fulda, the late eleventh-century *vita* of Hugh of Grenoble, two early twelfth-century *miracula* from Laon, and the twelfth-century *Life* of Christina of Markyate. Despite the evidence from ninth-century Fulda, Murray thus argued that regular lay confession originated as a reality in certain places in the late eleventh-century, promoted in certain key areas by a pastorally committed clergy.[64] Murray did not explicitly invoke the re-discovery of self-awareness in the twelfth century but it is implicit in his argument that only from the beginning of the long twelfth century, c. 1050–c. 1215, was there the right environment for the promotion of the self-awareness implicit in confession. Murray's paper has two signal virtues: it squarely addresses a problem occluded in much of the work undertaken on penance in both the early and late medieval periods, namely that prescriptive sources such as conciliar decrees, episcopal capitularies and penitentials, will not tell us what actually happened; and it suggests a way round the problem.[65] What Murray did not do was ask whether 'the discovery of the individual' was the reflection of new kinds of text produced in the twelfth century – a trick of the evidential light – or whether we can argue from the earlier silence.

A useful analogy is provided by the dearth of theological discussions of penance in the earlier medieval period; these do not start until the rise of the schools in the eleventh century.[66] But we cannot consequently assume that there was between the patristic age and the twelfth century no consideration of the theology behind penance. One of the earliest such discussions, *De vera et falsa poenitentia*, variously dated to the early or late eleventh century, argued that the humiliation and shame inherent in the act of confession constituted expiation of the sin itself.[67] This tract thus prefigured twelfth-century arguments for the importance of contrition to the making of satisfaction for sins.[68] If such terms as contrition and satisfaction are not to be found in the period 900–1050 that is because of the absence of theological treatises on penance and an absence of terminology; it need not necessarily mean a radical evolution in the nature of penance itself.[69]

---

[64] Murray's timetable thus reflects that of Anciaux, *Théologie*, 7–55, which was derived from more theoretical works.
[65] In this he was partly anticipated almost thirty years earlier by C. Vogel, 'La Discipline pénitentielle en Gaule des origines au IXe siècle: le dossier hagiographique', *Revue des sciences religieuses* xxx (1956), 1–26, 157–86 (repr. in his *En Rémission*, no. vi) who researched early medieval hagiography as a source for the history of penance.
[66] Anciaux, *Théologie*, 7.
[67] PL xl. 1113–30. For the earlier date see Müller, 'Umschwung in der Lehre von der Busse'; for a mid eleventh-century date see Anciaux, *Théologie*, 15 n. 2.
[68] Ibid. 15–55; Müller, 'Umschwung in der Lehre von der Busse'; Mansfield, *Humility*.
[69] See Poschmann, *Penance*, 158, for a survey of the orthodoxy on the beginning of doctrines of satisfaction. For a more detailed investigation see Anciaux, *Théologie*. A similar

Murray's work has, however, highlighted the major problems facing historians of penitential practice: the different source-genres from which the evidence is drawn and the different perspectives they each offer. He points out that most of the work to date has been distinguished by its concentration on material from one particular genre with only occasional oblique references to other evidence. Recent historians' focus on penitentials has thus inevitably led to a concentration in their accounts on 'secret', or at least less formal, penance. As Frantzen pointed out, historians still know very little about how penance was practised in the early medieval period or about the way in which penitentials were used.[70] Frantzen himself worked only on the Anglo-Saxon penitentials, prayerbooks and sources such as Ælfric's homilies and Old English poetry; he mostly ignored one important genre which would have given him evidence, albeit idealised, of the encounter between penitent and priest, namely the wholly liturgical sources such as the pontificals which existed by the tenth and eleventh centuries.

Mansfield showed just how valuable such liturgical evidence can be, yet with the exception of Jungmann and Vogel, early medievalists have largely ignored it.[71] As sources not only for penance but for medieval history as a whole, liturgical manuscripts form probably the largest single category of surviving medieval manuscripts.[72] Even Jungmann and, to a slightly lesser extent, Vogel, as Catholic historians, failed to exploit the full potential of this material because they both adopted a post-Tridentine viewpoint, focusing on how local liturgies evolved and contributed to the Roman liturgy.[73] Yet such local evidence is in itself fundamental to the history of penitential practice because it demonstrates that the penitential liturgies were a live issue for the local clergy who thought about them, evolving as a consequence their own regional rites. The interpretation of liturgical evidence has, of course, problems of its own. Take the example of the rite for the reconciliation of penitents on Maundy Thursday in the Romano-German pontifical (c. 950). Reconciliation plays a fairly minor part in a busy liturgical sequence: the day

---

criticism has been raised by several historians of Jacques le Goff's assumption that purgatory only came into existence as an idea in the afterlife once a noun, *purgatorium*, existed to refer to that belief, that is for an idea to exist and be commonly understood, it must have a name: J. Le Goff, *The birth of purgatory*, London 1984 (trans. by A. Goldhammer of *La Naissance du purgatoire*, Paris 1981) and the critique by G. Robert Edwards, 'Purgatory: "birth" or evolution?', *JEH* xxxvi (1985), 634–46.

[70] 'We do not have a full understanding of how the penitential was used, how widely penance was practised, or how the penitential interacted with other kinds of pastoral literature': Frantzen, *Literature*, 4.

[71] Jungmann, *Bussriten*; Vogel, 'Pénitence publique', and 'Les Rituels de la pénitence tarifée', in *Liturgia opera divina et umana: studi offerti à S. E. Mons. A. Bugnini*, Rome 1982, 419–27 (repr. in his *En Rémission*, no. xi).

[72] There are almost 1,000 liturgical manuscripts compiled before c. 1100 listed in *CLLA*.

[73] Jungmann, *Bussriten*. This Roman perspective explains why Vogel concentrated on the Romano-German pontifical, an antecedent of the Roman pontifical, in his 'Pénitence publique', and in *Le Pécheur au moyen âge*, 208–18.

is to start with the assembly of everything needed for the consecration of the chrism, then at the first hour the bishop should hold a synod of his priests and other interested parties, then at the third hour the bell should ring so that everyone comes to the church in which the chrism is to be consecrated, but preceding the consecration of the chrism, the bishop should reconcile the penitents.[74] Here then, the emphasis is placed not on the reconciliation of penitents but on the blessing and distribution of the sacred oil. Given that the bishop was also supposed to fit into his schedule a diocesan synod, we cannot assume that his Maundy Thursday was dominated by the rite for public penance, and therefore need to consider whether it was always practicable to include this rite in the annual liturgy. Other problems also need to be resolved: the differences in local liturgies cannot always be simply attributed to differences in local practice, since recorded variations in rites other than those for penance often seem to owe more to 'literary' interest than practical intention.[75] Nevertheless it is important to recognise that differences did exist between local liturgies and we must ask whether these suggest differing clerical attitudes to penitential practice in different localities. The problems associated with using liturgical evidence are discussed in further detail in chapter 4.

The aim of this study is to redress the failures and fill the gaps highlighted above by studying the practice of penance in the period 900–1050 and to do so by taking a holistic approach, reviewing all forms of penitential practice: public, private and mixed. Only by first focusing on the liturgical evidence and then bringing a range of other evidence to bear on the liturgy, following the two-way approach pioneered by Mansfield for the twelfth and thirteenth centuries, will we get a clearer sense of the usefulness or otherwise of the public/secret distinction.

The chronological limits of this study are determined both by the work of previous historians and by the sources. The history of penance has generally been written either at a micro-level, that of individual texts,[76] or a macro-level, that of general histories covering a wide geographic and histor-

---

[74] *PRG* xcix.222–302, ii. 59–85.
[75] On the literary nature of many early medieval liturgical books see N. K. Rasmussen, *Les Pontificaux des haut moyen âge: genèse du livre liturgique de l'évêque*, Louvain 1998; É. Palazzo, *A history of liturgical books from the beginning to the thirteenth century*, Collegeville 1998 (trans. by M. Beaumont of *Histoire des livres liturgiques: le moyen âge: des origines au XIIIème siècle*, Paris 1993). For a demonstration of this in another area, that of the *ordines* for holding a synod see MGH, *Ordines de celebrando concilio*. For a demonstration of this in the area of the penitential liturgy see the rite for entry into public penance on Ash Wednesday in the 'pontifical of Poitiers' which includes a lengthy exposition on the vices and how to remedy them which covers twenty-one pages of the printed edition; the rite itself takes up thirty-eight pages: *Il cosiddetto pontificale di Poitiers (Paris, Bibliothèque de l'Arsenal, cod. 227)*, ed. A. Martini, Rome 1979, 12–50; cf. the rite in the Romano-German pontifical which covers approximately seventeen full pages of the printed edition: *PRG* ii. 14–22, 59–67.
[76] For example, Kottje, *Bussbücher*; R. Folz, 'La Pénitence publique aux IXe siècle d'après les canons de l'éveque Isaac de Langres', in *L'Encadrement religieux des fidèles*, i. 331–43.

ical range.[77] Earlier scholars have concentrated either on late antiquity and the early medieval period up to and including the ninth century, or on the period beginning in the mid eleventh century leading up to the twelfth-century developments in scholastic theology and the Fourth Lateran Council of 1215. In the case of recent research on public penance, for example, Mansfield's researches did not extend back to the period 900–1050. De Jong's have not extended forward beyond the late ninth century. Equally historians of secret penance have also virtually omitted any detailed consideration of penance in the period 900 to 1050, despite the fact that the work of Poschmann, Jungmann and Vogel identified the tenth and eleventh centuries as periods of significant liturgical change for both secret and public penance.

Secret penance seems to have been a two-stage process in the ninth century: penitents were expected to return after their penance to be reconciled in a separate ceremony, and even if penance had been imposed by a priest, the penitent could only be absolved by his bishop. At some point penance became a one-stop process: Poschmann and Jungmann suggested that this development happened c. 1000 using evidence such as the *ordo* in Burchard of Worms's *Decretum* (c. 1020), although such evidence has now been shown to be more ambiguous than they thought.[78] Public penance also saw change in this period: Regino of Prüm, writing c. 906, is the first to describe the rite for the imposition of public penance on Ash Wednesday which culminates in the penitent's expulsion from the Church just as Adam was expelled from paradise,[79] whereas the Romano-German pontifical (c. 950) is one of the first texts to record in detail how the penitents should be received back into the Church on Maundy Thursday.[80] The curious historiographical hiatus between the Carolingian period and the long twelfth century means that the intervening period has been neglected. This study seeks to demonstrate that the development of penitential practice in the tenth and early eleventh centuries, whilst it owed a considerable debt to that under the Carolingians, also showed considerable independence, as witnessed by the changes recorded in the penitential liturgies of this period.[81]

---

[77] Lea, *Auricular confession*; Watkins, *History of penance*; Jungmann, *Bussriten*; Poschmann, *Penance*; Vogel, *Le Pécheur au moyen âge*.
[78] Jungmann, *Bussriten*, 190–7; Poschmann, *Penance*, 145. For recent reservations on whether this process had not occurred earlier than 1020 – the time of composition of Burchard's *Decretum* – that is in the ninth century, and also whether such a change is demonstrated by the *Decretum* see Kottje, 'Busspraxis', 391.
[79] Regino of Prüm, *Libri duo de synodalibus causis et disciplinis ecclesiasticis*, ed. F. Wasserschleben, Leipzig 1840, I.ccxcv, pp. 136–7; Vogel, 'Pénitence publique'.
[80] PRG xcix.224–51, ii. 59–67. Jungmann, *Bussriten*, 52–9; Vogel, 'Pénitence publique'.
[81] The tenth century, whilst in many ways merely continuing ninth-century developments, was a period which possessed a dynamic of its own in other ways too. On this see K. Leyser's review of H. Fichtenau, *Lebensordnung des 10. Jahrhunderts: Studien über Denkart und Existenz im einstigen Karolingerreich*, Stuttgart 1984, in *Francia* xiv (1986), 708–10.

INTRODUCTION

The liturgical sources which form the core of this study also helped to determine both its chronological and geographical limits. Liturgically this was a period of change, or at any rate of a huge explosion in the volume of the evidence. Regino of Prüm's material on penance has been considered significant by previous historians: he composed his collection for the archbishop of Trier c. 906 and therefore provides a starting date for this study.[82] I have already noted the importance of the Romano-German pontifical, composed in Mainz c. 950, and widely diffused throughout the *Reich* thereafter, for the development of public penance, but Vogel thought it similarly crucial for the development of one-stage secret penance.[83] The Romano-German pontifical, thanks to Vogel's work, is often presented as axiomatic for all tenth- and eleventh-century practice, but this study seeks to put it in its liturgical context, as reflected in liturgies found in Fulda, Lotharingia and northern west Francia, and northern and central Italy.[84] The end of this period, c. 1050, has been determined in part by my assessment of the significance of the papal reform movement in stimulating a re-evaluation of both canon law and of the Church's delivery of pastoral care.[85] That re-evaluation was to culminate in the *omnis utriusque* decree of the Fourth Lateran Council in 1215 enjoining annual confession for all Christians.

The importance of these three seminal texts – Regino of Prüm's *Libri duo de synodalibus causis et disciplinis ecclesiasticis*, the Romano-German pontifical and Burchard of Worms's *Decretum* – also helped to determine the geographical limits of this study, namely Italy, east Francia and Lotharingia, stretching into the province of Rheims in west Francia. For much of the tenth and eleventh centuries these areas, with the exception of west Francia, were ruled by kings and emperors of the Ottonian, then the Salian, dynasties. A shared ruler gave them a certain cohesion: east Frankish bishops appointed to Italian sees sometimes brought liturgical books with them,[86] and copies of Burchard

---

[82] On Regino's significance see Jungmann, *Bussriten*, 52–9; J. T. McNeill and H. M. Gamer, *Medieval handbooks of penance: a translation of the principal 'libri poenitentiales'*, New York 1938, 314–18; Vogel, 'Pénitence publique'; Mansfield, *Humiliation*, 171–2.

[83] Vogel, 'Pénitence publique', *Le Pécheur au moyen âge*, 206–18, and 'Pénitence tarifée'. Burchard's highly influential *Decretum*, composed in Worms c. 1020, has also been seen as signalling a crucial moment in the development of secret penance because it is a supposedly early witness to the movement away from a two-stage process in which first the penitent was awarded his penance and subsequently returned to be reconciled, combining both elements in a one-stop procedure: Jungmann, *Bussriten*, 52–9, 190; McNeill and Gamer, *Medieval handbooks*, 314–18, 321–43; Poschmann, *Penance*, 145; Vogel, 'Pénitence publique', and *Le Pécheur au moyen âge*, 80–113; Mansfield, *Humiliation*, 171–2.

[84] See ch. 5.

[85] For an introduction to the papal reform movement see Tellenbach, *Church*. On the re-evaluation of pastoral care in this period see Bolton, *Medieval reformation*.

[86] For example Poppo, patriarch of Aquileia (1019–42), took a Fulda sacramentary to Aquileia, now Udine, Biblioteca capitolare, MS 1: É. Palazzo, *Les Sacramentaires de Fulda: étude sur l'iconographie et la liturgie à l'époque ottonienne*, Münster 1994, 207–10.

of Worms's *Decretum* were quickly diffused in northern and central Italy.[87] The province of Rheims, which lay outside the empire, shared many links with neighbouring Lotharingia. It included the Lotharingian diocese of Cambrai, and a joint council was held by the provinces of Rheims and Trier in 948.[88]

By focusing on the area which provides us with the evidence for these changes I hope to emulate the micro-studies of people such as de Jong, Frantzen and Mansfield which have led in recent years to a partial chipping away at the 'grand narrative' of a three-stage development for the history of medieval penitential practice.[89] By considering a range of sources and taking account not only of the new texts written in this period, but also of the fact that many ninth-century texts were copied in the tenth century, and by studying the manuscript material in addition to the published texts, I hope to build up a picture of the many different forms of penitential practice available within a specific area at a specific time. And by focusing on this period of apparent change in penitential practice, I intend to build on recent work on the Carolingians and their attempts to introduce a standardised and widespread practice and to consider how far the tenth and eleventh centuries should be seen as sub-Carolingian – as merely continuing Carolingian ideas about penance in theory and practice – and how far they possessed their own dynamic.

But why does the history of penance matter? This question gets different answers from historians of different periods. For the sixteenth and seventeenth centuries, penance was an important weapon in the hands of both critics and defenders of the medieval Church. Medieval historians nowadays, whatever period of the Middle Ages they study, use penance as an *entrée* into the morals, attitudes and habits of lay people as well as the clergy and see the interaction of clergy and laity as centrally important.[90] Early medievalists

---

[87] The fundamental work on the manuscript history of Burchard's *Decretum* is still O. Meyer, 'Überlieferung und Verberitung des Dekrets des Bischofs Burhard von Worms', ZRG Kan. Abt. xxiv (1935), 141–83. For additional information on more recent work see the works listed in ch. 1, n. 40.

[88] Mouzon (948): MGH, *Concilia* VI, 132–4.

[89] For example, in *Humiliation* Mansfield demonstrated the importance of public penance in the twelfth and thirteenth centuries and the more muddled nature of much practice; de Jong has shown the importance of public penance to the Carolingian reformers; Frantzen, in *Literature*, has shown the importance of communication between 'national' Churches in the development of practice and texts. See also Dooley, 'Penance and confession' for her critique of Poschmann's model for the evolution from late antique to early medieval penance.

[90] Penance is thus merely one aspect of a wider debate about the relationship between the learned and the popular (however these terms are defined) in the early Middle Ages, or that between the 'literate' clergy and the 'illiterate' laity. For a consideration of the problems posed by these terms and on this debate in general see R. McKitterick (ed.), *The uses of literacy in early medieval Europe*, Cambridge 1990, and M. Richter, *The formation of the medieval west: studies in the oral culture of the barbarians*, Dublin 1994.

have recognised the significance of the surviving penitentials as a key source of evidence for the process of Christianisation of early medieval society.[91] Understandably they have focused on what has been seen as the practice of secret penance; unsurprisingly the wider significance of public penance, with the exception of *causes célèbres* such as Louis the Pious's penance at Soissons in 833, has been relatively ignored until recently. The exception was Karl Leyser who used the definitions established by the Carolingian councils of what was required from those doing public penance, namely to put down their weapons, abstain from riding on horseback, and from marriage, to illustrate the history of early medieval knighthood as both a secular and Christian ideal and practice.[92] Returning to issues of more general concern, namely the role of penance in Christianisation and the nature of Christianisation itself, the debate has often been framed in terms of two alternatives: seeing penance either as an instrument of social control, used by the Church, that is by the bishops, to enforce their values on and against the laity, or as an educational tool, designed to show and teach an ideal of Christian belief and behaviour. Was penance primarily a judicial weapon, used to enforce clerical justice, and impose clerical values, in episcopal courts, or was it primarily a pastoral practice, imposed in a spirit of co-operation and understanding upon an anxious laity?[93] This opposition, which first arose in the context of debates about the role of penance in the late medieval and reformation period, appears anachronistic when applied to that of the early Middle Ages. Terms such as the 'Church' and the 'laity' are convenient but misleading in this period,

---

[91] Beginning with the nineteenth-century German editions of penitentials: *Die Bussordnungen der abendländischen Kirche*, ed. F. W. H. Wasserschleben, Halle 1851; *Bussbücher I*; *Bussbücher II*. On the social significance of the penitentials see the pioneering work of T. P. Oakley: *English penitential discipline and Anglo-Saxon law in their joint influence*, New York 1923; 'Some neglected aspects in the history of penance', *Catholic Historical Review* xxiv (1938-9), 293-309; and 'The penitentials as a source for medieval history', *Speculum* xv (1940), 210-23. See also McNeill and Gamer, *Medieval handbooks*, 35-46. More modern works are numerous and include C. Vogel, 'Pratiques superstitieuses au début du XIe siècle d'après le *Corrector sive medicus* de Burchard, évêque de Worms (965-1025)', in *Mélanges E.-R. Labande: études de civilisation médiévale (IXe-XIIe siècles)*, Poitiers 1974, 751-61 (repr. in his *En Rémission*, no. x), and '*Libri paenitentiales*', 102-12; P. J. Payer, *Sex and the penitentials: the development of a sexual code, 550-1150*, Toronto 1984; J. Brundage, *Law, sex and Christian society in medieval Europe*, Chicago-London 1987; R. Meens, 'Children and confession in the early Middle Ages', in D. Wood (ed.), *The Church and childhood* (SCH xxxi, 1994), 53-65.

[92] Leyser, 'Early medieval canon law'.

[93] The origins of this debate go back at least to the late nineteenth century with Lea, *Auricular confession*, ii. 107-12, who viewed early medieval penance as punitive and coercive. For a more recent proponent of the social control view see Tentler, *Sin and confession*, and for opposition to his views concerning penance in the reformation period see Bossy, 'Social history', and *Christianity*. Kerff in '*Libri paenitentiales*' is the most recent exponent of the social control theory in this period. For the view of penance as a pastoral as well as a corrective exercise in the early medieval period see Frantzen, *Literature*, passim and 200-2. For a view of it as primarily pastoral in this period see Meens, 'Frequency'.

implying as they do an exclusivity of purpose amongst each of these two groups when in fact, as Leyser showed, bishops, kings and aristocrats worked closely together in the early medieval period; we cannot assume that the 'Church' was working to impose its own values on the early medieval society against the will of all members of the laity when such a separation did not yet exist.[94] The phrase 'the Church' itself rests on a misconception about the context in which the bishops and clergy worked in the early Middle Ages, assuming a unification of purpose and an acceptance of a degree of papal authority which did not occur before the twelfth century. We cannot assume that we know how far bishops saw their rural clergy, or how they understood their role, or what their role was. Before the twelfth century the early medieval Church seems more characterised by the diversity of the different areas and different groups within it than by any sense of unity. The positions in the debate about the social purpose of penance, control versus education, also appear based on a false premise, for education can be seen as a form of social control rather than as an alternative to it, being one of the means by which those hoping to impose their own values on a wider mass achieve their purpose.

If the debate to date has been framed in somewhat artificial terms, nevertheless it has led to a series of important and related questions concerning the level of participation in penitential practice both within and outside the clergy: was the practice of penance restricted to the elite, both lay and clerical, or was it more widespread than that?[95] Can we use the evidence of the surviving penitential texts to answer this question? Were they used by bishops and their deputies (archdeacons), or is there evidence that they were also used by local priests?[96] Did the clergy try to promote regular confession as a pastoral norm, and if so, when, where and how far were they successful in the early medieval period? Or did this only become feasible in the twelfth and thirteenth centuries when the combined growth in parish structures, and in clerical education, meant more trained clergy were available on the ground to

---

[94] Leyser, 'Early medieval canon law'.
[95] Both Frantzen, *Literature*, and Meens, 'Frequency', argue for the widespread nature of penance, on the basis that the evidence suggests that penitentials were available to those clergy below the level of bishop, i.e. the rural clergy.
[96] For the view that they were used only in an episcopal court context by bishops and their deputies see Kerff, '*Libri paenitentiales*'. For the counter-view see Meens, 'Frequency', where the author's analysis of 106 manuscripts of penitentials demonstrates (p. 141) that, 'while some manuscripts can indeed by identified as having been intended for an episcopal audience, the majority seems to have been used by simple priests in the daily work of pastoral care'. Both views are further evaluated in ch. 1. On the more general problem of how bishops related to their parish clergy and the problems faced by the parish clergy in this period see J. L. Nelson, 'Making ends meet: wealth and poverty in the Carolingian Church', in W. J. Sheils and D. Wood (eds), *The Church and wealth* (SCH xxiv, 1987), 25–36 (repr. in her *The Frankish world, c. 750 – c. 900*, London 1996, 145–53).

provide penance amongst other pastoral services?[97] How did early medieval people confess their sins: one to one with the priest in a manner resembling post-1215 confession,[98] or in a communal ritual like that of the mass, since participation in the eucharist was often associated with confession? Prescriptive texts obliged Christians to do penance as part of their preparation for the three main feasts of the liturgical year, Easter, Christmas and Pentecost.[99] Did this happen? If so, was it a communal act? If it was, how – if at all – did early medieval people distinguish between the different communal rituals for secret and public penance?

Possible solutions

This study uses a wide range of sources to examine the practices and perceptions of penance in this period in an attempt to answer these questions. Whilst the detailed problems associated with each genre are discussed as they arise, it is worth highlighting some more general difficulties here as, to a certain extent, they explain the structure of this work.

It takes a two-way approach in two senses. Chapters 1–5 consider the 'official', that is intentional, picture of penitential practice drawn in, for the most part, prescriptive sources; chapter 6 considers the 'unofficial' picture, that is individual accounts of penitential practice, derived mostly from narrative but also from documentary sources, which were not written in order to prescribe correct penitential procedure and which therefore might be assumed to convey a more 'realistic' picture; the methodological issues arising from such an approach are also discussed in more detail. In another sense too the approach is two-way, using the full spread of evidence which exists for penitential practice to reflect back on the liturgical material.

Chapter 1 offers a survey of the evidence provided by the canon law collections and penitentials for the penitential process itself. Inevitably, much of this material is derived from earlier collections and textual and codicological analysis suggests that many of these works were reserved for use at a high level of the ecclesiastical hierarchy, as reference and educational works.[100] Chapter 2 therefore considers in more detail how these statements

---

[97] On promotion in the early period see Frantzen, *Literature*, 15, and Meens, 'Frequency'. For the view that this only became feasible in the twelfth century see Murray, 'Confession'.
[98] As suggested by the stories recorded by Caesarius of Heisterbach (d. 1240). On Caesarius' accounts of confession see P. Biller, 'Confession in the Middle Ages: introduction', in Biller and Minnis, *Handling sin*, 1–35.
[99] On the association between penance and the eucharist see Avril, 'Remarques'. For a critical evaluation of Avril's views see Meens, 'Frequency'.
[100] For the view that this bias may reflect an institutional bias in favour of the preservation of the holdings of only high-level institutions see R. Meens, 'Priests and books in the Carolingian era', unpubl. paper delivered at the International Medieval Congress, University of Leeds, 15 July 1998.

on penitential practice were communicated to the clergy outside the school-room through a study of the councils held in this period, the synodal sermons read at them, and the episcopal capitularies composed. As in chapter 1, by comparing these texts with ninth-century precedents, it is possible to identify areas where episcopal legislators do seem to have innovated in ways that brought changes in the penitential process. These chapters have concentrated upon evidence composed for, and at least sometimes by, the secular clergy: but many of the narrative sources from this period were composed by monks. Because reliance is placed on monastic sources in chapters 4, 5 and 6, chapter 3 considers the role of penance in the regular life, and how authors' perceptions of penitential practice might have been influenced by their own experience of regular life. Chapters 4 and 5 establish the diversity of penitential rites available in the *Reich* and Italy through a survey of the liturgical material, identifying individual families of rites and placing them in the contexts for which they were composed and in which they were used. Chapter 4 examines the rites in the Romano-German pontifical, chapter 5 the range of other penitential rites which existed at the same time within the *Reich*. These two chapters are concerned with how and why such diversity arose. Whilst the rites themselves represented a clerical ideal, their diversity, it is argued, also reflects the fact that they were used; these rites allow us, in a way that the more prescriptive evidence does not, to examine the laity's experience of penance in conjunction with that of the clergy. Consideration of the liturgical evidence thus allows us to examine how the penitent and priest, layman and cleric, interacted in a ritual context.

Chapter 6 further seeks to redress the prescriptive bias of the previous chapters by examining the impact which penitential practice had upon the wider world through a study of actual cases of penance, starting at the top with the best known, those performed by kings, and moving down via cases amongst the clergy and nobility, to consider the possibility that penance was more widely practised than is often supposed by those at lower levels of society.

1

The Church Law of Penance: The Evidence of the Collections

The introduction to book xix, *De poenitentia*, of Burchard of Worms's *Decretum* demonstrates the two themes inherent in much of the penitential law of the time, that is the disciplinarian *Corrector* versus the pastoral *Medicus*:

> This book is called the Corrector and the Medicus since it contains ample corrections for bodies and medicines for souls and teaches every priest, even the less educated, how he shall be able to bring help to each person, ordained or unordained, poor or rich, boy, youth, mature or decrepit man, healthy or infirm, of every age and of both sexes.[1]

Usually, as here, the pastoral element predominated: penance was meant to help every Christian ensure his or her salvation. But the texts which prescribed penitential practice had more immediate objectives, namely to educate the priests who administered penance, and ensure that it was applied in a uniform manner. In this way the church law concerning penance is inextricably entwined with ecclesiastical discipline, and in particular with episcopal control over diocesan priests.

Much of book xix of the *Decretum* is dependent upon earlier penitentials including that of Halitgar, bishop of Cambrai (c. 829/30) and one of those attributed to Theodore, archbishop of Canterbury.[2] It is therefore important to understand the literary history behind individual canons in collections such as Burchard's *Decretum* before using them as evidence of penitential practice at a particular time or place. However, the nineteenth-century editions of such collections used by historians are faulty, based often on only a single manuscript; we often do not know when and where collections circulated, or what were their sources. Consequently whilst most surveys of early

---

[1] 'Liber hic Corrector vocatur et Medicus, quia correctiones corporum et animarum medicinas plene continet, et docet unumquemque sacerdotem, etiam simplicem, quomodo unicuique succurrere valeat, ordinato vel sine ordine, pauperi, diviti, puero, juveni, seni, decrepito, sano, infirmo, in omni aetate et in utroque sexu': Burchard of Worms, *Decretum*, PL cxl. 949. The manuscript tradition for the *Decretum* is confused but G. Fransen has argued that the Migne text is sufficient for most purposes: 'Le Décret de Burchard de Worms: valeur du texte de l'édition: essai du classement des manuscrits', *ZRG Kan. Abt.* lxiii (1977), 1–19 at p. 8.
[2] See the sources for individual canons listed in *Das Dekret*, 232–9.

medieval penance are grounded in the penitential handbooks and canonical collections of ecclesiastical law, they suffer because they are based on faulty editions of these texts.³ It is only in the last twenty years that these problems have started to be addressed as researchers have begun to investigate the specific, and often complex, manuscript histories of individual collections, their compilation and circulation.⁴ Even where the textual history of a particular penitential collection or handbook is known, the historian still faces considerable problems because, as Frantzen observed in his study of penitential literature in Anglo-Saxon England, historians imperfectly understand how such texts were used.⁵ With these two warnings in mind, this chapter considers the evidence for penitential practice as reflected in the church law of the approximate period 900–1050: first the collections will be examined, followed by some of the penitentials which were either composed or copied at this time.⁶ The next chapter will consider the evidence of church councils, episcopal capitularies and sermons. By examining not only the content of, but the manuscript evidence for, church law in this period, I hope to provide some reflections on the context in which this material was composed and preserved, and thus on the problems raised here.

---

3 Amongst other studies see Jungmann, *Bussriten*, 141–230, 265–316, esp. pp. 141–68; Poschmann, *Abendländische Kirchenbusse*, and *Penance*, 122–54; Vogel, *Le Pécheur au moyen âge*, 15–47, and 'Libri paenitentiales'; H. P. Forshaw, 'The pastoral ministry of the priest-confessor in the early Middle Ages, 600–1100: a study of the origins and development of the role of the priest-confessor in the administration of private ecclesiastical penance in the west', unpubl. PhD diss. London 1975; Frantzen, *Literature*.
4 Kottje, 'Busspraxis'. His project at the University of Bonn addresses this problem by seeking to investigate the textual history of the penitentials and to issue new editions. The aims of the project are outlined by him in 'Erfassung und Untersuchung der frühmittelalterlichen kontinentalen Bussbücher: Probleme, Ergebnisse, Aufgaben eines Forschungsprojektes an der Universität Bonn', SM 3rd ser. xxvi (1985), 941–50. The project's work has already yielded fruit in the form of new editions of several penitentials: *Paenitentialia Franciae, Italiae et Hispaniae saeculi VIII–XI*, i, ii. In addition the project has produced studies of the textual transmission of several texts including Kottje, *Bussbücher*; Hägele, *Das Paenitentiale Vallicellianum*, i; L. Mahadevan, 'Überlieferung und Verbreitung des Bussbuchs *Capitula iudiciorum*', ZRG Kan. Abt. lxxii (1986), 17–75; Meens, *Het tripartite boeteboek*.
5 'We do not have a full understanding of how the penitential was used, how widely penance was practised, or how the penitential interacted with other kinds of pastoral literature': Frantzen, *Literature*, 4. Excepting Frantzen's own contribution, there has been little progress on these topics until recently; see now the research of Rob Meens of the University of Utrecht: 'Frequency', and 'Priests and books in the Carolingian era' (unpubl. paper).
6 The *Collectio Anselmo dedicata* was compiled for the archbishop of Milan *c.* 885 and therefore will not be considered here as it falls outside the time limits of this study: HCC i. 235–43; J.-C. Besse, *Histoire des textes du droit de l'église au moyen âge de Denys à Gratien: Collectio Anselmo dedicata: étude et texte: extraits*, Paris 1960. The summary of contents does not suggest that this text is particularly concerned with penance, but as most of it remains unedited I have been unable to verify this at first hand. Also excluded, on the grounds that it falls outside the geographic limits of this study, is Abbo of Fleury's *Collectio canonum*, PL cxxxix. 473–508, composed at Fleury in western France 994x996, on which see M. Mostert,

The collections

The significance of the collections of Regino and Burchard in the history of penitential practice has long been recognised; Regino is one of the first works to record the elaborate ritual for the expulsion of public penitents from the Church which was such a feature of the tenth century,[7] whilst the *ordo* in Burchard has been interpreted as the earliest evidence for the unification of confession with the reconciliation of the penitent into a one-stop procedure.[8] Historians of penance have, however, paid little attention to the context in which both these collections were composed, nor to the methods used by their compilers.

Regino of Prüm (d. 915) compiled the *Libri duo de synodalibus causis et disciplinis ecclesiasticis* at the request of Rathbod, archbishop of Trier, c. 906, but dedicated it to the head of the German episcopate, Hatto, archbishop of Mainz, suggesting that a digest 'of diverse councils and decrees of the holy Fathers' might be useful to the archbishop when he was touring his diocese and did not have access to his own extensive library.[9] Based primarily on Carolingian material, Regino's collection contains descriptions of both public and secret penance; it was the basis for much of Burchard of Worms's *Decretum* compiled in the Rhineland c. 1020, especially book xix.[10] Burchard's collection was in turn an invaluable source for the late eleventh-century Italian reformers, Anselm of Lucca and Bonizo of Sutri, and later the

---

The political theology of Abbo of Fleury: a study of the ideas about society and law of the tenth-century monastic reform movement, Hilversum 1987, 70–6, 112–14. Abbo does not contain any explicit canons relating to penance, and those which do make reference to it, cc. 43–4, are citations, mostly from Gregory the Great. For the use Abbo made of Gregory's *Registrum* (*Registrum epistolarum*), ed. P. Ewald and L. M. Hartmann (MGH, Epistolarum i, 2nd edn, Berlin 1957), see ibid. 71–5.

[7] Jungmann, *Bussriten*, 52–60; Vogel, 'Pénitence publique'.

[8] Jungmann, *Bussriten*, 190–1. Jungmann's conclusions are cited by Poschmann, *Penance*, 145. Recent work, however, suggests that the evidence for a change to one-stop procedure c. 1000 is much less certain; Kottje in 'Busspraxis' suggests that there is evidence that the whole process began at least in the ninth century if not earlier and was much more gradual.

[9] 'Sciens, magnitudinem prudentiae vestrae non solum iuxta sacrorum canonum sanctiones totius provinciae sollicitudinem gerere, verum etiam totius regni utilitatibus per vigili cura insudare, misi vestrae celsitudini libellum, quem de synodalibus causis ecclesiasticisque disciplinis iussu hortatu Domini et reverendissimi Ratbodi archiepisopi, summo cum studio ex diversis sanctorum patrum conciliis atque decretis collegi atque coadunavi. . . . Sed quia vestra sapientiae supereminens celsitudo in disponendis rebus publicis assidue versatur, fortassis onerosum videtur, ut plurima conciliorum volumina semper vobiscum longe lateque deferantur, idcirco hunc manualem codicillum vestrae dominationi direxi, ut illum pro enkyridion habeatis, si quando plenitudo librorum vestrorum in praesentiarum non est': Regino, *Libri duo*, pref., 1–2; see also *HCC* i. 244–68.

[10] Traditionally dated c. 1008–c. 1012: ibid. i. 366–7. This dating has now been revised to c. 1020: *Das Dekret*, 12. On Burchard's sources see ibid. 165–276.

twelfth-century canonists Ivo of Chartres and Gratian.[11] Both Regino and Burchard drew on a wide variety of sources: royal and episcopal capitula, conciliar canons, penitentials, decretals and, most important, previous collections. It should be remembered that Carolingian collections also remained popular in this period, for many survive in tenth- and eleventh-century manuscripts, but their popularity did not prevent tenth- and eleventh-century ecclesiastics in Lotharingia, the Rhineland and Italy from compiling their own collections, and it is these which are the subject of this chapter.[12]

Burchard's *Decretum* reflects his aspirations as to what penance should and should not be, and was novel in its arrangement and selection of material.[13] An analysis of the sources for book xix by author and age demonstrates that the largest proportion came from various, mostly eighth- and ninth-century, penitentials; the other main source was Regino.[14] Anxious to make his work appear authoritative, Burchard falsified the authorities he cited for several of the chapters in the *Decretum*, especially those taken from various penitentials.[15] Although Burchard actually cited canons from nine penitentials in book xix, he attributed his canons to only three: the Roman penitential, and the penitentials of Theodore and Bede.[16] His choice was probably influenced by Regino who regarded only these three penitentials as authoritative.[17] Regino's prescription of specific penitential texts harked back

---

[11] HCC ii. 29, 143; W. Berschin, *Bonizo von Sutri: Leben und Werk*, Berlin–New York 1972, 63; Payer, *Sex and the penitentials*, 76–7, 85–6.

[12] For tenth-century (and later) manuscripts of ninth-century church law sources see McKitterick, *Frankish Church*, 18, 21–3. For evidence of twenty-five tenth- and eleventh-century manuscripts including parts of Halitgar of Cambrai's Penitential see Kottje, *Bussbücher*, 15–83. See also the tenth-century manuscripts in the list of 106 medieval manuscripts of tripartite penitentials (penitentials compiled from the Irish, Anglo-Saxon and Frankish traditions) compiled by Meens: 'Frequency', appendix A, pp. 55–61. This list is based on his research presented in full in his *Het tripartite boeteboek*, 220–66.

[13] P. Fournier, 'Études critiques sur le Décret de Burchard de Worms', *Nouvelle Revue historique de droit français et étranger*, 3rd ser. xxxiv (1910), 41–112, 213–21, 289–331, 564–84.

[14] *Das Dekret*, 232–9. Although Burchard included canons from Hohenaltheim (916) elsewhere in the *Decretum*, he failed to include its provisions on penance, for which see *MGH, Concilia VI*, 36.

[15] Fournier, 'Études critiques', 308–31, esp. pp. 327–9, and 'Le Décret de Burchard de Worms', *Revue d'histoire ecclésiastique* xii/1 (1911), 451–73, 670–701; HCC i. 378–81. Regino also falsely attributed his texts to make them appear more authoritative: ibid. i. 259–64.

[16] The nine are Halitgar of Cambrai's *Liber VI*; Excarpsus Bedae-Egberti; Penitential Bedae 'Duodecim'; Excarpsus Cummeani; Hrabanus Maurus' *Paenitentiale ad Heribaldum*, and his *Paenitentiale ad Otgarium*; the Penitentials of Theodore, Hubert and Egbert: *Das Dekret*, 232–9.

[17] 'Si habeat poenitentialem Romanum vel a Theodoro episcopo aut a venerabili Beda editum, ut secundum quod ibi scriptum est, aut interroget confitentem, aut confesso modum poenitentiae imponat': Regino, *Libri duo* i.96, p. 26. These three names all imply authority. Bede and Theodore were well-known figures in the western Church; the Roman penitential

to the early ninth-century reform councils at which the Carolingian bishops, after some reservations about them, sought to control the penitential texts in circulation.[18] Regino's prescription is included in his *inquisitio* for bishops to use to interrogate local priests whilst on a tour of their diocese. Bishops from the ninth to the early eleventh centuries regarded penance as an important aspect of a priest's pastoral duties, and one which they sought to control through regulation. The *Decretum*'s emphasis on authority, and the concern of its other nineteen books which cover topics such as incest and clerical discipline, suggest that, like Regino, it was intended primarily for an audience of bishops and their cathedral clergy.[19]

Regino's work is generally recognised as having an influential *Nachleben* but less attention has been paid to his immediate influence in the tenth century.[20] Drawing heavily upon Carolingian sources, his work also fits into a Carolingian tradition of episcopal handbooks intended to provide bishops, or their representatives, with the necessary knowledge for enforcing canon law at a local level.[21] The first book deals with matters concerning the clergy, the second with the laity. Both books are preceded by an *inquisitio* to be addressed in the first case to the local priest, and in the second to seven representatives of the *parochia*, by the bishop or his representative on his visitation of his diocese.[22] Regino's concern with clerical as well as lay discipline is shown by

---

did not exist but Halitgar of Cambrai attributed bk vi of his penitential, composed c. 829/30, to Rome to establish its credentials: 'Incipit liber sextus. Addidimus etiam huic operi exceptionis nostrae, paenitentialem romanum alterum quod de scrinio Romanae ecclesiae adsumpsimus, attamen a quo sit editus, ignoramus': *Bussbücher I*, 466; discussed by Kottje in *Bussbücher*, 157–67.

[18] Frantzen, 'The significance of the Frankish penitentials'.

[19] In his preface addressed to Brunicho, his provost, Burchard writes that he composed the book in answer to Brunicho's demand for a statement of clear teaching to aid young boys in study and to clear up the confusion which existed within the diocese: *Decretum*, 537–40.

[20] R. Pokorny reconsiders Regino's sources as well as his influence in W. Hartmann and K. Pennington (eds), *History of medieval canon law* (forthcoming). Unfortunately I have not been able to read his work but thank Professor Timothy Reuter for notifying me of its existence.

[21] Regino makes it clear in his prefatory letter to Hatto, archbishop of Mainz, that he intended his collection to act as a handbook; he is sending 'this handbook to your lordship so that you might have it as a guide when the abundance of your books is not at hand [Idcirco hunc manualem codicillum vestrae dominationi direxi, ut illum pro enkyridion habeatis, si quando plenitudo librorum vestrorum in praesentarium non est]': Regino, *Libri duo*, pref., 1–2. On the tradition of episcopal handbooks in the ninth century see McKitterick, *Frankish Church*, 36–43.

[22] 'Cum episcopus suam dioecesim circuit, archidiaconus vel archipresbyter eum praeire debet uno aut duobus diebus per parochias, quas visitaturus est, et plebe convocata adnunciare debet proprii pastoris adventum, et, ut omnes ad eius synodum die denominata impraetermisse occurrant, omnimodis ex auctoritate sanctorum canonum praecipere et minaciter denunciare, quod si quis absque gravi necessitate defuerit, procul dubio a communione Christiana sit repellendus. Deinde, adscitis secum presbyteris, qui illo in loco servitium debent exhibere episcopo, quidquid de minoribus et levioribus causis corrigere potest, emendare satagat ut pontifex veniens nequaquam in facilioribus negotiis fatigetur,

the inclusion in the section on penance in book i of a canon on how priests and deacons should do penance.[23]

The associated content of the codices in which Regino's text is preserved confirms that subsequent readers, like its author, regarded the *Libri duo* as an episcopal handbook. A manuscript from Mainz, which survives in its original binding, includes several other episcopal texts: a synodal sermon, three *ordines* for celebrating a synod, an account of a synod held by Archbishop Liutpert at Mainz, two works concerning excommunication, the statutes of the Council of Tribur (895) and a stemma for relations of consanguinity.[24] Regino's text survives in seven manuscripts, all tenth- or eleventh-century, which by their provenance suggest that it circulated mainly within eastern Frankia: in the province of Trier and its neighbouring provinces of Reims, Cologne, Mainz and Salzburg.[25] Traces of Regino's influence are found only in other tenth-century east Frankish collections, although as one manuscript now in Salzburg shows, they did not always adopt his penitential canons.[26]

---

aut ibi immorari amplius necesse sit quam expensa sufficiat': Regino, *Libri duo* ii.1, pp. 206–7. Bk ii makes little mention of penitential practice; its *inquisitio* is concerned to detect whether serious sins, which should be reported to the bishop, have been committed, and is followed by a set of appropriate canonical decrees, taken from a variety of sources, which include a list of possible commutations for penitential sentences. See Regino, *Libri duo* ii.5 (for the *inquisitio*), 446–54 (for commutations), pp. 208–16, 389–92.

[23] Ibid. i.316, pp. 151–2, taken from a decretal of Pope Leo I (P. Jaffé with W. Wattenbach, S. Loewenfeld, F. Kaltenbrunner and P. Ewald [eds], *Regesta pontificum romanorum ab condita ecclesia ad annum post Christum natum MCXCVIII*, 2nd edn, Leipzig 1885, no. 544). R. Pokorny reconsiders Regino's sources as well as his influence in his article in Hartmann and Pennington, *History of medieval canon law* (forthcoming).

[24] Wolfenbüttel, Herzog-August-Bibliothek, MS Guelf. 83. 21. Aug. fo. 2° (Mainz, s. xi), described by O. von Heinemann (ed.), *Die Handschriften des Herzoglichen Bibliothek zu Wolfenbüttel*, Wolfenbüttel 1900–13, ii. 65–6. On its attribution to Mainz see H. Hoffmann, *Buchkunst und Königtum im ottonischen und frühsalischen Reich* (MGH, Schriften xxx, Stuttgart 1986), i. 266, and also the description in MGH, *Ordines de celebrando concilio*, 222–3.

[25] HCC i. 267; Regino, *Libri duo*, pp. xx–xxi. One tenth-century copy from the cathedral library of Constance, now Stuttgart, MS HB VI 114 (s. x), is discussed in J. Autenrieth, 'Die kanonistischen Handschriften der Dombibliothek Konstantz', in J. Autenrieth and R. Kottje, *Kirchenrechtliche Texte im Bodenseegebiet: mittelalterliche Überlieferung in Konstanz, auf der Reichenau und in St Gallen*, Sigmaringen 1975, 7–21 at p. 14.

[26] The Collection in Four Books (Cologne, Dombibliothek, MS 124, s. xi) includes Regino's interrogation for use by confessors: HCC i. 283–90; F. Wasserschleben, *Beitraege zur Geschichte der vorgratianischen Kirchenrechtsquellen*, Leipzig 1839, 20–8. The Collection in 98 Chapters (Vienna, Österreichische Nationalbibliothek, Cod. 2198, and Bamberg, Staatsbibliothek, MS Can. 9) relies heavily on Regino for fifty-nine out of its ninety-eight chapters. Opening with an *ordo* for celebrating a council, it is particularly concerned with penance, listing the major crimes and their particular penance, and ends with an *ordo privata sue annualis penitentiae*: HCC i. 290–2; MGH, *Ordines de celebrando concilio*, 221–2. See also V. Krause, 'Die Akten der Triburer Synode 895', *Neues Archiv der Gesellschaft für ältere deutsche Geschichtskunde* xvii (1892), 51–82, 283–326 at p. 297. Both copies of this text were made in Freising: Hoffmann, *Buchkunst*, i. 418, 438, and his *Bamberger Handschriften des 10. und 11. Jahrhunderts* (MGH, Schriften xxxix, Hanover 1995), 123. Wolfenbüttel, Herzog-August-Bibliothek, Cod. Guelf. 451 Helmstadt, of unknown provenance, possibly

But other tenth-century east Frankish collections were compiled independently of Regino,[27] as were all the collections compiled in Italy at this time:[28] Regino's influence was localised chiefly within east Frankia.[29]

According to his preface, Burchard, bishop of Worms (1000–25), composed the *Decretum* for the instruction of the clergy of the diocese of Worms by presenting a clarification of existing laws, canons and penitential forms which had become confused and neglected.[30] He dedicated the collection to Brunicho, *praepositus* of the church of Worms, and requested that the collection should not pass out of the diocese. This local orientation corresponds to a passage in his *Vita*, written c. 1030, describing his work as a teacher:[31] the *Decretum* seems to have been intended as a textbook for

---

Strasbourg, also relies heavily on Regino. The other texts in the collection suggest a preoccupation with murder, especially within the family, for they include the letter attributed to Paulinus of Aquileia concerning his judgement of Astolph for the murder of his wife, and two papal letters on a similar question. Fournier suggested that it was probably a collection made by one man, either to meet a specific situation, or an especial interest: *HCC* i. 300–5. Salzburg, Bibliothek der Erzabtei St Peter, Cod. 32, is also dependent upon Regino for the section about a synodal tribunal, and the section about ecclesiastical judgements and marriages. The author chose, however, to rely on earlier, Carolingian authorities for his section on penance: *HCC* i. 305–10. On Regino's *Nachleben* see the article on Regino by Pokorny in Hartmann and Pennington, *History of medieval canon law* (forthcoming).

[27] For example, the collection preserved in Troyes, Bibliothèque muncipale, MS 1979 (east Frankia, s. x/xi), and Berlin, Staatsbibliothek, Phillips, Cod. 3711 (the latter has a Metz provenance); the collection in 77 chapters preserved in Munich, Bayerische Staatsbibliothek, Clm 3853 (s. x^2, Augsburg provenance (?)), Heilingkreuz, Stiftsbibliothek, MS 287, and Paris, BN lat. 3878 (s. x^{ex}, north-east Frankia); and the collection of St Emmeram, Regensburg, preserved in Munich, Bayerische Staatsbibliothek, Clm 14628: *HCC* i. 272–80, 292–300. It was recently suggested that the Collectio XII partium, which devotes bk xi to penance, preceded Burchard and was composed at Freising at the end of the tenth century: J. Müller, *Üntersuchungen zur Collectio duodecim partium*, Ebelsbach 1989. But Fournier's conclusions, that the work is dependent upon Burchard and was composed c. 1020–50 (*HCC* i. 434–42), have been reconfirmed by the recent detailed analysis of Hoffmann and Pokorny in *Das Dekret*, 87–107.

[28] Milan, Biblioteca Ambrosiana, Cods A. 46, G. 58; Verona, Biblioteca capitolare, MS LXIII (s. x $^{\text{med.-2}}$, north Italy – Verona?); and Vatican, BAV, MS 1349: *HCC* i. 330–47.

[29] P. Fournier, 'L'Oeuvre canonique de Réginon de Prüm', *Bibliothèque de l'École des Chartes* lxxxi (1920), 5–44 at p. 26.

[30] Burchard, *Decretum*, 537–40. The preface also survives in another version, on which see G. Fransen, 'Les Sources de la Préface du Décret de Burchard de Worms', *Bulletin of Medieval Canon Law* n.s. iii (1973), 1–9. Fransen also highlighted the preface's debt to the letter (c. 830) from Ebo, archbishop of Rheims, to Halitgar of Cambrai's requesting him to compose the penitential for which it is now the preface. For a recent discussion of Burchard's preface see B. C. Brasington, 'Prologues to canonical collections as a source for jurisprudential change to the eve of the Investiture Contest', *Frühmittelalterliche Studien* xxviii (1994), 226–42 at pp. 235–6. On Burchard in general see H. Fuhrmann, *Einfluss und Verbreitung der pseudoisidorischen Fälschungen von ihrem Auftauchen bis in die neuere Zeit* (MGH, Schriften xxiv, Stuttgart 1972–4), ii. 442–85.

[31] *Vita Burchardi episcopi wormatiensis*, ed. G. H. Waitz (MGH, SS iv), c. xviii, 840–1. For the argument that the *vita* was written with a didactic purpose for the clergy of Worms see S.

Worms's cathedral school and its clergy.[32] But Worms's tradition also recalled that the *Decretum*'s composition was a collaborative venture, involving five men. According to his *Vita* Burchard compiled the collection at the instigation of Brunicho and with the help of Walter, bishop of the neighbouring diocese of Speyer, a statement confirmed by the inclusion in the *Decretum* of a formula letter addressed to Walter.[33] The *Gesta abbatum Gemblaciensium*, written c. 1060, some forty years after the *Decretum*, records that Balderic, bishop of Liège, sent Olbert, a monk of Lobbes, to help Burchard with his collection.[34] Despite the relative lateness of the source it would be an odd detail to invent. Personal ties existed between Burchard and all his collaborators: Brunicho was an officer in his diocese; Burchard interceded with Henry II to obtain rights for the church of Speyer under Walter;[35] and a twelfth-century source suggests that Burchard was educated at Lobbes.[36] Burchard was thus able to draw upon the intellectual resources of three episcopal sees, situated in the provinces of Mainz and Cologne. He was probably responding to the early eleventh-century German Church's increased concern with co-operation and reform, witnessed by an increasing number of provincial and national councils, including the council held by Henry II at Dortmund (1005) attended by Burchard and Balderic's predecessor at Liège.[37] This early eleventh-century desire for reform generated a renewed need for authoritative, organised canon law collections: the late ninth-century north Italian canon law collection, the *Collectio Anselmo dedicata* appears, from

Coué, *Hagiographie im Kontext: Schreibanlass und Funktion von Bischofsviten aus dem 11. und vom Anfang des 12. Jahrhunderts*, Berlin–New York 1997, 26–40.

[32] Hoffmann and Pokorny argue that the glosses to the earliest manuscript of the *Decretum* suggest that it was produced at Worms for legal instruction in the cathedral school: *Das Dekret*, 65–8. This conclusion confirms the statement in Burchard's preface that it was intended for the instruction of students in the cathedral school: 'Et quia hoc res ita habet, eo me dilectio tua rogavit, ut opellam hanc congestam junioribus nostris legendam proponeram, quo ipsi in idonea nimirum, ea discant, quae vel senior aequalium nostrorum aetas modo assequi non possit, vel antecessorum negligentia non attigit. Utpote decentissimum fore existimans, ut quis cum omni probitate se discipulum prius exhibeat, quam doctoris auctoritatem apud vulgam temere praesumat. Et in scholis discat quod suae fidei commissos doceat': *Decretum*, 538.

[33] 'Eodem quippe tempore in collectario canonum in hac cella non modicum laboravit. Nam domino Walterio Spirensi episcopo adiuvante et Brunichone praeposito exhorante et suggerente, canones in unum corpus collegit; non pro ulla arrogantia, sed ut ipse dixit, quia canonum iura poenitentiumque iudicia in episcopatu suo omnino fuerant neglecta ac destructa. Hoc vero corpus sive collectarium distinxit et in viginti libros distribuit': *Vita Burchardi*, c. x, p. 837; for the letter see Burchard, *Decretum* ii.227, 663–4.

[34] *Gesta abbatum Gemblaciensium auctore Sigeberto*, ed. G. Pertz (MGH, SS viii), c. xxvii, p. 536.

[35] MGH, *Diplomatum regum et imperatorum Germaniae*, III: *Heinrici II et Arduini Diplomata*, ed. H. Bresslau and H. Bloch with M. Meyer and R. Holtzmann, Hanover 1900–3, no. cxc, pp. 224–5; Fournier, 'Le Décret de Burchard', 459.

[36] HCC i. 385–6.

[37] Thietmar of Merseburg, *Chronicon*, ed. R. Holtzmann (MGH, SRG n.s. ix, 1955), vi.18, pp. 294–7.

manuscript evidence, to have arrived in Germany at this time.[38] The *Decretum* was compiled in response to the same need, probably when the failings of the *Collectio* became clear; it has no section on penance, for example. The *Decretum* therefore seems, despite its preface, to have been compiled for a wider audience than the diocesan clergy of Worms.

Although one of its earliest manuscripts was written at and for Worms, two others were written in the Worms scriptorium for export, suggesting either that the collection was part of an official reform effort, or, at least, that it met a perceived need.[39] The rapid diffusion of the collection confirms that it became part of the reform initiative within the German episcopate; within thirty years of its compilation it was in the possession of several episcopal libraries both in Germany and Italy.[40] The *Decretum*'s size meant that it tended to circulate as an entire codex,[41] but several manuscripts include the educational *Admonitio synodalis* together with an *ordo* for the holding of a synod as an appendix.[42] The two major canonical collections of the tenth and eleventh centuries are therefore associated primarily with episcopal contexts and appear to have been composed for three purposes: for the education and for the discipline of the secular clergy, and as a legal reference text for the episcopal administration. Their influence was confined mainly to the area controlled by the Ottonian and Salian rulers.

---

[38] Fournier, 'Études critiques', 50–5; HCC i. 242–3; Müller, *Untersuchungen zur Collectio duodecim partium*, passim but esp. pp. 316–25.

[39] *Das Dekret*, 11–64.

[40] There are at least eighty manuscripts of Burchard's *Decretum* from the eleventh and early twelfth centuries. On its manuscript history see Meyer, 'Überlieferung', who identified seventy-four manuscripts. In addition to these see also those identified by F. Pelster, 'Das Dekret Bischof Burchards von Worms (1000–1025) in vatikanischen Handschriften', in *Miscellanea Giovanni Mercati II* (SeT cxxii, 1946), 114–57, and 'Das Dekret Burkhards von Worms in einer Redaktion aus dem Beginn der Gregorianischen Reform', *Studi Gregoriani* i (1947), 321–51; Fuhrmann, *Einfluss und Verbreitung der pseudoisidorischen Fälschungen*, 453–5; G. Fransen, 'La Tradition manuscrite du Décret de Burchard de Worms: une première orientation', in A. Scheuermann and G. May (eds), *Ius sacrum: Klaus Mörsdorf zum 60. Geburtstag*, Vienna 1969, 111–18, 'Les Sources de la Préface', and 'Le Décret'; H. Mordek, 'Handschriftenforschungen in Italien 1: zur Überlieferung des Dekrets Bischof Burchards von Worms', in *Quellen und Forschungen aus italienischen Archiven und Bibliotheken* li (1971), 626–51. See also those mentioned in Kottje, *Bussbücher*. The *Decretum* circulated quickly within eleventh-century Italy, being recorded in a library catalogue of 1035 from the ancient monastery of Nonantola: J. J. Ryan, 'Observations on the pre-Gratian canonical collections: some recent work and present problems', in *Collections de droit canonique médiéval: Louvain et Bruxelles 22–26 juillet 1958* (Bibliothèque de la Revue d'histoire ecclésiastique xxxiii, 1959), 88–103.

[41] For example, an early copy of the *Decretum* made in Worms c. 1020 (provenance, Bamberg cathedral), now Bamberg, Staatsbibliothek, MS Can. 6, comprises 312 folios and measures 26 by 33 cm.

[42] Meyer, 'Überlieferung', 171–3. The *Admonitio synodalis* is considered further in ch. 2.

Burchard and Regino on *paenitentia publica*

Burchard included in his *Decretum* this description of the process to be followed for public penance:

> At the beginning of Lent all penitents who undertake or who have undertaken public penance shall present themselves to the bishop of the city before the doors of the church dressed in sackcloth, barefoot, faces cast down to the ground, by their dress and expression proclaiming themselves to be guilty. Here the deans ought to be present, that is the archpriests of the parishes, that is the priests of the penitents, who should diligently examine their conduct, and they should enjoin a penance in the fixed degrees in accordance with the measure of guilt. After this let him (the bishop) lead them into the church, and he, prostrate on the ground and in tears, with all the clergy, shall chant the seven penitential psalms for their absolution. Then rising from prayer, according to what the canons order, let him lay hands on them, sprinkle holy water over them, first place ashes, then cover their heads with sackcloth, and with groans and frequent sighs he shall declare to them that just as Adam was expelled from paradise, so too they are banished from the Church for their sins. After this he shall order the ministers to drive them outside the doors of the church. The clergy shall follow them with the responsory, In the sweat of thy face thou shalt eat bread, so that seeing the holy Church disturbed and made to tremble at their sins, they shall not undervalue penance. At the sacred Lord's Supper, led back by their deans and priests, they are presented at the entrance of the church.[43]

This appears to be a description of public penance within the province of Mainz in the early eleventh century; Vogel noted its similarities to the *ordo* in the Romano-German pontifical composed c. 950.[44] But, as he also noted, it is taken almost wholly from Regino's collection compiled a century earlier for

---

[43] 'In capite Quadragesimae omnes poenitentes qui publicam suscipiunt aut susceperunt poenitentiam, ante fores ecclesiae se repraesentent episcopo civitatis, sacco induti, nudis pedibus, vultibus in terram prostratis, reos se esse ipso habitu et vultu proclamantes. Ibi adesse debent decani, id est, archipresbyteri parochiarum, id est, presbyteri poenitentium, qui eorum conversationem diligenter inspicere debent, et secundum modum culpae, poenitentiam per praefixos gradus injungant. Post haec in ecclesiam eos introducat, et cum omni clero septem poenitentiae Psalmos in terram prostratus cum lacrymis pro eorum absolutione decantet. Tunc resurgens ab oratione, juxta quod canones jubent, manus eis imponat, aquam benedictam super eos spargat, cinerem prius mittat, deinde cilicio capita eorum cooperiat, et cum gemitu et crebris suspiriis eis denunciet, quod sicut Adam projectus est de paradiso, ita et ipsi ab Ecclesiae pro peccatis abjiciuntur. Post haec jubeat ministris ut eos extra januas ecclesiae expellant. Clerus vero prosequatur eos cum Responsorio *In sudore vultus tui vesceris pane* etc ut videntes sanctam Ecclesiam pro facinoribus suis tremefactam atque commotam, non parvipendant poenitentiam. In sacra autem Domini coena, rursus ab eorum decanis et eorum presbyteris, ecclesiae liminibus repraesententur': *Decretum* xix.26, 984.

[44] Vogel, 'Pénitence publique', 137–8; *PRG* xcix.44–80 (Ash Wednesday), 224–51 (Maundy Thursday), ii. 14–23, 59–67.

the neighbouring province of Trier.⁴⁵ It is therefore difficult to accept this canon by itself as an accurate description of the public penitential process followed in the eleventh-century Rhineland without further investigation.

This canon illustrates the problems inherent in any study of church law. Texts produced at a particular time often repeat an earlier source as great emphasis was placed on precedent, not only in secondary collections of canons, but also in *fontes* like church councils and episcopal capitularies. Secondly, church law is usually aspirational; it represents only what the authorities wanted to happen, hence the reliance on precedent. Finally church law was not at this time universal: individual texts were produced in specific places for specific situations and often had only a limited circulation. Particular bishops might acquire or reproduce texts in accordance with their own needs, and particular occasions might evoke a search for an authoritative text.⁴⁶

Yet Burchard altered Regino's text in several ways not recognised by Vogel. He seems to have made a *précis* of the text he found in Regino in something of a hurry, producing a version which makes less sense: he omitted Regino's suggestion that the deans, that is the archpriests of the *parochiae*, ought to be present 'with witnesses, that is the priests of the penitents' and gave the deans responsibility for enjoining penance, whilst in Regino's version it is the bishop's reponsibility.⁴⁷ Burchard also added a phrase not found in Regino, that the penitents should be brought back on Maundy Thursday 'by their deans and priests'.⁴⁸ These differences, mostly omitted phrases, could have resulted from scribal errors but they are consistent throughout the five eleventh-century Burchard manuscripts which I have examined.⁴⁹ I have not been able to examine any of the Regino manuscripts, and Wasserschleben's edition may be faulty; this is, however, unlikely, as an identical reading is

---

⁴⁵ Regino, *Libri duo* i.295, pp. 136–7.
⁴⁶ For example, the contents of Wolfenbüttel, Herzog-August-Bibliothek, Cod. Guelf. 451 Helmstadt suggest that it was produced in connection with a parricide case. See n. 26 above.
⁴⁷ Compare 'ubi adesse debent decani, id est archipresbyteri parochiarum, cum testibus, id est presbyteri poenitentium, qui eorum conversationem diligenter inspicere debent. Et secundum modum culpae poenitentiam per praefixos gradus injungat' (Regino, *Libri duo* i. 295, p. 136) with 'Ibi adesse debent decani, id est, archipresbyteri parochiarum, id est, presbyteri poenitentum, qui eorum conversationem diligenter inspicere debent et secundum modum culpae, poenitentiam per praefixos gradus injungant' (Burchard, *Decretum* xix.26, 984).
⁴⁸ Compare 'In sacra autem Domini coena rursus ecclesiae liminibus repraesententur' (Regino, *Libri duo* i.295, p. 137), with 'In sacra autem Domini coena rursus ab eorum decanis et eorum presbyteris ecclesiae liminibus repraesententur' (Burchard, *Decretum* xix. 26, 984). There are a further two minor textual differences: (1) Regino: 'Tunc surgens ab oratione'; Burchard: 'Tunc resurgens ab oratione'; (2) Regino: 'ita et ipsi ab ecclesia ob peccatas eiicantur'; Burchard: 'ita et ipsi ab ecclesia pro preccatis abjiciuntur'.
⁴⁹ London, BL, MS Cotton Claudius C. vi (Canterbury cathedral, s. xi); Bamberg, Staatsbibliothek, MS Can. 6 (Bamberg cathedral, <1030); Vatican, BAV, MS lat. 7790 (s. xi); BAV, MS lat. 4880 (s. xi/xii); BAV, MS lat. 1355 (s. xi).

found in the interpolated version of Regino's text printed by Migne.[50] As my review of eleventh-century Burchard manuscripts includes a copy made in Worms before 1030, these differences must have entered the Burchard tradition at an early stage. They are significant: in Burchard's version it is the deans who enjoin penance, in Regino's it is the bishop. Burchard's variants may therefore be due to deliberate change, reflecting a difference in practice between Trier c. 906 and Worms c. 1020; or, perhaps, to original scribal errors which were not corrected by subsequent scribes. Thus in Burchard's version the two connecting sentences, concerning the imposition of the penance by the deans and the penitents' entry into church, led by the bishop, have different subjects; in Regino's the subject of both sentences is the bishop. If they were scribal errors, however, we must question whether this canon was consulted or followed by Burchard's eleventh-century readers.

There is no textual precedent for Regino's (and thus Burchard's) text. In outline he appears to be following Carolingian practice: Hincmar, archbishop of Rheims (d. 882) also delegated the supervision of public penitents' penance to deans and priests.[51] Following the traditional penitential liturgy, Regino prescribed that the bishop should lay his hands upon the penitents when receiving them into penance.[52] However, he introduced an innovation, namely the expulsion of the penitents at the end of the Ash Wednesday service as an echo of Adam's expulsion from paradise.[53] Although, as we shall see in chapter 4, the mid tenth-century Romano-German pontifical's *ordo* for entry into penance also included the penitents' expulsion, it excluded the laying on of hands; the Romano-German pontifical represents either a different version of a common tradition, or the evolution of Regino's text, following dramatic logic by removing any contact between the bishop and the penitents from a service which culminated in their expulsion from the Christian community. In either case, by following Regino Burchard recommended a different service from that prescribed in the Romano-German pontifical; yet the pontifical was widely circulated within the province of Mainz (which includes Worms) and beyond.[54] It is likely but we cannot be certain, given Regino's reliance elsewhere on Carolingian precedents, that this chapter is a description of local practice in early tenth-century Trier; it cannot be accepted as evidence of practice in early eleventh-century Worms or beyond.

Regino's text also demonstrates the bishop's attempts to re-enforce his control over the penitential process: the penitents are brought before the bishop by the deans and priests of the penitents for him to enjoin penance upon them, demonstrating his control over the diocesan hierarchy. Other

---

[50] PL cxxxii. 185–400.
[51] Hincmar, Capitulare III, c.i, MGH, *Capit. Ep. II*, 73–4.
[52] Regino, *Libri duo* i.295, pp. 136–7; see Vogel, 'Pénitence publique', 138–9. It was also prescribed by Hincmar, Capitulare III, c.i, MGH, *Capit. Ep. II*, 73–4.
[53] Mansfield, *Humiliation*, 173.
[54] See the analysis in ch. 4 and appendix 1 of the manuscripts of the Romano-German pontifical for further detail as to its distribution.

incidental references to public penance in both works also suggest a connection between public penance and episcopal authority: Regino included, in a section about the behaviour of priests, a chapter from Hincmar's first capitulary against priests who are reticent about the guilt of sinners, or about bringing penitents for reconciliation, a chapter which is obviously intended to address the problems caused by the bishop's inevitable reliance on his priests for the instigation of the public penitential process.[55] In his section on penance, Regino followed the *ordo* for secret penance with a canon from Halitgar of Cambrai's penitential (*c.* 830) ordaining that bishops (not priests) should decide the length of a penance according to the sin.[56] Referring perhaps, but not explicitly, to public penance, he stated that no priest should reconcile a penitent before he has been interrogated by the bishop, unless it is necessary in the bishop's absence;[57] that no priest should receive a penitent from another town or reconcile him without the testimony of his bishop or priest;[58] that a penitent should abstain from both secular affairs and war, even after he has ceased to be a penitent.[59] These texts are all based on earlier precedents. Regino ends this section with canons culled from Paul, Augustine and Gregory concerned with ensuring that any penance performed was a true penance.[60] Regino's debt to the Carolingian bishops, both their councils and their capitularies, may account for his concern to retain episcopal control of the penitential process; this emphasis upon the bishop seemingly represents a move from the use of public penance as a tool of central royal govern-

---

[55] '*De presbyteris qui culpas peccantium reticent vel minus digne poenitentes ad reconciliantionem adducant.* Ut nemo presbyterorum xenium vel quodiunque emolumentum temporale, immo detrimentum spirituale a quocunque publice peccante vel incestuoso accipiat, ut episcopo vel ministris eius peccatum illius reticeat, nec pro respectu cuiusque personae aut consanguinitatis vel familiantibus, alienis communicans peccatis, hoc episcopo innotescere detrectet, nec a quoquam poenitente aut gratia aut favore munus suscipere praesumat ut minus digne poenitentem ad reconciliationem adducat et ei testimonium reconciliationis ferat et quocunque livore alium quemlibet dignius poenitentem a reconciliatione removeat, quia hoc simoniacum et Deo et hominibus contrarium est': Regino, *Libri duo* i.215, pp. 107–8; Hincmar, Capitulare I, xiii, *MGH, Capit. Ep. II*, 40–1.
[56] Regino, *Libri duo* i.305, p. 148. See Halitgar, *Paenitentiale* iii.1, *Bussbücher II*, 275.
[57] Regino, *Libri duo* i.310, p. 150; source: Council of Africa (419), c. x. See also Burchard, *Decretum* xix.70, 999; *Das Dekret*, 236.
[58] Regino, *Libri duo* i.313, pp. 150–1. Cf. Burchard, *Decretum* xix. 62, 998 (source: Felix III, Ep. c. 6. 1, in Jaffé-Kaltenbrunner, *Regesta pontificum romanorum*, no. 609; text edited in PL lviii. 624); source given in *Das Dekret*, 236.
[59] Regino, *Libri duo* i.317–25, pp. 152–4. These canons are also found in the ninth-century texts of Halitgar, *Paentientiale* iii.5, 6, 7, 8, *Bussbücher II*, 276–7; Hrabanus Maurus, *Poenitentium liber ad Otgarium*, cc. xxxix–xl, PL cxii. 1424, and his *Paenitentiale ad Heribaldum episcopum Antissiodorensem*, cc. xv–xvi, PL cx. 483–4. All these ninth-century texts cite Leo I's decretal: Jaffé-Kaltenbrunner, *Regesta pontificum Romanorum*, no. 544. These canons were also taken up by Burchard, *Decretum* xix.95, 1003.
[60] '*Qualis sit vera poenitentia. Poenitentiam certam non facit, nisi odium peccati et amor Dei. Quando sic poenites ut tibi amarum sapiat in animo, quod antea dulce fuit in vita, et quod te prius obiectabatur in corpore, ipsum te cruciet in corde, tunc vere poenites*': Regino, *Libri duo* i.327, p. 155. Source: Pseudo-Augustine, *Sermo* cxvii.2, PL xxxix. 1977.

ment in the ninth century to its becoming a local and episcopal one, a means of control over a local district, in the early tenth century. Such concern may also explain Burchard's preoccupation with penance; he seems from the evidence of other sources to have exercised tight control over the city of Worms and its environs.[61] He certainly regarded episcopal control of the penitential process as important for he incorporated a text, not found in Regino, against bishops dealing with a penitent from another see without the permission of the penitent's bishop.[62] Penance was important to episcopal authority not only over the laity but also the clergy: Burchard included five canons, not found in Regino, concerned with whether clerics who have done penance can resume their office, suggesting that the collection was compiled for those involved with enforcing clerical discipline.[63] He also stressed the role of the priest, interpolating canon xxxiii of the Council of Châlon (813) which allows for confession to God alone, with an assertion attributing this argument to the Greeks and thereby implicitly condemning such practice.[64] His stress on the role of the priest reflects the preoccupation of the *Decretum* with defending both the authority of the secular clergy and the bishop's control over his diocesan hierarchy.[65]

Regino and Burchard on *paenitentia secreta*

Both Regino and Burchard start their sections on penance by instructing priests to tell all their parishioners to come to confession on Ash Wednesday: those who are 'stricken with the mortal wound of sin' ought to confess the evil they have committed and receive a penance in accordance with canonical authorities, and 'every person who recognises he has soiled with the stain of sin the immaculate robe which he received in baptism' should confess all his trangressions 'to his own priest' and very carefully observe what is enjoined on him.[66] Burchard copied Regino's text but glossed it with a

---

[61] See his *Lex familiae ecclesiae wormatiensis* (c. 1023x25), ed. L. Weiland, MGH, *Constitutiones I*, 639–44; J. Pétrau-Gay, 'Burchard de Worms', in *Dictionnaire de droit canonique*, ii. 1141–57; M. Kerner, 'Burchard, Bischof von Worms: kirchenrechtliche Sammlung und Hofrecht', in *LMA* ii. 947–51.

[62] Burchard, *Decretum* xix.62, 998. Source: Felix III, Epistola, c. 6. 1, in Jaffe-Kaltenbrunner, *Regesta pontificum romanorum*, no. 609, edited in PL lviii. 924. For this attribution see *Das Dekret*, 236.

[63] Burchard, *Decretum* xix.43 (for source see Hrabanus Maurus, *Paenitentiale ad Heribaldum*, c. x, PL cx. 476A–9A); xix.49–50 (for possible source see *Collectio Anselmo dedicata* v.116, 137); xix. 150–1 (from Hrabanus Maurus, *Paenitentiale ad Heribaldum*, c. x, PL cx. 474A–6B), 988–91, 994–5, 1012; attributions made in *Das Dekret*, 235, 239.

[64] Burchard, *Decretum* xix.145, 1011. On the implications of this canon for Burchard's methodology and outlook see Vogel, *Le Pécheur au Moyen Age*, 202–3.

[65] Fournier, 'Le Décret', 451–73.

[66] 'Presbyteri admonere debent plebem sibi subiectam et omnis, qui sentit se mortifero peccati vulnere sauciatum, feria quarta ante quadragesimam cum omni festinatione recurrat ad vivificantem matrem ecclesiam, ubi quod male commisit cum omni humilitate, et

chapter from Theodulf of Orléans's first capitulary (c. xxxvi): the priests of the *plebes* should call the people before them, and reconcile the contentious by canonical athority and settle all quarrels, and then give penance to those who confess, so that before the beginning of the fast, all those who have confessed, having accepted their penance, are free to say, 'and forgive us our trespasses as we forgive those who trespass against us'.[67] Burchard emphasised that rural priests should ensure that all those guilty of known sins did penance; it is unclear what sort of penance he is referring to. The text he shares with Regino is similarly unclear, merely suggesting that there are two sorts of confession on Ash Wednesday: for those guilty of major, and for those guilty of minor sins. Ash Wednesday is therefore seen as a day of universal confession for all Christians.

Both Regino and Burchard then selected texts culled from Halitgar of Cambrai's preface to book vi of his penitential; Halitgar composed his work in six books at the request of Archbishop Ebo of Reims c. 829/30 in order to provide a practical guide for confessors and a justification for penance in 'one volume'.[68] The manuscript history of Halitgar's collection suggests that it circulated mainly within an episcopal milieu; it is not therefore surprising to find both Regino and Burchard citing from Halitgar on secret penance in their own episcopal collections.[69] Regino's selection was much fuller: he included Halitgar's injunction that no one except a bishop or a priest should presume to give penance or hear confession, although he followed Halitgar in allowing that a deacon might hear confession in an emergency.[70] Burchard was also anxious to defend the secular clergy's control over penitential rites, quoting instead a canon from Theodore's penitential (c. 690xc. 740), falsely attributed to a Mainz council.[71] But Regino and Burchard both adopted

---

contritione cordis simpliciter confessus suscipiat remedia poenitentiae secundum modum canonicis auctoritatibus praefixum, tradaturque Satanae in interitu carnis, ut spiritus salvus sit in die Domini. Non solum autem ille, qui mortale aliquid commisit, sed etiam omnis homo, quicunque se recognoscit, immaculatam Christi tunicam, quam in baptismo accepit, peccati macula polluisse, ad proprium sacerdotem festinet venire et cum puritate mentis omnes transgressiones omniaque peccata quibus Dei offensam se incurrisse meminit, humiliter confiteatur, et quicquid ei a sacerdote fuerit iniunctum, ac si ab ipso omnipotentis Dei ore esset prolatum, ita diligenter intendat et cautissime observet': Regino, *Libri duo* i.292, p. 135; Burchard, *Decretum* xix.2, 949. Despite the problems with the Migne edition noted by Fransen, 'Le Décret' (see n. 1 above), its text of the *ordo* accords with one of the earliest copies of the text made at Worms c. 1030: Bamberg, Staatsbibliothek, MS Can. 6, fos 242r–60r. This manuscript was written c. 1020 and a Bamberg hand added the text of the Council of Seligenstadt (1023) in the second quarter of the eleventh century: *Das Dekret*, 16–18; Hoffmann, *Bamberger Handschriften*, 122.

[67] Burchard, *Decretum* xix.1, 949; Theodulf of Orléans's capitula I, c. xxxvi, *MGH, Capit. Ep. I*, 133–5. On the problems of what is meant by a *plebs* in this period see ch. 2.

[68] Halitgar, *Paenitentiale*, pref., *Bussbücher II*, 265.

[69] On Halitgar's episcopal audience see Meens, 'Frequency', 40.

[70] Regino, *Libri duo* i.299–300, pp. 138–9; Halitgar, *Paenitentiale* vi: pref., *Bussbücher II*, 291.

[71] Burchard, *Decretum* xix.142, 1010, attributes the text to a Mainz council, 'ex concilio

Halitgar's injunction that, as part of the bishop's or priest's preparation for hearing the confession of the faithful, they should humble themselves and pray, with groans and tears, for both their own faults and those of all Christians; only Regino included Halitgar's justification of this action: if the penitent saw the priest weeping for his deeds, this should increase his own fear of God and horror at his own sins.[72]

Burchard's *ordo* is not, therefore, a straight copy of Regino despite their superficial similarities. Both begin their *ordo* with an interrogation of the orthodoxy of the penitent's beliefs followed by a penitential *interrogatio* concerning various sins with their appropriate penance. Topics covered included homicide, perjury, theft, adultery, rape, sodomy, intercourse at the forbidden times and pagan practices, and are presented in a questionnaire. Thus, to take one of the questions in Burchard: 'Have you violated a grave, by which I mean, after you see someone buried have you gone at night, broken open the grave, and taken his clothes? If you have, you should do penance for two years on the appointed fast days.'[73] Pierre Payer made a strong case for Regino's interrogation being dependent upon that in the Bede–Egbert double penitential.[74] Burchard's version owes much of its overall structure to Regino but is more elaborate, covering 180 questions about possible sins and their appropriate penances.[75] One of the more original elements of the *Decretum* is that it contains material not found in previous penitentials, such as specific questions about superstitious beliefs and practices.[76] The arrangement of the *interrogatio* is, however, confused; there are, for example, two separate

---

Mogunt. cap. 2', but it comes from the penitential of Theodore known as that of the *discipulus Umbriensium* II.vi.16: *Die Canones Theodori Cantuariensis und ihre Überlieferungsformen*, ed. P. Finsterwalder, Weimar 1929, 321. The *discipulus Umbriensium* is a problematic text. For the most recent discussion of its history see T. Charles-Edwards, 'The penitential of Theodore and the *Iudicia Theodori*', in M. Lapidge (ed.), *Archbishop Theodore: commemorative studies on his life and influence*, Cambridge 1995, 141–74, where it is dated to the mid eighth century.

[72] 'Videns autem ille, qui ad poenitentiam venit, sacerdotem tristem et lacrymantem pro suis facinoribus, magis ipse timore Dei perculus amplius tristatur et exhorescit peccata sua': Regino, *Libri duo* i.303, p. 140. For the broader instruction see ibid. i.302, p. 140. This canon is also found in Burchard, *Decretum* xix.2, 949–50. The source is Halitgar, *Paenitentiale* vi: pref., *Bussbücher II*, 291–2. All three authors include the preparation prayer 'Domine Deus omnipotens propitius esto mihi peccatori ut condigne tibi possim gratias agere', found in other *ordines* for the giving of penance, for example PRG xcix.45, cxxxvi.3, ii. 14–15, 234–5, and SF, nos 55 (347) and 437 (2375), pp. 43, 281. See chs 4, 5 for further details.

[73] 'Violasti sepulcrum, ita dico, dum aliquem videres sepelire, et in nocte infringeres sepulcrum et tolleres vestimenta ejus? Si fecisti, II annos per legitimas ferias poeniteas': Burchard, *Decretum* xix.5, 960C.

[74] Payer, *Sex and the penitentials*, 79. For the text of the Bede–Egbert double penitential see *Bussbücher II*, 679–701. On the date of this so-called double penitential see Frantzen, *Literature*, 69–77, 107–10, for a summary of the arguments given in full in his 'The penitentials attributed to Bede', *Speculum* lviii (1983), 573–97.

[75] Burchard, *Decretum* xix.5, 951–76; Fournier, 'Études critiques', 323–5.

[76] Vogel, 'Pratiques superstitieuses'.

sections concerning incest, representing, perhaps, the unsuccessful fusion of two different sources.[77] This repetition, together with Burchard's debt to his predecessors, suggests that book xix was intended as a reference work rather than for practical use. After the penitent has confessed his sin and received the appropriate penance the priest should recite the eight principal sins and their derived sins, and the eight virtues which cure them.[78] Then the penitent should prostrate himself on the ground and formally acknowledge his own sinfulness before God and beg His forgiveness. The priest prostrates himself with the penitent and sings Psalms xxxvii, cii, l, liii and li followed by prayers in which he invokes God's forgiveness; in Regino's version, the priest only sings Psalms lvii, l and liii.[79] The *ordo* concludes with the priest asking God's forgiveness on behalf of the penitent: 'May almighty God be your helper and protector and grant forgiveness of your sins past, present and future. Amen.'[80] Burchard's *ordo* is therefore a close, not a carbon, copy of Regino's. The absence of a reference to explicit absolution in both *ordines* suggests, however, that if absolution were sought, it would have been delayed until Maundy Thursday. It is less than clear that it was an element in this particular process.[81]

Both Regino and Burchard included detailed and seemingly partially original *ordines* in their collections, suggesting that they regarded penance as an important aspect of the priest's duties and one they sought to regulate. But Burchard's eleventh-century manuscript tradition suggests that different centres took different attitudes to this *ordo*. In one eleventh-century copy an alternative reading has been added later above the line so that the prayers refer to plural penitents in addition to the singular penitent of the original text, suggesting that the text was read and reflected upon, if not used;[82] conversely another centre was so indifferent to the *ordo* that c. vii, its terminating chapter, was omitted by their copyist.[83]

Although dependent on earlier legislation for much of their work, both collectors demonstrated more originality in their lists of how penitential

---

[77] Burchard, *Decretum* xix.5, 957d–9c, 965d–7d.
[78] Ibid. xix.6–7.1, 976–8, parallels the version in Regino, *Libri duo* i.304, pp. 146–7. The classification of eight principal sins owes much to the early fifth-century text of John Cassian, *De institutes coenobiorum et de octo principalium vitiorum remediis libri XII*, ed. J.-C. Guy, in *Jean Cassien: institutions cénobitiques* (SC cix, 1965).
[79] Burchard, *Decretum*, xix.7, 977–8.
[80] 'Deus omnipotens sit adiutor et protector tuus, et praestet indulgentiam de peccatis tuis, praeteritis, praesentibus, et futuris. Amen': ibid. xix.7, 978. In Regino's version, it is followed by a text, taken from the Bede–Egbert penitential, outlining the need to take into account the penitent's personal circumstances before awarding him penance: Regino, *Libri duo* i.304, p. 148.
[81] Poschmann, however, viewed the *ordo* in Burchard as evidence for a one-stage penitential process of confession followed immediately by reconciliation: *Penance*, 145.
[82] Vatican, BAV, MS Vat. lat. 4880, fos 149v–61v. For example, 'huic famulo' was amended to 'his famulis' at fo. 161r.
[83] Ibid. MS Vat. lat. 1355, fos 249v–68r.

sentences could be commuted. Penance was measured in days fasting on bread and water but Regino allowed for those to be commuted to the recital of psalms, or almsgiving or physical punishment: thus a day's fasting is worth a meal for two or three poor men, one denarius in alms, the recital of a whole psalter in summer, or fifty psalms in winter, spring and autumn, or twelve strokes.[84] Burchard's prescriptions were more varied, and comprise some of the most original parts of book xix, less than 6 per cent of which is original.[85] For him, like Regino, commutation did not indicate an evasion of personal responsibility.[86] Prayers could be undertaken personally, through the singing of the psalms or by reciting the Pater Noster; the number of psalms to be sung would vary with the length of the penance to be redeemed, and the posture and position of the penitent: the number increased if he was standing, rather than kneeling, and in a convenient place rather than church.[87] Alternatively, the penitent could commission a priest to say mass, the equivalent of one year's penance, but the penitent must confess his sins, if they were *crimina capitalia*, attend mass and abstain from wine, meat and fat on that day.[88] Redemption through the payment of money was means-tested.[89] Burchard's apparent invention of ways to discharge penance suggests an effort to meet demand. He himself was aware of his innovation: he ended his description of what the penance for homicide entails and the possible ways to redeem it, thus: 'We concede these things to you from mercy, not according to the severity of the canons, for the canons prescribe thus: If anyone on purpose and through desire commits murder, he shall renounce the world and go into a monastery of monks and there serve God always.'[90] But he was often strict: he included an injunction of the Council of Châlon (813) that pilgrimage to Rome does not dispense with the confessor's penance,[91] intended to discourage people from appealing to the pope against the penance imposed

---

[84] Regino, *Libri duo* ii.451, p. 391.
[85] Burchard, *Decretum* xix.14–16, 18.2, 21, 982–3. These canons have no known source: *Das Dekret*, 233.
[86] On commutation in general see C. Vogel, 'Composition légale et commutations dans le système de la pénitence tarifée', *Revue du droit canonique* viii, ix (1958, 1959), 289–318, 1–38, 341–59 (repr. in his *En Rémission*, no. v).
[87] Burchard, *Decretum* xix. 18, 982.
[88] Ibid. xix.21, 983.
[89] Ibid. xix.15, 22, 982, 983. The source for c. 22 is Regino, *Libri duo* ii.446, pp. 389–90 (ultimately derived from Excarpsus Bedae-Egberti, c. 41). For these attributions see *Das Dekret*, 233.
[90] 'Ista secundum misericordiam concedimus tibi, non secundum canonum censuram: quia canones sic praecipiunt. Si quis per industriam et per cupiditatem homicidium fecerit, saeculum relinquat et ingrediatur monasterium monachorum et ibi iugiter Deo servat': *Decretum* xix.5, 952B. The canonical prescription has its ultimate origin in Gregory the Great; see ch. 2 for further consideration of this prescription.
[91] *Decretum* xix.51, 995; Council of Châlon (813), c. 45, MGH, *Concilia II*, i. 282–3; HCC i. 392. This injunction was taken up by the Council of Seligenstadt (1023), cc. xvi, xx, MGH, *Constitutiones I*, 638–9. This council is discussed in chapter 2; its canons were often copied with Burchard's *Decretum*.

on them.⁹² Pilgrimage was seen here not as a way to redeem penance but as a challenge to episcopal authority. Burchard's concern with commutation is part of his overall pastoral preoccupation: the canons on commutation follow his seemingly original definition of the activities required of, or denied to, the penitent for a seven-year penance.⁹³ A year's penance meant fasting on bread and water on Monday, Wednesday and Friday, eating only beans, vegetables, fruit and beer on Tuesday, Thursday and Saturday, and on Sundays and feast days eating the same food as everyone else although the penitent should take care on these occasions not to over-indulge. His innovation suggests that he intended the penances outlined in the *interrogatio* to be applied, and anticipated the need to define what was meant by penance: such a concern with definition also confirms what Burchard stated in his preface, namely that the work was designed as an educational aid for teaching potential priests in the cathedral school.

Both Regino and Burchard cited the so-called Carolingian dichotomy: in Burchard's words, priests should distinguish between 'him who has sinned publicly and done penance publicly, and him who has sinned secretly and voluntarily made confession'.⁹⁴ Burchard inserted these words into his *interrogatio*. This clear distinction could suggest that the *interrogatio*, and hence the *ordo*, was to be used for the administration of public as well as secret penance; the *ordo* was a stage through which all penitents had to pass, before it was decided whether they should do public penance. Alternatively, Burchard may have included this passage because the purpose of the *interrogatio* was educational: it was intended to help priests memorise the appropriate penances and this was seen as an equally important piece of information. Or the *Decretum* may have been intended solely as a reference work for bishops and cathedral clergy concerned with the administration of the penitential system. Whilst Regino omitted any reference to the dichotomy in his *interrogatio*, both collections inserted the same reference to it, a canon from the Council of Mainz (847), shortly after their prescriptions of the public penitential process.⁹⁵ The dichotomy explains the apparent contradiction between priests' responsibility for imposing penance for mortal sins, and

---

92 On early medieval penitential pilgrimage see C. Vogel, 'Le Pélérinage pénitentiel', *Revue des sciences religieuses* xxxviii (1964), 113–53 (repr. in his *En Rémission*, no. vii).
93 *Decretum* xix.9–10, 980–1; *Das Dekret*, 233.
94 'In istis omnibus supradictis debent sacerdotes magnam discretionem habere, ut discernant inter illum qui publice peccavit et public poenituit et inter illum qui absconse peccavit et sua sponte confessus est': *Decretum* xix.5, 971c.
95 'Sed discretio servanda est inter poenitentes qui publice et qui absconse poenitere debeant': Council of Mainz (847), c. xxxi, MGH, *Concilia* III, 176, which is itself taken from the Council of Reims (813), c. xxxi, MGH, *Concilia* II, i. 256. Compare 'Sed discretio servanda est inter poenitentes publice et absconse. Nam qui publice peccat, oportet, ut publica multetur poenitentia secundum ordinem canonum pro merito suo excommunicetur et reconcilietur': Regino, *Libri duo* i.296, p. 137. This canon follows directly on from the description of public penance, and is also found in Burchard's *Decretum* xix.28, 985.

the bishop's assumption of responsibility for public penitents. Neither author thought it necessary to discuss what signifies a public sin.

Despite the inclusion by Regino and Burchard of *ordines* for the administration of secret penance, which give an air of pastoral concern to their works, investigation of both their context and content suggests that they were composed as aids for the higher clergy, as reference aids for the administration of penance by the bishop and his cathedral clergy. In Burchard's case there are some hints in book xix that support his stated aim of producing a work for use in the training of clergy in the cathedral school at Worms.

Penitentials

That canon law collections were composed for and used by members of the higher clergy is unsurprising. But it is less clear who comprised the readers and users of tenth- and eleventh-century penitentials. Recent research means that we know more about the textual history of certain penitentials and their sources, but still very little about how penitentials were used. Penitentials evolved in conjunction with the development of secret penance, emerging in the sixth-century in Ireland whence they spread rapidly to England and the continent.[96] They began as collections of penitential canons, but an *ordo* for hearing confession and giving penance was added from the late eighth century, perhaps the most influential being that of Halitgar of Cambrai's early ninth-century penitential (c. 829/30).[97] Their use was debated by the early ninth-century Carolingian reform councils, but they were accepted and promoted by the Frankish Church; their popularity is demonstrated by their survival in at least 300 manuscripts from before 1000.[98] Scholarship to date has concentrated on their early history with relatively little attention being paid to penitentials produced or copied in the tenth and eleventh centuries except for the work of Frantzen, who demonstrated that the introduction of Frankish penitentials into England played an important part in the tenth-century reform movement.[99] Despite studies of individual manuscripts, no overview exists of penitentials copied or produced in any of the areas under review for the tenth and eleventh centuries.[100] What follows is not a

---

[96] Frantzen, *Literature*, 19–93.
[97] The earliest examples are in the *Poenitentiale floriacense* (s. viii ex) and the *Poenitentiale sangallense* (s. ix 2/4): *Die Bussordnungen*, 422–9, discussed by Frantzen in *Literature*, 103–6.
[98] This figure is derived from Murray, 'Confession', 60. On the attitude of the Frankish reformers of the early ninth century see Frantzen, *Literature*, 97–110, and 'Significance of the Frankish penitentials', where he argues that the reformers accepted and promoted certain penitentials, thereby refuting the argument that the reforms took effect against the penitentials, put forward by Pierce [McKitterick], 'The "Frankish" penitentials'.
[99] Frantzen, *Literature*, 122–50.
[100] A partial exception is Rob Meens's recent study of 106 manuscripts containing tripartite penitentials which covers this period but concentrates on the ninth century:

detailed study of all the penitentials used in this period, but rather a review, not only of some of the texts of penitentials composed, but also of the associated content with which they and certain ninth-century penitentials were copied in this period, followed by a comparison of my findings with the conclusions reached by historians specialising in the material from the earlier period. This review thus contributes to, rather than solves, the larger problem of how penitentials were used in the early medieval period.

The established view sees penitentials as handbooks used by priests in the course of delivering pastoral care throughout the early Middle Ages. This view is supported by the considerable number of manuscript copies of penitentials associated with missionary centres such as St Gall and Rheims, as well as the injunctions to priests in Carolingian legislation to possess such books.[101] But Franz Kerff has challenged this view of their pastoral purpose, arguing that penitentials should be seen as collections of canon law made with a specific aim: to aid the bishop in the conduct of his synodal inquisitions.[102] They are thus juridical rather than pastoral in intent, more concerned with penance as a punishment than as a cure for sinners. Penitentials were episcopal handbooks made to support the bishop as governor of his diocese, rather than handbooks to aid rural priests in the delivery of pastoral care. Strong arguments, however, have been put forward for the pastoral use of penitentials at a level beneath that of the episcopate in the ninth century: the inclusion of an *ordo* with the canons meant that they not only recorded moral standards, as in canon law collections, but also sought to enforce them.[103] And Rob Meens's important recent study of the associated content of 106 medieval manuscripts of tripartite penitentials (that is penitentials drawn from the Irish, Anglo-Saxon and Frankish traditions) confirms this view of the majority of ninth-century manuscripts as priestly handbooks; but as his own work suggests, the picture is rather different for the tenth century when the majority of manuscripts in his sample appear to have been copied in juridical or episcopal contexts and seem far removed from their original pastoral environment.[104] Thus the inclusion of canons from penitentials in

---

'Frequency'. Payer examined the history of certain penitential canons in this period but did not consider the codices themselves: *Sex and the penitentials*, 72–83.

[101] Meens, 'Frequency', 39–40 n. 28. On St Gall see R. Kottje, 'Kirchenrechtliche Interessen im Bodenseeraum vom 9. bis 12. Jahrhundert', in Autenrieth and Kottje, *Kirchenrechtliche Texte*, 23–41; on Rheims see Kottje, *Bussbücher*, 84–5.

[102] F. Kerff, 'Mittelalterliche Quellen und mittelalterliche Wirklichkeit: zu den Konsequenzen einer jüngst erschienenen Edition für unser Bild kirchlicher Reformbemühungen', *Rheinische Vierteljarhrsblätter* li (1987), 275–86, and 'Libri paenitentiales'. This juridical context is also assumed in H. Lutterbach's work, 'Intentions – oder Tathaftung? Zum Bussverständnis in den frühmittelalterlichen Bussbüchern', *Frühmittelalterliche Studien* xxix (1995), 120–43.

[103] A. J. Frantzen, 'The tradition of penitentials in Anglo-Saxon England', *Anglo-Saxon England* xi (1983), 23–56.

[104] Meens, 'Frequency', 45–6.

tenth-century canon law collections such as those compiled by Regino and Burchard suggests that such penitential texts were also now seen as reference works for use in a juridical context. Perhaps as a legacy of the distrust of penitentials exhibited by the early Carolingian reform councils, both authors were reluctant to acknowledge their penitential sources: Burchard even went so far as to give false attributions to those of his canons derived from penitentials.

One popular penitential handbook was that composed by Halitgar, bishop of Cambrai. He sought to rectify the confusion demonstrated by late eighth-century continental handbooks which contain a contradictory synthesis of tariffs from earlier penitentials.[105] Halitgar was not especially influential among his contemporaries but he was often copied in the tenth and eleventh centuries, surviving in more than twenty-five manuscripts from this period.[106] Many of these are partial copies: books i and ii on the virtues and vices were often omitted, books iii, iv and v on the administration of penance and canonical penances for the laity and the clergy were the most widely copied parts; book vi, a guide to the confessor for the administration of penance, containing an *ordo confessionis* with a synthesis of canons from earlier penitentials, was not especially popular.[107] Perhaps this is because Halitgar conceived his work as an instructive text to be disseminated by the bishops to their clergy.[108]

It is therefore perhaps not surprising to find that Halitgar was copied into tenth- and eleventh-century episcopal handbooks, such as that which Kottje has identified as belonging to Adalbert, bishop of Prague (d. 997).[109] This

---

[105] Halitgar wrote his penitential in six books at the request of Ebo, archbishop of Rheims, who in a letter, which with Halitgar's reply acts a preface to the work, complained about the confusion in penitential practice generated by the circulation of unauthorised and often contradictory penitentials: *Bussbücher II*, 264–5. Halitgar's penitential thus fits into the more general concern expressed by Carolingian bishops in the early ninth century about the nature of the penitentials in circulation which were regarded as lacking authority and as sometimes allowing priests to go against canonical practices. In 829 the council of Paris condemned (c. xxxii) those penitentials which allowed priests to go against canonical authority and ordained that bishops seek out and burn erroneous booklets within their own diocese: *MGH, Concilia II*, ii. 633; Frantzen, *Literature*, 97–107. As Frantzen has demonstrated the Frankish reforms did not lead to the suppression of the penitentials: 'The significance of the Frankish penitentials'.

[106] Kottje, *Bussbücher*, 15–83.

[107] Although bk vi did circulate on its own with Hrabanus' *Penitentiale ad Heribaldum*: Kottje, *Bussbücher*, 134–9.

[108] *Bussbücher II*, 264–5. In 'Libri paenitentiales' Kerff based his argument for an episcopal context for the penitentials on a study of manuscripts of Halitgar. As Meens suggests, it is not surpising to find Halitgar's text preserved in an episcopal context as it was written as part of the episcopal movement to clarify penitential practice in the late 820s and early 830s: 'Frequency', 40.

[109] Heiligenkreuz, Stiftsbibliothek, MS 217 (south German, s. x^{ex}): Kottje, *Bussbücher*, 25–8. Kottje's attribution is made on the grounds of the inclusion of letters from the pope and Duke Boleslav concerning Adalbert, bishop of Prague, c. 992, but it might equally have

includes not only books iii–v of Halitgar's penitential, but also the Bede–Egbert double penitential, Hrabanus Maurus' penitential for Heribald, letters of Hrabanus Maurus and Gregory the Great, canons from the Councils of Mainz (852) and Worms (868), a canonical collection, and also secular laws, the Lex Alemannorum together with Ansegis's collection of Carolingian royal capitularies.[110] Such mixed collections continued into the late eleventh century: a Saint-Gallen codex contains the Gregorian Collection in LXXIV Titles together with book vi of Halitgar and Hrabanus Maurus' penitential for Heribald.[111] Halitgar was also copied in a collection with a more pastoral tone, which was also probably compiled for a bishop because, for example, it includes an *ordo* for the reconciliation of penitents on Maundy Thursday. Written probably in north Italy, or possibly southern France, the tenth-century codex also includes together with the first five books of Halitgar, *ordines* for giving penance and the reconciliation of the dying, Theodulf's first set of *capitula* and two treatises on baptism.[112] Nevertheless we cannot always assume that penitentials were copied for the purpose suggested by their pastoral content. Halitgar's book vi was often omitted: his work was valued as a reference guide on penance rather than as instruction for specific practice. His penitential was copied for use in cathedral libraries, for educative or reference purposes, not for use in the field. But as Meens has argued, this is not unexpected: Halitgar's penitential seems always to have been intended for an episcopal audience; it was written at the request of Archbishop Ebo of Reims as a result of the Carolingian reform councils and combines material from the late antique councils with that from the penitential tradition.[113]

Few new penitentials were composed in tenth-century east (or west) Frankia.[114] Earlier penitentials continued to be copied but the milieu for which they were copied changed. There seems to be an abrupt change

---

been compiled by Adalbert's successor. Other episcopal handbooks include one from Augsburg, Munich, Staatsbibliothek, Clm 3853 (s. x²), ibid. 38–9, and one produced at Corvey which includes the *Leges Saxonum, Francorum* and *Thuringorum*, the *Capitula Angilramni*, Halitgar's penitential (bks iii–v), the Bede–Egbert double penitential, and various ninth-century councils amongst other works: Münster, Staatsarchiv, MS VII. 5201 (s. x¹), on which see ibid. 45–7, and G. Theuerkauf, *Lex, speculum, compendium iuris: Rechtsaufzeichnung und Rechtsbewusstsein in Norddeutschland vom 8. bis zum 16. Jahrhundert*, Cologne–Graz 1968, 67–97.

[110] For a description of this manuscript see *Collectio capitularium Ansegisi*, ed. G. Schmitz (MGH, Capitularia regum Francorum n.s. i, Hanover 1996), 93–6.

[111] St Gall, Stiftsbibliothek, Cod. 676 (c. 1080–1100): Kottje, *Bussbücher*, 60–1. Meens classified it as a juridical manuscript: 'Frequency', 59.

[112] Barcelona, Biblioteca de la Universidad, MS 228 (s. x²): Kottje, *Bussbücher*, 15–16. This collection is classified by Meens as pastoral: 'Frequency', 56.

[113] Ibid. 40.

[114] Neither the Arundel penitential (s. x/s. xi) – BL, MS Arundel 201, *Bussbücher I*, 437–65 – nor the *Poenitentiale pseudo-Fulberti* (s. xi) – BL, MS Arundel 173, ibid. 773–4 – includes penitential *ordines* or other specific guidance on practice.

between the ninth century, when the majority of penitentials were copied for use in a pastoral context, and the tenth century when the majority of manuscripts were written for a juridical or episcopal context.[115] Whether this change means a decline in standards of pastoral care is less clear. Did clerics choose instead to compose new penitential *ordines* complete with detailed lists of tariffs in liturgical books rather than continuing in the old penitential medium, such as that in a tenth-century ritual from the ancient monastery of Bobbio, or were they content with the many ninth-century copies in existence, or did they turn to the new collections for penitential canons?[116] These issues require much more research before we can hope to answer the question of what guidance, if any, local rural priests followed in administering penance.[117]

But this model of a move away from penitentials in the tenth century, whilst true for northern Europe, is not a universal one: several new penitentials, based on Frankish penitentials, were composed in Italy in the tenth and eleventh centuries.[118] Six of these include penitential *ordines*, each of which seems unique to that text, suggesting that some attempt was made to tailor these penitentials to meet pastoral needs.[119] One such which follows the Frankish format of *ordo* followed by penitential canons is in a Vatican

---

[115] Meens, 'Frequency', 41–6.

[116] Vatican, BAV, MS Vat. lat. 5768 (s. x), fos 17r–41v; Hägele, *Das Paenitentiale Vallicellianum*, i. 94. *Ordines* accompanied by penitential canons are also found in the following liturgical manuscripts: the eleventh-century sacramentary from S. Lorenzo in Damaso, Rome (Rome, Biblioteca Vallicelliana, Cod. E. 15, fos 170v–84v), edited in *Bussbücher I*, 239–47; the early eleventh-century *rituale* from S. Abundio, Como (Rome, Biblioteca nazionale, Cod. 2116 (Sessor. 136), fos 19v–50v), described by A. Ebner, *Quellen und Forschungen zur Geschichte und Kunstgeschichte des Missale Romanum im Mittelalter: Iter Italicum*, Freiburg-im-Breisgau 1896, 170–2; and that in the late eleventh- or early twelfth-century pontifical from Arezzo (Vatican, BAV, MS Vat. lat. 4772, fos 190v–230v) where the *ordo* for giving penance is followed by penitential canons taken from Burchard's *Decretum*, bk xix: *Bussbücher II*, 403–7. Later north European examples may yet come to light, but current research into the tenth- and eleventh-century evidence confirms the idea of a move away from the use of penitentials in a pastoral context to their use only in a canonical one in northern Europe.

[117] I intend to study the evidence for penitential rituals found in the liturgical collections of pastoral rites known as *rituales* in greater detail in the future.

[118] New penitentials were also composed in Old English in tenth-century Anglo-Saxon England: Frantzen, *Literature*, 122–50.

[119] In addition to the two mentioned in the text see: (i) Rome, Biblioteca Vallicelliana, Cod. E. 15 (s. ix ^{ex} – s. x ^{med}): *Bussbücher I*, 239–342; see also Hägele, *Das Paenitentiale Vallicellianum I*, 93–4, esp. n. 47. The manuscript itself is early eleventh-century; (ii) Rome, Biblioteca Vallicelliana, Cod. E. 62 (central Italy, s. xii), fos 269–84. Although fos 1–268 comprise a *rituale*, written in a s. xi hand, the penitential *ordo* and the canons which follow it begin on a new quire and are written in a proto-Gothic hand, suggesting a twelfth-century date for this text; it is edited by Wasserschleben in *Die Bussordnungen*, 550–66; (iii) Monte Cassino, Cod. 372 (s. ix/x): *Bussbücher I*, 397–432; (iv) Vatican, BAV, MS Vat. lat. 5768 (s. x, Bobbio), fos 17r–41v (the final folio/s from this quire appear to be missing). On this text see Hägele, *Das Paenitentiale Vallicellianum*, i. 94.

manuscript of unknown provenance which was probably compiled in Rome c. 1000.[120] It was copied in a *libellus* which also includes a *Passio sanctae Luciae* and a lectionary for various Marian feasts: its liturgical, not canonical/legal, context suggests that it was used in a practical liturgical manner which may explain the *ordo's* innovatory nature. The canons themselves are copied (ultimately) from a north-eastern west Frankish source but were rearranged to make a shorter, clearer collection.[121] The *ordo* is a variation on a ninth-century recension, and includes an *interrogatio* and shares several features with that found in a collection of pastoral liturgical rites from eleventh-century southern Italy.[122] It begins with the priest reminding the penitent to fear God and spelling out the correct way to do penance. The priest should then prostrate himself before the altar, rise and ask the penitent if he wishes to confess all his sins since baptism; the penitent should then recite a confession prayer. There is no *interrogatio*. The priest then admonishes him to keep the Ten Commandments, and to visit the sick, bury the dead, be diligent in charity, honour priests and implement their orders in all things. The process seems more akin to that identified by Frantzen as devotional confession than the administration of secret penance, for no provision is made to confess a specific sin nor award a specific penance, a function presumably supplied by the subsequent set of penitential canons.[123] However, other pastoral penitentials must have been made for a bishop: Vallicelliana B. 58 is a composite text but includes an *ordo* for public as well as one for secret penance together with a penitential.[124] Until we know more about the provenance and purpose of these manuscripts, we cannot study the differences in these *ordines* and the reasons behind them. But these differences, their adaptations and innovations, suggest that they were regarded as effective working texts, for use in a pastoral environment.

Other Italian penitentials of this period were compiled in a more juridical context. Neither Vallicelliana, Cod. C. 6 nor Vallicelliana, Cod. F. 92 contains an *ordo*,[125] and one of the most famous collections of penitential texts was compiled in tenth-century northern Italy for a monastic context:

---

[120] Vatican, BAV, MS Archivio S. Pietro H. 58, fos 109r–17v: Körntgen, 'Ein italienisches Bussbuch'.

[121] Körntgen argues, ibid, that these canons came via north Italy. He gives a summary of them with their sources at pp. 198–205.

[122] 'Incipit quomodo debet esse mediator sacerdos infra deum et hominem sive penitentiam dans. Quotienscumque Christiani ad poenitentiam accedunt.' On this text see Körntgen, *Studien zu den Quellen*, 130–8. The *ordo*, at fos 109v–12r, has not been edited but has several similarities with that in *Ein Rituale in beneventanischer Schrift: Roma, Biblioteca Vallicelliana, Cod. 32: Ende des 11. Jahrhunderts*, ed. A. Odermatt (Spicilegium Friburgense, xxvi, 198), 283–96.

[123] Frantzen, *Literature*, 170.

[124] These rites are edited by Schmitz in *Bussbücher I*, 774–9.

[125] Rome, Biblioteca Vallicelliana, Cod. C. 6, fos 180r–3r, 189r–95v (Rome, s. xi[in]), edited in *Bussbücher I*, 350–88; Rome, Biblioteca Vallicelliana, Cod. F. 92 (Italy, s. xi), edited in *Die Bussordnungen*, 682–8.

Berlin, Staatsbibliothek (Haus 1), Cod. Hamilton 290.[126] These collections fit well with Hägele's suggestion that Italy's tenth-century interest in penitentials may be seen as part of the interest in canon law evinced in the manuscripts produced or copied in the large cathedral schools of Milan, Parma, Pavia, Verona and Vercelli.[127] But, as he pointed out, the belated Italian interest in reworking Frankish penitential canonical material went hand in hand with the compilation of new penitential *ordines* which fit less easily with an academic interest. The manuscript evidence of texts suggests that some Italian penitentials were used in a more pastoral context,[128] but cathedral schools existed to train the secular clergy in practice as well as law. Although there may not be one single explanation for the Italians' belated interest in Frankish penitentials, it is none the less possible that, as in late Anglo-Saxon England, their interest was part of a more general concern with ecclesiastical reform. Nevertheless the Italian evidence presents a somewhat different picture to that shown by the eastern Frankish evidence where penitentials had become transformed into canonical collections. But in both cases the evidence points the same way: penitentials were ceasing to be seen as pastoral texts and were coming to be considered rather as texts to be used in a more formal context, either that of the cathedral school or the episcopal court and synod.

From the major to the minor, all the canonical collections produced in this period seem to be as much judicial and academic as pastoral in their intent. They were produced within an episcopal environment, and appear more concerned with asserting control over the diocesan clergy than with ensuring the provision of penance for the Christian community. These collections remain dry, prescriptive texts which seem remote from the practice of penance in this period. But if they were not widely available to the more general clergy, how did the the clergy, in particular the bishops, set about promoting the practice of penance? And how did the bishops seek to train their clergy in the practice of penance? These questions will be pursued in the next chapter.

---

[126] Kottje, *Bussbücher*, 16–18.
[127] Hägele, *Das Paenitentiale Vallicellianum*, i. 93–5.
[128] See n. 116 above: Vatican, BAV, MS Vat. lat. 5768 (s. x); Rome, Biblioteca Vallicelliana, Cod. E. 15; Rome, Biblioteca nazionale, Cod. 2116 (Sessor. 136); Vatican, BAV, MS Vat. lat. 4772. To which can be added the two *libelli* composed in Rome c. 1000, now Vatican, BAV, MS Archivio S. Pietro H. 58 on which see in addition to Körntgen, 'Ein italienisches Bussbuch', P. Salmon, 'Un *Libellus officialis* du XIe siècle', *Rev. Bén.* lxxxvii (1977), 257–88, and his 'Un Témoin de la vie chrétienne dans une église de Rome au XIe siècle: le "liber officialis" de la Basilique des Saints-Apôtres', *Rivista di storia della chiesa in Italia* xxxiii (1979), 65–73.

2

Education and Communication: Councils, Synodal Sermons and Capitularies

The size and nature of the canon law and penitential collections which survive from this period represent a considerable investment of both time and money; most could only have been owned by wealthy individuals and institutions: bishops, cathedrals and monasteries.[1] Inventories from the previous century, however, suggest that some, but not all, rural churches in the dioceses of Rheims and Freising owned texts of both penitentials and collections of canons.[2] The lack of similar evidence from the tenth and eleventh centuries for the ownership of such manuscripts at a level beneath that of the cathedral clergy is probably a product of a behavioural change: the later period did not share the Carolingian enthusiasm for the careful written administration of church goods.[3] More concrete evidence is hard to come by in either period: whilst some historians have argued that certain surviving codices were composed for use at this level, such as the manuscript now Paris, BN, MS Lat. 1207(I), written in Trier in the second half of the eleventh century, which includes a penitential, fragments from an episcopal capitulary on baptism and burial, a sermon on the Last Judgement, and a little summary

---

[1] An example is the early copy of Burchard's *Decretum*, written in Worms in about 1020 for Bamberg cathedral (Bamberg, Staatsbibliothek, MS Can. 6) which comprises 312 folios measuring 26 by 33 cm: *Das Dekret*, 16–19; Hoffmann, *Bamberger Handschriften*, 122. In addition there is the central Italian eleventh-century penitential collection (Rome, Biblioteca Vallicelliana, Cod. B. 58) which comprises 189 folios measuring 19 by 25 cm, and the north Italian tenth-century collection in Berlin, Deutsche Staatsbibliothek, MS Hamilton 290, which appears to be another episcopal handbook, combining penitential texts with extracts from capitula and other pastoral texts: H. Boese, *Die lateinischen Handschriften der Sammlung Hamilton zu Berlin Staatsbibliothek zu Berlin-Preussischer Kulturbesitz*, Weisbaden 1966, 142–3; Kottje, *Bussbücher*, 16–18.

[2] Out of the eight Bavarian churches which included books in their inventories, only three held a penitential and one a book of canons. Out of six churches owned by St Remigius of Rheims, two owned either a penitential or a book of canons, and two owned both a penitential and a book of canons: C. I. Hammer, Jr, 'Country churches, clerical inventories and the Carolingian Renaissance in Bavaria', *Church History* xlix (1980), 5–17. Rob Meens has suggested that this may be an underestimate as codices which included several texts were probably classified in inventories after the first text in the volume: 'Priests and books in the Carolingian era'.

[3] The relative decrease in the use of the written word in the Ottonian, compared with the Carolingian *Reich*, has been noted by several historians. See, for example, K. Leyser, 'Ottonian government', *EHR* xcvi (1981), 721–53 (repr. in his *Medieval Germany and its neighbours, 900–1250*, London 1982, 69–101).

of Christian dogma, others regard such texts as episcopal handbooks as they also include episcopal capitularies.[4] In any case codices such as this one, which might have been owned by parish priests, are in the minority; the codicological evidence represents an inevitable bias in favour of large institutions, because institutional continuity protected their holdings against dispersion, those of rural churches being more vulnerable to loss and destruction. Even if we accept that penitential and canonical texts were available in some country churches, the ninth-century evidence suggests this would not have been the case for all churches. How then would the rural clergy know how to administer penance correctly?

Before trying to answer this question, we need to ask another: what do we mean by the 'rural clergy'? The history of church provision much below the level of the cathedral is very murky in this period. There seems to be considerable variation between different areas of Europe.[5] In Italy, England and perhaps also parts of France and Germany, services were delivered following a two-tier system: teams of clergy were based in a mother church to which dues and baptismal rights belonged but might visit and administer certain services from dependent chapels scattered in the surrounding area. From c. 800 attempts were made to introduce a one-tier system whereby the local church enjoyed full pastoral rights. At the same time lords often built chapels on their own lands, so-called *Eigenkirchen*, and appointed the clergy to them,

---

[4] An example cited by Meens, 'Frequency', 42–3, who argues for it being seen as one of a series of books for parish priests. For the view of such texts as episcopal handbooks see Kerff, 'Libri paenitentiales', 46. The position is complicated by the existence of codices such as Vatican, Archivio St Pietro H. 58 – composed in Rome, probably for the basilica of S. XII Apostoli, or possibly the church of S. Apollinarius, in s. xi: Salmon, ' "Libellus officialis" ', and 'Témoin de la vie chrétienne'. The codicology of this manuscript may be more complicated than Salmon allows as it seems to be an amalgamation of two *libelli*, both of which seem to have been compiled with a pastoral intent; on the *libellus* which includes a penitential see Körntgen, 'Ein italienisches Bussbuch'.

[5] In general see G. W. O. Addleshaw, *The development of the parochial system from Charlemagne (768–814) to Urban II (1088–1099)*, London 1954; S. Reynolds, *Kingdoms and communities in western Europe, 900–1300*, Oxford 1984, 79–100. See also the essays in *Le istituzioni ecclesiastiche della 'Societas christiana' dei secoli 11–12: diocesi, pievi e parrocchie: atti della 6a settimana internazionale di studio, Milano, 1–7 settembre 1974* (Miscellanea viii, 1977); V. Bo, *Storia della parrocchia: i secoli dell'infanzia (sec. VI–XI)*, Rome 1990; Tellenbach, *Church*, 26–8. On monastic ownership of local churches see G. Constable, *Monastic tithes: from their origins to the twelfth century*, Cambridge 1964, and 'Monasteries, rural churches and the *cura animarum* in the early Middle Ages', in *Cristianizzazione ed organizzazione ecclesiastica delle campagne nell'alto medioevo: espansione e resistenze* (Settimane xxviii, 1982), 349–89. For provision in Italy see C. Boyd, *Tithes and parishes in medieval Italy: the historical roots of a modern problem*, Ithaca 1952. For England see J. Blair, 'Introduction: from minster to parish church', in J. Blair (ed.), *Minsters and parish churches: the local church in transition, 950–1200*, Oxford 1988, 1–19, and 'Debate: ecclesiastical organisation and pastoral care in Anglo-Saxon England', *EME* iv (1995), 193–212; E. Cambridge and D. Rollason, 'Debate: the pastoral organisation of the Anglo-Saxon Church: a review of the "minster hypothesis" ', ibid. 87–104; and the essays in J. Blair and R. Sharpe (eds), *Pastoral care before the parish*, Leicester 1992.

leading to clerics whose first loyalty was to their lord, secular or religious; for with gifts of lands to monasteries by the faithful came the local churches already built on them, so abbots often had control over rural churches.[6] Although it is difficult to generalise from local case studies, it seems that both systems continued to co-exist in this period.[7] Thus bishops could not expect to have unrivalled control over the appointment of secular clergy within their diocese and often sought, not wholly successfully, to reassert their control over the clergy of mother churches, *capellae* and *Eigenkirchen* and to assess their performance. In his collection Regino included an *inquisitio* addressed to the seven representatives of the *parochia*, asking them about their priest's conduct, as well as their own and that of the community.[8] Obviously not all bishops were conscientious nor concerned with standards of pastoral care, but reformist bishops existed in every age and it is with their aspirations that this chapter is concerned.

Given that canon law collections were not available to all rural clergy for consultation, this chapter aims to examine the other evidence for indications of the guidance they could have received from their bishops in the administration of penance. Education of the clergy was not a new issue when it was taken up by the eleventh-century reformers: it had been a recurrent concern for conscientious bishops from late antiquity onwards.[9] Bishops communicated with their clergy at various levels: through councils, through the sermons preached at such synodal assemblies, and through episcopal capitularies. By studying the sources for communication at these three levels, this chapter aims to establish how bishops sought to educate their clergy about the penitential process.

Councils

Councils were held at a variety of different levels within the Church and consequently with differing purposes. They might be held at a national level, often with the aim of launching a grand reform programme of the entire Church, as the Anglo-Saxons did at the Council of Clovesho in 747, or the Carolingians at the Synod of Frankfurt in 794.[10] Such councils were attended

---

[6] Tellenbach, *Church*, 77–84, 289–90.
[7] On the patchy nature of provision in one diocese see M. C. Miller, *The formation of a medieval church: ecclesiastical change in Verona, 950–1150*, Ithaca–London 1993, 136–7. On the problems of generalising see Reynolds, *Kingdoms*, 81–8. On the problems of seeing the history of parish provision as developmental with one system succeeding another see ibid. and also Cambridge and Rollason, ' "Minster hypothesis" '.
[8] Regino, *Libri duo* ii.2–5, pp. 207–16.
[9] McKitterick, *Frankish Church*, esp. ch. ii; Nelson, 'Making ends meet'; C. Cubitt, *Anglo-Saxon church councils, c. 650–c. 850*, London–New York 1995.
[10] For a consideration of Clovesho see ibid. 99–124. For the text of the Council of Frankfurt see MGH, *Concilia II*, no. xix, i. 110–71.

by the bishops and (sometimes) abbots of the kingdoms.[11] Then they could be held at provincial and diocesan levels, where their aims were more modest: to ensure uniformity of practice, to instruct their clergy about their own duties, and those of all Christians, including penance, and to discipline those under their jurisdiction by calling clerics and laymen to account for specific actions and delivering appropriate penitential sentences. Only their general instructions will be studied here; individual cases are considered in chapter 6. It is unclear who attended provincial synods but diocesan synods were attended by all the clergy of the diocese; indeed the rural clergy had to collect the chrism (for baptism) from the cathedral on Maundy Thursday and Holy Week was a favoured time for such meetings.[12] How far such meetings were attended by the laity is less clear, although they would probably have done so merely as observers; a greater distinction seems to have been made within the kingdom of east Frankia between ecclesiastical synod and secular assembly than was normal in either the Anglo-Saxon kingdoms or western Frankia.[13]

Sixty-seven councils are recorded as being held in Germany and Lotharingia in the period 900–1055.[14] Thirty-eight councils are recorded for Italy in the same period.[15] These overall totals may be broken down further for the period 916–1055: sixty-six German and Lotharingian councils are recorded of which ten were held at diocesan level, fifteen at provincial, thirty-nine at national and two between pope and emperor; thirty-five Italian councils are recorded, none at diocesan level,[16] the majority being papal councils held in or outside Rome, the rest being either provincial councils or *Reich* synods.[17] Isolde Schröder's list of synods held in west Frankia between 888 and 987 suggests that three diocesan and eighteen provincial synods for the Rheims province were held between 900 and 987.[18] Many of these synods, at provincial and national as well as diocesan level, left no canonical

---

11 Rulers and leading members of the laity undoubtedly attended synods, at least at a national and provincial level, although rulers rarely presided over these gatherings. King Conrad I, for example, did not preside over the Council of Hohenaltheim in 916. Royal involvement became more pro-active in the eleventh century. King Henry II, for example, established a prayer-confraternity with his bishops at the Synod of Dortmund in 1005: Thietmar, *Chronicon* vi.18, pp. 294–6.
12 I. Schröder, *Die westfränkischen Synoden von 888 bis 987 und ihre Überlieferung* (MGH, Hilfsmittel iii, Munich 1980), 46–9. The Council of Nicaea ordained that one of the two synods to be held annually should meet before Easter, the other in the autum: Cubitt, *Anglo-Saxon church councils*, 26.
13 T. Reuter, *German in the early Middle Ages, c. 800–c. 1050*, London 1991, 103; Cubitt, *Anglo-Saxon church councils*, 44–59.
14 H. Wolter, *Die Synoden im Reichsgebiet und in Reichsitalien von 916 bis 1056*, Paderborn–Munich–Vienna–Zurich 1988, to which may be added one council for the period 900–16 from Mansi, *Concilia*, xviii.
15 Wolter, *Synoden*, to which may be added three councils from Mansi, *Concilia*, xviii.
16 Pavia (955) is perhaps an exception; it is ignored by Wolter, *Synoden*.
17 This analysis is based on Wolter's work ibid.
18 Schröder, *Westfränkischen Synoden*. One provincial synod overlaps with Wolter's analysis being a joint synod held with the province of Trier at Mouzon in 948.

record; they are known only from references in chronicles, or from charters of privileges which were issued at the council.[19] Many more may have left no trace: diocesan synods, which church law required be held biannually, are especially under-recorded.[20] However, the existence of 110 manuscript copies of *ordines* for celebrating a church synod made in the *Reich* in this period suggests that most bishops made provision for holding such meetings, even if they failed to do so, or left no record.[21] But the proceedings of those synods which left a record should be treated with caution; they may not be representative of universal norms but rather of the reforming aspirations of that particular assembly. The temptation to extrapolate general developments from the evidence of these canons should be dismissed; instead they provide evidence for ideas about penance in a particular place at a particular time, although only a minority of the councils held in this period deal with penance. Their conciliar *acta* will now be examined methodically for the light they cast on penitential practice.

The conciliar canons issued in this period show very clearly the reiterative nature of law: new law is not declared, but old law is repeated as part of the Church's perpetual cycle of renewal and reform. Conformity to existing law was seen as the solution to current troubles. Thus in 909 Archbishop Heriveus (900–22) held a provincial council for Rheims at Trosly. His opening sermon recalled the tribulations brought upon the region by the Viking raids and the consequent breakdown of order, which was seen as God's punishment for sinful behaviour, due not only to the laity but to the bishops who had neglected to preach to them. Heriveus published fifteen *capitula* to remedy the situation which are all heavily based on, and cite, existing law.[22] Not surprisingly, given his sermon's premise, penance featured heavily amongst pleas that the king attend to his duties, monasticism be revived, priests avoid sinful behaviour, ecclesiastical property and rights be respected. Much of Heriveus' text recalls the works of his predecessors, Fulk and Hincmar.[23] Penance is not described explicitly as a practice or a duty, only

---

[19] For example, that of Trosly (921) is recorded only by Flodoard in his *Annales*, ed. P. Lauer, Paris 1905, a. 921, and his *Historia remensis ecclesiae*, ed. J. Heller and G. Waitz (MGH, SS xiii), iv.16; that of Fismes (935), again recorded only by Flodoard in his *Annales*, a. 935 and *Historia* iv.25. The provincial Rheims' synod of Mont-Notre-Dame (972/3) is known from incidental references: Schröder, *Westfränkischen Synoden*, no. lvi, pp. 290–301.

[20] For biannual requirement see, for example, Burchard, *Decretum* i.43, 561. Schneider's work suggests that many bishops owned *ordines* for celebrating church councils; 110 out of the 312 manuscripts he used for his edition are from this area in this period: MGH, *Ordines de celebrando concilio*.

[21] Diocesan synods are under-recorded throughout Europe before the thirteenth century, presumably because they did not issue legislation before then. On the origins of synodal statutes see O. Pontal, *Les Statuts synodaux* (Typologie xi, 1975).

[22] Sources include Pseudo-Isidore, Benediktus Levita, the *Relatio episcoporum* (829) and Hincmar's *Capitula* I and II: G. Schmitz, 'Das Konzil von Trosly (909): Überlieferung und Quellen', DA xxxiii (1977), 341–434.

[23] M. Sot, *Un Historien et son église au XIe siècle: Flodoard de Reims*, Paris 1993, 229–31.

prescribed as a punishment: anyone guilty of sacrilege against the kingdom of God should restore the stolen goods and do public penance. Only after making satisfaction may he receive the imposition of the hands of the bishop and reconciliation.[24] Penance is also prescribed as a punishment for those who do not respect priests,[25] and for theft,[26] perjury, homicide and the killing of a cleric.[27] Heriveus ends with a call that they should all do penance. Penance is therefore seen as a necessary component of the reform cycle.[28]

The east Frankish synod held at Hohenaltheim in 916 combined the reformist aspect of Trosly with an overt political purpose which threatened to overshadow its proceedings.[29] It was attended by most of the east Frankish bishops and a papal legate, although seemingly not by the Saxon and Suabian bishops, and only perhaps by King Conrad I; it is unclear whether the papal legate or the archbishop of Mainz presided. According to its preface the canons were intended not only to correct those bishops attending the council but all Christian people.[30] The council was concerned with both reform – according to canon viii bishops should not set a bad example to the people – and with strengthening the king's position.[31] None of the canons deal with penitential practice in detail: canon xxxiii (*de paenitentia*) is a compilation of *auctoritates* about the asceticism and attitude required for true penance, thus supporting and justifying the practice.[32] These texts appear to have been mediated through more recent sources: a quotation from Gregory, for example, is found in the proceedings for the reform Council of Châlon in 813.[33] But the

---

[24] Mansi, *Concilia*, xviii. 274–5.

[25] c. v, ibid. xviii. 275–9.

[26] 'c. vii: *De rapinis*. Sciat ergo unusquisque raptor agat, restituat primum quod injuste abstulit, si veram poenitentiam agere et veram Dei misericordiam obtinere cupit': ibid. xviii. 285.

[27] c. xiii, ibid. xviii. 297–302.

[28] This emphasis on penance, and its connection with the restoration of peace, was a component of earlier reform councils. See Cubitt's discussion of the influence of Alcuin's ideas on the Anglo-Saxon councils of 786 (and also of the *Admonitio generalis* of Charlemagne): *Anglo-Saxon church councils*, ch. vi.

[29] MGH, *Concilia* VI, 19–40. See also H. Fuhrmann, 'Die Synode von Hohenaltheim (916) – Quellenkundlichbetrachtet', DA xliii (1987), 440–68; Wolter, *Synoden*, 11–20.

[30] 'Capitula infra notata ad correctionem tam nostram quam christiani populi statuendo collegimus': MGH, *Concilia* VI, 20.

[31] c. viii, ibid. 22–3; c. xx (p. 28) is headed explicitly, '*Item de robore regis*'; G. Bührer-Thierry, *Évêques et pouvoir dans le royaume de Germanie: les églises de Bavière et de Souabe, 876–973*, Paris 1997, 92–104.

[32] '*De Penitentia*. Sanctus Paulus apostolus instruit penitentiam dignam agere in ieiuniis, vigiliis et orationibus cum elemosinis [2 Cor. 6, 5]; sanctus Gregorius: quem caro laeta traxit ad culpam, afflicta reducat ad veniam [*In evangelia homilia* 16, 5 – PL lxxvi. 1137D]; sanctus Augustinus: penitentiam certam non facit, nisi odium peccati et amor dei; sicque penitere, ut tibi amarum sapiat in animo quod antea dulce fuit in vita [Pseudo-Augustine, Sermo cxvii, c.ii, PL xxxix. 1977]': c. xxxiii, MGH, *Concilia* VI, 36.

[33] c. xxxvi, MGH, *Concilia* II, i. 280–1. That from Paul is found in Regino, *Libri duo*, app. I, c. xxxiii, pp. 404–5; that attributed to St Augustine ibid. app. I, c. xxxiv, p. 405.

authors of the Hohenaltheim decrees, following earlier precedents taken from Visigothic councils and penitentials, obviously regarded the performance of penance as an appropriate punishment for failure to obey church law. It could be applied to both bishops and the laity: any bishop who communicated with an excommunicate should do penance, as ordained by Gregory the Great in his *Register*, in a monastery, but secretly because he cannot do it publicly.[34] This is because public penance invalidates sacerdotal orders.[35] Similar provisions were made for a member of the laity guilty of the same offence.[36] The way in which penance should be carried out is not specified. Canon xxi enjoined a similar penance upon Erchanger of Suabia and his associates for sins both against the king and sacrilege against church property: they should leave the world, put down their arms and enter a monastery where they should do penance all the days of their life.[37] Perpetual monastic penance was a sentence often used by Merovingian and Carolingian rulers against their political rivals: it rendered them politically neutral without killing them.[38] But at Hohenaltheim the sentence was issued by the bishops rather than the king (who may have been absent), presumably as part of their attempt to restore peace to the kingdom by using their strongest weapon.[39] It did not, however, prevent Conrad from beheading Erchanger in 917. A similar penance was enjoined against those who commit perjury against the king, anyone who injures or murders a monk or a priest or his own father, and perjures himself, but an additional refinement, taken from the *Dionysiana*, was added: the penitent might be allowed to enter church and stand in the place of the auditors after three years, and be gradually reintroduced into communion with the Church, although he should abstain from meat and

---

[34] 'VIII. Ut non malum exemplum sint populo episcopi. Bonum exemplum populis se ipsos episcopi et sacerdotes debent praebere et ostendere, non solum dictis, verum et factis. Propter hoc enim statuimus, ut minime umquam in posterum contra sacra statuta aliquomodo communicemus excommunicatis; et diiudicamus nosmet ipsos, quatinus in futuro non iudicemur a domino. Sequi cupimus dicta et statuta sancti Gregorii papae et paenitentiam dignam agere volumus secrete in monasterio, quia publice nequivimus, in futuroque predicta omnibus modis deo propitio vitare. Eandemque legem statuentes presbiteris, diaconibus et omni clero, si de gradu deponi noluerint, ut fideliter observent et aliis servare predicent': MGH, *Concilia VI*, 22–3. See Gregory I, 'tunc ex nostra auctoritate non solum dominici corporis et sanguinis communione privatus sit, verum etiam in monasterio, ubi poenitentiam agere debeat, retrudatur ut criminis sui maculas convenienti valeat apud aeternum iudicem lamentatione purgare': *Registrum epistolarum*, ed. P. Ewald and L. M. Hartmann (MGH, Epistolarum i, 2nd edn, Berlin 1957), reg. iii.27 at i. 185. See also 'Et sit ita repperit ab honoris sui et ipsos milites gradu deiecat et in monasteriis ubi digne valeant agere paenitentiam deputet': reg. ix.25, ibid. ii. 58. On the sources for Hohenaltheim see Fuhrmann, 'Synode von Hohenaltheim (916)'.
[35] This issue is explored further in ch. 3.
[36] c. ix, MGH, *Concilia VI*, 23.
[37] c. xxi, ibid. 28–9. On this case see Leyser, 'Early medieval canon law', 64.
[38] de Jong, 'What was public', 877–87.
[39] Bührer-Thierry, *Évêques*, 92–104.

wine all the days of his life.[40] These canons seem to be unique to Hohenaltheim.[41] Perjury was previously the concern of penitentials, episcopal *capitula* and royal legislation rather than church councils. By including measures against perjury the bishops seem, in their attempt to restore stability, to be trying to substitute ecclesiastical for royal justice and thereby shore up royal authority.[42] Unlike Trosly, the bishops assembled at Hohenaltheim seem concerned not with the reform of the Church but rather with the correction and assertion of episcopal authority in the face of the king's failure to do so.

The canons promulgated at Hohenaltheim apparently describe penitential practice in detail but in fact are quoting from the Fathers, principally Gregory the Great, often using Regino as their immediate source, although they usually have ninth-century precedents as well. These canons may not therefore reflect practice, promulgating instead an ideal view of church life, based on that of the church Fathers. But these particular canons were generated by a specific situation: opposition to King Conrad I's rule from Arnulf of Bavaria and Erchanger of Suabia.[43] Arnulf was summoned to answer charges before the next council, whilst Erchanger was condemned for rebellion against the king and for attacking Salomon, bishop of Constance. All the canons relating to perjury and communication with excommunicants, not just those specifically referring to Arnulf and Erchanger, can be seen as consequences of this situation. Hohenaltheim's *acta* were thus influenced by their immediate political context, although as pastoral canons they influenced later German councils.[44]

The canons of the provincial synod of Trier held in 927 or 928 under Archbishop Ruotger (915–31) appear wholly pastoral in their intent and do not acknowledge their sources so explicitly.[45] (Ruotger was also the author of a capitulary which will be considered later in this chapter.) Although the canons bear a close resemblance to Ruotger's *capitula* their treatment of penance is sufficiently different to require separate consideration. One set of canons is concerned with the services which should be provided to all Christians – baptism, confirmation and communion three times a year – including one on annual confession which has no known source although it is also

---

[40] cc. xxii–v, MGH, *Concilia* VI, 29–32; c. xxii cites directly c. viii from the 'Council of Ankyra 314', recorded in the *Dionysiana II*. For this attribution see ibid. 29 n. 84.
[41] Canons xxii, xxiii and xxv on perjury are found in an appendix to the penitential attributed to Pseudo-Egbert. Fuhrmann and Hehl have argued that the Hohenaltheim decrees antedate this appendix: MGH, *Concilia* VI, 3–4; Fuhrmann, 'Synode von Hohenaltheim (916)', 448–52.
[42] Bührer-Thierry, *Évêques*, 94–6.
[43] Ibid. On the political circumstances leading up to the council see Reuter, *Germany*, 131–6. On the echoes between the prescriptions of Hohenaltheim and those of ninth-century legislation see Leyser, 'Early medieval canon law', 64.
[44] For example, Erfurt (932) echoes Hohenaltheim cc. vi–ix: MGH, *Concilia* VI, 109.
[45] MGH, *Concilia* VI, 79–88; Wolter, *Synoden*, 23–5.

found in Ruotger's *capitula*.⁴⁶ The priest should ensure that all his parishioners make their confession, and in the case of people who live in several places, he should check with their neighbouring priests to ensure that they have confessed. Priests should use both the stick and the carrot to ensure that all their parishioners make their confession, by emphasising the penalty for refusing to confess, namely anathematisation, and the advantage, that confession washes away sin.

This canon is followed by a more elaborate version of Ruotger's *capitulum* concerning the giving of penance, the beginning of which is originally taken from Radulf of Bourges's *capitula*, composed c. 853–66.⁴⁷ At the beginning of Lent confessions should be heard and penances given, presumably by the priest, and on Ash Wednesday those performing public penance led before the bishop. At the ninth hour of Ash Wednesday, when the bishop put the ashes on the heads of Christians, he should come to the doors of the church and having prayed to the east, the priest should call his parish's penitents by name. The bishop should then sprinkle blessed water over them and puts the ashes on their heads, saying 'Remember that thou art dust and to dust thou wilt return' (Job xxxiv.15). And then with his right hand the bishop should send them to the door.⁴⁸ Similarly on Maundy Thursday, before the blessing of the holy chrism, the penitents are to be sent by the hand of the bishop into the church. The priest should then admonish the penitents to beware the vices and show humility and contrition, begging Christ's mercy with tears and frequent fasts, and showing a downcast face. Others entering church should pray for them, saying 'May Almighty God be merciful to you'. In passages derived from Radulf's ninth-century capitulary, the penitents should note that penance is like a second baptism which guards them against vice and sin, whilst the priest should note that he is not allowed to give public penance as public sins are reserved for episcopal penitential judgement, but only minister to those whose faults are hidden and who should therefore do secret penance.⁴⁹ Whilst these canons were based on Radulf, they give much more detail about the administration of public penance.⁵⁰ Ruotger's description of public penance also differed from that found in Regino of Prüm because of his concentration on the reconciliation on Maundy Thursday, which was virtually omitted from Regino's account, but both men emphasised

---

⁴⁶ cc. xi–xiv (on regular confession see c. xiv), MGH, Concilia VI, 82–3; cf. Ruotger, Capit., c. xxvi (regular confession), c. xxvii (administration of Lenten confession), MGH, Capit. Ep. I, 70, discussed below.
⁴⁷ Trier, c. xv, MGH, Concilia VI, 83–4; Ruotger. Capit., c. xxvii, MGH, Capit. Ep. I, 70; Radulf, Capit. c. xxxii, ibid. 258–9.
⁴⁸ For a parallel with the north-central liturgy see ch. 5.
⁴⁹ See Radulf, Capit., cc. xxxiii–iv, MGH, Capit. Ep. I, 259–60.
⁵⁰ Radulf, Capit., c. xxxii (confess to priest in week before Lent), c. xxxiii (seven ways to remedy sin), c. xxxiv (public penance), MGH, Capit. Ep. I, 258–60. These chapters are all repeated in Trier (927), c. xv, MGH, Concilia VI, 83–4.

episcopal authority.⁵¹ The parallels with Regino's account of the expulsion of penitents on Ash Wednesday, written for the archbishop of Trier some twenty years earlier, are equally striking. Taken together, they suggest that Regino and Ruotger were both describing public penance as practised in early tenth-century Trier.

Ruotger distinguished between confession, an annual duty, like communion, required of all Christians, and public penance, for which he thought a detailed description necessary. Perhaps he regarded public penance as a mechanism through which he could maintain his relations with his rural priests, ensuring he met with them regularly. Hincmar, archbishop of Rheims, had some seventy years earlier in 856 envisaged a parallel system of upward reporting to ensure that major sins committed in the *parochiae* were reported by their priests to the bishop's officers.⁵² Hincmar recognised that the priests' co-operation was fundamental to the whole system.⁵³ This explains the concern of several authors of *capitula* to prohibit priests from accepting money for public sins, incest or penance, that is for bribes against the imposition of public penance.⁵⁴ Ruotger saw penance not only, through confession, as an important part of every Christian's liturgical year but, through public penance, as a means of controlling his diocese.

The provincial synod of Mainz (950x4) also promoted annual confession and regular communion: a priest should admonish all Christians to confess their sins to one another in Lent before Easter and at Christmas, on Maundy Thursday, and Good Friday and communicate on Easter Sunday.⁵⁵ The bishops assembled at Mainz, like those at Trier, saw confession and communion as essential to an individual's membership of the Christian community; their ultimate source was in both cases c. 33 of the Council of Châlon (813).⁵⁶ But the process for confession is not described. Confession's link to communion was established in the Carolingian era: it was a necessary part of the preparations for receiving the eucharist.⁵⁷ Bishops seem not so much concerned to promote regular or annual confession but rather regular

---

51 For Regino's account see ch. 1.
52 Hincmar, Capit. III.1, MGH, *Capit. Ep. II*, 73–4.
53 Atto of Vercelli also made provision in his capitulary to ensure that reports were made to the bishop: c. xc, MGH, *Capit. Ep. III*, 296–7. He appears to have arrived at this system independently as his text is not dependent on Hincmar's capitulary.
54 For example, Ruotger, Capit., c. xx, MGH, *Capit. Ep. I*, 68. Only Hincmar envisaged a punishment procedure for priests too lazy or corrupt to bring such cases to the bishop's attention: Capit. III.1, MGH, *Capit. Ep. II*, 74. See also Trier (927/8), c. ix, MGH, *Concilia VI*, 82; Radulf, Capit., c. xviii, MGH, *Capit. Ep. I*, 247.
55 'Admoneaturque universa plebs catholica, quo castitate servata sicut in quadragesima ante pascha alterutrum confiteantur peccata secundum apostolum dicentem: Confitemini alterutrum peccata vestra et sancto die navitatis Christi sicut in cena domini et in parasceve et sabbato sancto in dieque resurrectionis communicet': MGH, *Concilia VI*, 176–7; Wolter, *Synoden*, 62–4.
56 MGH, *Concilia II*, i. 280.
57 Avril, 'Remarques', 349–50; Meens, 'Frequency', 37–8.

communion; nevertheless they emphasised the importance of regular Lenten confession for membership of the Christian community.

The next council to refer to the procedures for penance is that of the Council of Seligenstadt (near Frankfurt) which met in 1023. One of a series of reforming councils held by the Emperor Henry II, it aimed to establish uniformity of worship and clerical discipline.[58] It supported episcopal control over the penitential process, but a description of the process was thought unnecessary. The canons emphasise the priest's responsibilities for the day-to-day supervision of penitents; no priest, on pain of anathema, should allow a penitent to interrupt his fast except in the case of illness;[59] all penitents must stay in the place where they were given their penance so the priest can be a witness to their penance, although they may move in time of war.[60] As at Trier the priest should report to the bishop on the penitent's conduct. Reconciliation remained an episcopal prerogative: no priest, except with the bishop's permission, might reconcile anyone excluded for his faults,[61] nor should anyone appeal to Rome in the hope of papal pardon without first completing their penance and then only with their bishop's permission.[62] These last two canons arose specifically from the case of Otto and Irmengard of Hammerstein who had appealed to Rome against their excommunication at the Council of Nijmegen (1018) on the grounds that their marriage was incestuous.[63] Seligenstadt seemingly assumed that the public penitential system was in place and felt no need to prescribe the process itself nor to define it as public penance as such; its attempts to defend that system against circumvention by reluctant penitents suggests a vigorous tradition of public penance.

Whilst Seligenstadt was concerned with clerical responsibility and control over the penitential process, a synod held two years later by Gerard, bishop of Cambrai, returned to the theme found in the early tenth-century synods, namely that confession was necessary for membership of the Christian community. Gerard preached a sermon against the opinions of some Italian heretics he encountered in Arras who rejected baptism, the eucharist, penance, marriage and the saints.[64] It is impossible to use these records as evidence for the heretics' actual belief, influenced as Gerard was by earlier models of heresy,[65] only for what Gerard defined as orthodoxy, and of this

---

[58] Concilium Seligenstadense (12 Aug. 1023), MGH, Constitutiones I, 636; Wolter, Synoden, 297–306.
[59] c. xvii, MGH, Constitutiones I, 638.
[60] c. xix, ibid. 638–9.
[61] c. xx, ibid. 639.
[62] c. xvi, ibid. 638.
[63] This case is considered in more detail in ch. 6.
[64] PL cxlii. 1271–312; R. I. Moore, The origins of European dissent, 2nd edn, Oxford 1985, 9–18; M. Lambert, Medieval heresy: popular movements from the Gregorian reform to the Reformation, 2nd edn, Oxford 1992, 22–5.
[65] See Moore, Origins, 14–18.

penance was an essential part: confession was necessary for salvation. But it is unclear whether the heretics even attended the synod; his sermon was aimed as much at the assembled clergy as at them. It has been described as a summary of a handbook for the education of priests, using citations from Hrabanus Maurus, for example, against the heretics' views on baptism.[66] It therefore fits into the existing tradition of synodal education.

Penitential processes were not of much concern to the remaining councils in the period covered by this study.[67] The reform councils had no need to concentrate on penance, as they had already inherited a large body of pastoral material, in both canonical and liturgical collections. The councils which seem most concerned with prescribing penitential processes – Trier (c. 927–8) and Mainz (c. 950x4) – are both provincial councils; as such they were, perhaps, more low key, aimed at imposing uniform practice across the province in a manner very similar to those used in episcopal *capitula*. By contrast those less concerned with process, Hohenaltheim (916) and Seligenstadt (1023), were both attempts to hold a synod of the whole east Frankish Church. Whilst reform was often, especially in the earlier Middle Ages, the preoccupation of national synods, it is perhaps not surprising that by this period they were less concerned with issues which had become the preoccupation of other genres, namely episcopal *capitula*, church law collections and the liturgy.

Council decisions in this period usually enjoyed only a limited circulation. Those of Trosly (909) are recorded in only one medieval manuscript from Saint-Rémi;[68] those of Hohenaltheim (916) are also recorded in a single manuscript probably from Freising cathedral, together with those of Coblenz (922), Erfurt (932) and Mainz (950).[69] That manuscript was partially assembled in northern Italy but the Hohenaltheim canons are recorded in a mid tenth-century Bavarian hand. Individual canons circulated outside Germany: cc. xvii and xxiii–xxv are recorded in a north Italian codex written in the second half of the tenth century,[70] and c. xxv is also found in another Freising

---

[66] R. Gorre, *Die ersten Ketzer im 11. Jahrhundert: religiöse Eiferer – soziale Rebellen? Zum Wandel der Bedeutung religiöser Weltbilder* (Konstanzer Dissertationen iv, Constance 1982), 130–64.

[67] Gregory VII's Rome council (1078) issued canons concerning false penance and against bishops poaching others' penitents: Mansi, *Concilia*, xx. 507–10. The former was taken into the canonical tradition: J. T. Gilchrist, 'The reception of Pope Gregory VII into the canon law (1073–1141)', *ZRG Kan. Abt.* lix (1973), 35–82 at p. 71 (repr. in his *Canon law in the age of reform, c. 11th–c. 12th*, Aldershot 1993, no. viii).

[68] Vatican, BAV, MS Reg. lat. 418, fos 1r, 3r–73r; Schröder, *Westfränkishen Synoden*, 189–97; Schmitz, 'Das Konzil von Trosly', 347–59.

[69] Munich, Bayerische Staatsbibliothek, Clm 27246, described in N. Daniel, *Handschriften des zehnten Jahrhunderts aus der Freisinger Dombibliothek: Studien über Schriftcharakter und Herkunft der nachkarolingischen und ottonischen Handschriften einer bayerischen Bibliothek*, Munich 1973, 107–9, and also in MGH, *Concilia VI*, 6–10.

[70] Berlin, Deutsche Staatsbibliothek, MS Hamilton 290. For dating see Boese, *Lateinischen Handschriften*, 142–3; MGH, *Concilia VI*, 10.

manuscript.[71] A century later some were also taken up into Burchard's *Decretum*, although not book xix, and thence entered the works of Anselm of Lucca, Bonizo of Sutri, Ivo and Gratian.[72] For the first century after they were issued their influence remained confined to those areas under Ottonian control; those of Trier (927/8) were discovered amongst a sermon collection in a late eleventh-century manuscript.[73] The surviving evidence for the tenth-century councils suggests that conciliar decisions were not widely circulated.[74] Whilst some, such as those of Hohenaltheim, came to have a posthumous significance, they provide very limited evidence of contemporary thought, limited to a certain area at a certain time.

Synodal sermons

The decrees from the diocesan synod held by Ruotger, bishop of Trier, in 927/8 were unknown before their discovery in a Viennese manuscript almost twenty years ago; in it the decrees are entitled *Sermo in synodo faciendus*, showing the association drawn by contemporaries between canonical decrees and the usually formulaic synodal sermons preached by the bishop to his assembled clergy.[75] One such sermon on their duties and behaviour as priests was preached by Bishop Rather to the clergy of his diocese of Verona at a Lenten synod in 966.[76] He berated them for their ignorance and instructed them in the faith and the life and duties of a priest, including his penitential ministry, in terms drawn from a pre-existing text, the *Admonitio synodalis*, which Rather incorporated into his sermon. Priests should not profit from their office either by pawning sacred vessels and sacerdotal garments, or obtaining the reconciliation of penitents in return for payment.[77] This is obviously an incidental reference to the problems caused by the procedure of public penance, in which the priest's report on the penitent's conduct is vital

---

[71] Munich, Bayerische Staatsbibliothek, Clm 6425, MGH, *Concilia* VI, 10. Bührer-Thierry builds on Fuhrmann's work to suggest that canons xxii–xxv, which are all concerned with perjury, whilst they are based on the penitential of pseudo-Bede-Egbert, the eighth-century councils of Toledo and Regino's collection, represent an attempt by the council to restore order and reaffirm the importance of royal justice and the penalties for going against it: *Évêques*, 94–6.
[72] MGH, *Concilia* VI, 13.
[73] Vienna, Österreichische Nationalbibliothek, Cod. 1529; R. Pokorny, 'Die Kanones der Trierer Synode des Jahres 927 (?): ein Textfund zu den Capitula Ruotgers von Trier', *DA* xxxviii (1982), 1–25.
[74] In the absence of a modern edition for councils post 967 this analysis has not been attempted for the later period.
[75] MGH, *Concilia* VI, 79; *in synodo faciendus* was added by a slightly later hand.
[76] Rather, *Synodica*.
[77] Ibid. 132; cf. *Admonitio synodalis*, nos xlv–xlvi, p. 53.

to the bishop's decision as to whether to reconcile him. Priests should forbid penitents communion unless they give alms at the same time; this seems to be an oblique reference to commutation.[78] Amongst a series of injunctions concerned with the laity's duties – knowledge of the Lord's Prayer and the Creed, observation of the Rogation Days' fast, communion four times a year at Christmas, Maundy Thursday, Easter and Pentecost[79] – is one that the priest should invite the people to confession on the fourth day before Lent, and enjoin a penance upon them in accordance with their sin, based not upon his own views, but upon what is written in a penitential.[80] Thus the penances awarded should not be arbitrary. This part of Rather's sermon was not original but taken from the list of duties prescribed in the *Admonitio synodalis*.

The *Admonitio synodalis* was very popular; it survives in more than 125 manuscripts of episcopal capitularies and *ordines* for holding a synod.[81] Its origins are much debated. It shares several issues with the *Inquisitio* addressed to the clergy in book i of Regino, which in turn owed much to the ninth-century episcopal capitularies of Theodulf of Orléans, Gerbald of Liège and Hincmar of Rheims. Amiet, the editor of the *Admonitio*, therefore suggested that it was composed in the early ninth century and adopted by Regino.[82] But there are no witnesses to the text before the early tenth century and this, together with the fact that the textual parallels with Regino are not all-inclusive, led Lotter to argue that both Regino and the *Admonitio* were derived from a common source.[83] More recently Rodolf Pokorny has suggested that the *Admonitio* is dependent upon Regino and was thus not composed before the first decade of the tenth century.[84]

The confusion surrounding the *Admonitio*'s origins is symptomatic of one of the fundamental problems of church law: the emphasis on precedent and the reluctance to innovate make it difficult to use law as evidence for change. Many of the provisions of the *Admonitio* have precedents in earlier sources; for example, similar prohibitions against payment for church services, including the reconciliation of penitents, are found in the *capitula* of both

---

[78] 'Nullus penitentem invitet carnem manducare et bibere vinum, nisi pro eo ad praesens eleemoysnam fecerit': Rather, *Synodica*, 133; cf. *Admonitio synodalis*, no. lviii, p. 57.
[79] Rather, *Synodica*, 133; cf. *Admonitio synodalis*, nos lxi–lxii, lxiv, pp. 58–9.
[80] Rather, *Synodica*, 133; cf. *Admonitio synodalis*, no. lxiii, p. 58.
[81] P. Brommer, 'Capitula episcoporum: Bemerkungen zu den bischöflichen Kapitularien', *Zeitschrift für Kirchengeschichte* xci (1980), 207–36 at p. 219 n. 70.
[82] *Admonitio synodalis*, 71–7.
[83] F. Lotter, 'Ein kanonistisches Handbuch über die Amtspflichten des Pfarrklerus als gemeinsame Vorlage für den Sermo synodalis "Fratres presbyteri" und Reginos Werk "De synodalibus causis" ', *ZRG Kan. Abt.* lxii (1976), 1–57.
[84] R. Pokorny, 'Nochmals zur Admonitio synodalis', ibid. lxxi (1985), 20–51.

Hincmar and Radulf of Bourges.[85] All three penitential provisions are found in Regino's *Inquisitio*.[86]

One way of surmounting the problem is to look for clues as to how contemporaries interpreted the provisions of the *Admonitio*. A closer study of the additions Rather made to it in his sermon to the Veronese clergy, for example, indicates how these provisions were understood by one mid tenth-century bishop.[87] Rather gave his sermon an educational aspect, seeking through his clergy to promote the proper observance of the Christian life by the laity: thus Lent, Advent and the octaves of other important feasts should be observed through fasting and sexual abstinence, and on the Monday until Thursday of Holy Week a fast should be kept until the ninth hour, excepting children and the very old, and on Maundy Thursday at the ninth hour all, *omnes*, must come to the Mother Church to be reconciled.[88] This incidental reference suggests that for Rather anyway Maundy Thursday was the time when all penitents should be reconciled, a time for universal reconciliation rather than the specific reconciliation of public penitents. After his prescription for Holy Week observance, he reminded his priests of the episcopal perogative over public penance: 'Know that you may give penance for hidden sins, but for public sins you should defer to us.'[89] Similar provisions are found in the Council of Mainz of 847 and Regino of Prüm as well as tenth-century legislation.[90] Although his additional instructions also have Carolingian precedents, their presence outside the received *Admonitio* text suggests that they represent Rather's own aspirations.[91]

Rather was bishop of Verona on and off between 931 and 967, encountering opposition from both the imperial court and the Veronese clergy led by the cathedral chapter.[92] He was not a native of Verona; he entered the

---

85 *Admonitio synodalis*, nos xxxiv, lxvi, pp. 50, 53. For similar provisions see Hincmar, Capit. I.xiii, and Capit. V.ix, *MGH, Capit. Ep. II*, 40–1, 88; Radulf, Capit. c. xviii, *MGH, Capit. Ep. I*, 246–7.

86 *Admonitio synodalis*, nos xlvi, lviii, lxiii, pp. 53, 57–8, correspond to Regino, *Libri duo* i.38, 51, 59 (inquisitio) and II.lxv.5 (inquisitio), pp. 22–3, 214.

87 Rather's sermon was not itself influential; it survives in three tenth-century manuscripts, all written in Verona under Rather's supervision, only one of which was exported (Munich, Bayerische Staatsbibliothek, Clm 6340) to Bishop Abraham of Freising who had an interest in sermons. For their manuscript history see *Ratherii Veronensis opera minora*, ed. P. L. D. Reid (CCCM xlvi, 1976), pp. viii–xi; Munich, Clm 6340 is described by Daniel in *Handschriften*, 101–5.

88 'Quinta feria hora nona ad ecclesiam matrem omnes reconciliandi venite': Rather, *Synodica*, 136.

89 'De occultis peccatis poenitentiam vos dare posse scitote, de publicis ad nos deferendum agnoscite': ibid. 137.

90 Council of Mainz (847), c. xxxi, *MGH, Concilia III*, 176–7; Regino, *Libri duo* i.296, p. 137; and Trier (927), c. xv, *MGH, Concilia VI*, 83–4.

91 Rather's views on penance in all his works were conventional: B. Schwark, *Bischof Rather von Verona als Theologe: ein Beitrag zur Geschichte der Theologie im Zeitalter der Ottonen*, Königsberg 1916, 60–74.

92 On Rather's career see G. Monticelli, *Raterio vescovo di Verona (890–974)*, Milan 1938.

Lotharingian monastery of Lobbes as a child and came to Italy with the exiled bishop of Liège (and former abbot of Lobbes), Hilduin. Initially appointed to Verona by Hugh of Provence in 931, his intermittent episcopate (932–5, 946–7, 961–8) corresponds with the vagaries of Italian politics at this time. This 966 synod was held at a particularly stormy point. Rather had regained the see with the help of Otto I in 961 but lost imperial support when he sought to finance a new school to train the lesser clergy from lands previously used as fiefs for military retainers; he was consequently put on trial by the imperial *missus*, the count of Verona.[93] At the same time (965) he annulled the ordinations performed (in his *interregnum*) by his rival for the see; the Veronese clergy turned on him and damaged the episcopal palace. In the immediate aftermath, when order was (temporarily) restored, he held this synod. But he retired to Lotharingia in 967. Although ultimately unsuccessful, his overall aim in 966 was to establish his episcopal authority over a rebellious clergy by reminding them of their duty.[94] But he was also, as his doomed plans for a *scuola* show, interested in their education.

The *Admonitio* is part of a continuous tradition of episcopal education and exhortation of the clergy, exemplified in another form by Regino's *Inquisitio*. This tradition continued into the eleventh century; Gerhard considered it worth recording in his portrait of Udalrich of Augsburg (923–73) as a model bishop that he held a diocesan synod at which he reminded the assembled clergy of how they should serve God in terms remarkably similar to those of the *Admonitio*.[95] Rather thus used the *Admonitio* in very unusual circumstances. It is more often preserved in legal and liturgical sources with capitularies, as an appendix to Burchard's *Decretum*,[96] and in *ordines* for holding a synod, than with other sermons.[97]

Synodal sermons were not always used to educate an ignorant clergy. In the aftermath of an early tenth-century Hungarian attack a *chorepiscopus* of Augsburg preached at what was probably a diocesan synod held in Augsburg cathedral in which he called on the assembled people, both lay and clerical, to propitiate God by repenting their sins to atone for their recent troubles.[98]

See also the introduction by P. L. D. Reid (trans.) to *The complete works of Rather of Verona*, Binghamton, NY 1991, 3–11.
[93] F. Weigle, 'Il processo di Raterio di Verona', *Studi storici veronesi* iv (1953), 29–44, and 'Ratherius von Verona im Kampf um das Kirchengut 961–68', *Quellen und Forschungen aus italienischen Archiven und Bibliotheken* xxviii (1937–8), 1–35; Miller, *Formation of a medieval Church*, 160.
[94] Weigle ignored the sermon in his study of Rather's attempts to reform the Veronese clergy: 'Ratherius von Verona'.
[95] Gerhard, *Vita Sancti Oudalrici*, c. vi (MGH, SS IV), 394–5. Gerhard, Udalric's provost, composed his life in the late tenth century.
[96] Meyer, 'Überlieferung', 171–3.
[97] For example, PRG lxxx.51, i. 286–9.
[98] H. Schneider, 'Eine Freisinger Synodalpredigt aus der Zeit der Ungarneinfälle (Clm 6245)', in H. Mordek (ed.), *Papsttum, Kirche und Recht im Mittelalter: Festschrift für Horst Fuhrmann zum 65. Geburtstag*, Tübingen 1991, 95–115 (the text is edited at pp. 107–15).

Anyone who had deviated from the Christian life through diabolical works should go to church, and make a pure and tearful confession to God and his priest, and accept his penance, do good works and live a Christian life.[99] This rare surviving text of a synodal sermon is preserved in an eleventh-century manuscript; it shows that penance was seen as a necessary prelude to the greater peace. This sermon also reminds us that synods were attended by the laity as well as the clergy.

Both types of sermon are essentially formulaic, and both preserve a simple view of penitential practice. Although Tellenbach has rightly cautioned against assuming that diocesan synods were held regularly, anonymous texts like the *Admonitio synodalis* probably provide a more accurate picture than do the great canon law collections of the sort of information which was communicated to the rural clergy on a regular basis.[100] If the canon law collections were, at least in part, teaching and reference texts for priests, especially bishops and cathedral clergy, then the *Admonitio* and related texts represent the equivalent of refresher courses for the rural clergy.[101] Of course, not all bishops held synods, not all bishops delivered such talks to their clergy, and not all clergy listened to their bishops, but such sermons are likely to represent the state of penitential practice on the ground, or at least the content of episcopal instructions about it.

Episcopal *capitula*

The *capitula episcoporum* have similar aims to the synodal sermons: to train priests in their duties and conduct and to establish and maintain internal diocesan structures. They thus demonstrate the importance of penance in the pastoral and administrative aspects of episcopal office.

Bishops probably initially addressed their *capitula* to their clergy at a diocesan or provincial synod; only later did they become a source for canonical reference.[102] They originated in the ninth-century reforms of the Frankish Church, and ninth-century texts, especially, are often preserved with peni-

---

[99] 'Quae omnia sunt diabolica opera et omnibus christianis devitanda, et quae ducunt homines ad perditionem aeternam. Ideoque pensate vosmetipsos, et si aliquis vestrum de his supra dictis aliquid gestum habet, veniat ad ecclesiam et ibi deo et sacerdoti suo puram et lacrimabilem confessonem faciat et dignam poenitentiam accipiat et bonis operibus se ornet, ut cum diabolo non pereat, sed cum Christo vivat semper in aevum, quia non prodest, ut bona faciamus, nisi mala devitamus': Schneider, 'Eine Freisinger Synodalpredigt', 111.
[100] Tellenbach, *Church*, 31.
[101] Lotter described the *Admonitio* as a canon law handbook on the official duties of the parish clergy: 'Ein kanonistisches Handbuch', 1.
[102] *Capitula episcoporum* is an artificial term: P. Brommer, *Capitula episcoporum: die bischöflichen Kapitularien des 9. und 10. Jahrhunderts* (Typologie xliii, 1985), 10–13. For Burchard's use of the *capitula* of Theodulf and Hincmar in the *Decretum* see *Das Dekret*, 256, 274.

tential texts or texts on the liturgy in practical collections, so-called 'episcopal handbooks', perhaps intended for consultation by the cathedral clergy.[103] *Capitula* are thus direct evidence of communication between bishops and their clergy.

Rosamond McKitterick noted over twenty years ago that episcopal *capitula* had been neglected as a source for the Carolingian reform movement.[104] Whilst this is no longer the case for the ninth century, a similar complaint can be raised for studies of the tenth- and early eleventh-century Church,[105] although it is also true that fewer *capitula* were produced in this period. The decline in production was probably due to the large number of ninth-century episcopal *capitula* surviving in tenth- and eleventh-century copies, reducing the need for bishops to compose their own.[106]

But some bishops did; their capitularies are considered here in chronological and geographical order. Although ninth-century *capitula* were important to later clergy, as witnessed not only by their manuscripts but by their use as sources for church law collections, councils as well capitularies, they are not evidence for the ways in which penance was viewed in this period, and so will be considered only where they are a direct source for the later *capitula*.

Lotharingia: the province of Trier

Ruotger, archbishop of Trier (915–31), composed his *capitula* for a provincial synod sometime between 915 and 929.[107] The text survives in one tenth- and two twelfth-century manuscripts, one with an east Frankish, and two with a north-west Frankish provenance.[108] Despite the fact that the manuscript

---

[103] McKitterick, *Frankish Church*, 45–79. At least one manuscript of Atto of Vercelli's *capitulare*, Vercelli, Biblioteca capitolare, MS XXXIX, was probably copied for his cathedral clergy since it contains several marginal notes to other relevant canonical precepts in a different but contemporary hand, suggesting it was read and reflected upon: S. Wemple, *Atto of Vercelli: Church, State and Christian society in tenth-century Italy*, Rome 1979, 186–7. Tellenbach has cautioned against assuming that rural priests had access to copies of capitularies: *Church*, 31. Meens, on the other hand, has argued that it is probable that they did, although he offers no concrete proof: 'Frequency', 43.

[104] McKitterick, *Frankish Church*, 45.

[105] Tellenbach, *Church*, 30.

[106] P. Brommer, 'Die bischöfliche Gesetzgebung Theodulfs von Orléans', ZRG Kan. Abt. lx (1974), 1–120. For a list of manuscripts see MGH, *Capit. Ep.* I, 76–99, 145–7. On tenth-century decline see Tellenbach, *Church*, 30. McKitterick noted the correlation between the increase in the issue of episcopal *capitula* in the second half of the ninth century and the decline in the number of 'general' church councils but, as general councils were not popular in the tenth century, this explanation will not work for this period: *Frankish Church*, 50.

[107] MGH, *Capit. Ep.* I, 57–8. Ruotger's *capitula* has several canons in common with the Synod of Trier (927). For further detail see Pokorny, 'Kanones von Trierer Synode'.

[108] North-west Frankia: Antwerp, Museum Plantin-Moretus MS M 82 (66) (s. xii), and

provenance cannot be pinned down more precisely, it is doubtful whether it circulated much outside the province of Trier.

Ruotger introduces his *capitula* with a letter to his clergy in which he reminds them of their role as pastors: they should take care both of their own salvation and of those committed to them through setting a good example.[109] The *capitula* which follow are concerned on the one hand to guide the priest in the correct conduct of his life and in his responsibilities towards his flock,[110] and on the other to assert his own episcopal authority: priests should attend the diocesan synod,[111] collect the chrism on Maundy Thursday,[112] respect parish boundaries and not poach each others' parishioners.[113]

The *capitula* concerned with penance are a product of these two concerns. Firstly, Ruotger forbids his priests to accept payment for administering baptism, burial, penance or the eucharist: if any priest ignores this prohibition, he will incur the vengeance of canonical sentence.[114] This pastoral injunction to ensure that the Church's 'sacraments' were freely available, as we have already seen, has several ninth-century precedents; the inclusion of the threat against the priest is, however, novel.[115] Secondly, priests should ensure that everyone in their *parochia*, from the smallest to the greatest, comes to confession: those who do not wish to come should be excommunicated.[116] This threat also has no parallel amongst the other episcopal *capitula*. They should also prevent those who hold land in several *parochiae* from evading making their confession by checking with neighbouring priests; this provision is also found in the Council of Trier (927x8).[117] Thirdly, Ruotger instructs his priests on how to give penance to the faithful: in the week before Lent the faithful should confess to the priest all their sins, in both word and thought, and accept penance for them. Peace should be restored, all grudges and disputes abandoned, for in the words of the Lord's Prayer, 'Forgive us our

---

BL, MS Cotton Cleopatra C. viii (s. xii); east Frankia: Leiden, Bibliothek der Rijksuniversiteit, MS Vulcan. 94 B (s. xii): MGH, *Capit. Ep. I*, 59–60.

[109] Ibid. 61–2.

[110] The priest should be chaste and sober (c. ix); know the prayers, the mass, the office and psalms (cc. viii, x); preach regularly (c. xiv); ensure his flock know the Lord's Prayer, the Creed and the days when they should communicate (cc. xxii, xxv): ibid. 64–6, 68–9. Sources: Radulf, Capit., cc. viii, x, xiii, xxii, xxix, ibid. 239–40, 242–3, 250–1, 256–7; *Admonitio synodalis*, c. lxi–lxv, pp. 58–9.

[111] c. xii, MGH, *Capit. Ep. I*, 65. Source: Radulf, Capit. c. xii, ibid. 241. Archpriests should also hold councils: c. xiii, ibid. 65. For earlier parallels with this text see Hincmar, Capit. I.xv, and Capit. III.i, MGH, *Capit. Ep. II*, 42–3, 73–4.

[112] c. xv, MGH, *Capit. Ep. I*, 67. Source: Radulf, Capit., c. xiv, ibid. 243–4.

[113] c. xvi, ibid. 67. Source: Radulf, Capit., c. xv, ibid. 244–5.

[114] 'Si quis vero sacerdotum hoc, quod prohibemus, fecerit, canonicae sententiae vindictam suscipiet': c. xx, ibid. 68.

[115] Hincmar, Capit. I.xiii and Capit. V.ix, MGH, *Capit. Ep. II*, 40–1, 88; Radulf, Capit., c. xviii, MGH, *Capit. Ep. I*, 246–7; Riculf of Soissons, Capit., c. xi, MGH, *Capit. Ep. II*, 105.

[116] c. xxvi, MGH, *Capit. Ep. I*, 70.

[117] c. xiv, MGH, *Concilia VI*, 83.

trespasses as we forgive those who trespass against us.' They are reminded that this is appropriate behaviour for Lent, and that penance is a second baptism. In order to hear someone's confession the priest should inquire carefully about the type of sin committed, and give a penance which is commensurate with the guilty deed. The priest should then admonish the penitent to confess his bad thoughts, reminding him of the eight vices, and accept his confession.[118] Fourthly, Ruotger reminds his priests about the different penitential remedies recorded in the ancient canons, Holy Scripture and the penitentials. Finally he reminds them that there are seven ways of remitting sin.[119]

These last two canons are taken almost directly from the capitulary of Radulf of Bourges, composed 853–66.[120] Ruotger made extensive use of Radulf's work, except that on public penance, a subject he omitted from his *capitula*, leaving it to his council (927x8).[121] Ruotger regarded annual confession as necessary to the life of all Christians, hence his inclusion of the threat of excommunication; those who fail to confess are excluded from the Christian community. Coercion was not associated only with public penance. His description of the administration of confession cannot be accepted uncritically as depicting practice in the province of Trier in the 920s as it is described in exactly the terms used some sixty years earlier by an archbishop in relatively distant Aquitaine. Given Ruotger's reliance on Radulf elsewhere in his capitulary (and his synodal decrees), these chapters probably represent Ruotger's aspirations, inspired by his model, as much as reality.

North-eastern France: the province of Rheims

The capitulary evidence from the province of Rheims is slighter than that for Trier. *Capitula* are preserved in four manuscripts, *Sangallensia*, *Cottoniana*, *Antwerpensia* and *Trosleiana*, but only the first two contain references to penitential practice.[122] Both the provenance and date of the *Capitula Sangallensia* are uncertain: somewhere in northern France, sometime between the mid ninth and early tenth centuries. But it is the only text from northern Europe to refer to the use of writing in the administration of penance: the names of the penitents and their sins should be recorded on schedules so that the bishop (presumably) has enough information to know how they should be

---

[118] c. xxvii, MGH, *Capit. Ep. I*, 70.
[119] The seven are baptism, martyrdom, almsgiving, forgiving the sins of others, preaching, charity and penance, but the text breaks off before reaching penance: c. xxviii, ibid. 70.
[120] Radulf, Capit., cc. xxxi–xxxiii, ibid. 257–60. On Radulf's work see McKitterick, *Frankish Church*, 59–61.
[121] Ruotger's *capitula* are, however, incomplete (see c. xxviii) and may possibly have originally included public penance.
[122] For the latter see MGH, *Capit. Ep. III*, 104–9, 141–6.

punished and when the penitent should be reconciled.[123] This chapter, which has no penitential context, seems to refer to public penance; the bishop should be presented with a report before he enjoins penance on the penitent. The *Capitula Cottoniana*, from late ninth- or early tenth-century Rheims, include only the standard prohibition, inherited from the ninth century, against priests accepting money for public sins or incest or penance.[124]

The Rheims *capitula* thus provide little evidence of concern for penance but, as the Council of Trosly (909), and Flodoard's and Richer's descriptions of individual incidents suggest, penance was an important concern of, and disciplinary tool used by, tenth-century archbishops of Rheims.[125] The absence of *capitula* may instead be due to the survival of the Carolingian *capitula* of Hincmar and Theodulf of Orléans in Rheims's well-stocked archives.[126]

East Frankia: the province of Mainz

Surviving from this province is only one set of tenth-century *capitula*, which were probably written in early tenth-century Mainz but based upon Regino, giving a date post-906.[127] The only canons concerning penance appear under the heading: 'what they (the priests) should tell the people'.[128] The priest should, firstly, order his people to take communion three times a year, at Christmas, Easter and Pentecost, unless they are penitents,[129] and, secondly, ensure that they know the Creed and the Lord's Prayer and come to confession in Lent.[130] The former is based upon a canon in Regino, itself taken from Ansegis's collection.[131] The latter is equally grounded in ninth-century traditions.[132] Both are similar to provisions made in the

---

[123] 'Ut nomina paenitentum eorumque scelera unusquisque in scedula describat et iugiter previdere satagat, qualiter peniteant, quatenus testis tempore reconciliacionis esse valeat': c. viii, ibid. 117. For southern Europe see below.

[124] c. xvi, ibid. 139.

[125] For example see the discussion of the synod of 923x924 which issued a penitential ordinance after the battle of Soissons (922) in ch. 6.

[126] Two Hincmar manuscripts have a Rheims provenance: Paris, BN, MS lat. 4287 (s. ix$^{3/4}$), and Vatican, BAV, MS Reg. lat. 418 (s. x^1), MGH, *Capit. Ep. II*, 30. One manuscript of both Hincmar's and Theodulf's capitularies (Paris, BN, MS lat. 3878) was copied in north-eastern France/the western Rhineland in the eleventh century: MGH, *Capit. Ep. I*, 90; MGH, *Capit. Ep. II*, 30.

[127] MGH, *Capit. Ep. III*, 181–6.

[128] 'Quid plebi denuntiare debeant': ibid. 186.

[129] c. ix, ibid.

[130] c. xi, ibid.

[131] 'Ut tribus vicibus laici in anno communicent. Ut si non frequentius vel ter laici homines in anno communicent nisi forte quis maioribus quibuslibet criminibus impediatur, id est in Pascha, Natali Domini et Pentecoste': Regino, *Libri duo* i.334, p. 158. For the source see *Collectio capitularium Ansegisi* ii.43, p. 562.

[132] On the need to instruct the laity see Theodulf, Capit. II, cc. i–ii, MGH, *Capit. Ep. I*, 148–9; Hincmar, Capit. I, c. i, MGH, *Capit. Ep. II*, 34–5; Regino, *Libri duo* i.275, pp. 128–9.

Admonitio synodalis.[133] These canons demonstrate that penance was important to an individual's membership of the community; he or she affirms his (or her) membership through regular communion and confession, and is temporarily excluded through penance.[134] The *capitula*'s debt to Carolingian legislation may explain why no further sets of *capitula* were composed in the tenth-century province of Mainz: they were already well supplied with Carolingian texts, both as original texts[135] and in the summary of Carolingian legislation provided by Regino's collection and so had no need to generate further material.

Northern Italy: the province of Milan

Copies of Carolingian episcopal *capitula* were also made in Italy in this period.[136] But one mid tenth-century bishop in the province of Milan, Atto, bishop of Vercelli (924–c. 960), felt it necessary to draw up his own lengthy capitulary.[137] His *Capitulare* was of little interest to either his episcopal contemporaries or successive generations; it survives in only two tenth-century manuscripts, both written in Vercelli on Atto's orders.[138] It is, however, a useful case study for the knowledge of canon law and for contemporary practice in a mid tenth-century north Italian diocese.

Atto drew on four main sources, principally the *Collectio Anselmo dedicata*, but also the *Capitulare* of Theodulf of Orléans, the *Dionysio-Hadriana* and *Pseudo-Isidore*.[139] His is a personal compilation and certain themes predominate; in particular Atto was keen to assert the importance of episcopal authority, and to emphasise the bishop's role in the workings of the diocese.

---

133 *Admonitio synodalis*, nos lxi, lxiii–iv, pp. 58–9.
134 Avril, 'Remarques'.
135 For example, a collection including the *capitula* of both Haito of Basle and Theodulf was compiled, probably at St Gall, in the tenth century: St Gallen, Stiftsbibliothek, Cod. 677, MGH, *Capit. Ep. I*, 92. A late ninth-century southern German copy of Theodulf's first capitulary survives, now Bamberg, Staatsbibliothek, MS lit. 131, and a mid ninth-century copy of Theodulf survives from Fulda, now Basle, Universitätsbibliothek, MS F. III. 15: ibid. 77–8.
136 North Italian manuscripts of the capitularies of Theodulf and Haito include Barcelona, Bib. Univ. MS 288 (s. x^{ex}); Monza, Bib. Cap. MS b. 23/141 (s. x); Vatican, BAV, MS Vat. lat. 1146 (s. xi). Central Italian manuscripts include Vatican, BAV, MS Vat. lat. 1147 (s. xi^2); Vienna, Österreichische Nationalsbibliothek, Cod. 914 (s. xi^2): MGH, *Capit. Ep. I*, 78, 83, 93–4, 99.
137 MGH, *Capit. Ep. III*, 243–304.
138 Vatican, BAV, MS Vat. lat. 4322 (s. $x^{med.}$) and Vercelli, Biblioteca capitolare, MS XXXIX (s. $x^{2/4}$), described in MGH, *Capit. Ep. III*, 259–60, and Wemple, *Atto*, 185–7. Wemple notes that the texts from the *Capitulare* were recorded in one contemporary collection, but gives no evidence for her statement.
139 S. Wemple, 'The canonical resources of Atto of Vercelli (926–960)', *Traditio* xxvi (1970), 335–50, and *Atto*, 201–17. Atto's own library included the *Dionysiana*, the *Collectio*, and *Pseudo-Isidore*: ibid. 38.

Atto may not have relied on previous sources for all his canons; the source for ten chapters, 10 per cent of the work, has not been traced.[140] In particular no source has been identified for the chapter concerned with the administration of penance by priests, c. xc: *Qualiter presbiteri erga penitentes agant:*[141]

A priest should not impose rules of penance without respect of person or case; the times of penance or of reconciliation he should leave to the bishop's decision. Just as a priest should not reconcile a penitent without consulting the bishop (unless by the bishop's permission) so rather priests who are ordained among the people should take great care lest their parishioners fall into criminal faults. If this should happen they should make careful inquiry, both from the parishioners themselves and from all their neighbours, about how the events occurred, and should not delay writing this down. They should be zealous in encouraging them often to have recourse to the satisfaction of peace and penance. The senior priest of that congregation – or whoever is more learned after him – should come together with them bringing with him what he has written. If the penitents defer appearing, the priest should be at the chief seat of the bishop on Ash Wednesday, together with what he has written and should produce this for his bishop to consider what he should do. If the penitents appear he should once more give an account of the rules which are imposed on them as penance, and should show the greatest concern for them, to know their behaviour as well as possible. If he perceives that anyone is bowed down by his penance, so that there is some expectation of danger from increased weakness, or if infirmity weighs heavily on anyone, the priest should return to his bishop so that remedies may be granted to the penitent through his agency. If the bishop is not present he should refer the matter in the meantime to the cardinal priests of the chief see. On Maundy Thursday, the day of reconciliation, he himself should return to give a most complete account of what each has done; and again similarly on the Wednesday after the octave of Pentecost he should make haste to appear together with them so that he should learn and write down what has been imposed on them.[142]

---

[140] Ibid. 211.
[141] MGH, *Capit. Ep. III*, 296–7.
[142] 'Non debet presbiter iniungere penitentiae leges sine aliquo respectu personae aut causae, sed tempora penitentiae aut reconciliationis episcopi arbitrario concedat. Et ut presbyter inconsulto episcopo non reconciliet penitentem, nisi episcopo permittente. Sed potius presbiteri, qui in plebibus ordinantur, providentiam magnam habeant, ne eorum parroechiani in criminalia incidant delicta. Quod si evenerit, tam ab ipsis quam ab omnibus vicinis diligenter, qualiter acta sunt, inquirant et scriptis notare non differant eosque admonere frequenter studeant, ut ad pacis et penitentiae satisfactionem citissime currant; et cum ipsis primus eiusdem plebis presbiter, aut qui doctior post ipsum fuerit, veniat idemque, quod scripserat, secum adferat. Quodsi hiidem penitentes venire distulerint, ipse in capite ieiunii ad primam eiusdem episcopii sedem esse nullo modo cum eodem dissimulet scripto suoque hoc suggerat episcopo, ut, quod ei exinde agendum sit, consideret. Si autem etiam penitentes adfuerint, leges, quae illis penitentiae imponuntur, rursus describat curamque et sollicitudinem erga eos maximam gerat, ut eorum conversationem plenissime cognoscere possit. Quodsi obnixe aliquem penitentiae viderit incumbere aut debilitate incurrente periculum speretur aut si infirmitas quempiam oppresserit, ad suum presbiter recurrat episcopum, ut illi per ipsum remedia concedantur. Qui si defuerit, cardinalibus prime sedi

This is obviously a description of public penance: the priest should investigate criminal faults amongst his parishioners. Yet this chapter is concerned to maintain episcopal authority over the penitential process:[143] the length of penance and the timing of the reconciliation should be left to the bishop; he should monitor the penances imposed by the priest; on Ash Wednesday the senior priest of each parish should present all the penitents in his *plebs* to the bishop, who should then assess whether their penance is appropriate. A penitent's penance may only be altered after consultation with the bishop, or the bishop's cardinal priests in his absence.[144] The priest must return to the bishop on Maundy Thursday to give an account of the conduct of each penitent, and again on the Wednesday after the octave of Pentecost.

Hidden beneath this emphasis on episcopal authority are some interesting pointers to penitential practice in mid tenth-century Vercelli. The priest should follow the *penitentiae leges*, suggesting that he should have access to a penitential. Penance was, in fact, an expression of the judicial authority exercised by the Church, perhaps explaining the parallels between the description given by Atto and the secular judicial process.[145] The priest should investigate the circumstances surrounding a crime and write a report. He should present his report, if possible with the penitent, to the bishop on Ash Wednesday in order to allow the bishop to approve the action taken. This emphasis on the written word may reflect a level of literacy also expected by the secular judicial system within Italy.[146] But as a similar demand for written reports on penitents can be found north of the Alps in the early tenth-century northern French *capitula Sangallensia*, Atto's requirement probably owes less to Italy's *Schriftlichkeit* than to his concern, as a conscientious bishop and legislator, to devise a watertight penitential system. The priest should return to give an account of the penance performed by each penitent on Maundy Thursday, presumably before they were reconciled by the bishop. Although some eighth- and ninth-century evidence suggests that penitents were incarcerated for the period of their penance, Atto envisages some form of community service, whereby penitents perform their penance as part of the village community.[147] Their penance may not always end on Maundy

---

presbiteris interim sucgeratur. Ad diem namque reconciliationis, id est caena domini, ipse quoque recurrat singulorum acta plenissime indicandum. Similiter etiam quarto die post octavam pentecosten cum ipsis pariter adesse festinent, ut rursus, quae illis iussa fuerint, cognoscere et describere possit': c. xc, MGH, *Capit. Ep. III*, pp. 296–7.

[143] Watkins, *History of penance*, ii. 686.

[144] Cathedral clergy were often referred to as cardinal clergy outside of Rome in the ninth and tenth centuries: K. F. Morrison, 'Cardinal', in *New Catholic encyclopedia*, iii. 104–5; C. G. Fürst, 'Kardinal', in *LMA* v. 950–2.

[145] Bougard, *La Justice*, 239–43.

[146] C. Wickham, 'Land disputes and their social framework in Lombard-Carolingian Italy, 700–900', in W. Davies and P. Fouracre (eds), *The settlement of disputes in early medieval Europe*, Cambridge 1986, 105–24 at pp. 114–15.

[147] For the evidence of the incarceration of penitents see Poschmann, *Penance*, 137; de Jong, 'What was public?', 877–87.

Thursday, for the priests return for an update-report on the Wednesday after the octave of Pentecost: a penitent given a seven-year penance might be reconciled at the end of the first Lent of his penance, but continue to serve his penitential sentence.

Atto's other canons on penance have precedents in earlier canonical collections: penitents should genuflect daily; those who die as penitents should be buried by the Church; penitents should abstain from worldly affairs.[148] Atto may have based c. xc on an existing authority, now lost; in its absence, it seems likely that he wrote down contemporary practice, albeit in an idealised form, following the same path seemingly taken twenty or thirty years earlier by Regino in Lotharingia and the author of the *capitula Sangallensia*.

Although Suzanne Wemple has argued that Atto in his other, more theoretical, works underplayed both the role of the Church as an institution for penance and the juridical power of priests, the importance he attached to both in the *Capitulare* suggest his ideas were more traditional when formulated for a practical context.[149] In emphasising that reconciliation of penitents should be restricted to bishops, Atto of Vercelli merely echoed the provisions made by earlier clerics: the Council of Pavia (850) ordered that the priests in every town and village should monitor the way in which penitents undertook their penance, not only physically by observing the precepts, but also mentally by expressing contrition. The priest has freedom to determine the length of the penance – if it is being performed in a negligent manner, it may need to be extended, if diligently, it may be curtailed. But the reconciliation of penitents is reserved exclusively to the bishop: the priest should consult the bishop, even if he is absent, before reconciling the penitent, for only bishops have the power to reconcile penitents through the imposition of hands.[150] Whilst Pavia echoes earlier descriptions, the picture is very similar to that drawn by Atto a century later.[151] But whilst Pavia envisages the priest determining the type and length of penance, Atto gave the priest no such autonomy – he was to leave such matters to the bishop's decision. The parallels between Pavia and Atto are not overt: Atto did not cite Pavia directly, and although there is a slight possibility that he may have seen a copy of the canons of Pavia, he almost certainly did not own them.[152]

---

[148] cc. xci–xciii, MGH, *Capit. Ep. III*, 297–8. For cc. xci–xcii see *Statuta ecclesiae antiqua*, cc. lxvii, lxvi respectively; c. xciii is taken partially from Leo I's *Epistola ad rusticum*, preserved in both the *Dionysio-Hadriana*, cc. xxiii–iv, and the *Collectio Anselmo dedicata* vii.98–9, with several unattributed and untraced lines inserted. For all these attributions see Wemple, *Atto*, 211–14.
[149] Ibid. 8.
[150] Council of Pavia, c. vii, MGH, *Concilia III*, 222–3.
[151] Watkin, *History of penance*, ii. 719. For echoes of Halitgar and canons of the Council of Carthage 390 see MGH, *Concilia III*, 223 nn. 31–4.
[152] The manuscript tradition for the complete text of the Council of Pavia is limited to four manuscripts, none of which have a direct association with Vercelli. But canon xxiv of the

It is therefore likely that both Pavia and Atto reflect the ideal to which the bishops of northern Italy aspired. How far these aspirations were realised is less clear but none of Atto's successors found much need to copy or produce their own versions of the *capitulare*. How far penance was, or continued to be, practised in the way described by Atto is therefore open to doubt.

Unlike their ninth-century counterparts, tenth-century *capitula* were not widely distributed; their evidence is therefore highly localised. Yet their authors, like their predecessors, demonstrate the aspirations of individual bishops, suggesting a number of conclusions about the practice of penance: firstly, that it was regarded as one of the crucial rituals by which a Christian demonstrated his (or her) membership of the Christian community, just like baptism and Christian burial; secondly, that public penance was clearly differentiated from annual confession; and thirdly, that bishops saw in public penance a useful mechanism for the control of their dioceses.

Although there is much overlap and repetition between these three genres, this is actually evidence of widespread episcopal concern with penitential practice. Firstly, of a desire on the part of the bishops to educate their clergy; such repetition demonstrates not only the reiterative nature of medieval law, but was itself a form of education for the clergy concerned. Secondly, reiteration shows the great importance the bishops attached to the central precepts regarding penitential practice, and the different ways in which they sought to get them across.

The evidence for penitential practice examined so far – penitential and canon law collections, conciliar *acta*, episcopal *capitula* and synodal sermons – was produced mainly for and by bishops and their secular clergy. Yet they constituted only one section of the clergy. The regular clergy, both monks and canons, played a leading part in the Church at this time, as well as writing many of the surviving records from this period. The next chapter therefore examines the role of the regular clergy in the history of penitential practice in this period.

---

council is recorded in a manuscript of Pseudo-Isidore which was known and used by Atto, now Vercelli, Biblioteca capitolare, MS LXXX. For the manuscript history of the Council of Pavia see ibid. 218–19. For Atto's knowledge of Vercelli, Biblioteca capitolare, MS LXXX see Wemple, *Atto*, 207–8.

3

Penance and the Regular Life

Historians have long recognised the important contribution made by monks to the history of the penitential, and thence to the history of *paenitentia occulta*, in the very early Middle Ages (c. 600–c. 800), but have paid little attention to the role of penance within the monastic life itself.[1] This *lacuna* owes something to the monks' own view of their life which saw penance as peculiar to laymen; monks by entering the religious life had undergone a second baptism, similar to that of penance, by swearing to live a life without sin, and thus had foregone the need for penance.[2] Yet for any community living in accordance with a rule there had to be a procedure for those who offended against it. And as the evidence reviewed in this chapter demonstrates, the records for such discipline, for both the monks and canons of this period, share a common vocabulary and repertoire of gestures with those for the practice of canonical penance administered to all Christians. This is of especial interest to this study because members of the regular clergy were largely responsible for the transmission of the evidence for the practice of penance in this period: they composed and copied canonical collections,[3] penitential liturgies,[4] sermons about penance,[5] and *vitae* and chronicles which included accounts of people undertaking penance.[6] How far therefore did the regular clergy's own experiences of penance influence the accounts they gave of it? This chapter seeks to address this question through an examination of the role of penance in the lives of the regular clergy, that is canons as well as monks, for the boundaries between the two were not impermeable: for example, many monastic reformers in the tenth century were trained in houses of secular canons.[7] Further, it examines the part which they played in

---

[1] For the contribution of monks to the early history of *paenitentia occulta* and the penitential see, amongst others, the comments by Poschmann, *Abendländische Kirchenbusse*, 27–31, and *Penance*, ch. ii, esp. pp. 129–32; Vogel, *Le Pécheur au moyen âge*, 20–4; Frantzen, *Literature*, esp. chs ii–iii.
[2] Pseudo-Augustine, *Sermo III: ad monachos: de poenitentia*, PL lviii. 875–6.
[3] See ch. 1.
[4] See chs 4, 5.
[5] For example the sermon on penance written for Maundy Thursday attributed to Bern, abbot of Reichenau: extracts edited in C. Erdmann, *Forschungen zur politischen Ideenwelt des Frühmittelalters*, Berlin 1951, 116–17.
[6] See ch. 6.
[7] J. Siegwart, *Die Chorherren- und Chorfrauengemeinschaften in der deutschsprachigen Schweiz von 6. Jahrhundert bis 1160 mit einem Überblick über die deutsche Kanonikerreform des 10. und 11. Jahrhundert*, Freiburg 1962, ch. iv, esp. pp. 156–62; G. Constable, 'Monastic

the delivery of pastoral care, thus exploring one avenue through which ideas about penance left the cloister and permeated the secular world.

Both monks and canons played distinctive yet important roles in the Church in this period, although the difference between them may not always have been clear to outsiders.[8] Both groups supposedly lived their life according to a rule: the most popular for monks being some version of that of Benedict, for canons that composed in the mid eighth century by Chrodegang, bishop of Metz, for the canons of his cathedral. This picture was, however, more complicated for both groups, as we shall see.

Despite much work in recent years, the history of canons remains much more obscure than that of monks. This obscurity reflects the fact that most canonical foundations lacked the institutional longevity of most monastic houses, and consequently the institutional consciousness which was to produce the great early modern Benedictine historians, such as Jean Mabillon, whose work was to prove so influential on the course of nineteenth- and twentieth-century historiography. Yet regular canons were numerous and played an important role in church life in the tenth and eleventh centuries. They differed principally from monks in being, in the main, but not always, ordained clergy.[9] Like monks they supposedly shared a common life, eating and sleeping together, but they were allowed to retain private property. They often constituted the cathedral chapter, and as such had regular pastoral contact with the laity, administering both public and secret penance. But they could, and did, live in much smaller, more rural communities, where they were seemingly involved in delivering pastoral care.[10] In the tenth century such canonical communities were often unreformed associations of married and hereditary clergy, living in separate

---

possessions of churches and "spiritualia" in the age of reform', in *Il monachesimo e la riforma ecclesiastica (1049–1112): atti della quarta settimana internazionale di studio Mendola, 23–29 agosto 1968* (Miscellanea vi, 1971), 304–31.

[8] On this point see Reuter, *Germany*, 243.

[9] The exceptions included houses of female canons: M. Parisse, 'Les Chanoinesses dans l'empire germanique (IXe–XIe siècles)', *Francia: Forschungen zur westeuropäischen Geschichte* vi (1978), 107–26. The most detailed study of canons and canonesses in this period is the local study by Siegwart, *Chorherren*, ch. iv, which also places Swiss activity within a broader context.

[10] Thus the ninth-century external schools of Fulda, which acted as centres for the education of priests in the area, became in the tenth century houses of canons but, seemingly, continued to deliver pastoral care: M. Hildebrandt, *The external school in Carolingian society*, Leiden–New York–Cologne 1992, 119–29. Those in favour of the 'minster' hypothesis in Anglo-Saxon England also envisage teams of clergy involved in the delivery of pastoral care, although how far these teams were regular clergy, and how universal this system was is a matter of considerable debate: Blair, *Minsters and parish churches*; Blair and Sharpe, *Pastoral care before the parish*. For a recent review of the debate see Cambridge and Rollason, 'Debate: the pastoral organisation of the Anglo-Saxon Church', and Blair, 'Debate: ecclesiastical organisation and pastoral care in Anglo-Saxon England'.

houses, and such canons were of sufficient importance that their reform was an important concern of the eleventh-century reform movement.[11]

Whilst the canonical life, although often unreformed, was popular in the tenth century, this period is more renowned as a time of monastic reform: monks in conjunction with certain members of the episcopate, powerful laymen and women, sought to reform existing monasteries, and establish new ones run on reformist lines, in a series of movements concentrated in the heartlands of Burgundy, Flanders and Lotharingia but spreading over the course of the tenth and eleventh centuries to the rest of west Frankia, into Italy and England and into east Frankia in the eleventh century. However, many of the older monasteries in this period, such as the east Frankish houses of St Gallen, Reichenau, Fulda and Corvey, as well as the north Italian houses of Bobbio and Nonantola, continued to maintain their customary form of monasticism.[12] Research in the last forty years has revised Kassius Hallinger's bipartite model of reform spreading out, domino-like, from the twin centres of Cluny in Burgundy and Gorze in Lotharingia to create two rival networks of affinity across Europe, each adhering to a common set of customs (*consuetudines*) derived from their mother house.[13] Rather than imposing an anachronistic twelfth-century model of networks of rival orders, akin to those of Cluny and Clairvaux, on the tenth century, the monastic reform of that period is now seen in terms of what Gerd Tellenbach has described as a series of 'centres from which impulses of renewal and intensification went out to other monasteries, to abbots and monks, to the laymen and bishops who helped to support monastic life by founding patronising and venerating monasteries'.[14] Gorze and the monasteries which formed part of its reform group is perhaps the prime example of this, starting in Lotharingia in the 930s but then spreading to Fleury in west Frankia, Anglo-Saxon England and into east Frankia.[15] Individual institutions, such as the monas-

---

[11] The most famous example of an unreformed community of canons is that recorded at Arezzo: *Historia custodum aretinorum* (MGH, SS xxx/2), 1471–82, analysed by R. W. Southern in *The making of the Middle Ages*, London 1953, repr. London 1987, 125–7. The introduction of reformed canons regular did not reach Germany until the late eleventh or early twelfth centuries: Reuter, *Germany*, 242. For a convenient summary of the reform of canons see C. Morris, *The papal monarchy: the western Church from 1050 to 1250*, Oxford 1989, 74–8. For more detail see *Istituzioni monastiche e istituzioni canonicali in occidente (1123–1215): atti della settima settimana internazionale di studio Mendola, 28 agosto – 3 settembre 1977* (Miscellanea ix, 1980). On the history of canons before the eleventh century see F. Poggiaspalla, *La vita comuna del clero dalle origino alla riforma gregoriana*, Rome 1968; R. Schieffer, 'Kanoniker', in *LMA* v. 903–4; Siegwart, *Chorherren*.
[12] Tellenbach, *Church*, 109.
[13] K. Hallinger, *Gorze – Kluny: Studien zu den monastischen Lebensformen und Gegensätzen im Hochmittelalter*, Rome 1950.
[14] Tellenbach, *Church*, 110. See also R. Kottje, 'Einleitung: monastische Reform oder Reformen?', in R. Kottje and H. Maurer (eds), *Monastische Reformen im 9. und 10. Jahrhundert*, Sigmaringen 1989, 9–13.
[15] On the foundation of the Gorzian monasteries see J. Nightingale, 'Monasteries and their

tery of Fleury in west Frankia, building on different sets of institutional and personal relationships, were subject to influences from more than one source – in Fleury's case, from Gorze certainly, but also from Cluny (we know that Odo, abbot of Cluny visited and reformed the monastery in 930 but he does not seem to have left much mark on the abbey's customs) and, of course, by the traditions inherited from the ninth-century Carolingian reformers.[16] Fleury in turn was to influence the tenth-century Anglo-Saxon reformers at the council in 970 which issued the *Regularis concordia*.[17] In other cases individual figures, such as William of Volpiano of Saint-Benigne, Dijon, or Gerard of Brogne, created reform 'groups' of monasteries centred on their personality and vision of monastic life.[18] The great Burgundian monastery of Cluny itself stood in contrast to these movements in that rather than the connections between Cluny and those houses loosely affiliated with it being due to personal connections with the founder, they were due to a common allegiance to a Cluniac way of life.[19] But whilst the nature of the Cluniac empire in the tenth century has been overstated (Fleury is now known to have been much more independent than used to be thought), as has the extent of Cluniac expansion in the eleventh century, Cluny did influence some of the houses in the area under consideration – for example the central Italian monastery of Farfa, reformed by Odo in the 930s, received a set of Cluny's customs in the mid eleventh century.[20] As important as contemporary influences were those of the past; all the tenth-century monastic

---

patrons in the dioceses of Trier, Metz and Toul, *circa* 850–1000', unpubl. DPhil. diss. Oxford 1988. On Gorze as a centre of influence see, in addition to Hallinger, *Gorze–Kluny*, M. Parisse, *La Nécrologie de Gorze: contribution à l'histoire monastique* (Annales de l'est. Memoire xl), Nancy 1971. On Gorzian monasticism, once it had spread into the empire in the eleventh century, see P. Jestice, *Wayward monks and the religious revolution of the eleventh century*, Leiden 1997.

[16] On the Gorzian influence on Fleury see A. Davril, 'Points de contact entre la *Vita Iohannis abbatis Gorziensis* et les *Consuetudines Floriacenses antiquiores*', in M. Parisse and O. G. Oexle (eds), *L'Abbaye de Gorze au Xe siècle*, Nancy 1993, 183–92. On the Carolingian influence see J. Nightingale, 'Oswald, Fleury and continental reform', in N. Brooks and C. Cubitt (eds), *St Oswald of Worcester: life and influence*, London–New York 1996, 23–45.

[17] Ibid.

[18] On William of Volpiano of Saint Benigne, Dijon, see N. Bulst, *Untersuchungen zu den Klosterreformen Wilhelms von Dijon (962–1031)*, Bonn 1973. On Gerard of Brogne in Flanders see J. Wollasch, 'Gerard de Brogne und seine Klostergründung', *Rev. Bén.* lxx (1960), 62–82, 224–31.

[19] J. Wollasch, *Mönchtum des Mittelalters zwischen Kirche und Welt*, Munich 1973. On Cluny in the tenth century see B. Rosenwein, *Rhinoceros bound: Cluny in the tenth century*, Philadelphia 1982; G. Constable, 'Cluny in the monastic world of the tenth century', in *Il secolo di ferro* (Settimane xxxviii, 1991), 391–437; and N. Hunt (ed.), *Cluniac monasticism in the central Middle Ages*, London 1971.

[20] On Odo's work in Italy see B. Hamilton, 'Monastic revival in tenth-century Rome', *Studia Monastica* iv (1962), 35–68 (repr. in his *Monastic reform, Catharism and the crusades (900–1300)*, London 1979, no. ii). For the customary see *Liber tramitis aevi Odilonis abbatis*, ed. P. Dinter (CCM x, 1980).

reformers inherited a substantial legacy, in terms of legislation about, and commentaries and other writings on, the monastic life, from the Carolingian reforms embodied by the Aachen decrees of 816–17 and other works associated with the circle of Louis the Pious's adviser, the monastic reformer Benedict of Aniane.[21] The reformers thus perceived themselves as taking part in what was an ongoing reform cycle. And the ultimate authority, and ideal, for all these monastic reformers was the rule of Benedict.[22]

Monks

The rule of Benedict of Nursia was the most influential of the late antique monastic rules on western monasticism. Composed c. 500–c. 550, it did not remain in constant use unchanged, but instead became both the spiritual and practical ideal to which monastic reformers constantly sought to return.[23] Monastic reformers prescribed their reforms at a general level in church councils, as Louis the Pious did on the advice of Benedict of Aniane at the councils of Aachen in 816 and 817, and at a more local level in the customaries. These latter supplemented the rule by describing the practice of a particular house, giving details of how the divine office should be celebrated and instructions for other aspects of the monastic life.[24] Commentaries were also written on the rule which sought to explain and justify its prescriptions.

But it is the Benedictine rule which is the starting point for drawing a picture of penitential discipline within the monastic life, for it was the predominant source for internal monastic discipline throughout western Europe in this period: in a community that lived according to a rule there had to be a procedure for those who offended against it.[25] The rule established a

---

[21] J. Semmler, 'Das Erbe der karolingischen Klosterreform im 10. Jahrhundert', in Kottje and Maurer, *Monastische Reformen*, 29–77. See also Constable, 'Cluny in the monastic world', 397–400.
[22] Rodulfus Glaber, a pupil of William of Volpiano, traced Cluny's customs directly to the Benedictine rule: *Rodolfi Glabri historiarum libri quinque*, ed. J. France, Oxford 1989, III.v, pp. 120–6.
[23] On the rule of Benedict as a source for the Carolingian reforms of the early ninth century see M. de Jong, 'Carolingian monasticism: the power of prayer', in R. McKitterick (ed.), *New Cambridge medieval history*, II: c. 700–900, Cambridge 1995, 622–53 at pp. 629–34.
[24] For example the Councils of Aachen in 816 and 817: MGH, *Concilia II*, i. 307–466. See also the English reform council of 970: *Regularis concordia Angliae nationis monachorum sanctimonialumque*, ed. T. Symons, London 1953.
[25] There is less evidence concerning the rule followed by female houses, but one copy of the rules of Benedict and Caesarius of Arles (Bamberg, Staatsbibliothek, MS Lit. 142) was made for the abbess of Niedermünster, c. 995, at the request of Henry of Bavaria, father of Henry II, as his father was buried there and his mother stayed at the house until her death: *Vor dem Jahr 1000: abendländische Buchkunst zur Zeit der Kaiserin Theophanu: eine Ausstellung des Schnütgen-Museums zum Gedenken an den 1000. Todestag der Kaiserin Theophanu*, Cologne 1991, no. 13, 68–9.

two-fold classification, set out in cc. xxiv and xxv, between lesser and graver faults. Lesser faults should result in the brother being excluded from eating with the rest of the community and from taking a leading part in the oratory.[26] Grave faults should result in the brother being excluded from both the refectory and the oratory altogether, and from communicating with the rest of the community: 'He is to be alone at the work enjoined him, continuing in the sadness of penance.'[27] It is the abbot's duty to determine the nature of the fault.[28] If a fault is committed in public, the offender is less severely disciplined if he comes immediately before the abbot and the community to make spontaneous satisfaction than if he leaves his fault to be revealed by someone else. However, if a concealed fault is a sin of the soul, then the brother should make it known only to the abbot or the spiritual seniors who will know how to cure it, rather than uncover and broadcast it.[29] This disciplinary system was for infringements of monastic discipline, not sinful behaviour. Yet the distinction made in the rule between faults committed in secret and in public was echoed by the so-called Carolingian dichotomy, that public sins deserve public penance, secret sins secret penance; indeed the rule was perhaps one of the influences defining this dichotomy.

The terminologies of monastic discipline and canonical penance overlap: the punishment for faults is known as *excommunicatio* (excommunication), that is exclusion from involvement in the monastic community.[30] If any other monk communicated with an excommunicate brother he too was to be excommunicated;[31] this provision, concerning communication with excommunicates, owes much to the late antique Church's system for internal discipline. As early as the fourth century excommunication was prescribed for clergy who had contact with excommunicates, and as early as the fifth century with regard to the laity.[32] The rule also adopts the medical language often associated with penitential practice, citing from Matthew's Gospel, 'they that be whole need not a physician but they that are sick'.[33]

The disciplinary procedure for grave faults ends either with the excommu-

---

[26] RB, c. xxiv, ii. 544.
[27] 'Solus sit ad opus sibi iniunctum, persistens in paenitentiae luctu': ibid. c. xxv, ii. 546.
[28] Ibid. c. xxiv, ii. 544.
[29] 'Si animae vero peccati causa fuerit latens, tantum abbati aut spiritalibus senioribus patefaciat, qui sciat curare et sua et aliena uulnera, non detegere et publicare': ibid. c. xlvi, ii. 596.
[30] 'Qualis debet esse modus excommunicationis?': ibid. c. xxiv, ii. 544; 'De excommunicatione culparum': ibid. c. xxiii, ii. 542.
[31] Ibid. c. xxvi, ii. 546–8.
[32] E. Vodola, *Excommunication in the Middle Ages*, Berkeley–Los Angeles–London 1986, 8–10, esp. n. 41.
[33] Matthew ix.12; RB, c. xxvii, ii. 548. See also Luke v.31. Texts concerned with penance often used medical analogies, for example '*Incipit prologus de medicinae salutaris animarum. De remediis uulnerum secundum priorum patrum diffinitiones dicturi sacri tibi eloqui, mi fidelissime frater, antea medicamina conpendi ratione intimemus*': *Paenitentiale Cummeani*, in *The Irish penitentials*, ed. L. Bieler with D. A. Binchy, Dublin 1975, 108; 'Liber hic

nicate being expelled, if he refuses to make amends,[34] or being reconciled, if he makes satisfaction for his fault.[35] He should do so by lying prostrate outside the oratory doors during prayer and prostrating himself at the feet of all the other members of the community as they leave the oratory. When the abbot judges that satisfaction has been done,[36] the excommunicate should appear and prostrate himself at the feet of the abbot and all the community and then he may be accepted back into the community, and follow the regime for those guilty of lesser faults: he may not take a leading part in the oratory, and must prostrate himself on the ground after the Office at each of the Hours. The chapter concludes by prescribing that those guilty of minor faults should be excommunicated from the table only, but not from the oratory, and make satisfaction in the oratory, that is prostrate themselves after the Office each time, until the abbot gives the order. Again the rule shares a common vocabulary with canonical penance; the errant monk must make satisfaction in order to be restored to communion. They also share a physical language of gesture: the errant monk has to prostrate himself before the abbot and the community, just as the penitent must prostrate himself in the liturgy for both public and secret penance before the officiating priest and an audience.[37]

Yet modern monastic historians have distinguished monastic regular discipline from penance, accepting the monks' own views both of their lives as a form of penance, and of their own work in performing a vicarious penance on behalf of their benefactors.[38] But the ambiguities caused by a common vocabulary meant that the distinction between discipline and penance was less obvious to tenth- and eleventh-century monks, as demonstrated both by their customaries and by the existing commentaries on the rule. Only two such commentaries were available in this period, and both were composed in the ninth century: that of Smaragdus, abbot of the Lotharingian monastery of St Mihiel, Verdun (from c. 809), and that of Hildemar of the north Italian monastery of Civate (d. c. 850). Yet their respective manuscript traditions suggest that they were both copied and read at this time. And the texts themselves suggest how the rule's prescriptions were perceived not only by their authors but also by the audiences which read or heard them.

The *Expositio in regulam S. Benedicti* by Smaragdus is the earliest commentary on the rule, although it is compiled mostly from the works of earlier writers, including Gregory the Great, Cassian, Isidore and the rules of Basil and the Master.[39] The *Expositio* is associated, like Smaragdus' other works,

---

Corrector vocatur et Medicus, quia correctiones corporum et animarum medicinas plene continet': Burchard, *Decretum*, 949.

[34] *RB*, c. xxviii, ii. 550–2.
[35] Ibid. c. xliv, ii. 592–4.
[36] 'Usque dum abbas iudicaverit satisfactum esse': ibid. c. xliv, ii. 592.
[37] See ch. 5 for consideration of the audience for secret penance.
[38] For example Tellenbach, *Church*, 106.
[39] Smaragdus, *Expositio in regulam s. Benedicti*, ed. A. Spannagel and P. Engelbert (CCM viii, 1974).

with Benedict of Aniane's early ninth-century monastic reform movement.[40] It survives in at least eleven manuscripts dating from the ninth to the eleventh centuries, mostly from northern France and southern Lotharingia, although it is also found in Cologne, northern Spain and Italy.[41] Smaragdus' works were probably not known universally, but there is sufficient evidence to suggest that they were known to tenth- and early eleventh-century monks, especially to those involved in the Lotharingian monastic reform movement.

In what is overall a conservative work, Smaragdus merely amplified the position on penance established in the rule. Thus, following the rule, Smaragdus shared a common vocabulary with canonical penance: commenting on c. xxvii, he defined satisfaction as humility of both the heart and body brought about through the fruits of penance.[42] He was anxious to stress that c. xxiii prescribed the punishment for lesser faults against the rule but that the monk was subject to public penance for graver faults which should be imposed immediately rather than only after two secret warnings by his superiors have failed.[43] Here public penance obviously refers to public punishment, namely excommunication from the refectory and the oratory. But the potential possibilities which existed for confusion between monastic discipline and canonical penance generated by a shared vocabulary were more fully realised in Hildemar's commentary.

Hildemar was a monk of the west Frankish monastery of Corbie who, with Abbot Leudegar, was given the task by Archbishop Angilbert II of Milan (824–60) of reforming Italian monasticism; as part of his work, as schoolmaster of the community at Civate near Lecco on Lake Como, Hildemar dictated his commentary to his pupils in 845.[44] It thus survives in three versions,[45] all thought to be ninth-century, and probably based on three inde-

---

[40] F. Rädle, 'Smaragdus von St Mihiel', in *LMA* vii. 2011–12.

[41] W. Witters, 'Smaragde au moyen âge: la diffusion de ses écrits d'après la tradition manuscrite', in R. Louis (ed.), *Études Ligériennes d'histoire et d'archéologie médiévales: mémoires et exposés présentés à la semaine d'études médiévales de Saint-Benoit-sur-Loire de 3 au 10 juillet 1969*, Auxerre 1975, 361–76 at p. 370. The manuscript diffusion for Smaragdus' *Diadema monachorum*, a florilegium concerning the monastic life, is very similar: ibid. 367–70.

[42] '*Et provocent eum ad humilitatis satisfactionem. Humilitatis satisfactio est, quando se cognoscit homo per superbiam peccasse, et humiliato corde et corpore pro peccatis suis fructus dignos poenitentiae facit*': Smaragdus, *Expositio in regulam*, c. xxvii, p. 227. See also c. xxv where *disciplina* is used as a synonym for *poenitentia*: '*Cibi autem refectionem solus percipiat mensura vel hora qua praeviderit abbas ei conpetere. Provide enim considerare debet abbas, cui qualis conueniat disciplina vel poenitentia*': ibid. 225.

[43] '*De gravioribus enim criminibus sub publicam poenitentiam regulariter subiciendus est monachus, non semel et secundo a senioribus admonendus*': ibid. c. xxiii, 217.

[44] M. de Jong, 'Growing up in a Carolingian monastery: Magister Hildemar and his oblates', *Journal of Medieval History* ix (1983), 99–128 at p. 99. For further analysis of Hildemar's commentary see also her *In Samuel's image: child oblation in the early medieval west*, Leiden–New York–Cologne 1996.

[45] The fullest version of the text is edited in *Expositio regulae ab Hildemaro tradita*, ed. R. Mittermüller, Regensburg 1880, the earliest manuscript of which is eleventh-century and

pendent sets of lecture notes.[46] The manuscript distribution is chiefly confined to the empire, and suggests that Hildemar's commentary was more influential there than Smaragdus', possibly because of his links with Corbie.

Whilst Hildemar followed the conventional two-fold classification set out in cc. xxiv and xxv of the rule between lesser and graver faults, he also incorporated a Carolingian tract, often attributed to Benedict of Aniane, which contained a four-fold classification of sins:[47]

Class I   Minor breaches of the rule
Class II   Sins of the spirit against the rule, for example disobedience, pride
Class III External failings requiring public acknowledgement (defined by the *Rule of Benedict*, c. xlvi)
Class IV   Sins of the body, for example theft, drunkenness, sexual intercourse

Hildemar followed the rule: it was the abbot's duty to establish whether a fault was light or grave and then award the penalties specified by the rule. But sins within the same class were not always equal, and the abbot should use his discretion to establish the exact level of gravity and thus the manner in which the brother should be admonished.[48]

Hildemar also followed the rule in distinguishing the treatment given for public versus secret minor faults.[49] Repeating existing tradition, he argued that those brothers guilty of minor faults should follow the seven steps of

---

from Dijon (BN, MS lat. 12637) but it also survives in five other medieval manuscripts, all with an imperial provenance (one twelfth-century, two thirteenth-century and two fifteenth-century manuscripts): W. Hafner, *Der Basiliuskommentar zur Regula S. Benedicti: ein Beitrag zur Autorenfrage karolingischer Regelkommentare*, Münster 1959, 25–37. Hildemar's commentary also survives in an abridged version which was attributed by its nineteenth-century editor to Paul the Deacon: *Pauli Warnefridi diaconi casinensis commentarium in regulam Benedicti*, Monte Cassino 1880. Out of ten medieval manuscripts of this version (one late ninth-century, two tenth-century, five eleventh-century and two thirteenth-century), eight have an Italian provenance: Hafner, *Der Basiliuskommentar*, 37–51. The third version goes no further than c. lxi of the rule and is recorded in two ninth-century manuscripts, both from Reichenau (Karlsruhe, Landesbibliothek, MSS Augiensis clxxix, cciii), and an eleventh-century manuscript (Einsiedeln, MS ccliii): ibid. 7–25.

[46] K. Zelzer, 'Überlegungen zu einer Gesamtedition des frühnachkarolingischen Kommentars zur Regula S. Benedicti aus der Tradition des Hildemar von Corbie', *Rev. Bén.* xci (1981), 373–82.

[47] 'Modus penitentiarum Benedicti abbatis Anianensis (ante 821)', ed. J. Semmler, in K. Hallinger (ed.), *Initia consuetudines Benedictinae consuetudines saeculi octavi et noni* (CCM i, 1963), 565–82. This text is often known by the title given in the Migne edition, *Excerptus diversarum modus paenitentiarum*, PL ciii. 1417–20.

[48] Hildemar, *Expositio regulae*, 350–3.

[49] 'V. gr. inuentus est frater, qui illud peccatum secrete fecit: pro hac non duabus vicibus est admonendus secrete, sed solummodo post unam uicem secretam transire ad publicum. Et hoc intuendum: siue secundum sensum primum, siue secundum, in modo leuioris culpae est faciendum': ibid., 393–4. See also p. 574.

correction, a system of graduated stages through which the transgressor had to pass: if he did not make amendment after stage one, he went on to stage two, and if he failed to make amendment after stage two to stage three and so on. These seven stages are taken from cc. xxiii, xxiv, xxviii and xxx of the rule, and are included in 'Benedict of Aniane's' *Excerptus*.[50] They are: secret admonition, public correction, excommunication, severe fasts, corporal punishment, prayer and, finally, expulsion. According to Hildemar secret admonition, stage one, could only be delivered if the fault was committed in secret; if the fault were public, the admonition should be public. Whilst secret admonition might be delivered twice, public admonition could only be delivered once. He also defined what he meant by secret and public; secret admonition could be delivered before as many as four or five brothers, but for correction to be public it should be delivered before the whole brotherhood, in either the monastic chapter, the refectory or the oratory.[51] Hildemar thus elaborated on the provisions in the rule.[52] But he followed c. lxii of the rule in recognising that a monk-priest also came under the bishop's jurisdiction, and should appear before the bishop before being expelled. Whilst a monk should go through seven steps for a light fault before being expelled, a monk-priest must go through eight: the first six are the same, the seventh is appearance before the bishop, followed by expulsion.[53]

But despite his conservatism, Hildemar argued that the rule's requirements in c. xxv for a grave fault, which echoed those for public penance being expressed in the same language, were analogous to them: he described this chapter as having a common origin with the sacred canons which separate a man from the Church,[54] according to which no-one may be ordained after doing public penance; if he performs public penance after ordination he should be deposed. Public penance is that which a monk endures alone in sorrow separated from the church, the refectory and the companionship of all

---

[50] A. Schroll, *Benedictine monasticism as reflected in the Warnefrid-Hildemar commentaries on the rule*, New York 1941, 92.
[51] 'Regularis disciplina est: si secreta fuerit illa defensionis culpa, secreto admoneatur semel et secundo et reliq. usque ad sextum gradum, h.e. usque ad orationem. Si vero publica culpa contentionis fuerit, publice arguatur. Et hoc animadvertendum est, ut coram quot fratribus deliquit, coram eisdem fratribus satisfaciat, nam publica culpa est coram totis fratribus, veluti cum est in capitulo, in refectorio, in oratorio et reliq. ubi omnes insimul consuetudo est convenire': Hildemar, *Expositio regulae*, 136 (commentary on c. iii of the *Rule of Benedict*); Schroll, *Benedictine monasticism*, 92–3.
[52] *RB*, c. xlvi, ii. 594–6.
[53] 'Quod iste sacerdos per octo gradus duci debet, non per septem, sicut alius monachus non sacerdos, id est primus gradus est secreta admonitio, secundus publica correptio, tertius gradus est excommunicatio simplex, quartus est nimiis jejuniis, quintus gradus est, si dignus est, flagellum, sextus gradus est oratio, septimus episcopus, deinde expulsio': Hildemar, *Expositio regulae*, 574. Cf. *RB*, c. lxii, ii. 640–2.
[54] 'Inde etiam sacri canones, qui hominem ab ecclesia separant tracti sunt': Hildemar, *Expositio regulae*, 350. See also 'Sed sciendum est, quia istud capitulum de canonica auctoritate tractum est': ibid. 352.

his brothers.⁵⁵ Therefore Hildemar argued that the abbot should consider carefully before inflicting punishment on a monk for a grave fault, and where possible should avoid it, as this would prejudice his vocation to the priesthood or his continuation in sacerdotal office.⁵⁶ Hildemar thus blurred the strictures of canonical public penance with those of the monastic discipline also known as public penance: it was a commonplace of church teaching that priests should be deposed instead of undergoing public penance.⁵⁷ The ambiguities of a shared language no doubt contributed to his view. But confusion arose only on this issue: elsewhere Hildemar was content to use *poenitentia* to mean monastic discipline, for example when outlining the procedure to be followed on the return of a monk who had fled before completing his penance.⁵⁸ Hildemar was, however, prepared to deal with the problems generated by his new interpretation; aware that his views were at variance with Benedict's prescription, he explained why Benedict had considered how satisfaction should be made for grave faults in terms of symmetry: 'Consider, that it was not necessary for him to pronounce on satisfaction for grave faults, but because he was about to speak of satisfaction for minor faults, he discussed also the satisfaction for grave faults.'⁵⁹ But why was Hildemar prepared to challenge Benedict on this issue? Elsewhere in his work Hildemar showed he wished to encourage the development of a pure elite based on oblates, brought up in the community, who were to become its monk-priests.⁶⁰ Hildemar was bothered by anything which might challenge that purity, but his confusion may also have existed in others' minds: the barriers between monastic and canonical public penance were not rigid ones in the minds of all early medieval clerics.

Evidence for the connection between public and monastic penance recurs two centuries later in the penitential ordinance issued by the Anglo-Norman bishops after the battle of Hastings in 1066 in which they imposed a penance on all those members of the army of William, duke of Normandy, who had

---

⁵⁵ 'Si autem ipsa culpa gravior talis fuerit, unde eum canones non prohibeant, ad ordinem clericatus accedere, et ipsa persona sive ordinatus sit sive adhuc non sit, et tamen potest provehi – iste talis pro huiuscemodi peccato non debet publice poenitere pro dicta canonica auctoritate – eo quod canonica auctorictas est, quia, qui publicam poenitentiam egit, nec presbyter nec diaconus esse potest, si vero in presbyteratu vel diaconatu constitutus publicam poenitentiam egerit ab ordine removeri debet; publica poenitentia est in qua monachus separatus ab ecclesia et a refectorio vel a consortio omnium fratrum solus in poenitentiae luctu consistit': ibid. 346.
⁵⁶ Ibid. 346–53.
⁵⁷ É. Amann, 'La Pénitence primitive', 832; Poschmann, *Abendländische Kirchenbusse*, 172–203.
⁵⁸ Hildemar, *Expositio regulae*, 366–7.
⁵⁹ 'Animadvertendum est, quia non oportuerat dicere de satisfactione gravium culparum, sed tamen, quia dicturus erat de levium culparum satisfactione, ideo dixit de gravium culparum satisfactione': ibid. 467.
⁶⁰ de Jong, 'Growing up in a Carolingian monastery', 120–2.

taken part in the campaign.[61] Different penances were assigned according to the status and degree of involvement of those taking part in the battle and it was also agreed that determining the penance for those monks who had taken part was the responsibility of their abbot and not that of the authors of the ordinance.[62] Although this provision smacks of a compromise between the conflicting legislatures of the episcopate and abbatiate, it also suggests that, for the eleventh-century Norman clergy, monks had to be seen to do penance as did their secular counterparts and that such penance could not be determined by the bishops but only by the abbot. It was, however, to be equivalent to episcopal penance.

Public penance was not, however, the only penitential institution associated with the monastic life: the development of the practice of non-public, reiterable confession, accompanied by penitentials, is associated with monasticism, especially Irish monasticism.[63] It is not, however, widely discussed in the commentaries or customaries. The rule mentions confession only once: in order for a monk to reach the fifth rung on the ladder of humility he must confess to his abbot all his bad thoughts and deeds, following the exhortation of the psalmist to confess to the Lord.[64] Smaragdus interpreted this as confession to the abbot, resulting in penance.[65] Hildemar discussed it only with reference to how an abbot should know whether a monk was a suitable candidate for ordination: he should ask the candidate's confessor if he knew of any reason why the candidate was unworthy. If he did, the confessor should try to dissuade the abbot without breaking the seal of the confession.[66] This is the only place where Hildemar alludes to liturgical confession; otherwise he follows the rule and Smaragdus in regarding confession as referring to spiritual direction from the abbot and as a means of (monastic) penance.[67]

These commentaries were read and copied in the tenth and eleventh centuries, as shown both by their surviving manuscripts and by the traces Hildemar, for example, left on the eleventh-century customs of Farfa.[68] Such customaries, produced by individual monasteries as supplements to the rule, provide, perhaps, a more contemporary perspective on the role of penance in

---

[61] *Councils and synods with other documents relating to the English Church*, i/2: *1066–1204*, ed. D. Whitelock, M. Brett and C. N. L. Brooke, Oxford 1981, 581–4.
[62] 'Paenitentia monachorum secundum regulam suam et abbatum iudicia statuantur': ibid. 583.
[63] Frantzen, *Literature*, 19–60.
[64] RB, c. vii, vv. 44–8, i. 484. The *Rule* cites Psalms xxxvi.5, cv.1, cxvii.1, and xxxi.5.
[65] 'Id est *revela* per confessionem abbati quem tibi dominus pro se vicarium dedit actiones tuas, in quibus peccati conscientia latet, et *spera* in dominum qui tibi veniam de commissis misericorditer donet': Smaragdus, *Expositio*, c. vii, 183. In both this chapter, and c. xvi of his *Diadema monachorum*, he also talks of confession as medicine but does not give explicit instructions about how confession should be administered, nor how it relates to monastic discipline: PL cii. 613.
[66] Hildemar, *Expositio regulae*, 570–1; Schroll, *Benedictine monasticism*, 85.
[67] Ibid. 87.
[68] Zelzer, 'Überlegungen'.

the monastic life in this period; nevertheless, Barbara Rosenwein's warning that customaries are 'paradigms not portrayals' must be borne in mind.[69] As Hildemar's commentary found only the punishment for grave faults to be analogous to that of canonical penance, the following discussion concentrates on the customaries' instructions for the procedure to be followed when a brother has committed a grave fault.

Several customaries survive from the area under consideration in this period and provide a comprehensive picture of monastic customs. The earliest is that of Saint Emmeram, Regensburg, which preserves a version of the Gorze customary from c. 980–90.[70] That of the west Frankish monastery of Fleury was written down in the early eleventh century for the edification of Bishop Bernward of Hildesheim (993–1022) by Theoderich of Amorbach, who had stayed at Fleury under Abbot Abbo (988–1004).[71] Although Fleury was reformed by Odo of Cluny c. 930, recent research suggests that it was more independent of Cluny than earlier historians had supposed; its customary shows more parallels with what is known of Gorzian monasticism and also the ninth-century reforms of Benedict of Aniane than with what we know of tenth-century Cluny.[72] The customary of the east Frankish monastery of Fulda also owes a great deal to the Gorzian milieu, being based upon practice in Trier and composed c. 1000–18.[73] The customary of the central Italian monastery of Farfa provides the earliest definite evidence of Cluniac practice, being a copy of Cluny's customs, dating from Odilo's abbacy (994–1048), and probably produced in the early fifth decade of the eleventh century.[74] Lastly, there is the first direct record of Cluny's customs composed by Ulrich c. 1083 for Abbot William of the east Frankish monastery of Hirsau who wished to reform his own abbey along Cluniac lines.[75]

---

69 Rosenwein, *Rhinoceros bound*, 96.
70 This is more concerned with the liturgical requirements of the monastic year than with monastic behaviour: *Redactio Sancti Emmerammi dicta Einsidelensis*, ed. M. Wegener, C. Elvert and K. Hallinger (CCM vii/3, 1984), 187–256. On the date of this text see K. Hallinger (ed.), *Consuetudines saeculi X/XI/XII monumenta: introductiones* (CCM vii/1, 1984), 426–9.
71 On dating see Davril's comments ibid. 333–6. For a text of the customs see *Consuetudines floriacenses antiquiores*, ed. A. Davril and L. Donnat with M. Wegener, C. Elvert and K. Hallinger (CCM vii/3, 1984), 7–60. On Theoderich's career see A. Davril, 'Un Moine de Fleury aux environs de l'an mil: Thierry d'Amorbach', in Louis, *Études ligériennes*, 97–104.
72 On the parallels between Fleury's customary and Gorze see Davril, 'Points de contact'; on parallels with Carolingian texts, including the Aachen decrees, see Nightingale, 'Oswald, Fleury and continental reform'.
73 *Redactio fuldensis-trevirensis*, ed. M. Wegener, C. Elvert and K. Hallinger (CCM, vii/3, 1984), 257–322. For the date of the text see Hallinger, *Consuetudines saeculi X/XI/XII*, 429–33. Gorze's customs were introduced to Fulda after Henry II instigated reform there in 1013: J. W. Bernhardt, *Itinerant kingship and royal monasteries in early medieval Germany c. 936–1075*, Cambridge 1993, 122.
74 See *Liber tramitis*, pp. xxi–lxix, for further discussion of the date and transmission of the text.
75 Ulrich, *Antiquiores consuetudines cluniacensis monasterii*, PL cxlix. 643–778. Bernard's

The Fulda–Trier customary explicitly compared the excommunication procedure followed in the case of those who had committed grave faults to that followed by the bishop for public penitents: those guilty of grave faults are punished by being pushed out from the company of their peers, just as an episcopal sentence segregates them from the company of the faithful.[76] This connection may not have been made in all cases as other customaries are less explicit. Although accounts vary in detail, the procedures outlined in the customaries for dealing with those guilty of grave faults are all remarkably similar, owing to their common origin in the rule.

Following the process outlined in the Fulda–Trier customary the offender was first flogged, then banished from the community. He might not eat, sleep or pray with the community. No one in the congregation was allowed to speak to him, except those seniors sent by the abbot, in accordance with the rule, to bring him the remedy of consolation. He might not participate in the divine office but must attend, standing outside the doors of the church. As the brothers went out, he must prostrate himself fully on the ground. It was up to the abbot to determine for how long he should be excluded from the congregation. The offender's restoration to the community followed a similarly set pattern. He was introduced as if he were a novice. He prostrated himself before the abbot and begged forgiveness, and promised that he wished to correct himself. He was then told to sit in the last place. All the brothers then entered the church, prostrated themselves, and sang the seven psalms and the litany.[77] This process was known as making 'satisfaction'.[78]

Monastic practice was not, however, uniform: the procedures at Fleury deem corporal punishment sufficient, and make no reference to exile from the community, whilst the 'Farfa' customary omits any mention of flogging.[79] Flogging is, however, a prominent feature in Ulrich's late eleventh-century account of Cluniac practice.[80] According to Ulrich the offender should not enter church, but hear mass from the corner of the chapter nearest to (i.e. outside) the church, prostrating himself outside the doors of the church both before and after the service. According to the Fulda customary he should not enter the chapter except to be exiled from and restored to the community.

---

customary, composed c. 1075 for Abbot Hugh of Cluny (1049–1109), is not considered as it provides evidence only for practice within Cluny, which is outside the geographic and chronological remit of this study: ibid.

76 'Si vero prevaricatores precepti existant, ad verbera seu graviorem culpam perveniunt. Qui pena huiuscemodi dampnationis gravantur, equali exertatione puniuntur velud is, qui episcopali sententia segregatur a fidelium turma': *Redactio fuldensis-trevirensis*, c. xvi, 279. A similar observation is made earlier in the chapter: 'Nulla in monasteriis castigatio equalis huic esse conspicitur, nam episcopali exertatione similis fore comprobatur': ibid. 278.

77 Although not specified in the text, it seems reasonable to assume that the seven referred to are the penitential psalms.

78 'De eius satisfactione': *Redactio fuldensis-trevirensis*, c. xvii, 280.

79 *Consuetudines floriacenses*, c. xxxii, 50–1.

80 Ulrich, *Consuetudines cluniacensis* III.iii, 734–5.

The 'Farfa' customary refers to the process of return into the community as 'reconciliation',[81] and the offender's period in excommunication from the community as his 'penance': he passes out from his penance, and appears naked and barefoot before the chapter. After he has received judgement, he takes his cowl and tunic back and prostrates himself at the feet of all his brothers, starting with the abbot. He then leaves, dresses himself and returns to seek pardon before the abbot, and on his command he takes his place as the newest recruit.[82] This service thus has parallels with the entry of a novice into the order.[83] Once restored to the community, the offender remains unable to communicate with his fellows or to participate through reading or singing in the liturgy; a clear distinction is drawn between a period of penance, and the period of punishment by the community; the two are not co-terminous. Thus whilst the procedure for punishment of grave faults set out in the customaries shared several features with that for canonical penance, it was also clearly seen as being distinct from it.

Liturgical confession was also seen as distinct from the confession which was part of monastic discipline. At the same time the parallels between the two processes are very strong. Ulrich's customary is the only one to refer to confession, merely indicating the gesture a brother should use to indicate that he wishes to confess – placing his right hand on his chest; the priest should then lead the way into chapter where the penitent should prostrate himself, then rise up and say the seven penitential psalms or, if he does not know them, the Lord's Prayer, and afterwards he should do what the priest orders. He should not read the Gospel text nor make the peace nor make the offering that day.[84] He obviously needed to expiate his faults, a reminder of the parallels which existed with liturgical penance. The monastic procedures for both internal discipline against those who break the rule and for confession were distinct from the Church's penitential procedures and yet the parallels which existed between the two processes offered scope for confusion, and Hildemar, as we have seen, seems in one instance to have confused the two.

Shifting the focus from the individual, the offender, to the community as a whole, what role did penance play in the internal liturgical life of the monastery? Penance, after all, was supposed to play a significant part in the secular Church's annual liturgy – all Christians were meant to confess to their priest before the start of Lent. Yet it was much less important in the liturgy of the monastic year.

---

81 'Sicque tandiu faciat donec ad reconciliationem in conuentum uocatus fuerit': *Liber tramitis*, c. xx, 218.

82 Ibid. 218.

83 G. Constable, 'The ceremonies and symbolism of entering religious life and taking the monastic habit, from the fourth to the twelfth centuries', in *Segni e riti nella chiesa altomedievale occidentale* (Settimane xxxiii, 1987), 771–834.

84 Ulrich, *Consuetudines cluniacensis* II.xii, 706–7; G. de Valous, *Le Monachisme cluniacien des origines au XVe siècle: vie intérieure des monastères et organisation de l'ordre*, Paris 1935, i. 357–8.

THE PRACTICE OF PENANCE

The Benedictine rule itself paid only brief attention to the Church's annual liturgical cycle.[85] This omission was rectified in most of the tenth- and eleventh-century customaries which included detailed descriptions for the observance of the major festivals, including Ash Wednesday and Maundy Thursday. The liturgy was one of the most obvious ways in which different monastic houses, and different families of monasteries, distinguished themselves from each other.[86] Yet the way in which all monasteries chose to observe Ash Wednesday is remarkably similar.

According to the 'Farfa' customs, on Ash Wednesday after the hour of Sext the brethren should take off their shoes, wash their hands and enter the church for a special service at which the priest blessed the ashes, sprinkled holy water over them, and put them on the heads of all the brothers.[87] This service is followed by a procession and then mass. The 'Farfa' service makes no connection between the service and penance because it did not need to; the connections between the two were axiomatic and part of general monastic consciousness. Gregory the Great in his *Moralia in Iob*, when commenting on Job xlii.6, 'Wherefore I abhor myself and repent in dust and ashes', drew an explicit link between the ashes and repentance which was repeated in the ninth century by Smaragdus in his *Diadema monachorum*.[88] The tenth- century Romano-German pontifical (*c*. 950) also made provision for the blessing and imposition of ashes on the congregation as part of the Ash Wednesday penitential *ordo*, a procedure which took place after the penitent had been expelled from the Church.[89] The Romano-German pontifical's *ordo*, like the 'Farfa' Ash Wednesday service, was not an *ordo* for entry into penance but rather an initiation service in which the entire congregation entered into Lent. As the diffusion of the Romano-German pontifical in the eleventh century was much more limited than has hitherto been assumed, the parallels between the two services must owe something to

---

[85] RB, cc. x–xv, xlix, ii. 512–24, 604–6.
[86] Hallinger's distinctions between Cluny and Gorze have been modified to produce a more complex picture but one that still allows for distinctions between the two groups, especially on grounds of liturgy: Hallinger, *Gorze–Kluny*, 869–976, esp. pp. 892–959; Tellenbach, *Church*, 101–21.
[87] *Liber tramitis* I.v, pp. 51–3.
[88] 'Idcirco ipse me reprehendo et ago poenitentiam in favilla et cinere': Job xlii.6; cf. 'In favilla enim et cinere poenitentiam agere est, contemplata summa essentia, nihil aliud quam favillam se cineremque cognoscere. In cilicio asperitas et compunctio peccatorum, in cinere autem pulvis ostenditur mortuorum. Et idcirco utrumque adhiberi ad poenitentiam solet, ut in compunctionis cilicio cognoscamus quid per culpas fecimus, et in favilla cineris, perpendamus quid per judicium facti sumus': Smaragdus, *Diadema monachorum*, c. xv, 611; cf. Gregory the Great's comments on Job xlii.6: *Moralia in Iob*, ed. M. Adriaen (CCSL cxliii.B, 1985), lib. xxxv.vi, pp. 1777–8.
[89] PRG xcix.74–80, ii. 21–3. This is discussed in further detail in ch. 4. Although the practice of the imposition of ashes on all Christians as part of the rite for entry into Lent was obviously normative in the tenth century, it was first given papal approval only in 1091: Mansfield, *Humiliation*, 182.

a common ninth-century heritage and suggest that we might look for the origins of the Romano-German pontifical's *ordo* in monastic practice, for the imposition of the ashes signified the entry of the whole community into Lent, a time when monks should, following the rule, pursue the ascetic life even more rigorously than usual.[90]

However, one text makes a direct connection between penance and the imposition of ashes on Ash Wednesday: the tenth-century Anglo-Saxon *Regularis concordia*. Its Ash Wednesday service differs from the general tradition in several respects: it places the service later, after None, and attributes the blessing and imposition of the ashes to the abbot, not a priest, 'because it is his (duty) to impose penance on them'.[91] The *Regularis concordia* is a code of monastic observance agreed by an assembly of abbots and abbesses held at Winchester under King Edgar in 970, with the advice of monks from Fleury and Ghent.[92] The resulting text combined different aspects from the monastic customs of Fleury, and Gorzian monasticism, as well as showing a common debt to the ninth century.[93] However, as its editor noted, the Ash Wednesday service appears to be unique.[94] This apparent uniqueness may be a peculiarly Anglo-Saxon aspect of the text, but as there are no records at this date of either the Fleury or Gorze (or indeed Cluniac) customs it may instead be due to a continental liturgical tradition which has since been lost. As we have seen there is certainly a contemporary continental tradition linking the imposition of ashes with the imposition of penance: the *ordo* for entry into public penance on Ash Wednesday in the Romano-German pontifical, composed in Mainz c. 950, makes this connection.[95]

But none of the monastic customaries make provision for the reconciliation of penitents on Maundy Thursday, although an early twelfth-century manuscript of the Romano-German pontifical from northern Germany includes in the margins of its *ordo* for that service directions for how the lord abbot should preside over a service of the brethren.[96] The important role

---

[90] On the diffusion of the Romano-German pontifical see ch. 4 and appendix 1. On the behaviour expected of monks in Lent see *RB*, c. xlix, ii. 604–6.
[91] 'Quarta feria Capitis Ieiunii, Nona decantata, abbas stola ornatus benedicat cineres; quibus benedictis eat ipse abbas et imponat capitibus singulorum, quia eius est paenitentiam illis imponere, canentes interim antiphonam *Exaudi nos Domine*, psalmum *Saluum me fac Deus* (ii) et *Gloria*, *Kyrie eleison*, *Pater noster*, psalmus *Deus misereatur nostri* et preces et collectam': *Regularis concordia*, c. iv, 32.
[92] Ibid. Proem., c. v, 3.
[93] For the role of Gorzian influence see T. Symons, 'Regularis concordia: history and derivation', in D. Parsons (ed.), *Tenth-century studies: essays in commemoration of the millenium of the Council of Winchester and Regularis concordia*, London 1975, 37–59. On the debt to Fleury, and Fleury's debt to the Carolingians, see Nightingale, 'Oswald, Fleury and continental reform'.
[94] *Regularis concordia*, 32 n. 5.
[95] PRG cxix, ii. 14–23.
[96] Wolfenbüttel, Herzog-August-Bibliothek, Cod. Guelf. 141 Helmstadt, fo. 21r. This manuscript has a late medieval provenance to the monastery of St Michael, Lüneburg, in

played by monks as composers of liturgical *ordines* and administrators of penance will be discussed later in chapters 4 and 5. However, the prescriptive sources under consideration suggest that liturgical penance, as it was known and practised in the secular Church, had only a minor role in the internal liturgical life of the monasteries in this period.[97]

Perhaps it is because the monastic life was supposed to be one of constant penance that the evidence for the terms and manner in which that life was conceived seems to be more concerned with the punishments associated with monastic discipline than liturgical (or secular) penance. Nor is this surprising: the rule was composed as a guide to the monastic life, and shaped both the commentaries upon it, and the customaries which sought to apply the rule to the running of individual communities. But liturgical penance did have an impact on life within these houses; for as these prescriptions for the monastic life show, the relationship between the monastic life, as lived within the community, and liturgical (or secular) penance was a complex one. The shared terminology of the monastic disciplinary and liturgical penitential procedures, as we have seen, allowed Hildemar in the ninth century to assimilate the consequences of monastic discipline with those for canonical public penance. The early eleventh-century Fulda–Trier customary drew a similar analogy between the two procedures. The abbot's position as head of his community placed him in an ambivalent situation: he was responsible for enforcing both monastic discipline and, in certain situations, penitential practice. It is not suprising that the distinction between the two is less defined than it at first appears, or was supposed, to be. We have thus seen how ideas and practices about secular penance could enter the cloister: it is time to see how far monastic concepts of penance and confession moved from the cloister into the world in this period.

Monks and the delivery of pastoral care

Although monks traditionally saw themselves as living a life which was closer to God and more remote from the sinful world of laymen, the secular world played a vital part in the role which they constructed for themselves.[98] The monks of the Gorzian reform movement drew on traditions which had

---

the diocese of Verden: *OR* i. 420. This text is discussed in ch. 4. The abbot of Evesham c. 1300 also apparently presided over a service of solemn penance: *Officium ecclesiasticum abbatum secundum usum Eveshamensis monasterii*, ed. H. A. Wilson (HBS vi, 1893), 60–7, 71–80.

[97] Modern accounts of the monastic liturgy tend to ignore penance: B. Rosenwein, 'Feudal war and monastic peace: Cluniac liturgy as ritual aggression', *Viator* ii (1971), 129–57. Even older accounts, such as that of de Valous in *Le Monachisme clunisen*, deal only with confession (pp. 357–8).

[98] 'Si, inquit, monachi perfecti sunt, beatis angelis assimilantur: sin vero ad saeculare desiderium revertuntur, apostaticis angelis, qui suum domicilium non servaverunt, per suam

existed from the time of Gregory the Great, if not earlier, to promote a more active attitude towards their role in the world than that conceived at Cluny.[99] Conversely Odo of Cluny in his *Vita Geraldi* promoted a specific model of sanctity for laymen.[100] Recent work on France and Lotharingia has further demonstrated the impact which monasticism had upon lay life, both economically, in terms of the relations established between monasteries and families,[101] and in terms of piety, as noble men and women sought not only to be commemorated by these communities, but also to be buried in them.[102] Monasteries also played an important part in the political life of the kingdom, providing in tenth- and eleventh-century Germany essential logistical support to an itinerant ruler.[103] This interaction between the secular and monastic worlds was not new. Monasteries had, for example, become, from the sixth and seventh centuries, places where public penance was undertaken, and where inconvenient political opponents were exiled to do penance for their political offences.[104] Given this background, what opportunities existed for monks to promote their values and practices amongst the laity?

Opportunities existed at two levels: the institutional and the missionary. At an institutional level church law sought to restrict monks administering pastoral care. It was not, however, consistent: sometimes it prohibited monks from ministering at all to the laity, at other times it sought to subject monks involved in such care to episcopal authority. The Council of Koblenz (922) decreed that monks who owned parishes ought to obey their bishop, whilst Burchard included a decree against monks giving penance to *seculares*.[105] The issue resurfaced in the late eleventh century;[106] several councils outside the *Reich* ordained that no abbot or monk should enjoin a penance on anyone

---

utique apostasiam jure comparantur': Odo of Cluny, *Vita sancti Geraldi Auriliacensis comitis* II.viii, PL cxxxiii. 675.

[99] P. G. Jestice, 'The Gorzian reform and the light under the bushel', *Viator* xxiv (1993), 51–78.

[100] S. Airlie, 'The anxiety of sanctity: St Gerald of Aurillac and his maker', *JEH* xliii (1992), 372–95; J. L. Nelson, 'Monks, secular men and masculinity, c. 900', in D. M. Hadley (ed.), *Masculinity in medieval Europe*, London–New York 1999, 121–42.

[101] C. Bouchard, *Sword, miter and cloister: nobility and the Church in Burgundy, 980–1198*, Ithaca–London 1987; B. Rosenwein, *To be the neighbour of Saint Peter: the social meaning of Cluny's property, 909–1049*, Ithaca–London 1989; S. D. White, *Custom, kinship and gifts to saints: the 'laudatio parentum' in western France, 1050–1150*, Chapel Hill–London 1988; Nightingale, 'Monasteries and their patrons'.

[102] M. Bull, *Knightly piety and the lay response to the First Crusade: the Limousin and Gascony, c. 970–1130*, Oxford 1993; M. McLaughlin, *Consorting with saints: prayer for the dead in early medieval France*, Ithaca–London 1994.

[103] Bernhardt, *Itinerant kingship*.

[104] de Jonge, 'What was public', and *In Samuel's image*, 259–64.

[105] Council of Koblenz, c. vi, MGH, *Concilia* VI, 70; 'Quod monachi secularibus poenitentiam dare non debeant': Burchard, *Decretum* xix.142, 1010.

[106] On this issue in general see Constable, *Monastic tithes*, and also his 'Monastic possession of churches and "spiritualia"'.

without an episcopal grant of *cura animarum*.[107] Against this tide of episcopal restriction, two false papal decrees authorising pastoral works by monks were composed in mid eleventh-century Italy; both circulated amongst monastic communities and were included with three other false decretals in a mid twelfth-century treatise from southern Germany written in defence of monks' ownership of tithes and performance of pastoral works, that is preaching, the administration of baptism and the enjoining of penance.[108] The exercise of a pastoral ministry by monks seems, on the basis of these councils, to have been a recurrent issue, suggesting that it was a continual practice throughout this period.

The historiography to date has concentrated on the legal evidence of church law and charters, resulting in a confused picture: on the one hand, the episcopate perennially sought to restrict monastic pastoral activity; on the other, monks themselves abstained from direct involvement. Joseph Avril's study of the charter evidence for northern France for relations between dependent houses of monasteries and the parishes in which they were situated, usually owned by the monastery, suggests that whilst in a few cases monks themselves appear to provide parish services, in the majority of cases the dependent house was separate from the parish; the monastery was responsible only for the appointment of a parish priest.[109] His conclusions seem to be echoed in central Germany, where Fulda's external schools, which existed in the ninth century to train parish priests, in the tenth became canonries.[110]

---

107 Council of Poitou (1078), c. v, Mansi, *Concilia*, xx.498; Council of Poitou (1100), c. xi, Mansi, *Concilia*, xx.1124. The First Lateran Council (1123), c. xvi, forbade monks from exercising any ministry: *Decrees of the ecumenical councils*, i. 193.

108 G. Constable, 'The treatise "Hortatur nos" and accompanying canonical works on the performance of pastoral works by monks', in his *Religious life and thought (11th–12th centuries)*, London 1979, no. ix. The treatise is entitled 'Ratio quod liceat monachis predicare, baptizhare et penitentiam iniungere'. The treatise *Apologeticus monachorum adversus canonicos*, in defence of monastic priests' rights to administer sacraments, including penance, attributed to Peter Damian is spurious: *Die Briefe des Petrus Damiani*, ed. K. Reindel (MGH, Die Briefe des deutschen Kaiserzeit iv, Munich 1983–93), i. 61.

109 J. Avril, 'Recherches sur la politique paroissiale des établissements monastiques et canoniaux (XIe et XIIIe s.)', *Revue Mabillon* lix (1980), 453–517, and 'Paroisses et dépendances monastiques au moyen âge', in *Sous la règle de Saint Benoît: structures monastiques et sociétés en France du moyen âge à l'époque moderne: abbaye bénédictine Sainte-Marie de Paris 23–25 octobre 1980*, Geneva–Paris 1982, 95–105. On monks and parish churches in general see idem, 'La Paroisse médiévale: bilan et perspectives d'après quelques travaux récents', *Revue d'histoire de l'église de France* liv (1988), 91–113; G. Devailly, 'Le Clergé régulier de le ministère paroissial', *Cahiers d'histoire* xx (1975), 259–77; J. F. Lemarignier, 'Encadrement religieux des campagnes et conjoncture politique dans les régions du royaume de France situées au nord de la Loire, de Charles le Chauve aux derniers Carolingiens (840–987)', in *Cristianizzazione ed organizzazione ecclesiastica*, 765–800. For a useful summary of the literature up until the early 1980s see H. Platelle, 'La Paroisse et son curé jusqu'à la fin du XIIIe siècle: orientations de la recherche actuelle', in *L'Encadrement religieux des fidèles*, 11–26.

110 Hildebrandt, *The external school*, 128–9. Fulda also continued its pastoral work in the tenth century, albeit more indirectly, through the production of liturgical texts, as discussed

But in the eleventh-century Rhineland, Conrad of Regensburg, abbot of Siegburg, created several priories where monks were employed in pastoral ministry and the bishop of Liège allowed monks and canons to perform the *cura animarum* in the remoter districts of his diocese in the late eleventh and twelfth centuries.[111] Thus not all houses were actively involved in the pastoral ministry, but some chose to minister to the laity, and this ministry included hearing confessions.

Episcopal privilege, that is exemption from episcopal authority, also allowed certain monasteries to control the pastoral ministry on their lands. The abbot was not only free to choose the bishop whom he wished to ordain his monks priests but could also exercise his own quasi-episcopal jurisdiction over lands and churches owned by the monastery; the exact nature of this jurisdiction is less clear, but the liturgical evidence from Fulda, where the abbot enjoyed this privilege, suggests it included the right to administer public penance.[112] Abbot Gervinus of St Riquier (1045–75) was awarded a personal episcopal privilege. According to the late eleventh-century chronicler of St Riquier, Hariulf, Gervinus was an active preacher and confessor, anxious to save sinners in northern and western France and even in Hungary.[113] However, his activities incurred the displeasure of some clerics, whereupon he was called to Rome where he preached before Pope Leo IX (1048–54). The pope granted him permission to hear confessions, impose penance and grant absolution, and also to preach, the latter signified by a gift of (papal) sandals.[114] The granting of such *pontificalia* meant exemption from episcopal jurisdiction; perhaps as many as a hundred abbots enjoyed the right to wear the symbols of episcopal authority in the period 900–1100.[115] Gervinus thus represents the missionary aspect of a monastic ministry to the

---

in ch. 5. St Gall, too, used monk-priests in its *Eigenkirchen* from 802 until 956: T. L. Amos, 'Monks and pastoral care in the early Middle Ages', in T. F. X. Noble and J. J. Contreni (eds), *Religion, culture and society in the early Middle Ages: studies in honour of Richard E. Sullivan*, Kalamazoo 1987, 165–80 at p. 173.

111 For Siegburg see U. Berlière, 'L'Exercice du ministère paroissial par les moines du XIIe au XVIIIe siècle', *Rev. Bén.* xxxix (1927), 340–64 at p. 352. For Liège see G. Constable, 'Monasteries, rural churches and the *cura animarum*', 372.

112 See ch. 5.

113 'Praeterea tanta illi erat in convertendis atque salvandis peccatorum animabus curae instantia, ut peccaminum fasce oppressis mirabiliter compatiens et concurrens, videretur illius spiritu gubernari, qui dixit, "Filioli mei, quos iterum parturio", non solum vero hujus nostratis patriae, si quos cognovisset, homines scelestos, corrigebat, sed etiam Neustriam et Flandriam, Galliam quoque et Aquitaniam, necnon Hungariam, pia gyrans sedulitate criminosorumque confessiones acceptans': Hariulf, *Chronique de l'abbaye de Saint-Riquier*, ed. F. Lot, Paris 1894, IV.xxvii, p. 250. See also J. Hourlier, 'La Spiritualité à Saint-Riquier d'après Hariulf', *Revue Mabillon* 1 (1960), 1–20 at p. 17; Constable, 'Monasteries, rural churches and the *cura animarum*', 372–3.

114 Hariulf, *Chronique* IV.xxvii, p. 253.

115 Constable, 'Monasteries, rural churches and the *cura animarum*', 378.

laity, which sought to promote penance through preaching and which had a long tradition stretching back at least to Gregory the Great.[116]

Monks could also act on an individual level, as confessors, as both the Latin monk Romuald and the Greek monk Nilus are said to have done for Otto III.[117] There is evidence that dying in a monastery, accompanied by the monastic last rites which included confession, was a privilege increasingly sought by the laity in this period.[118] Individual monks, such as Rather of Verona in the tenth and Peter Damian in the eleventh century, also became bishops, and as such were in a position to bring monastic values to bear upon their office. How far they left a permanent mark is more open to question. It is, however, worth remembering that the dividing line between the secular and monastic clergy was not impermeable, and could be and often was crossed.

There is therefore evidence that pastoral care, and in particular the administration of penance, was seen as a part of the pastoral duties which some monks were called to administer; that monks administered penance as part of their missionary activities; that they sometimes provided clergy, monk-priests, often based in priories, for rural churches owned by them; that they trained parish clergy in external schools, and may have continued to do so. But there is also evidence from this period that monks abstained from pastoral activity, delegating it to parish priests. Not all houses were actively involved in the pastoral ministry, but whilst the majority of monk-priests were probably occupied in saying private masses, some ministered to the laity, and this included administering penance. In addition, monks influenced both the penitential liturgy and practice of private prayers, and composed most of the surviving accounts of penance undertaken by laymen as well as monks. Detection of monastic influence is therefore an underlying theme of this study.

Canons

The Benedictine rule was not, however, the only form of regular life in this period; the canonical life was also popular. The lives of canons were mostly based upon the mid eighth-century rule composed by Chrodegang, bishop of Metz (742–66), for the canons of his cathedral, and two decrees issued at the Council of Aachen (816) held by Louis the Pious and his religious adviser,

---

116 Amos, 'Monks and pastoral care'; A. Thacker, 'Monks, preaching and pastoral care in early Anglo-Saxon England', in Blair and Sharpe, *Pastoral care before the parish*, 137–70.
117 S. Hamilton, 'Otto III's penance: a case study of unity and diversity in the eleventh-century Church', in R. Swanson (ed.), *Unity and diversity in the Church* (SCH xxxii, 1996), 83–94.
118 Bull, *Knightly piety*, 143–6; F. Paxton, *Christianizing death: the creation of a ritual process in early medieval Europe*, Ithaca–London 1990.

Benedict of Aniane, to promote the reform of the regular life within the Frankish *regnum*: the *Institutio canonicorum*, for canons, and *Institutio sanctimonialium*, for canonesses.[119] The Aachen decrees were drawn from a variety of patristic sources and were intended to replace Chrodegang's rule and to ensure that canons, and their female counterparts, followed the same pattern of life throughout the kingdom. Although the manuscript history of the *Institutio canonicorum* suggests that the rule for canons was widely distributed it did not succeed in eliminating Chrodegang's rule, and indeed, in the later ninth or early tenth century, probably in Lotharingia, someone compiled a recension of Chrodegang's rule interpolated with passages drawn from the *Institutio canonicorum* which survives in several manuscripts, including a version in Old English.[120]

Despite the considerable *lacunae* which exist in the history of the canonical movement, when compared to that of their monastic colleagues, it is clear that houses of canons (and canonesses) continued to be founded in the tenth century and at an increased rate in that time for reform and growth, the eleventh century.[121] What rule individual houses followed is less certain. Copies of Chrodegang's rule continued to be made in the tenth and eleventh centuries, as did copies of the Aachen decree for canons; as we have already seen Chrodegang's text was subject to alteration over the course of the ninth century, and the Aachen decrees were not exempt from some judicious editing to fit in with the prevailing *mores*. For both Chrodegang's rule and the Aachen decree allowed canons to possess private property, to the later distress of the eleventh-century reformers.[122] Unsurprisingly, the Vatican Library contains two eleventh-century manuscripts of the rule of Aachen which omit the offending decree about the ownership of private property.[123] And it was almost certainly the presence of problems such as this in the

---

[119] Chrodegang I. The text of the Aachen decrees is at MGH, *Concilia II*, i. 307–464. For a general introduction to the Aachen decrees see J. Semmler, 'Institutiones Aquisgranenses', in *LMA* v. 451–2.

[120] For an edition of the interpolated rule see Chrodegang II. On the complex textual history of Chrodegang's rule, which survives in four main recensions, see the fundamental work by A. Werminghoff, 'Die Beschlüsse des Aachener Concils im Jahre 816', *Neues Archiv der Gesellschaft für ältere deutsche Geschichtskunde* xxvii (1902), 607–75 at pp. 646–51. See also C. Hocquard, 'La Règle de saint Chrodegang: état de quelques questions', in *Saint Chrodegang: communications présentées au colloque tenu à Metz à l'occasion du douzième centenaire de sa mort*, Metz 1967, 55–89. For the Old English recension (a version of the late ninth-century interpolated rule), with parallel Latin text, see *The Old English version of the enlarged rule of Chrodegang together with the Latin original: an Old English version of the capitula of Theodulf together with the Latin original: an interlinear Old English rendering of the epitome of Benedict of Aniane*, ed. A. S. Napier (Early English Text Society cl, 1916).

[121] *Istituzioni monastiche e istituzioni canonicali*, especially the article by R. Locatelli, 'Les Chanoines et la reforme dans le diocèse de Besançon (vers 1050–1150)', at pp. 704–18.

[122] Chrodegang I, c. xxxi, pp. 20–3; Council of Aachen (816), cc. cxv, cxx, MGH, *Concilia II*, i. 397–400.

[123] C. Egger, 'La regole seguite dai canonici regolari nei secoli XI e XII', in *La vita comune del clero nei secoli xi e xii: atti della settimana di studio, Mendola, settembre 1959* (Miscellanea iii,

prevailing *regula* for canons which led to the introduction of the rule of Augustine in northern France at the end of the eleventh century.[124] In the period 900–1050 the rules available for canons were Chrodegang's rule and the Aachen decrees, which despite being amalgamated in the late ninth or early tenth century also continued to circulate independently.

The recensions of Chrodegang's rule and the Aachen decrees both provide for regular confession and for atonement through penance for serious sins on the part of the canons. According to the original recension of Chrodegang, each canon should confess to the bishop at least twice a year.[125] If he has committed a minor sin, according to the original recension he should make a spontaneous confession to the bishop; the interpolated version adds that he should also abstain from participation in the mass and the office for that day.[126] According to both recensions, if the canon has committed a grave sin, such as murder, fornication, adultery, theft or similar major vices, he should first be flogged, then imprisoned, then do public penance in the monastic manner, that is be suspended from the oratory and the table and prostrate himself outside the doors of the church at each of the hours of the office.[127] Up until this point the interpolator had not felt it necessary to alter Chrodegang's original instructions in any significant way and had been content to maintain the difference between monastic punishment and secular penance. But this distinction begins to break down in the following chapter of the interpolated text, *de reconciliatione poenitentis capitale crimen*, which concerns the reconciliation of penitents for capital sins.[128] It describes

---

1962), ii. 9–12. The Lateran Council of 1059 considered the Aachen decrees but only a record of its comments on the ownership of property survives.

124 J. C. Dickinson, *The origins of the Austin canons and their introduction into England*, London 1950, 30–7; C. Dereine, 'Vie commune, règle de S. Augustin et chanoines réguliers au XIe siècle', *Revue d'histoire ecclésiastique* xli (1946), 356–406.

125 Chrodegang I, c. xiv, pp. 9–10. Much of this chapter is found in Chrodegang II, c. xxxi, cols 1071–2, but the requirement to confess to the bishop twice a year is omitted from the interpolated version.

126 'De his qui in quibusdam levioribus culpis delinquunt': Chrodegang I, c. xviii, p. 12; cf. Chrodegang II, c. xxviii, col. 1070.

127 'Egressus de carcere, si episcopo vel qui sub eo visum fuerit, agat adhuc publicam poenitentiam i.e. suspendatur ab oratorio simul et a mensa et omnibus canonicis oris, veniat ante ostium ecclesie, ubi prior iusserit, iacens, prostratus omni corpore ante ipsum limitum ecclesie usque dum ingrediuntur omnes': Chrodegang I, 'c. xv: De gravioribus culpis', p. 11, repeated in Chrodegang II: 'c. xxix: De gravioribus culpis', cols 1070–1. The Aachen decrees are less explicit; they enumerate the behaviour for which a canon should be admonished and finally excluded from the community, and also contain provisions for public penance in the event of serious sins: Council of Aachen (816), c. cxxxiv, MGH, *Concilia II*, i. 410–12.

128 'Ordo poenitentiam agentis publicam hic est: suscipies eum quarta feria mane in capite Quadragesimae, id est in capite jejuniorum, et cooperies eum cilicio, et orabis pro eo, et includes eum usque in Coenam Domini, qui eodem die praesentetur in gremio ecclesiae, qui dum vocatus venerit ad reconciliandum ante episcopum, vel clerum, cum omni humilitate prostrato omni corpore super terram ante absidam, petat ab omnibus veniam, et episcopus,

briefly the *ordo* for public penance, namely the imposition of a hairshirt on Ash Wednesday, and the penitent's confinement until Maundy Thursday, when he is brought before the bishop and all the clergy and the bishop says the prayers of reconciliation over him as he lies prostrate. This *ordo* appears to be connected to the previous chapter on how to deal with those guilty of grave faults. Here, by the late ninth or early tenth century, the monastic definition and procedure for public penance have been melded with the secular Church's liturgical procedures for public penance, perhaps because canons, as secular clergy, were subject to more general ecclesiastical discipline.

In the interpolated rule these chapters on public penance are followed by two on confession. The first is taken from the original recension of Chrodegang and cites the Bible on the importance and benefits of confession, urging the canon, if he thinks any bad thoughts, quickly to make confession to the bishop or the prior, suggesting that confession was reserved for minor faults.[129] The second is found only in the interpolated text and is a liturgical *ordo ad paenitentiam accipiendam et confessionem faciendam*.[130] A fairly conventional version of the *ordo* for secret penance, it is introduced as the prayer of penance and confession which is made before God and his priests at any time of the year, and by the faithful in the time before the three *quadragesimae*, that is Lent, Pentecost and Advent, to their priest, and by monks every Saturday to the bishop or prior.[131] Chrodegang, writing the original recension in the mid eighth century, had been content for the canons to confess twice a year; by the late ninth century the demands on them have, seemingly, been raised to confession once a week. Written for a single penitent, this *ordo* begins with a litany and is followed by an interrogation of the penitent about his beliefs followed by questions about his sinful behaviour and the award of a suitable penance. Liturgical private penance therefore had a role in the regular life of certain canons as both a devotional and disciplinary tool. The interpolated rule then returns to the text in Chrodegang's original recension, requiring the canons to confess their sins against the community: if they fail to atone they are excluded from the community which is exhorted to pray for them in terms taken from but expanding on c. xxiii of the Benedictine

---

vel qui sub eo est, det orationes super eum ad reconciliandum in quinta feria Coenae Domini': Chrodegang II, c. xxx, col. 1071.

[129] Chrodegang I, c. xiv, pp. 9–10; cf. Chrodegang II, c. xxxi, col. 1072.

[130] Chrodegang II, c. xxxii, cols 1072–3.

[131] 'Ordo ad paenitentiam accipiendam et confessionem faciendam. Haec est oratio poenitentiae et confessionis nostrae quae coram Deo et sacerdotibus eius a nobis pariter agendae sunt, id est, in unoquoque anno tribus vicibus, id est in tribus Quadragesimis populus fidelis suam confessionem suo sacerdoti faciat, et qui plus fecerit, melius facit. Monachi in unoquoque Sabbato confessionem faciant, cum bona voluntate, episcopo aut priori suo': Chrodegang II, c. xxxii, col. 1072. This is seemingly the only reference to *monachi* in the interpolated text which refers to the canons elsewhere as *clerici canonici*; this suggests the *ordo* was adopted from a monastic situation.

rule.¹³² But no distinction is made in the interpolated rule between the procedure to be used for lesser and that for greater faults.¹³³ However, what is clear is that by c. 900 the procedures for monastic discipline and liturgical penance had both become part of the canons' regular life.

The experience of canons and monks was, therefore, very different. Monastic procedures for infringements of the rule, on the whole, remained distinct from those for liturgical or canonical penance. Nevertheless because they both shared a common vocabulary and repertoire of gesture it was possible to confuse the two procedures, as both Hildemar's commentary and the Fulda–Trier customary reveal. Given the important part played by monks in the dissemination of the penitential liturgy and of accounts for the practice of penance, we need therefore to be alert to the possiblity of confusion between the two practices, especially when studying accounts of individual penitential acts. But penitential practice also encompassed confession and in the monastic life this too seems to have been seen as a process distinct from that for canonical penance. Yet monks were not isolated and, as this review has shown, the barriers between the monastic and wider world could be breached. And in addition to the conventional relationships generated by monastic patronage the involvement of some monks in the administration of pastoral care provides another means for cross-fertilisation between practices for monastic and canonical penance.

In contrast the distinction between internal discipline and penitential practice seems to have been much weaker for those following the canonical life. Thus the interpolated rule of Chrodegang includes an *ordo* for public penance as part of the disciplinary procedure for canons guilty of grave faults. The same source intended that a liturgical *ordo* for secret penance be used in the canons' weekly confession. Canons were more at the forefront of the delivery of pastoral care to the wider community than monks – especially those who acted as cathedral clergy – and this helps to explain, perhaps, the blurring of the distinctions. It also provides another channel through which monastic ideas about penance and punishment could permeate the wider community.

But one of the major conduits for the relationship between the regular clergy, both monastic and canonical, and the laity was through the liturgy. This chapter has shown that the liturgical influence on relations between the clergy and laity was in both directions: monks sometimes acted as pastors

---

132 Chrodegang II, c. xxxiii, col. 1073; but cf. Chrodegang I, c. xvii, p. 11, and RB, c. xxiii, ii. 542.

133 The *ordo* for giving penance and making confession ends 'Cavendum est utique ne hi qui in gravioribus peccatis incidunt, et hi qui in levioribus quibusdam delinquunt, aequaliter judicentur, sed secundum morbum adhibenda est medicina': Chrodegang II, c. xxxii, col. 1073, suggesting it was intended for those guilty of both lesser and grave faults. Presumably those guilty of grave faults also had to undergo public penance as outlined in Chrodegang II, cc. xxix–xxx, cols 1070–1.

outside their communities, but canonical penance also influenced monastic practice. The role of liturgy in shaping relations between the clergy and laity will be pursued in the more detailed examination of the penitential liturgy to be found in the next two chapters.

4

The Penitential Liturgy: Unity or Diversity?

The priest met the penitent when he administered the penitential rite. The idealised accounts of these encounters were recorded in the liturgy for both public and secret penance, and are the subject of this and the following chapter. Penance has a long liturgical history. Rituals for entry into public penance on Ash Wednesday followed by reconciliation on Maundy Thursday are first recorded in the Old Gelasian sacramentary,[1] an eighth-century manuscript thought to be based on seventh-century sources.[2] They also appear in the eighth-century or Frankish Gelasian texts.[3] Although the *Hadrianum*, the version of the seventh-century Gregorian sacramentary sent to Charlemagne from Rome in the late eighth century, had no rite for public penance, one was included in its ninth-century supplement attributed to Benedict of Aniane and also in later ninth-century revisions.[4] The tenth century saw a change: whilst the rites for public penance continued to be recorded in mixed Gregorian–Gelasian sacramentaries,[5] they also appeared in a new liturgical book, the pontifical. Intended mainly for episcopal use, the pontifical was a combination of the non-eucharistic *ordines*, instructions to the celebrant, with the corresponding prayers from the sacramentaries.[6] Although the pontifical first originated in the ninth century, the best known is the mid tenth-century Romano-German pontifical, which included not only *ordines* for the rite of public penance but also for secret penance.[7] *Ordines*

---

[1] *The Gelasian sacramentary: liber sacramentorum romanae ecclesiae*, ed. H. A. Wilson, Oxford 1894, xv–xvi, xxviii, pp. 14–15, 63–6.
[2] A. Chavasse, *Le Sacramentaire gèlasien (Vaticanus Reginensis 316): sacramentaire presbytéral en usage dans les titres Romains au VIIe siècle*, Tournai–Rome 1958.
[3] For example, *Das fränkishe Sacramentarium Gelasianum in alamannischer Ueberlieferung*, ed. L. C. Mohlberg, Münster, Westfalia 1918. On the eighth-century Gelasian sacramentaries see Vogel, *Medieval liturgy*, 70–8.
[4] 'XCVII: orationes et praeces super penitentem confitentem peccata sua more solito feria IIII infra L': SGR i. 451–2; 'XCVIII: orationes ad reconciliandum penitentem feria V in cena domini': ibid. i. 452–3. See also ibid. i. 694; iii. 113–18. For a brief review of the debate surrounding the date of composition of the *Hadrianum* and that of its supplement, and a history of their recension in Carolingian Frankia see Vogel, *Medieval liturgy*, 79–102. For further detail see Jean Deshusses's edition of the *Hadrianum* and its supplement: SGR.
[5] For example, the Fulda sacramentary (SF). For this identification see Vogel, *Medieval liturgy*, 102–4. For a review of mixed Gelasian–Gregorian sacramentaries see pp. 92–102.
[6] Ibid. 225.
[7] N. Rasmussen, 'Le "Pontifical" de Beauvais (IXe–Xe siècle)', in *Studia Patristica*, X: *Texte und Untersuchungen zur Geschichte der altchristen Literatur*, cvii, Berlin 1970, 410–18, and 'Unité et diversité des pontificaux latins au VIIIe, IXe et Xe siècles', in *Liturgie de l'église*

for secret penance have a shorter history: they are first recorded in ninth-century penitentials;[8] it is not until the tenth century that they find their way into the more formal liturgical books, the sacramentary and the pontifical.[9]

The rites which are the subject of these two chapters inherited a powerful textual legacy from previous centuries; in the case of those for public penance it was at least three centuries old. Textual tradition shaped both the form and the content of these rites. As with other areas of the liturgy, this textual inheritance generates pitfalls for the unwary historian because it is very difficult to use liturgical texts which have been in use over several centuries as historical evidence for a particular point in time.[10] Further, liturgical manuscripts are often seen as static compilations of texts, blindly copied and not much used.[11] This assumption underlies the approach taken by historians of liturgy; they have mostly been content to look for the sources of a liturgy, and more reluctant to consider that the compilation of a particular rite may be a result of deliberate choice at a particular time. But recent research has demonstrated that individual rites can be related to specific circumstances;[12] moreover, Mansfield's study of penitential rites has not only shown that major changes in the rites for public penance can be located to a particular time and place, but also demonstrated the importance of minor variations and discrepancies within the manuscripts of particular ritual families.[13] Such changes cannot be dismissed as minor differences between recensions. Instead a rite may be the product of the ideas of an individual: the author of the unfeasibly long and detailed *ordo* for public penance in the 'Poitiers' pontifical seems to have been driven by literary interest, a desire to compile a comprehensive collection of texts rather than a wish to compose a workable *ordo*. It is by no means certain that all textual differences represent different penitential practices. But they may, as Mansfield showed, reflect the contemporary liturgy. Whatever the case, they should be seen as evidence that these

---

particulière et liturgie de l'église universelle: conférences Saint-Serge XXIIe semaine d'études liturgiques, Paris, 30 juin–3 juillet 1975 (Bibliotheca 'Ephemerides Liturgicae' subsidia vii, 1976), 393–410. On the early pontificals see now his *Les Pontificaux de haut moyen âge*, and also Vogel, *Medieval liturgy*, 225–47.

[8] Kottje, 'Busspraxis', 388–92.

[9] For example, the Fulda sacramentary includes an *ordo* for secret penance which is discussed in ch. 5.

[10] 'In fact, it is very difficult, and very unsafe to attempt strict historical deductions from liturgical formulae, new or old': E. Bishop, *Liturgica historica: papers on the liturgy and religious life of the western Church*, Oxford 1918, 298.

[11] 'The medium itself had become the message': J. L. Nelson, 'Ritual and reality', in D. Baker (ed.), *The materials, sources and methods of ecclesiastical history* (SCH xi, 1975), 41–51 at pp. 44–5 (repr. in her *Politics and ritual*, 329–39).

[12] Idem, 'The rites of the Conqueror', in *Proceedings of the fourth Battle conference on Anglo-Norman studies*, Woodbridge 1982, 117–32, 210–21 (repr. in her *Politics and ritual*, 375–401), and 'The second English *ordo*', ibid. 361–74.

[13] Mansfield, *Humiliation*, 159–247.

manuscripts were not copied unreflectively, but instead with a purpose. The evolutionary nature of these rites suggests that, unlike the coronation *ordines* which were copied in the pontificals of late medieval French bishops long after they ceased to be of use to them, they were not redundant. Mansfield's approach has been adopted for my own study of the penitential liturgy. Her manuscript researches identified one distinctive family of rites for public penance peculiar to northern France, whilst my own examination of over forty manuscripts has revealed at least three distinctive families for the rites for public penance and greater variety amongst those for secret penance.

In this chapter therefore I study the penitential rites within the Romano-German pontifical; in the next I study the variety of other penitential rites which existed in this period. I start with the Romano-German pontifical because recent historians have taken it to be axiomatic of late tenth- and eleventh-century penitential practice throughout Europe.[14] Whilst it is the best known liturgical compilation from the period 900–1050, and was certainly popular – it survives in thirty-eight manuscripts – its present status amongst modern historians is due to three factors: it laid the foundations of the later Roman pontifical, making it a focus of interest for liturgical historians; it is easily available in a modern edition; and Vogel's research on penitential rites in this period, especially those for public penance, was based on the Romano-German pontifical.[15] But does this Mainz pontifical constitute the paradigm it has been taken to be?

The remainder of this chapter begins to address this question. It is divided into three parts: first it introduces the reader to the penitential liturgy in detail through a consideration of the texts for the rites for public and secret penance recorded in the Romano-German pontifical. This serves both to study the way in which these rites were perceived by all the parties involved, and also to provide a basis for comparison with the other contemporary liturgies which are the subject of the next chapter. In the second part I consider the evidence for who owned and therefore used the Romano-German pontifical, and in the last part the geographic distribution of its manuscripts. Can we, after all, view this pontifical as the universal liturgy of the *Reich*?

---

[14] Bull cites it in support of other, non-liturgical evidence for public penitential practice in south-western France although no manuscript copies of the Romano-German pontifical survive from this region: Bull, *Knightly piety*, 173 n. 77. Both he and Geoffrey Koziol rely on Vogel's account of public penance in this period and therefore implicitly on the Romano-German pontifical: G. Koziol, *Begging, pardon and favor: ritual and political order in early medieval France*, Ithaca 1992, ch. vi. But out of a total of seventeen surviving pontificals from tenth- and eleventh-century west Frankia, only four (possibly five) are copies of the Romano-German pontifical (see appendix 1).
[15] Vogel, 'Pénitence publique', and 'Pénitence tarifée'.

The Romano-German pontifical: the penitential *ordines*

Previous historians have studied the Romano-German pontifical's penitential rites in the context of the historical development of the penitential liturgy from late antiquity to the Council of Trent.[16] They therefore sought to establish the Romano-German pontifical's sources and to demonstrate which parts were new. Instead of repeating their work, it is the aim of this section to study the evidence within these rites for how penance was practised and understood by all the participating parties, clerical and lay.

Most rituals are, to some extent, polysemic; they communicate different messages at the same time, often to the different participants in the ritual.[17] It is therefore important to establish how many penitents and how many clergy participated in each rite and whether there was an audience which, whilst not directly involved, was nevertheless central to the way the rite worked; without an audience a coronation rite, for example, would have little validity, else who would know that the woman who had been crowned was queen?[18] It is also important to establish what messages were communicated during the rite, to whom, and how, for the method may give a clue as to the intended audience. Rituals are designed, but they also evolve over time; it cannot be assumed that the way in which these rituals worked and were understood is that intended by their designers. This is especially true for penitential rituals: those for public penance seem to have existed in some form by the fourth century, at least, although they were not formally recorded until the eighth century in the Gelasian sacramentary and not fully until the late ninth century.

One possible way towards understanding how these rites were practised and understood lies in the manuscript evidence. There is no single, uniform text of the penitential *ordines* as recorded in Vogel and Elze's edition of the Romano-German pontifical; my examination of sixteen manuscripts suggests that the copyists often introduced minor variations. It is now widely accepted by liturgical historians that we should not look for an *Urtext*, and that each liturgical text should be studied as valid in itself, not as a corrupt version of some unknown 'perfect' text.[19] More recently, Mansfield's research into minor textual variations in thirteenth-century *ordines* has demonstrated how such changes could be used as evidence for the way in which a rite was conceived of and used.[20] Such changes suggest that the scribe thought about the rite he was copying, and either introduced new changes, or adapted the

---

16 Jungmann, *Bussriten*, 212–13, 320–1; Vogel, 'Pénitence publique', *Le Pécheur au moyen âge*, 208–22, and 'Pénitence tarifée'.
17 V. Turner, *The forest of symbols: aspects of Ndembu ritual*, Ithaca–London 1967, 50–1; Koziol, *Begging*, 307–11.
18 Ibid. 289–324; Nelson, 'Ritual and reality'.
19 C. Vogel, 'L'Oeuvre liturgique de Mgr. M. Andrieu: un bilan provisoire', *Revue des sciences religieuses* xxxi (1957), 7–19 at p. 9.
20 Mansfield, *Humiliation*, 189–247.

rite he was copying according to his own perceptions of how penance should be practised,[21] or even adapted the rite to that practised within his own church. These textual variations will be considered as part of my study of the separate penitential rites.

Entry into penance on Ash Wednesday

The earliest evidence of a specific day for entry into (public) penance is seventh-century;[22] the earliest full rite for penance at the start of Lent is not recorded until the eighth-century Gelasian sacramentary.[23]

The Romano-German pontifical's *ordo* for entry into penance on Ash Wednesday comes in the section on the order of offices to be said throughout the year, at the start of the liturgy for Lent.[24] It was thus seen by the compilers of the Romano-German pontifical as part of the natural and pre-ordained sequence of events which make up the Church's liturgical year, rather than being set apart from it in a separate *ordo*. The Romano-German pontifical's *ordo* is long, complicated, repetitive and somewhat confusing. It is therefore important to outline the difficulties presented by the text before attempting to deal with them. In order to provide a way through the rite, table 1 provides a summary of its various stages.

It begins with an injunction that the deacon should call the people (*populus*) to hear the priest (*sacerdos*) admonish all Christians to make a true confession and receive penance at the beginning of Lent and return on Maundy Thursday to be reconciled. Exceptions were made for those who could not be reconciled on Maundy Thursday – anyone making a journey or whose profession did not allow it or who was too stupid should have both a Lenten and an annual penance enjoined on them and be reconciled immediately.[25] The rubric then deals with jurisdictional problems posed by a delay

---

[21] Rasmussen in 'Unité et diversité des pontificaux latins', argued that the pontifical of 'Poitiers' was not intended for actual use by its compiler but rather as a reference text.
[22] Jungmann, *Bussriten*, 44–5; Vogel, 'Pénitence publique', 139–40.
[23] '*Ordo agentibus publicam poenitentiam*. Suscipis eum iu feria mane in capite Quadragesimae, et cooperis eum cilicio, oras pro eo, et includis usque ad Coenam Domini. Qui eodem die in gremio praesentatur ecclesiae, et prostrato eo omni corpore in terra, dat orationem pontifex super eum ad reconciliandum in quinta feria Coenae Domini sicut ibi continetur': xvi, *The Gelasian sacramentary*, 15.
[24] 'In Christi nomine incipit ordo catholicorum librorum qui in ecclesia romana ponuntur': *PRG* xcix, ii. 1–141. The *ordo* for entry into penance on Ash Wednesday is only one part of the order for that day: 'Ordo in quarta ebdomada quadragesimae quae est in capite ieiunii', ibid. xcix.44–80, ii. 14–23. *Ordo* xcix is the same as *ordo* l of the *Ordines romani*: 'In Christi nomine incipit ordo catholicorum librorum qui in ecclesia romana ponuntur': *OR* v. 83–365. There is no evidence independent of the *PRG* for the appearance of *ordo* l.
[25] This apparent distinction between a penance which lasts just for Lent and one that last for the year is one also found in other texts. See, for example, 'Ordo priuatae seu annualis poenitentiae ita prosequendus est', *SF* lv, p. 42. It suggests that there was a penance which all

Table 1
The entry into penance on Ash Wednesday

PRG cxix.44–80, ii. 14–23

Entry into penance

1. Deacon's admonition to all Christians to come to penance (no. 44).
2. The priest's reception of the penitent and his/her entry into penance (nos 44–5).
3. The priest's interrogation of the penitent.
   Consults with penitent over his/her vices (no. 46).
   Considers penitent's status and circumstances when awarding penance (nos 47–9).
   Interrogates the penitent on the articles of faith and his/her willingness to do penance (no. 50).
4. Penitent's formal confession prayer (no. 50a) followed by priest's intercession prayer (no. 51) and priest's pastoral instruction on the eight vices (no. 52).
5. Penitent's act of contrition (no. 53).
6. Priest awards a formal penance (nos 54–5).
7. Priest's intercession on behalf of the penitent: seven penitential psalms followed by *preces* and intercessory prayers (nos 56–64).
8. Priest and penitent enter church and chant Psalms xxxvii and cii followed by Kyrie, *preces* and intercessory prayer (nos 65–6).

Missa post confessionem

After the complendum ashes are placed on the head of the penitent and s/he puts on sackcloth (nos 71–2).
The penitent is ejected from the church (no. 73).
The blessing of the ashes (nos 74–7).
Ashes are placed on the heads of the congregation (nos 78–9).
Procession to the next station (no. 80).

between the imposition of penance and the penitent's reconciliation; no one ought to usurp the judgement of an individual priest or a bishop in the administration of penance.[26] If it became necessary, and the priest was not present, the deacon might receive the penitent and give him holy communion, thus echoing the provisions made in canon law to ensure that a rival priest or bishop did not usurp jurisdiction over the penitent.[27] Presumably, both the liturgical and canonical strictures were intended to ensure that the penitent did a full penance. This provision suggests that the *ordo* could be administered by either a *presbiter* or *episcopus*; the remainder of the text refers to the minister as *sacerdos*, an ambiguous term which, although it may refer to either a priest or bishop, often refers to a bishop.[28] The *ordo* appears, however, in a

---

Christians were supposed to perform in Lent and a separate penance, which might last for more than one year, for those penitents with more serious sins.

[26] 'Sicut autem sacrificium offerre non debent nisi episcopi vel presbiteri quibus claves regni caelestis traditae sunt, sec nec iudicia ista alius usurpare debet': PRG xcix.44, ii. 14.
[27] Burchard, *Decretum* xix.40, 62, 70, 987–8, 998–9.
[28] M. Du Cange, suppl. D. P. Carpenterius and G. A. L. Henschel, *Glossarium mediae et*

collection made for episcopal use, and Regino of Prüm, some forty-five years earlier, described a similar *ordo* being administered by the bishop.[29]

The rubric then moved from the provisional to the actual: how the *sacerdos* should receive the penitent. If he is a layman, *laicus*, he should put down his stick, seemingly signifying his transition from lay to penitential status, and whoever he is, whether layman, cleric or monk, incline his head before the priest. Abandonment of the stick also implies the public nature of this rite, performed before all the Christian people. After this the priest recites a preparation prayer, requesting God to help him, and to look mercifully on His man- and maid-servants, *famuli* and *famulae*, who come to do penance and take refuge in His mercy.[30] The reference to female as well as male penitents suggests that, despite the references in the rubric to a layman and his stick, the *ordo* was intended for both men and women.

The priest then begins his interrogation of the penitent. He orders the penitent to sit next to him and questions him on the vices, so that nothing sinful remains in this heart.[31] The priest should then award him his penance, having taken into consideration his sex, age, condition, status and character; such penance could take the form of fasting, almsgiving, weeping whilst on his knees, standing in the form of cross or anything else which relates to the salvation of his soul.[32] The priest should distinguish between penitents according to their personal circumstances, between the rich and the poor, the free and the unfree, the child, the adolescent, the adult and the old man, between the intelligent and the mentally deficient, between laymen and clerics, between monks and bishops, priests and deacons, sub-deacons and readers, virgins and mature women, a canoness and a nun, between the lame, the healthy and the sick.[33] Although this list is to some extent formulaic, as similar lists are found in ninth-century penitentials, it too indicates that this *ordo* was intended to embrace women as well as men. The priest should also take into account the quality of the sin and of the man, whether he lives a continent or incontinent life, whether the sin was committed openly or in hiding, whether he was forced to commit his sin, and how much compunction he shows, and whether this was through necessity or voluntarily. This long rubric emphasises that each penitent should be judged on his own merits, and that penance is flexible and can vary according to both status and circumstance. Its echo of the canon law provisions may have had a didactic function and give a clue as to how they were enforced through the administration of the rite itself.

---

infirmae latinitatis, Paris 1840–50, vi. 9–10; J. F. Niermeyer, *Mediae latinitatis lexicon minus*, Leiden 1976, 925–6.
[29] See ch. 1.
[30] *PRG* xcix.45, ii. 14–15.
[31] Ibid. no. 46.
[32] Ibid. no. 47.
[33] Ibid. no. 48.

The following section is, like the minister's preparation prayer, fairly standard to all confession rites; the minister interrogates the penitent on his belief in the articles of faith.[34] If he believes this definition of trinitarian orthodoxy and is willing to repent, the priest should receive his confession and indicate to him his penance. And if he does not, the priest should not receive his confession. There then follows a very long confession prayer in which the penitent confesses before God, the angels and saints, in the presence of His altar and His priest, that he was conceived in sin, born into sin, nurtured in sin, and conversant with sin after baptism; sin is immediately associated with the human condition. An enormous catalogue of specific yet unspecified sins, such as pride, vainglory, jealousy, hatred, then follows. Covering two pages of the printed edition, this includes sins which apply perhaps more to the laity, such as adultery, and those which apply more specifically to the clergy, such as giving church property out in an unacceptable way: 'in dispensandis male rebus ecclesiasticis'. It is a formal affirmation of the penitent's sinful state, not a duplication of the interrogation which preceded the prayer. The re-enactment of this catalogue of sins reinforces for the penitent the extent of his guilt and the need for internal improvement. Such a declaration also demonstrates to a wider audience the penitent's sinful state and therefore his need for penance, suggesting that this *ordo* was performed in public; that the Romano-German pontifical's *ordo* for secret penance does not contain a similar prayer supports this suggestion.

The minister follows the penitent's confession with a brief prayer for the penitent's forgiveness. Whilst it starts in the third person with a request that God may demonstrate mercy towards the penitent, it then switches to the first person plural and asks that God may lead us equally into eternal life and guard us from all evil: 'Misereatur tui omnipotens Deus et dimittat tibi omnia peccata tua. Liberet te ab omni malo, conservet te in omni bono. Et perducat nos pariter ad vitam aeternam. Ab omni malo nos custodiat dominus.'[35] The priest not only asks for mercy on the penitent, he also allies the penitent with himself, acknowledging his own sinfulness. The use of the first person plural may also have been intended to involve the audience; it thus became a communal prayer in which the human community, inherently sinful, requested God's mercy for the sinner and His protection for themselves. It was also later regarded as an absolution prayer; a later hand in an early twelfth-century German manuscript described this prayer in the margin as 'absolutio'.[36] But there is no evidence that it was seen as more than an intercessory prayer in the tenth century.

The next stage seems to be primarily personal, an expression of pastoral care by the priest towards the penitent. The minister should encourage the penitent to memorise the vices recorded above, 'de suprascriptis vitiis', as a

---

[34] Ibid. nos 50–a, ii. 15–17.
[35] Ibid. no. 51.
[36] Wolfenbüttel, Herzog-August-Bibliothek, Cod. Guelf. 493 Helmstadt, fo. 9r.

precaution for his future.³⁷ There is no list of vices in the text of the Romano-German pontifical; Vogel interpreted the phrase as referring to a penitential, but there is no explicit reference to a penitential anywhere in the *ordo*.³⁸ This phrase may refer only to the sins outlined in the general confession prayer but a mid eleventh-century manuscript from Hildesheim provides a different explanation. In this version the general confession prayer is followed by lengthy instructions to the priest to explain the eight principal vices to the penitent invoking Ambrose and Jerome as authorities.³⁹ A similar text is found in the *ordo* for public penance on Ash Wednesday in the late ninth-century 'Poitiers' pontifical and an abbreviated version in the *ordo* for giving penance at the beginning of book xix of Burchard's *Decretum*.⁴⁰ The Hildesheim *ordo* may, therefore, represent an earlier tradition, rather than an interpolation to the Romano-German text, thus explaining this oblique reference.

The penitent should then make his act of contrition. Kneeling, weeping, on the ground, with his hands in supplication, he should look up at the priest who is standing over him, acknowledge his innumerable sins and humbly ask the priest to act as his intercessor.⁴¹ The penitent then prostrates himself full-length on the ground weeping and groaning with all his heart. The priest should then prostrate himself next to the penitent, thereby associating himself together with the penitent in the ritual; both are human, and as such must acknowledge their humility before God.⁴² Then the priest orders the penitent to rise up and when he is on his feet to await with fear and humility the priest's judgement.⁴³ Thus, gesture was used to underline the language of prayer. The penitent petitions the priest for help as his intercessor with God, through both word and gesture; the priest receives the penitent's supplications standing up, thus demonstrating his superiority, but he in turn prostrates himself before God, signalling that he too must petition God to show mercy to the penitent. Both then get up, showing that the petition has been successful. The theology underlying the *ordo* was thus communicated through changes in behaviour. The service probably had a didactic aspect for both the penitent and also, which is more often forgotten, the audience. The body

---

37 'Precavendum est tamen sacerdoti de suprascriptis vitiis, ut ei exhortationis gratia ad memoriam reducat, ne quid adversante diabolo occultum remaneat': *PRG* xcix.52, ii. 17.
38 'Le prêtre veillera à ce qu'aucun des péchés énumérés dans le pénitentiel ne demeure caché. Par son insistance, il les remettra en mémoire au pénitent': Vogel, *Le Pécheur au moyen âge*, 216.
39 Bamberg, Staatsbibliothek, Cod. Lit. 54, fos 88r–91.
40 *Il cosiddetto pontificale di Poitiers*, 17–40; Burchard, *Decretum* xix.6, 976–7.
41 *PRG* xcix.52–3, ii. 17.
42 'Quo perdicto, totum se in terram prosternat et gemitus atque suspiria vel lacrimas, prout Deus dederit, ab intimo corde producat. Sacerdos vero patiatur eum aliquantisper iacere prostratum iuxta quod viderit eum divina inspiratione compunctum': ibid. no. 54, ii. 18.
43 Ibid.

language of humility seems to have been universal in this period;[44] it was probably as important as the spoken language for communicating both theological ideas and the progress of the service to a penitent who may not have fully understood Latin. The audience would also have been able to follow the progress of the liturgy through watching the changes in posture of both the penitent and the priest.

The penitent's petition is successful provided certain conditions are met; the priest indicates to him the penance he is to receive, which should again be adapted to individual circumstances. After hearing the priest's sentence, the penitent then prostrates himself at the priest's feet, and asks that the priest pray for him, whilst he undertakes his penance, because he has received from the mouth of God these remedies for his salvation.

The penitent still prostrate at his feet, the minister recites the seven penitential psalms, followed by several responses from those psalms most concerned with petitioning the Lord for mercy, many of which are found in other *ordines* for the imposition of penance, and also in the office during Lent.[45] He then says one or more of eight alternative prayers which are concerned to petition God's mercy for the penitent.[46] Some are written in the third person singular, some in the first person plural; they do not appear to be intended for multiple penitents.[47]

The priest then orders the penitent to rise up from the ground, and he himself gets up from his seat, and if the time or the place allows, they should both enter the church, and on their knees or crawling sing several more psalms followed by *preces*.[48] The sequence concludes with a prayer in which the priest asks God to show His indulgence and mercy to this penitent who is named.[49] But absolution is reserved for Maundy Thursday.

A mass follows. The opening prayer, in which the priest petitions God to release His servant from sin, is taken from the Gelasian sacramentary where it is found amongst the prayers for the reconciliation of penitents on Maundy Thursday.[50] It thus demonstrates the relative fluidity which existed between the Maundy Thursday and Ash Wednesday rites; they were always seen as

---

[44] G. Althoff, 'Das Privileg der "deditio": Formen gütlicher Konfliktbeendigung in der mittelalterlichen Adelsgesellschaft', in his *Spielregeln der Politik im Mittelalter*, Darmstadt 1997, 99–125; H. Fichtenau, *Living in the tenth century: mentalities and social orders*, Chicago–London 1991 (trans. by P. J. Geary of *Lebensordnung des 10. Jahrhunderts: Studien über Denkart und Existenz im einstigen Karolingerreich*, Stuttgart 1984), 36–8; Koziol, *Begging*, 59–76 and passim.
[45] PRG xcix.56, ii. 18–19; Vogel, *Le Pécheur au moyen âge*, 217.
[46] PRG xcix.57–64, ii. 19–20. The initial rubric suggests that the priest should recite one prayer 'Post haec dicat sacerdos hanc orationem': ibid. no. 56. But the next rubric (no. 65) begins, 'Quibus dictis', suggesting that the priest is intended to recite more than one of the possible prayers.
[47] Ibid. nos 57–64.
[48] Ibid. no. 65, ii. 20.
[49] Ibid. no. 66.
[50] *Gelasian sacramentary*, 65; PRG xcix.67, ii. 20.

part of the same process and prayers could and did migrate between them. The Gospel refers to the parable of the proud Pharisee and the penitent tax collector which concludes, 'For everyone who exalts himself will be humbled, but the man who humbles himself will be exalted.'[51] The *secreta*, in which the priest begs for the gift of salvation for this Thy servant N., is also found in the Romano-German pontifical's *ordo* for the reconciliation of penitents on Maundy Thursday.[52] In the *complendum* the priest petitions God to avert the anger of His indignation and to forgive all the sins of this His servant.[53] The mass is therefore said specifically for the penitent, and should be seen as part of the penitential *ordo*. It is, however, a public affair; one early twelfth-century German manuscript includes neums with the antiphons, suggesting that these were sung as part of an elaborate ceremony.[54]

At the end of the *complendum* the priest puts ashes on the head of the penitent and says, 'remember man that you are dust and you will revert to dust'. Then he puts the hairshirt on the penitent and says, 'change your heart and humiliate your soul in ashes and a hairshirt. For God does not despise a contrite and humble heart'.[55] There then follows a prayer, written in the first person plural, which beseeches the Lord that He bestow the grace of salvation on His servant and that His anger be satisfied.[56] After this prayer the penitent is ejected from the church, with the words, 'Behold today you are ejected from the bosom of your holy mother church for your sin, as Adam the first man was ejected from paradise because of his transgression.'[57] There then follows the response which is taken from Genesis, 'With the sweat of your brow shall you eat your bread, you shall work the land, it will not give its fruits to you, it shall yield brambles and thistles. Because you have obeyed the voice of your wife rather than mine, accursed be the earth on which you work.'[58] The symbolic ejection of the penitent from the church suggests that this was a very public banishment. The penitent is, to some extent, a scapegoat; the community as a whole is purified through the expulsion of this sinner.[59]

---

[51] Luke xviii.10.
[52] PRG xcix.68, ii. 20–1.
[53] Ibid. no. 70.
[54] Wolfenbüttel, Herzog-August-Bibliothek, Cod. Guelf. 141 Helmstadt, fos 4v–7v.
[55] 'Hic mittendus est cinis super caput penitentis et dicendum: *Memento homo, quia puluis es et in puluerem reuertis*. Statimque imponendum cilicium et dicendum: *Convertere cor tuum et humilia animam tuam in cinere et cilicio. Cor enim contritum et humiliatum Deus non despicit*': PRG xcix.71, ii. 21.
[56] Ibid. no. 72.
[57] 'Ecce eieceris hodie a sinu matris tuae sanctae ecclesiae propter peccatum tuum sicut Adam primus homo eiectus est a paradiso propter transgressionem suam': ibid. no. 73.
[58] 'Sequitur responsum: *In sudore vultus tui vesceris pane tuo*, dixit dominus ad Adam, *cum operatus fueris terram, non dabit fructus suos, sed spinas et tribulos germinabit tibi*. Versus. *Pro eo quod obedisti voci uxoris tuae plus quam meae, maledicta terra in opere tuo. Non dabit*': ibid. This is a version of Genesis iii.17–20.
[59] M. Rubellin, 'Vision de la société chrétienne à travers la confession et la pénitence au

Whilst the penitent's involvement in the ceremony ends with his expulsion, it is not the end of the service for either the priest or the rest of the participating community. It is followed by the blessing of the ashes, in which the priest asks the Lord's mercy and blessing for the sinful.[60] After initial prayers, an antiphon requesting the Lord's mercy is sung, and the ashes placed on the heads of those present, whilst a further antiphon is sung asking God 'to be merciful and release us from our sins'.[61] This is followed by a prayer asking God to aid them in fasting and continence followed by a procession accompanied by another antiphon.[62] This final sequence echoes the previous sequence; just as the penitent has been instructed to fast, has changed into a hairshirt, and has had ashes placed on his head, so the faithful now repeat his behaviour as part of their own Lenten devotions. The physical trappings of penance are therefore seen as universal; penance is universal to all Christians, but only the public penitent is expelled from the church. This final sequence therefore brings the audience (of all Christians) into the picture properly for the first time, and emphasises that this is a communal and not just a personal service; it is directed not only at the penitent, but also at the whole population.

This account therefore suggests that it was a long, complicated and repetitive process: the penitent appears to be assigned his penance twice. This *ordo* is also highly ambiguous. There is no indication where the liturgy was to be performed; it is not until after the penitent has received his penance and prayers have been said for him, that the priest and penitent are instructed to enter the church, which suggests that the first stages of the penance need not have taken place inside the church. They could, indeed, have taken place in private. Further, there is no explicit rubric suggesting that this *ordo* should be administered by the bishop; the initial and subsequent rubrics merely refer to the *sacerdos*. Finally, although the initial call to penance is addressed to the whole parish, the *ordo* is concerned only with the single penitent.

Vogel attempted to resolve these problems by pointing to the similarities between this *ordo* and those for 'secret' or 'tariff' penance such as the Romano-German *ordo* cxxxvi; the interrogation about the articles of faith is found in other *ordines* for private penance for example, and, as we shall see, penance was seemingly assigned twice in *ordo* cxxxvi. Vogel suggested therefore that this *ordo* is in fact the awkward amalgamation of two *ordines*.[63] Up to

---

IXe siècle', in Groupe de la Bussiére (ed.), *Pratiques de la confession: des pères du désert à Vatican II: quinze études d'histoire*, Paris 1983, 53–70 at p. 63.

[60] PRG xcix.74–9, ii. 21–2.

[61] 'Interim ponendi sunt cineres super capita sicut antiphona testatur: *Immutetur habitu in cinere et cilicio ieiunimus et ploremus ante dominum, quia multum misericors est dimittere peccata nostra Deus noster*': ibid. no. 78.

[62] Ibid. nos 79–80, ii. 22–3.

[63] Vogel, *Le Pécheur au moyen âge*, 208–10. A. Martini argued, following Vogel, that a similar structure in the late ninth-century (so-called) 'Poitiers' pontifical also represented two *ordines*, one for private penance, followed by one for public penance: 'L'*ordo paenitentiae*

the final prayer before the mass it is an *ordo* for individual 'secret' penance, for all those who answer the deacon's call to penance. This prayer, however, marks the beginning of a new *ordo*, a rite of public penance, which includes the mass, the imposition of ashes and hairshirt, and the penitent's expulsion from the church.[64]

But Mansfield has argued that Vogel's suggestion is contradicted by the manuscripts which contain no indication that a new *ordo* starts with the mass. Moreover it is described as 'missa post confessionem', suggesting that in the minds of the Romano-German pontifical's compilers, at least, the mass was connected to the confession which had gone before.[65] She also suggested that rather than viewing the confession and assignment of penance as taking place in private, they should be seen as taking place outside the church, in the manner prescribed by Regino of Prüm for public penitents some forty-five years before. The Roman-German pontifical's *ordo* should therefore be seen as one public *ordo*, which, like the *ordo* for Maundy Thursday, takes place both in front of and inside the church. Mansfield's views are supported by my own comments on the significance of gesture for the communication of theological ideas and the progress of the *ordo* to an audience.

Confirmation of Mansfield's views exist in a copy of the Romano-German pontifical written for Besançon cathedral in the eleventh century in which the text of the 'missa post confessionem' is omitted;[66] the *ordo* runs straight from the final prayer of the first part to a rubric instructing the priest to sprinkle the holy ashes on the head of the penitent saying, 'memento homo quid pulvis es et in pulverem reverteris'.[67] The Besançon manuscript follows the text of the Romano-German pontifical except that the priest is instructed to sprinkle rather than put the ashes on the penitent's head. Neums were written above the responses which accompany the penitent's expulsion from the church, suggesting that a musical dimension was added to the liturgical drama. The final stage of the *ordo* contains a more explicit rubric than that in the Romano-German pontifical but is otherwise identical: 'Incipit benedictio cineris simul clero et populo collecto munum [sic] hora nona diei'.[68] Whilst

---

in feria quarta quinquagesimae del cosiddetto pontificale di Poitiers', in *Mens concordet voci pour Mgr A. G. Martimort*, Paris 1983, 629–38 at p. 631.

[64] In his analysis of the rite for Ash Wednesday Vogel assumes, without even citing his previous work, that the rite of public penance begins with the *missa post confessionem*: 'Pénitence publique', 138. He is presumably building on his argument, made in *Le Pécheur au moyen âge*, 207–18, that the rite prior to the mass was for tariff penance rather than public penance.

[65] Mansfield, *Humiliation*, 174–5.

[66] Wolfenbüttel, Herzog-August-Bibliothek, Cod. Guelf. 15 Weissenburg, fos 50r–3v. This manuscript was partly written in Besançon, partly in Germany; the Ash Wednesday *ordo* falls in the Besançon part. Mansfield seems to have been unaware of it.

[67] 'His finitis spargat sacerdos de cinere sancto super caput paenitentis dicens, Memento homo quid pulvis es et in pulverem reverteris': ibid. fo. 53r.

[68] Ibid. It replaces the Romano-German rubric: 'Eodem die fit collecta ad Sanctam Anastasiam. Et in primis agitur benedictio cineris': *PRG* xcix.74, ii. 21.

the Romano-German pontifical states that on that day the ashes should be blessed, the Besançon rubric makes it clear that in eastern France, at any rate, the ashes were blessed and distributed to both the clergy and the people at the same time ('simul') as the penitent was expelled from the church. The Besançon pontifical suggests that in one place at least the entire Romano-German penitential *ordo* was seen as part of a public ceremony which involved the whole community.

The differences from the Romano-German text in the Hildesheim pontifical, written in 1067, also suggest that the entire *ordo* was aimed at the whole community. The addition of what is almost a sermon on the eight vices following the penitent's confession prayer has already been noted above. A similar text is found in Burchard of Worms, and such an addition might suggest that the first part of the *ordo* belongs, as Vogel suggested, to the tradition of tariff penance, and is part of the pastoral care offered by the priest to the penitent.[69] But later in the same manuscript, after the expulsion of the penitent from the church, another didactic text was added on the seven ways by which sin is dissolved, that is by baptism, martyrdom, alms, living in accordance with God's law, preaching, charity and lastly penance.[70] The positioning of this last text demonstrates that both these texts were aimed at the audience as much as at the penitent himself. The public penance of one or several individuals is presented as an example and a reminder to the entire community of their own need for penance.

This rite was not new, as shown by the comparison with Regino. The only innovation the Romano-German pontifical's compilers made was to eliminate the episcopal laying on of hands.[71] This was replaced by the imposition of ashes as a sign of entry into public penance.[72] It was also a public rite, intended to communicate the basic tenets of penitential doctrine both verbally and visually, through gesture culminating in the dramatic explusion of the penitent from the church, which suggests that rather than seeing it as a narrow rite, enacted before a small number of clergymen, we should in fact see this as a very public act, performed outside the cathedral for a lay as well as clerical audience. All, not just the bishop, the clergy and the penitents, were participants in this ritual and all of them would have understood it in their different ways.

---

[69] Burchard, *Decretum* xix.6, 977–8.
[70] Bamberg, Staatsbibliothek, Cod. Lit. 54, fo. 93r.
[71] Mansfield, *Humiliation*, 173; Vogel, 'Pénitence publique', 139.
[72] Ibid.

Reconciliation of penitents on Maundy Thursday

Maundy Thursday was the traditional day for the reconciliation of penitents from at least the fifth century.[73] The earliest sacramentary, the eighth-century Gelasian, included a rite for the public reconciliation of a penitent who had been excluded from the church for the whole of Lent, but the first elaborate ritual for the readmittance of penitents into the church is not recorded until the late ninth century in the 'Poitiers' pontifical.[74] The Romano-German pontifical's rite is more straightforward than that for Ash Wednesday, but like that it is part of the annual liturgy, sandwiched between the blessing of the fire and the consecration of the chrism on Maundy Thursday. Table 2 summarises its main elements.

Table 2
The reconciliation of penitents on Maundy Thursday

PRG xcix.224–51, ii. 59–67

1. The presentation of the penitents.
   Penitents brought into the atrium of the church (no. 224).
   Archdeacon requests that the bishop look favourably on the penitents (no. 225).
   The bishop acknowledges his own sinfulness (no. 226).
   Archdeacon petitions the restoration of the penitents (no. 227).
   The penitents are called and approach the bishop (no. 228).
   The penitents are handed to the bishop (no. 229).

2. The reconciliation of the penitents.
   The bishop prostrates himself with the penitents during the recitation of the litany followed by *preces* (no. 229).
   The bishop intercedes on behalf of the penitents (nos 230–45).
   The absolution of the penitents (nos 246–50).
   Penitents are sprinkled with holy water and stand up (no. 251).

The service begins after the diocesan synod at the third hour, 9 a.m., when all (the clergy) come to the church in which the chrism is to be consecrated; the penitents are brought from the place where they have done penance so that they can be presented to the bosom of the Church.[75] Poschmann argued that this rubric, found in the Gelasian sacramentary onwards, suggested that public penance was principally performed by criminals, who were incarcerated for the duration of Lent in order to do penance, and then brought forth to be reconciled.[76] But his interpretation may be overstrict; not only the Romano-German Ash Wednesday *ordo* but also that for secret penance make no provision for the reconciliation of penitents before Maundy Thursday

---

[73] Ibid. 143.
[74] Jungmann, *Bussriten*, 78–83.
[75] PRG xcix.223–4, ii. 59.
[76] Poschmann, *Abendländische Kirchenbusse*, 118ff., and *Penance*, 137.

except in exceptional circumstances. The Romano-German *ordo* must, therefore, cover the reconciliation of all, not just public, penitents. The rubric also establishes that it was a public service at which the penitents were restored to communion with the Church. The action began outside the church: with the bishop seated before the doors of the church the penitent is brought into the yard (*atrium*) of the church.[77] Although the *ordo* never mentions an audience, the location of this service outside the church suggests the presence of spectators; it was held in a very public space.

The archdeacon requests the bishop to acknowledge the penitents' penance and sorrow, and to cure them in a petition beginning 'Adest o venerabilis pontifex', which presents the reconciliation of the penitents as a second baptism, referring to the occasion as the destruction of death and the beginning of eternal life, to being washed by water, that is the cleansing waters of baptism, and by tears, the cleansing properties of contrition.[78] Thus the service is linked to the blessing of the chrism which follows it, for chrism is used in both baptism and the reconciliation of the dying. Just as Christ through His death gave humanity a second chance for salvation, so penance allows Christians who have sinned a second chance.

The bishop responds by prostrating himself, acknowledging his own sinfulness and requesting that the Lord restore to him the joy of His salvation and strengthen him with the spirit.[79] Early on, therefore, the bishop acknowledges that he, like the penitent, is mortal, and prostrates himself before God. He acts as a mediator between the penitents and God, petitioning Him on their behalf, and, as Christ's minister on earth, is the agent for their reconciliation. Thus in the visual, behavioural language of the *ordo* the theological basis for the service is spelled out. This expression is made explicit in the next prayer in which the archdeacon petitions the bishop as God's minister to restore the penitent to God through the grace of divine reconciliation.[80]

The liturgical drama increases as the penitents approach the bishop in a formalised three-stage way, genuflecting whilst the bishop calls them to come in, 'venite'; after the third time, the penitents together with the deacon, who has acted as intermediary between the bishop and the penitents, move rapidly to the bishop's feet and prostrate themselves.[81] After this, whilst Psalm xxxiii is being sung, the penitents, still prostrate, are handed by the 'plebesani' to the archdeacon and from him to the bishop. Once they have touched or reached the bishop they are theoretically restored to the

---

[77] 'Tunc egreditur penitens de loco ubi penitentiam gessit, ut gremio presentetur ecclesiae. Sedente autem pontifice pro foribus ecclesiae, penitentibus in atrio ecclesiae eminus cum archidiacono iussum illius prestolantibus, antequam eos offerat, postulat archidiaconus his verbis': PRG xcix.224, ii. 59. For definition of *atrium* see Du Cange, *Glossarium mediae*, i. 465–6; Niermeyer, *Mediae latinitatis*, 67.
[78] PRG xcix.225, ii. 59–60.
[79] Ibid. no. 226, ii. 60.
[80] Ibid. no. 227.
[81] Ibid. no. 228, ii. 60–1.

Church.[82] This ceremony, in which the restoration of the penitents to the community is visually played out before the congregation, through the bishop calling the penitents into the church, and then through touching them with his hand, has been seen as the only major change which the compilers of the Romano-German pontifical introduced into the Maundy Thursday rite.[83]

The bishop chants an antiphon which again refers to penance as a chance to cleanse the heart of sin, and renew the spirit.[84] He then prostrates himself with the penitents whilst the clergy perform the litany followed by *preces*.[85] Thus, whilst the bishop is the only one with authority to reconcile the penitents, he again acknowledges the source of his authority, and implicitly acknowledges his equality with the penitents, now cleansed of sin, before God. Once the penitents are restored to the Church, the bishop chooses an intercessory prayer from the sixteen alternatives included in the fullest text of the Romano-German pontifical;[86] copiers often chose to omit some of these, presumably because they wished to reduce the list to more manageable proportions.[87]

There then follow the absolution prayers; some are intended for several penitents, some for only a single penitent.[88] They are all in the deprecative, not indicative; the bishop has not yet taken on personal responsibility for the absolution of penitents. But the *ordo* does not end with these prayers of absolution. Instead the *ordo* ends with a dramatic process. The bishop sprinkles the penitents with water, censes them, and commands them, 'rise up, you who are asleep, rise from the dead and Christ will give you light'.[89] The peni-

---

[82] 'Semper manuatim penitentes a plebesanis archidiacono, et ab archidiaconco redduntur episcopo, et ab episcopo restituuntur ecclesiae gremio': ibid. no. 229. Whilst the text in the Romano-German pontifical is slightly unclear, a twelfth-century copy from Augsburg suggests how it was interpreted by that period: 'manuatim paenitentes reddantur a plebe archidiacono et ab archidiacono ad manum episcopi et episcopus restituat eos gremio aecclesiae': Munich, Bayerische Staatsbibliothek, Clm 3909, fo. 200r.
[83] This ceremony is first recorded in the 'Poitiers' pontifical from the late ninth century but was popularised in the late tenth and eleventh centuries by the Romano-German pontifical: Jungmann, *Bussriten*, 100–9; Poschmann, *Penance*, 137–8; Vogel, 'Pénitence publique', 143–4; Mansfield, *Humiliation*, 173.
[84] PRG xcix.229, ii. 61.
[85] Ibid.
[86] Ibid. nos 230–45, ii. 61–5.
[87] Bamberg, Staatsbibliothek, Cod. Lit. 50, from Bamberg, and Bamberg, Cod. Lit. 54, from Hildesheim, omit nos 243–4; BL, MS Cotton Tiberius C. i omits nos 243, 248; Munich, Bayerische Staatsbibliothek, Clm 3909 (s. xii), from Augsburg, omits nos 232, 238, 240 and 243–7; Munich, Clm 6425 (s. xi^1), fos 73v–80v, from Freising, includes nos 222–9, 230, 238, 240, 245, 246, 248, 251, as well as two additional prayers not in the Romano-German pontifical; Paris, BN, MS lat. 1231, fos 136r–42v, from Regensburg, omits nos 232, 235, 241, 243–4, 248–50.
[88] 'Absolutio pluralis': PRG xcix.246–7, ii. 65; 'Absolutio singularis', ibid. nos 248–50, ii. 66.
[89] 'Hic aspergat eos aqua benedicta et turificet et postea dicat: Exurge qui dormis, exurge a mortuis et illuminabit te Christus. Post haec surgant penitentes et moneantur ab episcopo, ut quod paenitendo diluerunt iterando non revocent': ibid. no. 251, ii. 67.

tents who have been prostrate all this time then get up; they are restored both to the promise of eternal life and to the community of the Church. In the Middle Ages prostration was seen as essentially debasing and almost sub-human; by standing up the penitents are shown to have been restored to their status as human beings, as well as members of the Church.

A study of sixteen manuscripts of the Romano-German pontifical shows that, as with the *ordo* for Ash Wednesday, there was greater variety amongst copyists than the editors of the Romano-German pontifical suggest. When it comes to the absolution of the penitents one pontifical, copied in Hildesheim in 1067, makes several significant changes to the Romano-German *ordo*. First, a text given in the edition of the Romano-German pontifical as 'absolutio pluralis', is described as a blessing to be said over the prostrate penitents, 'benedictio super penitentes ad hunc prostratos'.[90] This is followed by a prayer described in the Romano-German pontifical as 'absolutio singularis' and in the Hildesheim codex as 'absolutio paenitentis', for which an alternative, as in the Romano-German pontifical, is given.[91] These two prayers are followed by a prayer which is not in the Romano-German pontifical, and which is described as 'absolutio generalis'. This prayer is particularly interesting because unlike the absolution prayers in the edited text of the Romano-German pontifical it is written in the first person plural indicative and not the subjunctive or optative: 'Nos etiam secundum auctoritatem nobis indignis adeo commissam absoluimus uos uinculo delictorum uestrorum ut mereamini habere uitam aeternam. Per.'[92] This is therefore evidence for the use of the indicative absolution in northern Germany by the mid eleventh century. This prayer is followed by two alternatives, found in the Romano-German pontifical under the rubric 'absolutio singularis', and then the sprinkling of the penitents with holy water. The modifications made by the scribe of the Hildesheim codex may help us to understand the Romano-German text more fully. Rather than seeing the absolution prayers as alternatives, for either several or a single penitent, we may perhaps see them as part of a progressive sequence. First the bishop blesses all the penitents, then he absolves a single penitent, then he absolves all who are present, thus incorporating the audience and other penitents into the rite.

The *ordo* is thus a dramatic visualisation of the theological ideas underlying it. The penitents have been cast out. They supplicate the bishop, who in turn supplicates God, for mercy. They are absolved, which is symbolised by their being sprinkled with water and incense. Then they are allowed to get up and be restored to the community.

---

[90] Bamberg, Staatsbibliothek, Cod. Lit. 54, fo. 9v. The prayer in question is *PRG* xcix.246, ii. 65.
[91] Bamberg, Staatsbibliothek, Cod. Lit. 54, fo. 10r. The prayers in question are *PRG* xcix.248 followed by no. 247, ii. 65–6.
[92] Bamberg, Staatsbibliothek, Cod. Lit. 54, fo. 10v.

Penance 'in the usual way'

This *ordo* appears in the Romano-German pontifical under the rubric 'Qualiter sacerdotes suscipere debeant poenitentes more solito [how priests ought to receive penitents in the usual way]'.[93] It is not part of the annual liturgy, but rather one of a series of *ordines* associated with life processes and administered in response to the needs of individual Christians: it is preceded by those for baptism, exorcism and various blessings and succeeded by those for the sick and the dying.[94] A similar cluster is found at the end of the contemporary Fulda sacramentary.[95] Although the title refers to plural priests and penitents, the prayers and rubrics within the *ordo* refer only to a singular penitent; like the other rites with which it is associated, this *ordo* was intended for individuals in need.

The rubric does not make explicit where the rite is to be performed. The only indication is the initial rubric which states that the priest should try and withdraw to a different place from the penitent, a *cubiculum*, in order to say the preparation prayer, and if he is unable to do so, he should say it secretly.[96] But the words of the rubric echo those of Matthew vi.6: 'But thou, when thou prayest, enter into thy closet [cubiculum], and when thou hast shut thy door, pray to thy Father which is in secret; and thy Father which seeth in secret shall reward thee openly.'[97] Was this description meant just to inform the priest of where he should prepare before giving penance, or were the resonances of Matthew vi.6 meant to be reawakened in his mind, reminding the priest of his connection to God through prayer? Whatever the case, it is one of the few hints we have of where penance should take place; the contemporary *ordo* in the Fulda sacramentary contains no indications as to place. Other, eleventh-century Italian evidence suggests that similar rites for secret penance took place in church. Peter Damian described how he heard the confession of the Empress Agnes 'under the *confessio* of St. Peter, before the holy altar'.[98] The evidence of eleventh-century Italian *ordines* which suggests

---

[93] PRG cxxxvi, ii. 234–45.
[94] Ibid. cvii–cxxxv, cxxxviii–clxx, ii. 155–233, 245–330.
[95] See ch. 5.
[96] 'Cum aliquis venerit ad sacerdotem confiteri peccata sua, mandat ei sacerdos, ut expectet modicum, donec intret in cubiculum adorare. Si autem non habuerit cubiculum, prius in secreto cordis sui dicat hanc orationem': PRG cxxxvi.1, ii. 234. This rubric is found in other rites for secret penance, for example 'Cum ergo venerit aliquis ad sacerdotem confiteri peccata sua, mandet ei sacerdos ut exspectet modicum donec intret Ecclesiam, aut in cubiculum suum ad orationem': Burchard, *Decretum* xix.2, 950. See also Halitgar, *Paenitentiale*, praef. and discussion of this rubric in Kottje, 'Busspraxis', 390.
[97] 'Tu autem, cum oraveris, intra in cubiculum tuum, et clauso ostio, ora Patrem tuam in abscondito: et Pater tuus qui videt in abscondito, reddet tibi': Matthew vi.6.
[98] 'Sed ut hii, qui ad apostolorum limina confluunt, sancta devocionis tuae salubriter imitentur exemplum, sub archana quoque beati Petri confessione ante sacrum altare me sedere fecisti, ac per lugubres gemitus et amara suspiria ab ipsa quinquennis infanciae tenera adhuc et nuper ablactata levitate coepisti': *Die Briefe des Petrus Damiani*, ep. civ, 141–58 at p.

Table 3
Penance in the usual way

('Qualiter sacerdotes suscipere debeant poenitentes more solito')

PRG, *ordo* cxxxvi, ii. 234–45

1. Priest's preparation prayer in secret (nos 1–3).
2. The priest's reception of the penitent.
   Reception prayer: 'Deus qui confitentium tibi corda purificas' (no. 4).
3. The priest's interrogation of the penitent.
   Interrogation on the articles of faith and affirmation that the penitent wishes his sins to be forgiven (no. 5).
   Assesses penitent's willingness and suitability for confession and penitential psalm xxxvii (nos 6–9).
   Priest's prayers for God's intercession alternated with penitential psalms (cii and l) (nos 10–12).
   Interrogation and confession of sins: list of questions with appropriate tariffs (no. 13).
4. Priest's instruction about the penitent's future behaviour.
   Advice on future conduct in accordance with rank (no. 14).
   Interrogation about minor sins (no. 15).
5. Priest's imposition of penance taking into account personal disposition and status (nos 16–18).
6. Priest's intercession.
   Penitent's formal affirmation of his confession of sins and confession of his sins in the vernacular (nos 19–23), followed by the recitation of *preces* and intercessory prayer by penitent (nos 24–5).
   Priest's intercessory prayers (nos 26–38).
   Mass (*Missa post confessionem*) (*ordo* cxxxvii, PRG ii. 245).

secret penance was often heard in church before other people will be considered in chapter 5. The fact that the priest is told to withdraw somewhere he can recite a secret prayer may suggest that the rite itself was performed in public but the evidence is unclear.

The *ordo* may thus be divided into six stages (summarised in table 3).[99] After preparation the priest receives the penitent; the rite contains two alternative prayers, one to be said on behalf of several penitents, 'pro famulis famulabusque', and one on behalf of a singular penitent, 'pro famulo tuo N. qui ad penitentiam venit'.[100] At the beginning, therefore, there is confirmation that the rite may be administered to more than one penitent at a time, and that the penitents may be of either sex. The rubrics and texts which follow, however, refer to only a singular penitent. Either the subsequent rite was administered to penitents individually, or, as in an eleventh-century

---

151; F. J. Fazzalaro, *The place for the hearing of confessions: a historical synopsis and a commentary*, Washington, DC 1950, 3.
[99] This division adapts that put forward by Forshaw, 'The pastoral ministry of the priest-confessor', 300–32.
[100] PRG cxxxvi.2–3, ii. 234–5.

Italian rite, administered to penitents in turn as part of a collective service.[101] There is not sufficient evidence in the Romano-German pontifical to reach any conclusion as to which, if either, practice was the case.

The priest then receives the penitent and says the prayer 'Deus qui confitentium tibi corda purificas' over him (suggesting that the penitent is kneeling or prostrate before the priest).[102] This prayer again refers to plural penitents, suggesting a partially communal service; a version of it is also used in the reconciliation *ordo* for Maundy Thursday, demonstrating how the different *ordines* drew upon a common pool of eighth- and ninth-century penitential prayers.[103]

The priest then begins his interrogation of the penitent by questioning him on the articles of faith, his willingness to confess and do penance, and whether he meets the eligibility criteria for penance.[104] The first aim is to make sure the penitent is in a suitable state of mind to do penance and profit from it; he is reminded, for example, that penance is not efficacious if one is still angry, and that he cannot receive penance until he has restored the profits of his crime.[105] The priest must also check that he is not a fugitive; if he is, the priest, following canon law, is not allowed to give penance as he trespasses on others' authority.[106] If he is incestuous, he cannot receive penance until he gives up this relationship.[107] The priest then recites three intercessory prayers interspersed by two penitential psalms, Psalm cii and Psalm l.[108] Whilst two of these refer to a singular penitent, one is a more general petition that God may 'heal the wounds of all so that just as none of us is free from fault so none should be a stranger to pardon'.[109] The priest should then make the penitent confess all his sins following a detailed interrogation.[110] This uses the same format as the interrogations found in penitentials, or that given in the *ordo* at the start of book xix of Burchard's *Decretum*: each sin is followed by the appropriate penance.[111] The interrogation covers a wide range of sins, from murder to perjury, adultery to sodomy, abortion and rape, failure to fast in Lent, drinking liquid in which a mouse or weasel has been found, and negligence of the Host. There is nothing very new about any of these sins; they are found in the earlier penitentials. But their

---

101 This rite is considered in ch. 5.
102 'Cum autem accesserit ad te, dic super eum hanc orationem': PRG cxxxvi.4, ii. 235.
103 Ibid. xcix.242, ii. 63.
104 Ibid. cxxxvi.5–9, ii. 235–6.
105 Ibid. no. 6, ii. 235.
106 'Interroga si fugitivus sit. Et, si est, ammone illum quia non licet ei poenitentiam agere': ibid. no. 8, ii. 236. Cf. Burchard, *Decretum* xix.62, 998: 'Ut nullus episcopus seu presbyter alterius poenitentem sine litteris sui episcopi suscipiat'.
107 PRG cxxxvi.9, ii. 236.
108 Ibid. nos 10–12, ii. 236–7.
109 'Cunctorum medere vulneribus, ut, sicut nemo nostrum liber est a culpa, ita nemo sit alienus a venia': ibid. no. 11, ii. 236.
110 Ibid. no. 13, ii. 237–40.
111 Burchard, *Decretum* xix.5, 951–76.

range suggests that this rite was intended to be universal, administered to both men and women, laity and clergy.

After this *interrogatio* the priest instructs the penitent as to his future behaviour. First he establishes the penitent's rank. The examples given are all lay offices: *comes, castaldius, ministerialis, negociator, massarius, monetarius, escarius*.[112] The priest then advises him on his future conduct, for example if he is a judge, he should not accept bribes; if he is married, he should not sleep with his wife on feast days, nor in Lent; in all cases he should pay the tithe. If the penitent is in religious orders, he or she should keep his or her vows. This *ordo* demonstrates its concern with pastoral care, being focused on the individuals and their future behaviour in a way which is missing from the Romano-German Ash Wednesday *ordo* for entry into penance. Their underlying aims are different: the Ash Wednesday *ordo* is conceived as a communal service which highlights the gravity of the penitents' sin, culminating in their expulsion from the Church, whilst this *ordo* seems to be conceived as a personal service to ensure the penitent's future salvation. The distinction between personal and communal, rather than between public and private, seems to underlie the difference between these two *ordines*. The priest then interrogates the penitent as to his minor sins, for example blasphemy and somnolence. This list carries monastic overtones which probably betray its origins in the conventual environment of St Alban's monastery, Mainz; for example, if the penitent has eaten before the hour, he should confess his sin.[113] If the penitent admits to any of these sins, he should be examined further, and if he is willing to amend, be given penance.[114] This section appears to belong with the *interrogatio* of the penitent; its place in the *ordo* reinforces the over-riding pastoral aim of 'secret' penance. Interrogation and advice are inextricably entwined.

Only after advising the penitent on his future behaviour does the priest award an appropriate penance, taking into account the penitent's circumstances. This may take the form of fasting, alms, prayer or genuflection through the day and night.[115] But before he imposes the penance, he ought to instruct the penitent on the ideas underlying penance: God is merciful and will forgive sin as long as the penitent changes his behaviour. Just as water washes everything away, so penance purges all sin, so that the penitent may be saved from the devil and the fires of hell, and enter into paradise.[116] Unlike the public rite for Ash Wednesday, the theological ideas underlying penance in this rite are communicated verbally rather than visually, confirming that it was intended as a personal, rather than a communal rite.

---

[112] PRG cxxxvi.14, ii. 240. The terminology used for these ranks, for example 'castaldius', seems to suggest an Italian origin in the office of *gastaldius* for this particular rubric.
[113] 'Si ante horam manducat', ibid. no. 15.
[114] Ibid. nos 15–16, ii. 240–1.
[115] Ibid. no. 17.
[116] Ibid. no. 18.

Such a distinction need not preclude the *ordo* from being administered to more than one penitent at once, but it suggests that it was not intended to be performed before a large audience as a public spectacle.

Finally the penitent makes a formal confession of his sins and the priest then intercedes with God on his behalf.[117] This *ordo* does not include a process for the reconciliation of the penitent; all penitents were reconciled on Maundy Thursday. The priest should first make sure that the penitent understands that by making a true confession God will remit his sins before formally awarding his penance. The penitent then confesses his sins in the vernacular: 'Deinde fiat confessio peccatorum rusticis verbis.'[118] The inclusion of a provision for confession in the vernacular suggests a high level of concern with pastoral care. By allowing the penitent to make his confession in his own everyday language, the authors of the *ordo* ensured that the penitent would have understood much of the proceedings, and have been aware of how he had sinned. Presumably most of the priest's interrogation and advice was also given in the vernacular although this is not made explicit in the text.[119] The penitent's confession is followed by several intercessory *preces* identical to those used in the other penitential *ordines* in the Romano-German pontifical, a direct intercessory prayer by the penitent himself addressed to the Lord, followed by one by the priest.[120] The penitent then prostrates himself at the priest's feet, and petitions him for judgement. The priest receives him, recites Psalm xii and then admonishes him with a suitable passage from Holy Scripture, and concludes with an intercessory prayer taken from a set of ten alternatives.[121] As with other prayers in the *ordo*, some of these can be found within the other penitential *ordines* in the Romano-German pontifical and most derive from a common ninth-century tradition. There is no indication that the penitent should get up from his prostrate position, just as there is no indication that the priest's petition has been answered; the penitent must wait until Maundy Thursday for his answer for this rite does not include an absolution prayer.

There then follows a mass which is identical to that in the Ash Wednesday *ordo*.[122] An early twelfth-century German manuscript omits this mass and instead includes the subsequent mass which in the Romano-German pontifical's edition is intended for the sick.[123] This may reflect the relative fluidity of

---

[117] Ibid. nos 19–23, ii. 241–2.
[118] Ibid. no. 23. For discussion of a similar provision in the Fulda sacramentary see ch. 5.
[119] The alternative to a vernacular confession would have been a formal confession prayer in Latin, such as that in the Fulda sacramentary, SF, no. 437 (2376), p. 282, discussed in ch. 5.
[120] PRG cxxxvi.24–6, ii. 242–3.
[121] Ibid. nos 27–38, ii. 243–5.
[122] Ibid. cxxxvii, ii. 245.
[123] Wolfenbüttel, Herzog-August-Bibliothek, Cod. Guelf. 493 Helmstadt, fos 238v–9r.

texts, and perhaps also that this *ordo* was intended for the sick, as its context in the Romano-German pontifical might also suggest; or the omission may be due to scribal error. The mass seems to be the conclusion to the rite. If this is the case, it suggests that the rite was, indeed, conducted in church. However, the mass is omitted from at least one early eleventh-century German manuscript, Bamberg, Staatsbibliothek, Cod. Lit. 53, where it is followed instead by the 'ordo ad visitandum infirmum'.[124] This would suggest that the mass was not regarded as fundamental to the rite.

Elaborate *ordines* are, for the most part, a product of the tenth century; it is therefore at least possible that this *ordo* for penance 'in the usual way' is a copy of an earlier, more primitive *ordo* than those for Ash Wednesday and Maundy Thursday, which is why it contains many fewer instructions about posture. But the concentration on verbal and vernacular communication, at the expense of non-verbal communication through changes in posture, suggests that the rite is primarily concerned with establishing a personal relationship between the priest and the penitent, in which the priest can offer pastoral advice to the penitent. It thus appears a much more personal and pastoral rite than those for Ash Wednesday and Maundy Thursday.

As these three *ordines* demonstrate, a clear distinction between public and private penance cannot be sustained. The three share several similarities: they all take place in and around the church; they may all be administered to more than one penitent; there is a high degree of overlap in their prayers. The *ordines* for entry into penance on Ash Wednesday and for penance 'in the usual way' share a common process – hearing the penitent's confession, awarding an appropriate penance and requesting God's mercy – and postpone reconciliation until Maundy Thursday. Rather than either rite being reserved for specific categories of sin, the *ordines* for Ash Wednesday and penance 'in the usual way' are both intended for serious sins – they apparently reflect the Carolingian dichotomy: public penance for public sins, private penance for private sins.[125] Nevertheless, the parallels between these different rites, and the absence of evidence for the compilers of the mid tenth-century Romano-German pontifical using private and public to distinguish between these two forms of penance, means we should rethink this terminology. 'Personal' and 'communal' seem to describe this distinction more accurately than public and private: the Ash Wednesday and Maundy Thursday services are communal services intended to involve the whole community in witnessing

---

The text parallels that included in the Romano-German pontifical under the heading 'Ordo cxxxviii: *missa pro infirmo de cuius salute desperatur*': *PRG* ii. 245–6.
[124] Fo. 167r.
[125] The latter may be administered to someone guilty of murder: 'Fecisti homicidium, aut casu, aut volens, sive pro vindicta parentum, vel per iussionem domini tui, aut in publico, vel facere voluisti et non fecisti vel servum occidisti? Septem vel quinque aut tres annos aut dies XL peniteas': *PRG* cxxxvi.13, ii. 237.

the shame of and praying for the penitent, whilst the *ordo* for penance 'more solito' is a personal one, primarily concerned with offering pastoral advice to the penitent.[126]

The Romano-German pontifical's users

The rites recorded in the Romano-German pontifical are, of course, an idealised representation of the penitential interface between cleric and penitent. As the Romano-German pontifical has been described as combining a practical with a didactic function, acting as a reference book of instruction for the clergy through the inclusion of juridico- and theologico-liturgical texts, it is important to examine the manuscript evidence for how the Romano-German pontifical was used and by whom; a reference text is less valuable as evidence of penitential ritual practice.[127]

The penitential texts recorded in the Romano-German pontifical were not uniformly adopted throughout the *Reich*. The eleventh-century pontifical written for Bishop Egilbert of Freising omits any form of penitential rite for Ash Wednesday, but the text for the blessing of the ashes on that day is followed by several descriptions of penance which were probably taken from Burchard's *Decretum*, including Burchard's description of public penance, pastoral instructions for the penitent's future conduct, and the remedies for sin, taken from Burchard and one of the penitentials attributed to Bede, and an *ordo* for penance 'in the usual way' which is also taken from Burchard.[128] The codex does not contain an alternative *ordo* for the giving of penance on Ash Wednesday or 'more solito', although it does include an *ordo* for the reconciliation of penitents on Maundy Thursday found in the Romano-German pontifical. These changes to the text of the Romano-German pontifical suggest that the copyist, or perhaps Bishop Egilbert himself, found the Romano-German pontifical's text unsatisfactory. This exchange between canon law and liturgical texts is not, however, proof that the Freising pontifical was intended for use as a didactic rather than as a liturgical text, as is more obviously the case with the twelfth-century pontifical from Augsburg (Munich, Bayerische Staatsbibliothek, Clm 3909) which contains on fos 1r–89r, in the same script as the following pontifical, a collection of canon law texts which are concerned with different aspects of the liturgy, including a copy of the *ordo* given in book vi of Halitgar's penitential.[129] The Freising

---

[126] For a similar distinction between the social and devotional in prayer and worship, and the overlap often found between the two see J. Bossy, 'Christian life in the late Middle Ages: prayers', *TRHS* 6th ser. i (1991), 137–50.
[127] Vogel, *Medieval liturgy*, 230.
[128] Munich, Bayerische Staatsbibliothek, Clm 6425, fos 14v–32r. The text is edited in OR v. 367–81; cf. Burchard, *Decretum* xix.2–7, 26, 949–78, 984; *Excerptum Bedae*, preface.
[129] 'Incipit liber poenitentialis ex scrinio romanae aecclesiae assumptus quomodo

codex is more complicated, because the canon law texts are included in the place of the Romano-German liturgical texts, as part of a sequence for the liturgical year, suggesting that it was intended as a guide to liturgical practice, although not a straight liturgical book. But the Romano-German pontifical's text was deemed unsatisfactory in some way, perhaps because it did not accord with local practice – Freising was in the province of Salzburg rather than Mainz, the home of the Romano-German pontifical – although the textual confusions of the Ash Wednesday *ordo* may also have contributed to its omission.

Theoretically the Romano-German pontifical was intended only for episcopal use as it contains texts for processes which are an episcopal prerogative, including not only public penance but also ordination. But whilst around twenty manuscripts have a cathedral provenance, suggesting episcopal use,[130] the Romano-German pontifical was also copied for monastic use.[131] Thus the monks of St Alban, Mainz, not only composed the Romano-German pontifical for export to various episcopal sees, but also, c. 1050, made a copy for their own use, now Vienna, Nationalbibliothek, Cod. lat. 701. It was not merely a library copy, to be used as a model for episcopal clients, for it includes a notice of the consecration of an oratory to St Alban in 1070, and in the litany the only name to be written in capitals is that of St Alban, the abbey's patron,[132] suggesting that this codex was intended for liturgical use within the abbey. Cambridge, Corpus Christi College, MS 163 was probably intended for use in a nunnery because it includes all the *ordines* for the consecration of women but ignores those for men.[133] Presumably it was kept in the convent but brought out when the bishop visited the nunnery to consecrate new members; it may only have been used on such occasions, for 'the manuscript gives scarcely a hint of use'.[134]

But there is evidence from the penitential *ordines* of how these apparently episcopal texts were adapted for use within a monastery. Otto, bishop of Bamberg (1102–39), commissioned one copy of the Romano-German pontifical for the nearby monastery of Michelsberg, now Bamberg, Staats-

---

paenitentes sint suscipiendi iudicandi sive reconciliandi': Munich, Clm 3909, fos 75v–89v. This manuscript is dated c. 1138–43: Kottje, *Bussbücher*, 39–40.

[130] See appendix 1.

[131] Monasteries were the usual source of liturgical books. See, for example, the sacramentaries produced by St Amand in the late ninth century: R. McKitterick, 'Manuscripts and scriptoria in the reign of Charles the Bald, 840–877', in *Giovanni Scoto nel suo tempo: l'organizzazione del sapere in eta Carolingia: atti del XXIV convegno storio internazionale: Accademia Tudertina*, Spoleto 1989, 201–34. See also the sacramentaries produced by Fulda in the late tenth century on which see ch. 5.

[132] OR i. 373–88.

[133] M. Lapidge, 'The origin of CCCC 163', *Transactions of the Cambridge Bibliographical Society* viii (1981), 18–28 at p. 23.

[134] D. Dumville, *Liturgy and the ecclesiastical history of late Anglo-Saxon England: four studies*, Woodbridge 1992, 73.

bibliothek, Cod. Lit. 55;[135] instead of the bishop, the abbot officiates over the blessing of the ashes on Ash Wednesday and their imposition on the brothers.[136] It thus provides liturgical evidence which seems to confirm the reality of the practices prescribed in the English *Regularis concordia* (c. 970), written some one hundred and fifty years earlier, but which, as we saw in chapter 3, was considerably indebted to continental monasticism. Another early twelfth-century manuscript, with a provenance of the monastery of St Michael's, Luneburg, in the north German diocese of Verden, includes in a slightly later hand a marginal addition to the reconciliation *ordo* for Maundy Thursday.[137] The margins have been cropped, making it difficult to reconstruct the text, but it appears to suggest that on Maundy Thursday the lord abbot should begin the seven penitential psalms as he enters the church with the priests. He should then say a Pater Noster. Then the abbot should put on his *stola*, speak with the brothers and say certain prayers which are marked in the main text by a sign in the margin, and which correspond to numbers 230, 231, 233, 234, 237, 242 and 245 in the edited text of the Romano-German pontifical.[138] The absolution prayers are not so marked, but one has been amended from the singular in the Romano-German pontifical's edited text to the plural in this copy.[139] By the beginning of the twelfth century some form of communal reconciliation after the communal penance of Lent had become the norm for this monastic community. Further research is required into many more monastic manuscripts before we can know whether this evidence for monastic adaptation of penitential rites in the early twelfth century is specific to this period, or whether, as seems probable, it is merely the first concrete evidence of practices only hinted at in earlier texts. These rites show, as was suggested in chapter 3, that penitential practices could be, and were, adapted by monastic communities for use amongst themselves. The penitential practices of the secular world penetrated the monastic one, and influenced life within these communities. But it was the monks of St Alban who composed the Romano-German pontifical: it was a two-way relationship. The Romano-German pontifical was thus not just an episcopal book but had a much wider ownership including monks, nuns and canons.[140] However,

---

[135] This tradition goes back to a note in a fourteenth-century hand on fo. 114v of the volume: OR i. 73.
[136] 'Deinde domnus abbas . . . cineres ita benedicit. . . . imponit cineres fratribus': fo. 82v.
[137] Wolfenbüttel, Herzog-August-Bibliothek, Cod. Guelf 141 Helmstadt, described in OR i. 419–29.
[138] Ibid. fo. 21r.
[139] Ibid. fo. 23r. This is equivalent to *ordo* xcix.250, PRG, ii. 66. This prayer is also recorded in the plural in Bamberg, Staatsbibliothek, Cod. Lit. 50, fo. 123v, and BL, MS Cotton Tiberius C. i, fo. 169v, which also have a monastic provenance (see appendix 1). But we should take into account the fact that the London manuscript was used by Sherborne which was both a bishopric and a monastery; we cannot always distinguish between these two types of institution.
[140] Vitry-le-François, Bibliothèque municipale, MS 36 is attributed to a house of canons regular.

it was an expensive and lengthy text, written by and for the higher cathedral and monastic clergy; it therefore provides no evidence of penance as it was administered by the lower clergy. This is an issue I shall return to in chapter 5.

The manuscript dissemination of the Romano-German pontifical

Although the Romano-German pontifical only provides evidence for the penitential liturgy administered by the higher clergy, this raises the question of whether it was used throughout Germany and Italy or only in particular provinces. The Romano-German pontifical was undoubtedly a best-seller; it survives in thirty-five manuscripts (of which twenty-nine are from the eleventh century) and four main recensions, and was copied not only in Germany, but also in Italy, northern France and England. But the detailed analysis of surviving manuscripts in appendix 1 presents a rather more complex picture.

As one would expect for a text produced in Mainz, the majority of manuscripts were written in Germany: twenty-five out of thirty-eight, of which sixteen were copied in the eleventh century.[141] Thus Michel Andrieu and Cyrille Vogel both argued that the Romano-German pontifical was produced by a team of editors at the behest of the imperial chancellor, Archbishop William of Mainz, and his father, the Emperor Otto I, in order to promote a single unified liturgy throughout the Ottonian *Reich*.[142] Vogel also argued that it exists in four recensions because of the speed of the redaction, generated by high demand.[143] But a closer examination of the surviving manuscripts suggests that the circulation of the Romano-German pontifical was more limited within Germany. The majority of the manuscripts (twenty-one out of twenty-five) come from the provinces of Mainz and Salzburg, none from that of Trier and only two (possibly) from Cologne. Of these the majority (fourteen) come from the province of Mainz. Yet other pontificals from other traditions have survived from both Trier and Cologne. Moreover, Archbishop Egbert of Trier (977–93) was a great patron of book production, especially for his own see.[144] It therefore looks as if the provinces of Cologne and more especially Trier resisted the adoption of the Romano-German pontifical whilst it was most successful in its home province of Mainz.

The answer to why the Romano-German pontifical was not more popular in the western provinces of the *Reich* may lie in the history of the

---

[141] See appendix 1, table 1.
[142] OR i. 507–9; C. Vogel, 'Le Pontifical romano-germanique du Xe siècle: nature, date et importance du document', *Cahiers de civilisation médiévale* vi (1963), 27–48, and *Medieval liturgy*, 235–6.
[143] PRG iii.29.
[144] *Egbert: Erzbischoff von Trier*, ed. R. J. Ronig, Trier 1993; Hoffmann, *Buchkunst*; H. Mayr-Harting, *Ottonian book illumination: an historical study*, London 1991, ii. 60–83.

tenth-century Ottonian Church. The primacy of the archbishop of Mainz was far from assured in the mid to late tenth century; the archbishops of Mainz, Cologne and Trier, in particular, and of Salzburg and Magdeburg to a lesser extent, were in dispute about who took precedence at councils and at coronations, and who acted as arch-chaplain. The archbishops of Trier were especially forthright in their claims c. 950–75, the period in which the Romano-German pontifical was composed and promoted.[145] Others also exploited Mainz's weakness: in 968 Magdeburg was given metropolitan status, making it independent of Mainz.[146] But Mainz's fortunes revived when Willigis became archbishop of Mainz in 975, and Trier's dwindled. In 977 Willigis obtained a personal privilege from Pope Benedict VII confirming his pre-eminence over the German episcopate.[147] It has been suggested that in an effort to revive Trier's fortunes, its archbishop, Egbert (977–93), looked west and not east; in 984–5 he supported Henry of Bavaria who had obtained the support of Lothar V of France by promising to cede Lotharingia to France. The saints of Trier, SS Maternus and Maximus, are also more prevalent in the west than in the east, suggesting that Trier's cultural and liturgical ties lay to the west rather than east of the Rhine.[148] This evidence suggests a political atmosphere in which the Trier episcopate might resist adopting a liturgy which had been produced in Mainz, and was promoted by its arch rival the archbishop of Mainz, hence the lack of manuscript evidence for the Romano-German pontifical there. Rather less is known about Cologne's role in these disputes. The papal privileges of 968 and 981 for the new archbishopric of Magdeburg described it as equal 'in the order of standing and sitting and in the discussion of all ecclesiastical affairs' with the archbishoprics of Mainz, Trier and Cologne.[149] Like Trier, Cologne may have been more resistant to a liturgy which was associated with Mainz. Or it may simply be that Cologne had its own strong liturgical traditions and was therefore in less need of the new pontifical. Such an explanation does not, however, explain why the Romano-German pontifical was reasonably popular in Salzburg. The overall evidence suggests a more complicated and restricted picture for the distribution of the Romano-German pontifical in Germany than that suggested in the work of Andrieu and Vogel.

---

[145] H. H. Anton, *Trier im frühen Mittelalter*, Paderborn–Munich–Vienna–Zurich 1987; Mayr-Harting, *Ottonian book illumination*, ii. 82–3.
[146] Reuter, *Germany*, 163–4.
[147] H. Büttner, 'Die Mainzer Erzbischöfe Friedrich und Wilhelm und das Papsttum des 10. Jahrhunderts', and 'Erzbischof Willigis von Mainz (975–1011)', both in his *Zur frühmittelalterlichen Reichsgeschichte an Rhein, Main und Neckar*, ed. A. Gerlich, Darmstadt 1975, 275–313.
[148] Mayr-Harting, *Ottonian book illumination*, ii. 82–3.
[149] Ibid. ii. 122; Fichtenau, *Living in the tenth century*, 11; H. Beumann, 'Die Bedeutung Lotharingiens für die ottonische Missionspolitik im Osten', in his *Wissenschaft vom Mittelalter: Ausgewählte Aufsätze*, Vienna 1972, 377–409.

We therefore need to revise their picture of Otto I exercising an all-encompassing authority over the Ottonian Church, promoting one liturgy, in the light of the pontifical's very limited circulation within the *Reich*. The research of Andrieu and Vogel is a product of its time: it was conducted c. 1920–60. Work in the past twenty years has produced a less confident view of the emperor's authority over the Ottonian Church, pointing to the limitations to imperial authority when making episcopal appointments, for example.[150] It has also been demonstrated that earlier Carolingian attempts to reform the liturgy did not intend a wholly universal liturgy, suggesting that liturgical diversity was the norm in the early medieval world.[151]

Diversity is again the case when we look at the reception of the Romano-German pontifical into Italy, which again is more complicated than the picture presented by Andrieu and Vogel. Attempts were obviously made to export it to Italy – at least three models lie behind the seven manuscripts copied in Italy which now survive. Quite when the Romano-German pontifical was introduced there is uncertain. Andrieu and Vogel suggested it was introduced to Rome by Otto I and his entourage in 960 but the evidence they adduced for its use in the ordination of Popes Leo VIII and John XIII in 963 and 965 has been undermined recently by Roger Reynold's work on the south Italian liturgy.[152] Reynolds demonstrated that the popes were ordained in accordance with the eighth-century Frankish ordination rite found in south Italian pontificals of the period. Nevertheless the Alessandrina codex, copied in the early eleventh century, possibly in Rome, provides evidence that the Romano-German pontifical was probably known in Rome in the first half of the eleventh century.[153]

However, the earliest concrete evidence that the Romano-German pontifical was known in Italy is Tuscan not Roman. The earliest surviving Italian copy is Lucca, Biblioteca capitolare, Cod. 607 which was copied in Lucca from a Mainz model probably in the early eleventh century.[154] It was in turn the model for a copy made for Lucca's neighbouring diocese of Pistoia.[155] But the Romano-German pontifical was seemingly not very influential in Tuscany; the late eleventh-century pontifical from the nearby diocese of Arezzo represents a different penitential tradition.[156]

---

150 T. Reuter, 'The "imperial church system" of the Ottonian and Salian rulers: a reconsideration', *JEH* xxxiii (1982), 347–74.
151 R. McKitterick, 'Unity and diversity in the Carolingian Church', in Swanson, *Unity and diversity in the Church*, 59–82.
152 OR i. 511–18; PRG iii. 46–51; Vogel, 'Le Pontifical romano-germanique du Xe siècle', 44–5, and *Medieval liturgy*, 237–9; R. E. Reynolds, 'The ritual of clerical ordination of the sacramentarium gelasianum saec. VIII: early evidence from southern Italy', in P. de Clerck and É. Palazzo (eds), *Rituels: mélanges offerts à Pierre-Marie Gy*, Paris 1990, 437–45.
153 Rome, Biblioteca Alessandrina, Cod. 173, described in OR i. 282–7.
154 Reynolds dates the Lucca manuscript to the early eleventh century in 'The ritual of clerical ordination'.
155 Pistoia, Biblioteca capitolare, Cod. 141.
156 Vatican, BAV, MS Vat. lat. 4772, described in P. Salmon, *Les Manuscrits liturgiques latins*

Use of the Romano-German pontifical in southern Italy was similarly restricted to only two codices. A different model to that used in Rome or in Tuscany, belonging to the A recension, lies behind the two copies made at Monte Cassino, the first in the second quarter or middle of the eleventh century, the second somewhat later.[157]

In northern Italy as well only two examples survive, both of which follow a Mainz exemplar; it is unclear whether the texts are related.[158] As in the south, the Romano-German pontifical failed to spawn any further imitations, perhaps because northern Italy had a strong tradition of local liturgies – the Milanese, Ambrosian and Aquileian rites – rendering the area relatively impervious to liturgical imports. But other German liturgical books were imported into northern Italy in this period: the Fulda sacramentary was taken to both Aquileia and Vercelli,[159] a Regensburg sacramentary was given to Verona.[160]

There is evidence of up to five possible German exemplars (now lost) which became the models for seven Italian manuscripts. The Romano-German pontifical was possibly more widely known within Italy: not all the copies may have survived. But its influence was limited: no exemplar led to more than two manuscripts. Despite the Romano-German pontifical's influence on the overall history of the Roman liturgy, its impact on eleventh-century Italian practice was more limited. There is no survey of the total number of Italian pontificals surviving from the tenth and eleventh century, and the problems of comparing different catalogue conventions make it difficult to arrive at even a 'guesstimate', but a preliminary survey suggests that there may be as many as forty-two pontificals, collections of *ordines* and what have been classified as sacramentary-rituals surviving for this period;[161] the seven copies of the Romano-German pontifical surviving

---

de la Bibliothèque Vaticane (SeT ccli, ccliii, cclxi, cclxvii, cclxx, 1968–72), no. 44, ii. 28–9. Arezzo possessed an eleventh-century sacramentary from Pistoia, Arezzo, Biblioteca Pubblica (Consorziale) VI. 3: R. Grégoire, 'Repertorium liturgicum Italicum', SM 3rd ser. ix (1968), 465–592 at p. 474.

[157] Monte Cassino, Abbey Library, Cod. 451; Rome, Biblioteca Vallicelliana, Cod. D. 5.

[158] Milan, Biblioteca Ambrosiana, Cod. z. 52 sup; Milan, Biblioteca capitolare, Cod. 53.

[159] Udine, Biblioteca capitolare, MS 1; Vercelli, Biblioteca capitolare, Cod. 181. For consideration of the Fulda sacramentary see ch. 5.

[160] Verona, Biblioteca capitolare, Cod. 87, written at St Emmeram, Regensburg, 993–4, for King Otto III and Bishop Wolfgang of Regensburg. It was acquired by Verona under Bishop Otbert (992–1008), perhaps as a gift from Bishop Wolfgang: K. Gamber, 'Liturgiegeschichte von Regensburg bis ins 16 Jahrhundert anhand der ehaltern Liturgiebücher', in *Liturgie im Bistum Regensburg von den Anfängen bis zur Gegenwart*, Munich–Zurich 1989, 13–37.

[161] This estimate of forty-two has been arrived at by taking all the manuscripts classified as pontificals, *ordines*, sacramentary-rituals, sacramentaries and missal-rituals, from the lists in Grégoire, 'Repertorium', and 'Repertorium liturgicum italicum: addenda I', SM 3rd ser. xi (1970), 537–56, of liturgical manuscripts written in Italy between the seventh and the twelfth centuries, supplemented as necessary from R. Amiet, 'Inventaire des manuscrits liturgiques conservés dans les bibliothèques et les archives de Rome', *Scriptorium* xxxix (1985), 109–18; L. Avitabile, M. C. di Franco, V. Jemolo and A. Petrucci, 'Censimento dei

from eleventh-century Italy form one-sixth of this total. The Romano-German pontifical was not therefore a total success, and it was also not the only rite imported into Italy from Germany.

The Romano-German pontifical was seemingly even less important in northern France and England. In neither country did it dominate liturgical production, constituting in both countries a minority, albeit a substantial minority, of the total number of surviving manuscripts.[162]

The Romano-German pontifical was therefore important, but its influence outside the German provinces of Mainz and Salzburg was limited. Even within the province where it was most successful, that of Mainz, there was room for independent activity, as the composition, production and dissemination of the Fulda sacramentary discussed in chapter 5 demonstrates. Further, several copies of the Romano-German pontifical do not contain all the penitential *ordines*: of the fifteen manuscripts I studied, only two contained a complete set,[163] a further seven contained the *ordines* for both Ash Wednesday and Maundy Thursday,[164] and two contained *ordines* for Maundy Thursday only.[165] In other words, far from containing three *ordines* which are representative of late tenth- and eleventh-century penitential practice, the Romano-German pontifical contributes only one element, albeit an important one, to a much more varied picture of liturgical practice. It is its influential *Nachleben* which has, perhaps, coloured historians' views of the Romano-German pontifical's role in the liturgical practice of the tenth and eleventh-century Church, assigning it an undeserved importance for this period.

---

codici dei secoli XI–XII', SM 3rd ser. ix (1968), 1115–94; CLLA; K. Gamber with B. Baroffio, F. dell'Oro, A. Häriggi, J. Janini and A. M. Triacca, *Codices liturgici latini antiquiores: supplementum*, Freiburg 1988; Salmon, *Manuscrits*.
[162] For further detail see appendix 1.
[163] Bamberg, Staatsbibliothek, Cod. Lit. 53, and Wolfenbüttel, Herzog-August-Bibliothek, Cod. Guelf. 493 Helmstadt.
[164] Bamberg, Staatsbibliothek, Cod. Lit. 50; BL, MS Add. 17004; MS Cotton Tiberius C. i; Munich, Bayerische Staatsbibliothek, Clm 3909; Clm 6425 (although its version for Ash Wednesday is based on canon law texts); Wolfenbüttel, Herzog-August-Bibliothek, Cod. Guelf. 15 Weissenburg; Cod. Guelf. 141 Helmstadt.
[165] Bamberg, MS Lit. 54; BN, MS lat. 1231.

5

The Penitential Liturgy: Regional Diversity

The previous chapter argued that the Romano-German pontifical was not the dominant liturgy, either within the western dioceses of Germany or more especially outside it, raising the question of which penitential rites were used instead. This chapter seeks to answer this question through three case studies of different families of penitential rites from different areas: Fulda, in the province of Mainz, which produced rites for both public and secret penance; Lotharingia, which produced rites for public penance; and northern and central Italy, which produced rites for secret penance.

These case studies were identified from my examination of almost eighty manuscripts (including sixteen of the Romano-German pontifical) preserved in various libraries in England, France, Italy and Germany. These manuscripts were selected for study on the grounds that they were written within the geographic and chronological limits of this study and known, from their manuscript descriptions or other references, to contain penitential rites. This selection does not pretend to be comprehensive: it is based on existing catalogues of liturgical manuscripts and those of major libraries supplemented by references from other sources.[1] But it covers the geographic area under consideration and provides some pointers, at least, towards a fuller and more complex picture of the penitential liturgy in this period.

The Fulda sacramentaries

If the Romano-German pontifical was one of the 'two major liturgical monuments' of the Ottonian renaissance, the other was the Fulda sacramentary;[2] the abbey of Fulda produced at least five sacramentaries over the period

---

[1] Catalogues of liturgical manuscripts include CLLA, and Gamber and others, CLLA Supplementum, for general coverage, although Gamber's work is notoriously error-ridden. Specific regional surveys include V. Leroquais, Les Pontificaux manuscrits des bibliothèques publiques de France, Paris 1938, on French library holdings; Salmon, Manuscrits, on the Vatican holdings; Amiet, 'Inventaire', on the holdings of the Rome libraries; and Avitabile, di Franco, Jemolo and Petrucci, 'Censimento'. On penance see also the texts edited by Schmitz in Bussbücher I and Bussbücher II, and Wasserschleben, Die Bussordnungen. For a general introduction to liturgical texts see Vogel, Medieval liturgy, and Palazzo, Liturgical books.
[2] The phrase is that of Cyrille Vogel: Medieval liturgy, 233.

c. 980–c. 1025 only two of which include penitential rites; several more sacramentaries survive as fragments.[3]

Fulda was one of the most important and powerful monasteries within the empire.[4] Its abbots were also powerful neighbours of the archbishops of Mainz, the Romano-German pontifical's backers. The links between Mainz and Fulda went back to the abbey's foundation in 744 by Boniface, the Anglo-Saxon missionary and archbishop of Mainz; its first abbot was his follower Sturm. They continued into the ninth, tenth and eleventh centuries with a significant exchange of staff at the highest level between the two centres: in this period Archbishop William (955–68), the supposed promoter of the Romano-German pontifical, was succeeded by Hatto II, abbot of Fulda (956–68) in 968; Erkanbald, abbot of Fulda (997–1011), succeeded Willigis as archbishop in 1011.[5] On the other hand there was a strong tradition of rivalry between Mainz and Fulda in the ninth century for control of the cult of Boniface, although it seems to have become more muted in the tenth century. Florence Mütherich therefore suggested that the abbots of Fulda conceived their sacramentary as a complement to the Romano-German pontifical: whilst the Romano-German pontifical was intended to be *the* collection of episcopal *ordines* for the empire, the Fulda sacramentary was intended as a compilation of the best of the Carolingian sacramentaries.[6] Its principal source was a sacramentary, perhaps with a supplementary *libellus*, from Saint-Amand, the principal supplier of sacramentaries in the second half of the ninth century, although it also contains traces of both insular influence and of that of Tours c. 800.[7] But as analysis of its penitential *ordines* will show, the Fulda liturgy for penance was uninfluenced by that of Mainz, contained in the Romano-German pontifical. It is unclear how far this was deliberate. The difference might instead be explained by genre: the Romano-German pontifical was just that, a collection of *ordines* combined with prayer

---

[3] G = Göttingen, Niedersächsishe Staats- und Universitätsbibliothek, Cod. theol. 231 (c. 975–80); U = Udine, Biblioteca capitolare, MS 1 (c. 975/80–90); B = Bamberg, Staatsibliothek, Cod. Lit. 1 (c. 990–1011); Ve = Vercelli, Biblioteca capitolare, Cod. 181 (c. 990–1011); Va = Vatican, BAV, MS Vat. lat. 3548 (c. 1015–25). The following fragments also survive: Berlin, Staatsbibliothek Preussischer Kulturbesitz, MS theol. lat., fo. 192 (s. x^{ex}/s. xi^{in}); Berlin, Staatsbibliothek Preussischer Kulturbesitz, MS theol. lat. qu. 231 (s. x ^{ex}); Fulda, Hessische Landesbibliothek, MS Aa 136, fo. 3 (s. ix^2/ s. x^{in} with additions in s. x^2 hand); Kassel, Landesbibliothek und Murhardsche Bibliothek, 2° MS Theol. 54 (s. ix); Palazzo, *Sacramentaires*, 5–9, 183–92, 199–203, 206–13, 216–20, 223–4.
[4] Bernhardt, *Itinerant kingship*, 265–89; K. Schmid (ed.), *Die Klostergemeinschaft von Fulda in früheren Mittelalter*, Münster 1978.
[5] Palazzo, *Sacramentaires*, 177–8. Several abbots of Fulda were appointed to the archbishopric in the ninth as well as the tenth and eleventh centuries: Reuter, *Germany*, 63.
[6] F. Mütherich, L. Grodecki, J. Taralon and F. Wormald, *Le Siècle de l'an mil*, Paris 1973, 116.
[7] Palazzo, *Sacramentaires*, 149–53. On Saint-Amand see R. McKitterick, 'Carolingian book production: some problems', *The Library* 6th ser. xii (1990), 1–33.

THE PRACTICE OF PENANCE

texts, intended for bishops (but, as we saw, used by the regular clergy as well), the Fulda sacramentary a collection of only the prayer texts the presider needs for the celebration of mass, the administration of the sacraments and other liturgical services. But in order to consider the Fulda penitential liturgy fully we need to explore how it differed from the Romano-German pontifical; examine its sources; and identify its intended users.

Although copies of the Fulda sacramentary were made for use outside the abbey, the only two which include penitential *ordines* appear to have been produced for use within Fulda itself. G (Göttingen, Niedersächsishe Staats- und Universitätsbibliothek, Cod. theol. 231) was produced c. 975–80 and Va (Vatican, BAV, MS Vat. lat. 3548) composed as much as fifty years later, c. 1015–25.[8] G appears to be the *Urtext* for all the subsequent sacramentaries. A large and prestigious compilation of 256 folios, it includes one *ordo* for admission to public penance, one for the reconciliation of penitents, and two for secret penance; Va contains only one *ordo* for secret penance which nevertheless differs from either of those in G.[9] Va makes no provision for the reconciliation of penitents.

The first *ordo* is for private or annual penance: 'ordo priuatae seu annualis poenitentiae ita prosequendus est'. This *ordo* (A) was integrated into the services for the liturgical year and is included at the beginning of Lent.[10] It begins with instructions to the *sacerdos* to call all those who are accustomed to confess to renew their confession at the beginning of Lent and be reconciled on Maundy Thursday. If for any reason the penitent is prevented from attending the Maundy Thursday reconciliation then, as in the Romano-

---

[8] The provenance of G is not known before it entered the Helmstedt University Library c. 1600 and thence Göttingen University Library in the early nineteenth century. Its editor, Richter, suggests that it remained at Fulda until the sixteenth century: SF, p. xi. See also Palazzo, *Sacramentaires*, 188. Va's provenance is also unclear but it seems to have remained at Fulda until c. 1049. Marginal additions mention various members of the Byzantine imperial family including Constantine IX Monomachus (d. 1055), Theodora, daughter of Constantine VIII (d. 1056) and the Empress Zoe (d. 1050). Palazzo suggested that these additions related to the Synod of Mainz (October 1049) at which Ekbert, abbot of Fulda (1047–58), supported the Byzantine emperor, Constantine IX, against Henry III: Palazzo, *Sacramentaires*, 202 esp. n. 2. Gamber asserts it was produced for Fritzlar but provides no supporting evidence: CLLA, no. 975, p. 424. The provenance of the remaining completed Fulda sacramentaries is as follows: U was probably made for the see of Hamburg–Bremen but was in Aquileia by 1031, probably having been taken there by Poppo, the German patriarch of Aquileia (1019–42): Palazzo, *Sacramentaires*, 207–10; Gamber, CLLA, no. 979, p. 424; Hoffmann, *Buchkunst*, 169–70; B was probably made under Abbot Erkanbald (997–1011) for either Henry II's cathedral at Bamberg or the abbey of Michelsberg in Bamberg: Hoffmann, *Buchkunst*, 139–40, and *Bamberger Handschriften*, 141–2; Palazzo, *Sacramentaires*, 183–6. It had entered the cathedral library by s. xi. Ve was made under Abbot Erkanbald (997–1011) for Henry, bishop of Würzburg (995–1018), who in turn gave it to Otto III's chancellor, Leo, bishop of Vercelli (999–1027): ibid. 212–13.

[9] For an edition of G see SF. Va remains unedited. The penitential rite is at fos 33v–6v.

[10] SF, *ordo* lv, pp. 42–6.

German pontifical's *ordo* for entry into (public) penance on Ash Wednesday, the priest should award him both his annual and his Lenten penance and reconcile him immediately. And as in the Romano-German pontifical's *ordo* for (public) penance, the penitent should put down his stick before approaching the priest as a supplicant to begin the rite.[11] This initial wording, whilst similar, differs slightly from that in the Romano-German pontifical and as it continues the Fulda rite differs more markedly, both in text and in order, from that of the Romano-German pontifical.

The penitent is ordered to sit next to the priest and is interrogated on the orthodoxy of his beliefs and his willingness to renounce sin. If he is willing, the priest should receive his confession and indicate to him his penance. Then the penitent should kneel on the ground, holding his hands out in supplication, and weeping, acknowledge his sins and petition the priest to intercede for him. He then prostrates himself full-length on the ground with groans, sighs and tears. After some time the priest orders him to rise and, abject and trembling, receive his penance. The penitent then prostrates himself again to hear the priest's pastoral advice on the need to perform his penance, followed by one of a set of intercessory prayers. After this the priest should order the penitent to get up and he himself should rise from his sedile and they should both enter the church and sing the seven penitential psalms together with prayers and *capitula* whilst on their knees. This is followed by the office and a 'missa post confessionem'.[12]

The inclusion of the office suggests that *ordo* A was intended for use within the monastic community at Fulda. It appears to describe a semi-public ritual enactment of the act of confession and the award of penance; it is as much an act of affirmation as of confession. It is also very similar to that outlined in the Romano-German pontifical's *ordo* for entry into penance on Ash Wednesday. The order (although not all the texts) of the Fulda *ordo* closely resembles those in part I of the Romano-German pontifical's *ordo* and, as in that rite, the 'missa post confessionem' is an integral part of it. Where Fulda's *ordo* A differs from the Romano-German pontifical's rite is that it makes no provision in the mass for the imposition of ashes and sackcloth nor for the expulsion of the penitents from the church. Despite the close parallels with the Romano-German pontifical's rite for entry into seemingly public penance on Ash Wednesday the Fulda rite was, as its title suggests, intended only as part of the procedure for annual or private Lenten penance. The compilers of the Fulda rite thus distinguished it from the subsequent *ordo* for public penance,[13] suggesting that there was one ritual for annual penance, to be embraced by all

---

[11] Ibid. 42; cf. *PRG* xcix.44, ii. 14. The *ordo* in the *PRG* does not specify what type of penance it refers to, but the description accords well with descriptions for public penance given in the Gelasian sacramentary and Regino's *Libri duo*; it also contrasts to *PRG*, *ordo* cxxxvi for penance 'in more solito', which refers to a more personal form of penance.
[12] 'Sequitur officium': *SF*, 45.
[13] 'Incipit ordo agentis publicam paenitentiam': ibid. lvi, p. 46.

those who are accustomed to confess and who come to renew their confession at the beginning of Lent, to be distinguished from the shameful ritual for public penitents.[14]

For the G text also contains a brief *ordo* for entry into public penance ('ordo agentis publicam paenitentiam') which follows the *ordo* for annual penance and is taken directly from the Gelasian tradition: on the morning of Ash Wednesday the priest should receive the penitent, cover him with sackcloth and cast him out.[15] The full text of the intercessory prayers is not given; instead the reader is referred 'ut supra' to the previous *ordo*, suggesting that this *ordo* was not much used. Half a century later the copyists felt no need to include it in *Va*.

Ordo A erased the role of the bishop from the rite for entry into penance on Ash Wednesday and in doing so turned it into a rite for *poenitentia privata*. The bishop was similarly excised from G's rite for the reconciliation of the penitent on Maundy Thursday: 'reconciliatio poenitentis in caena domini'. Like *ordo* A, it appears to be a rite peculiar to Fulda; unlike that for entry into public penance, it is not taken directly from the Gelasian sacramentary, and instead seems intended for use within the monastery.[16] Unlike that in both the Gelasian and the Romano-German books, it omits the presentation of the penitents by the archdeacon to the bishop ('Adest o venerabilis pontifex'). Rather it begins with the chanting of Psalm l, followed by the antiphon 'Cor mundum crea in me deus et spiritum rectum innoua in uisceribus meis [Create in me a clean heart, O God, and renew a right spirit within me]', followed by the Kyrie, the Pater Noster and several penitential *preces*. This sequence, including the text and order of the *preces*, is exactly that found in the Romano-German pontifical's *ordo* for Maundy Thursday after the penitents have entered into the church and been handed to the bishop who has restored them to the church community; it is not found in the earlier Gelasian or Gregorian sacramentaries.[17]

The intercessory prayers which follow are not coterminous with nor as numerous as those recorded in the Romano-German pontifical – there are only eight as opposed to twenty-one. The Gregorian sacramentary is seemingly the source for all eight; the Gelasian contains only three.[18] But between the composition and circulation of the *Hadrianum* with the *Aniane Supple-*

---

[14] 'Praemonere debet omnis sacerdos eos, qui sibi confiteri solent, ut in capite ieiunii concurrere incipiant ad renouandum confessionem': ibid. lv, p. 42.
[15] 'Suscipis eum IIII. feria mane caput quadragesime et cooperies eum cilicio et recludis has orationes dicens': ibid. lvi, p. 46. Cf. *ordo* xvi, in *The Gelasian sacramentary*, 15, which does not include specific prayers, but the Fulda rite in G accords with the fuller rite recorded in the Gelasian sacramentary from St Gallen given at ibid. 325 (although the last of the five intercessory prayers is omitted from G).
[16] SF ci, pp. 76–8.
[17] PRG xcix.229, ii. 61. The final *prex*, 'Domine exaudi orationem meam', is omitted from the Fulda rite.
[18] SF ci.654, 658–9, pp. 77–8, correspond to *The Gelasian sacramentary*, 64–5.

ment in the early ninth century, and the composition of G in the late tenth century, some prayers had crossed over from the *ordo* for giving penance, for of these eight only four are found in the prayers for Maundy Thursday;[19] the other four are found in the 'Orationes ad dandam paenitentiam'.[20] All eight also feature in the Romano-German pontifical but again they are split: the first six prayers of the Fulda *ordo* may be found in the Romano-German pontifical's reconciliation *ordo*, but the last two prayers in the Fulda *ordo* are located in the Romano-German pontifical's *ordo* for private penance.[21] Both the Romano-German pontifical and the Fulda sacramentary are presumably derived from a common Gregorian tradition, and the relative ease with which prayers moved across the different penitential rituals suggests continuing flexibility in their composition. After all, these prayers all perform the same function, namely to ask for God's forgiveness of the sinner. A clue to the origins of the Fulda reconciliation *ordo* may be found in the late ninth-century so-called 'Poitiers' pontifical which contains all the intercessory prayers in the Fulda *ordo*, albeit in a different order.[22] The 'Poitiers' pontifical omits the initial sequence but, like the the Romano-German pontifical, gives the intecessory prayers as for plural penitents whilst those in both the Gregorian and Fulda sacramentaries are for single penitents.[23] The Fulda *ordo* therefore probably has its origins in a late ninth-century liturgical tradition; hence its similarities to the 'Poitiers' pontifical.

Unlike the 'Poitiers' pontifical, however, it makes no mention of the bishop's role in the service;[24] this apparently deliberate omission suggests that the Fulda *ordo* was intended for use by the abbot rather than a bishop. And the abbot had to seek alternative ways to demonstrate the reconciliation of the penitents: the reconciliation *ordo* is followed by a mass intended for penitents, suggesting that it was integrated into the monastery's activities: 'Sequitur officium'.[25] It concludes with a prayer to be said over the penitents (now in the plural) after they have communicated, which specifically asks for

---

[19] SF ci.654, 658–9, 661, pp. 77–8, correspond to SGR, nos 3963–5, 3969. The *Hadrianum*, a version of the seventh-century Gregorian sacramentary, was sent to Charlemagne by Pope Hadrian c. 784 x 791. The 'Aniane' supplement was composed in the early ninth century.
[20] SF ci.655–7, 660, pp. 77–8, correspond to SGR, nos 3951, 3958–60.
[21] SF ci.654–9, pp. 77–8, correspond to PRG xcix.230–5, 245, ii. 61–2, 64–5. SF ci.660–1, p. 78, correspond to PRG cxxxvi.34–5, 10, ii. 244, 236.
[22] SF ci.654–61, pp. 77–8, correspond to nos 293, 297–8, 295–6, 294, 299 in *Il cosiddetto pontificale di Poitiers*. The 'Poitiers' pontifical was composed for St Pierre de Vierzon, s. ix[2]: Leroquais, *Pontificaux*, i. 267–70. On this text see now Rasmussen, *Pontificaux*.
[23] For example, 'Praesta quaesumus domine huic famulo tuo dignum paenitentiae fructum': SF ci.658, p. 77; 'Praesta quaesumus domine his famulis tuis': PRG xcix.235, ii. 62.
[24] One prayer requests God's support for the minister of this rite in carrying out His service but makes no explicit reference to a bishop: 'Adesto domine supplicationibus nostris et me, qui etiam misericordia tua primus indigeo, clementer exaudi, et mihi, quem non electione meriti, sed dono gratiae tuae constituisti operis huius ministrum da fiduciam tui muneris exequendi et ipse in nostro ministerio quod tuae pietatis est operare': SF ci. 654, p. 77.
[25] Ibid. cii, pp. 78–9.

the absolution of the penitents from the fetters of iniquity: 'accusantes suas conscientias ab omni uinculo iniquitatis absoluis [absolve their accusing consciences from every fetter of iniquity]'.[26] The reconciliation of the penitents with the Church was thus signalled by their receiving communion rather than through contact with the bishop and this may explain the emphasis of the rubric for this prayer: 'oratio super penitentes, postquam communicauerunt'. Although the monks of Fulda chose to emphasise the significance of the penitents' communion, it was quite usual for mass to follow the reconciliation rite, as it did in both the Romano-German pontifical and the 'Poitiers' pontifical.[27]

Fulda obviously adapted the existing rites to formulate their own rites for the formal entry into penance and the reconciliation of penitents by excluding the bishop from these rites: why? The compilers recognised that these rites were not for public but private or annual penance. In this they were in accordance with canon law: the administration of public penance and the reconciliation of penitents was reserved to the bishop.[28] These rites were recorded in a codex (G) made for use within Fulda and it is probable that the abbot had quasi-episcopal responsibility for those living both within the monastery and on monastic land in its immediate vicinity. Abbots were often awarded privileges which gave them the right to wear pontifical regalia and exempted their monastery from episcopal control; Fulda was placed under the direct control of the papacy in 751, and the monks periodically renewed their privilege.[29] In 999 Pope Sylvester II re-confirmed Fulda's existing privileges, which provided, amongst other things, that no abbot should presume to receive consecration except from the apostolic see, that no bishops, archbishops nor patriarchs might celebrate mass on an altar under the abbot of Fulda's protection, that no prince might have authority over any of the monastery's possessions, and that the abbot of Fulda should come under the criminal jurisdiction of the pope only. Further, he granted to Abbot Erkanbald (997–1011) and his successors the right to call upon the apostolic

---

[26] Ibid. cii.670, p. 79. Three out of the four prayers in the mass are listed in the prayers for the reconciliation of penitents in the Gregorian sacramentary and all four can be found in the Maundy Thursday reconciliation *ordo* in the Romano-German pontifical. SF cii.662, 664, 670, pp. 78–9, correspond to SGR, nos 3966–8. Prayers cii.662–4, 670, SF, pp. 78–9, correspond to PRG xcix.236, 238, 237, 242, ii. 62–3. Only one (SF cii.663, p. 78) appears in the 'Poitiers' pontifical where it is listed amongst the prayers to reconcile penitents, at the beginning of the mass: *Il cosiddetto pontificale di Poitiers*, no. 235, pp. 150–1.

[27] In the 'Poitiers' pontifical the reconciliation of penitents is integrated into the mass, following on from the Gospel; the restoration of the penitents to the Church is followed by the offertory: ibid. 168–79.

[28] For example, 'Quod monachi secularibus poenitentiam dare non debeant': Burchard, *Decretum* xix.142, 1010. See also ibid. iii.240, 724–5.

[29] The level of forgery at Fulda inevitably raises problems for historians, but on the papal privileges see the review by H. Jakobs of M. Rathsack's thesis, 'Fuldaforfalschkningerne: en retshistorisk analyse af Klostret Fuldas pavelige privilegier 751–ca. 1158', Copenhagen 1980: 'Zu neuen Thesen über die Fuldaer Papsturkunden', DA xxxvii (1981), 792–5.

see to defend himself and his church, 'according to the custom of bishops'.[30] Whilst this privilege (and also its predecessors) does not contain an explicit grant of all episcopal privileges to Fulda, it suggests that bishops were effectively excluded from having any control over the monastery. The bishop of Würzburg, in whose diocese Fulda lay, was presumably responsible for the consecration of those monks who became priests, and should, theoretically, have had penitential jurisdiction over both the monks of Fulda and the men and women living on the lands of the monastery. But Sylvester's privilege excluded both bishops and archbishops from saying mass at any altar owned by the monastery, presumably including parish churches on monastic lands.[31]

Evidence exists from elsewhere for abbots administering public penance. We have already seen that several copies of the Romano-German pontifical have a monastic provenance.[32] Mary Mansfield has argued, on the basis of thirteenth-century northern French evidence, that the inclusion of rites for solemn (that is public) penance in six abbatial pontificals suggests that certain abbots, principally of monasteries located in population centres where there was no episcopal see, expelled and received penitents.[33] Fulda was situated in a region where there were not many sees, and was perhaps therefore involved in a more direct pastoral role towards the monastery's tenants in the surrounding area.[34] The repetition of the sacerdotal penitential prerogative in canon law adds credence to the suggestion that abbatial control over penance may have been a more common phenomenon than previously thought although it is unclear whether it refers to public or secret penance. In Fulda's case, at least, the community seems to have evolved a hybrid rite, for a formal secret penance.

There is, however, nothing in the text of the whole reconciliation *ordo* to suggest that it was intended for public penitents. The tenth century is a period of transition in the administration of secret penance, from a two-stage process to a one-stop procedure in which absolution is given at the same time as penance. The Fulda reconciliation *ordo* probably applied the old, two-stage procedure to the reconciliation of all penitents, both public and secret. But in that case why, fifty years later, was no provision made for the reconciliation of penitents in *Va*? Perhaps by the time the rite in *Va* was composed secret

---

[30] 'Liceat etiam tibi, charissime fili, tuisque successoribus abbatibus ejusdem monasterii episcoporum more apostolicam sedem ac defensionem tui tuaeque Ecclesiae appellare ac contra omnes aemulos vestros Romanae majestatis scuto vos defensare': ep. ii, PL cxxxix.272.
[31] 'Nulli episcoporum, archiepiscoporum, patriarcharum temere, nisi a vobis accepta licentia, super altare vestri patrocinii missarum solemnia celebrare liceat': ibid. 272.
[32] See ch. 4.
[33] Mansfield, *Humiliation*, 165–7. Monks in eleventh-century south-west France often administered public penance in conjunction with bishops against enemies of the monastery: Bull, *Knightly piety*, 174–9.
[34] Fulda's pastoral role is discussed in greater detail later in this chapter.

penance had become a one-stop procedure. There is still much we do not know about penance as practised at Fulda.

The G codex also contained another *ordo* (B) headed 'Incipit ordo ad dandum peniteniam more solito feria IIII. infra quinquagesimam'. It is included towards the end of the manuscript in the pastoral section of rituals for life-stages between two *ordines* for the visitation and anointing of the sick. It has no preliminary rubric and begins with the priest's preparation prayer, 'Domine deus omnipotens propitius esto mihi peccatori.'[35] The priest then interrogates the penitent on his beliefs and willingness to renounce sin. If he is willing to renounce sin (and not guilty of incest) the penitent should prostrate himself abjectly on the ground in the sight of God and ask Blessed Mary and all the apostles, martyrs, confessors and holy virgins to intercede for him so that God may grant him true forgiveness and perfect patience for the confession of his sins. After this preparation the penitent should get up and recite his sins; the priest should inquire of him diligently and make him confess his faults. And the penitent should then formally ask all the saints to intercede with God for his salvation. After a blessing from the priest the penitent recites a confession prayer in the vernacular,[36] followed by an intercessory prayer from the priest in which he begs that God may bless the penitent, guard him and grant him remission of all his sins so that he may enjoy eternal life. The seven penitential psalms are then sung, each interspersed by a Kyrie, *preces* and an intercessory prayer.

Ordo B is much shorter than A; it could be recited more quickly. Unlike A, its rubrics give no indication of location, but apparently it did not have to be administered in church. It is also not integrated into the liturgical day by either the office or the mass which suggests it was intended to be used in a less ritualised way than A. *Ordo* A, in contrast, describes a highly ritualised ceremony in which the actions of both participants, down to the facial expression of the penitent, are prescribed in sometimes seemingly unnecessary detail: thus the priest should rise from his chair ('sed ipse surgat de sedili suo'). Although its location is unclear (only after the penitent has confessed his sins and received his penance do both he and the priest move into the church to sing the seven penitential psalms), it was a very public ceremony, hence the reference to the priest's *sedile*, and seemingly began outside the church before moving into it. The recital of the seven penitential psalms led directly into a communal rite: the office followed by the mass.

The third penitential rite (*ordo* C) was recorded in Va perhaps as many as fifty years after those in G.[37] Although Va, like G, is a luxury codex, unlike G its decoration programme was never completed; this includes the rubrication for *ordo* C where only the initial rubric was scratched in. The absence of

---

35 SF ccccxxxvii.2375, p. 281.
36 My interpretation of 'Et sacerdos benedicat oret et dicat'. *Incipiat confessio*: ibid. 282.
37 Vatican, BAV, MS Vat. lat. 3548, fos 33v–6v.

rubrication from *ordo* C suggests that this penitential *ordo* was little used, especially as several other texts in the codex were rubricated.

Its text is similar to that of *ordo* B. But there are some differences: the wording of the priest's interrogation of belief follows that in *ordo* A rather than B. The wording of the instructions about the penitent's willingness to renounce sin (not rubricated) following this interrogation seems to be an amalgam of that found in *ordines* A and B, beginning with a sentence from A, 'si uult dimittere suscipias eius confessionem' but continuing with the version given in B, beginning at 'si uero uult, tunc prosternat se humiliter in conspectu dei in terram ad orantem'.[38] Whilst a Latin confession prayer precedes the Germanic vernacular prayer in *ordo* B, the order is reversed in *ordo* C, and the Latin confession prayer is a slightly amplified version of that in *ordo* B. More significantly, in *ordo* C, unlike B, a set of *preces* follow the seven penitential psalms, all but one of which may be found amongst those in *ordo* A; there are none in common with those found at the end of *ordo* B. Finally, *ordo* C concludes with five petition prayers, all of which are found in A and only four in B. The inclusion of an additional *prex* suggests that rather than editing *ordines* A and B together, the compiler of *ordo* C possibly had another source. He did not copy from G but either used a different exemplar, itself a modification of G's texts, or made his own modifications to the text, perhaps in line with current practice at Fulda.

It is, however, possible that the Fulda *ordo* evolved as a result of external influences, the most obvious of which, given its supposed dominance and Fulda's connections with Mainz, is the Romano-German pontifical, which antedates G by perhaps twenty years and *Va* by seventy. But comparison of the Romano-German pontifical's *ordo* for penance 'in more solito' with the three Fulda *ordines* suggests no closer a relationship than some shared common elements from their common ninth-century inheritance.[39] As already acknowledged, the overlap between the Romano-German pontifical's *ordo* for entry into public penance and *ordo* A is greater. The wording of the interrogation of belief and the willingness to dismiss sin is virtually identical, although *ordo* A contains additional instructions about the penitent's posture but omits the pastoral instruction give on the vices by the priest in the Romano-German pontifical. But all seven of the prayers which the Romano-German pontifical and *ordo* A have in common are also found in

---

[38] Ibid. fo. 34; *SF*, *ordines* lv, ci, pp. 42, 281. The confessors and holy virgins have been omitted from the list in *ordo* B of saints petitioned by the penitent.

[39] *Ordo* A shares only seven elements out of a total of thirty-eight in the Romano-German pontifical – the priest's preparation prayer and a similarly worded interrogation of the penitent's beliefs, and five intercessory prayers: *SF* lv.347, initial interrogation, 348–9, 351–3, pp. 42–3, correspond to *PRG* cxxxvi.2–3, 5, 29, 36, 31–3, ii. 234–44. *Ordines* B and C share these two elements, two *preces*, four intercessory prayers, and make provision for vernacular confession: *SF*, nos 2375, 2377–82, pp. 281–4, correspond to *PRG* cxxxvi.2 or 3, 5, 23–4 (2 out of 7 psalms), 29, 31–3, ii. 234–45.

the Gregorian sacramentary.⁴⁰ Whilst both *ordines* have certain *preces* in common, the Romano-German pontifical contains three *preces* which are not in *ordo* A, which in turn includes two not found in the Romano-German pontifical. This analysis suggests, therefore, that it is more likely that *ordo* A was composed separately from the *ordo* for entry into (public) penance on Ash Wednesday in the Romano-German pontifical. The overlap between *ordines* B and C and the Romano-German pontifical's *ordo* for Ash Wednesday is also limited to prayers from the ninth-century Gregorian tradition. The degree of overlap is unsurprising: all the *ordines* originate from the same ninth-century liturgical tradition, and all fulfil the same function, the administration of penance at the beginning of Lent. But there is no substantial evidence that the Romano-German pontifical had any direct influence on the liturgy at Fulda.

Instead Fulda seems to have constructed its own liturgy. Although G contains two *ordines* (A and B) for ordinary or annual Lenten penance, they were not identical.⁴¹ Why, therefore, were they both included in a single codex? The answer seems to be because the monks of Fulda distinguished between formal private penance (*ordo* A) and more informal 'confessional' penance (*ordines* B and C).

But who was the intended audience for Fulda's *ordines*? We have already seen that the abbots probably had powers over their tenants. But are there any clues in the manuscripts themselves as to whether they were intended for use outside the cloister?

G contains two *ordines* for non-public penance, one, A, integrated into the Church's liturgical year, the other, B, placed towards the end of the manuscript as part of a pastoral section on rituals for life-stages: baptismal rites, the visitation of the sick and rites for the dying. This last section may have originated as a *libellus* supplement to the sacramentary proper.⁴² Since G is a large and prestigious volume, highly decorated and illustrated with several miniatures, Henry Mayr-Harting has suggested that these pastoral rites were copied down in turn into *libelli* for pastoral use but that the codex itself was used only on important occasions.⁴³ Nor can these rites have been for use solely within the monastic community as the inclusion of a wedding ceremony,⁴⁴ a mass for

---

⁴⁰ Appendix 2, table 1.
⁴¹ As neither of the *ordines* for the sick make provision for hearing the confession of the dying, unlike those in the Romano-German pontifical, Poschmann argued that *ordo* B showed the incorporation of the anointing of the sick into existing penitential rites. But its title suggests that the compilers of G viewed *ordo* B specifically as Lenten penance and some fifty years later the compilers of Va placed *ordo* C, which is very similar to *ordo* B, in its order in the liturgical year i.e. at the beginning of Lent: Poschmann, *Penance*, 244–5. See also Jungmann, *Bussriten*, 114–15.
⁴² This suggestion is put forward in Palazzo, *Sacramentaires*, 153.
⁴³ Mayr-Harting, *Ottonian book illumination*, ii. 133–4.
⁴⁴ 'Incipit actio nuptialis': SF, *ordo* cccclxvii, pp. 323–7, follows a series of different masses for the dead (*ordines* cccxl–cccclxvi).

a sterile wife,[45] a mass to celebrate the birth of a child[46] and *ordines* for baptism,[47] testifies.

Fulda had a strong missionary and pastoral tradition from the time of its foundation; the writings of its abbot Hrabanus Maurus (822–42) show the continuing importance of this tradition in the ninth century.[48] He attached great importance to the administration of Fulda's *Eigenkirchen*, and it has been suggested that he was running a pastoral as well as a property organisation; some monastic estates, especially where there were churches, were run by priests.[49] This pastoral tradition continued after his death; necrologies from the 870s suggest that six of Fulda's dependent houses were schools, staffed by monk-priests and housing groups of scholars.[50] These schools seem to have been intended to educate candidates for ordination. As Fulda also had its own 'internal' school within the monastery, it seems likely that these schools were intended to provide pastoral care and charity to the people living in the vicinity. Those houses furthest from Fulda had the highest number of scholars to monks; they were presumably intended to provide education and ministry to an area which was too far from Fulda to be served directly by the community. The tradition failed to continue directly into the tenth century; at least two of these houses were destroyed *c.* 915 whilst the others became canonries. But Fulda may not have abandoned its pastoral ideals; canons rather than monks may have become the agents for education, with Fulda continuing to play a role as a supplier of liturgical books, as suggested by the production of at least two, and possibly three, codices for its own use over the course of half a century.[51] Fulda was held in high repute in the ninth century for its performance of the mass and the tenth-century evidence suggests that more of its monks became priests than at other houses in the *Reich*, generating a need for sacramentaries.[52] But the inclusion of a set of pastoral rites at the end of the G codex suggests continued pastoral concern.

Ordines B and C both contain a vernacular confession prayer in which the penitent confesses to almighty God and all the saints his bad thoughts and acts against God's will, including perjury, curses, whoring, homicide, drunkenness, envy and greed, as well as failure to observe proper Christian practice: he never went to church, never kept the fast, did not do penance, did not confess his sins, did not honour the saints on holy days and blasphemed and knowingly deserted God whether he intended to or not.

---

[45] 'Missa pro sterilitate mulierum': ibid. *ordo* cccclxviii, pp. 327–8.
[46] 'Missa in natale genuinum': ibid. *ordo* cccclxix, pp. 328–9.
[47] Ibid. *ordines* cccclxxv–vi, pp. 343–54.
[48] J. M. Wallace-Hadrill, *The Frankish Church*, Oxford 1983, 315–22.
[49] M. Sandmann, 'Wirkungsbereiche fuldischer Mönche', in Schmid, *Klostergemeinschaft*, ii. 743–4; Mayr-Harting, *Ottonian book illumination*, ii. 133.
[50] Hildebrandt, *The external school*, 119–29.
[51] Codices G, *Va* and possibly B.
[52] Mayr-Harting, *Ottonian book illumination*, ii. 154–5.

Fulda was not unique in producing a confession in the German vernacular; related texts survive from Mainz, whilst both Lorsch and nearby Würzburg appear to have produced independent confession prayers.[53] All these prayers have been dated to the ninth century, that from Fulda to c. 825–50, to a time when, probably inspired by the Carolingian reforms, East Frankish clerics sought to promote penance. Unlike Romance, there was little connection between the Germanic vernaculars and Latin, the prevailing language of prayer; hence the relative volume, in comparison to Romance, of vernacular prayer texts.

The inclusion of a vernacular confession prayer suggests therefore that these two *ordines* were intended to be administered not just to the noble-born monks of the Fulda community who knew and understood Latin, but to those who could not follow Latin. The prayer's text, moreover, suggests that it was intended for a member of the laity: the penitent has to acknowledge that he has failed to attend church, hardly probable if the penitent was a lay brother or other member of the community who might not be expected to have very good Latin. The order of sins, including perjury and whoring, also suggests a lay milieu. Whilst this catalogue of sin has a certain finality, suggesting it was intended as a deathbed confession, its formulaic nature, including the failure to observe proper Christian practice, can also be seen as part of a pastoral effort to reinforce good Christian observance. This text's presence in both *ordines* therefore suggests that Fulda's pastoral tradition was still vigorous in the tenth century.

The lay audience for *ordo* B, at least, is confirmed by the miniature depicting the giving of penance which heads the vernacular prayer (see frontispiece). The earliest example of this act in western medieval art, it is one of a series illustrating the rites for visiting the sick, extreme unction and the scrutiny before baptism which come at the end of G.[54] G is the only one of the Fulda sacramentaries to include illustrations of liturgical scenes.[55] Although stylistically they seem to follow ninth-century models, their inclusion suggests that Fulda still took its pastoral role very seriously in the tenth century, for these rites had the potential for bringing the Fulda community into contact with the surrounding people.[56] In this miniature the clergy are shown delivering the penitential rite to both lay men and women. On the left-hand side is the priest, either a bishop, as he is holding a crosier, or an abbot with the *pontificalia*, immediately behind him is a man in a different garb, possibly the archdeacon, and then five clerics.[57] On the right-hand side

---

53 C. Edwards, 'German vernacular literature: a survey', in R. McKitterick (ed.), *Carolingian culture: emulation and innovation*, Cambridge 1994, 141–70 at p. 146.
54 J. Timmers, 'Busse, Buss-Sakrament', in *Lexikon der christlichen Ikonographie*, ed. E. Kirschbaum, W. Braunfels and others, Rome 1968–76, i. 344.
55 Palazzo, *Sacramentaires*, 97.
56 For example, the baptismal rites in G: *SF* cccclxxv–vi.2680–723, pp. 343–54.
57 For the identification of the clerics see Palazzo, *Sacramentaires*, 97–8.

is a group of seven men in lay dress, behind whom stand a group of five women also in lay dress; both groups are advancing towards the clerical group, inclining themselves in petition. This position may correspond with the rubric at the start of *ordo* A that the penitent should incline himself in supplication before the priest.[58] But penance is portrayed as a communal rather than a solitary affair; it may therefore represent the instruction in *ordo* A that the priest should instruct everyone who is accustomed to confess to make renewal of their confession.[59] But the illustration is actually for *ordo* B which contains no such instructions; the miniature could, on stylistic grounds, be a copy of a ninth-century model and therefore need not correlate with the text. But although the artist may have followed a ninth-century style, he need not have followed a ninth-century model.[60] In any case it was not thought inappropriate for *ordo* B, suggesting that this *ordo* was perceived of as a communal rather than personal service.

The production at Fulda of a family of sacramentaries c. 975–1025 suggests that the liturgical dominance of the Romano-German pontifical was not yet a foregone conclusion. Fulda's penitential liturgy appears to have developed independently from a ninth-century base. Although it seemingly evolved over the period, as witnessed by the differences between *ordines* B and C, it remained uninfluenced by the Romano-German pontifical, changing instead with reference to its own internal traditions. Its penitential *ordines*, both formal and informal, were composed by a monastic community and as such reflected its needs: the reconciliation of penitents at Fulda did not require a bishop. But the parochial nature of these *ordines* was also recognised by the compilers of the Fulda sacramentaries: those sacramentaries which were produced for immediate export, the U, Ve and possibly B codices, are 'pure' sacramentaries without any *ordines* although they were probably all produced for episcopal use; penitential *ordines*, both public and secret, would have therefore been of use to their owners.[61] The exclusion of such texts from sacramentaries written for export suggests that the Fulda community regarded them as peculiar to their own house and as unsuitable for export. As at least two of the rites, *ordines* B and C, seem to have been intended for the laity, it is unlikely that they were excluded as being peculiar to monastic use, although these particular rites may have been excluded on the grounds that the vernacular confession prayer was written in a local dialect and thus incomprehensible outside Fulda's immediate area.

The evidence of the G codex suggests that the Fulda community c. 975

---

[58] 'Cum autem accesserit penitens ad sacerdotem, si laicus est dimisso baculo, quisquis vero ille est, sive laicus sive clericus sive monachus, suppliciter se inclinet ante sacerdotem': *SF*, 42.
[59] 'Praemonere debet omnis sacerdos eos, qui sibi confiteri solent, ut in capite ieiunii concurrere incipiant ad renovandam confessionem': ibid.
[60] This possibility is raised by Mayr-Harting, *Ottonian book illumination*, ii. 130–1.
[61] The B codex may have been produced for either the monastery of St Michael, Bamberg, or for the bishop of Bamberg.

conceived of three types of penance: public penance; a highly ritualised, semi-public ceremony for entry into formal private or annual penance (*ordo* A) on Ash Wednesday; and penance 'in the usual way' which was also entered into on Ash Wednesday (*ordo* B). The distinction between *ordines* A and B is abstruse; it seems to have disappeared over the course of the next half century for *ordo* C in the *Va* codex demonstrates the evolution of a single, simpler, and shorter rite for penance at the beginning of Lent. This evolution also demonstrates the Fulda community's continued interest in penance: penance remained a matter for contemporary concern rather than a relic of the ninth-century pastoral tradition.

The north-central family

Jungmann first identified what he called the 'nordfranzösischen' and Mansfield the 'north-central' family of rites for public penance.[62] This family is principally distinguished from other *ordines* for public penance by its rite for the reconciliation of penitents on Maundy Thursday in which the order of events is a reversal of that in the Romano-German pontifical. In the Romano-German pontifical the penitents are presented to the bishop outside the church, led back into the church and then restored to communion with the metaphysical Church.[63] In the north-central rite the penitents are first physically reintroduced to the church, then presented to the bishop, and only after this are they restored to the metaphysical Church.[64]

Jungmann identified the north-central family of penitential rites from a set of thirteenth- and fourteenth-century manuscripts; he thus concluded that these rites originated in the twelfth century.[65] Through her more recent research Mansfield refined Jungmann's work and identified twenty manuscripts containing these rites in the period 1150–1350, and one, the pontifical of Beauvais (B_1) from the eleventh century; she concluded that the rite was developed in the eleventh century.[66] My researches have discovered three more versions surviving in eleventh-century manuscripts.

The penitential rites for Ash Wednesday and Maundy Thursday in the Beauvais pontifical (B_1) survive only in Martène's eighteenth-century edition of ecclesiastical rites as Beauvais cathedral's library was pillaged at the Revolution.[67] Martène's text was probably taken from the pontifical of Roger I, bishop of Beauvais (998–1022) which, according to a seventeenth-century partial transcription of various rites, although not unfortunately of

---

[62] Jungmann, *Bussriten*, 98–100; Mansfield, *Humiliation*, 192–6.
[63] PRG xcix.224–9, ii. 59–61.
[64] For example CP, nos 389–409, pp. 98–103.
[65] Jungmann, *Bussriten*, 98–100.
[66] Mansfield, *Humiliation*, 189–247.
[67] Martène, *Ritibus*, i. 793–7.

the penitential ones, was a mixture of the Gelasian and Romano-German traditions.[68]

The second codex (P) (Paris, BN, MS lat. 13313), is in two parts. The first is a pontifical copied by four scribes, three from Mainz and one from Lotharingia, probably Metz,[69] and includes an *ordo* for the reconciliation of penitents.[70] A supplement written in a second Lotharingian hand was added in the second half of the eleventh century.[71] This includes two *ordines* for giving penance and an *ordo* for the ordination of an abbot; the latter contains a promise of obedience by the abbot to the bishop of Cambrai. The entire manuscript was probably in use in the diocese of Cambrai by the end of the eleventh century, although the supplement may only have been copied from a Cambrai model, for both the early modern provenance and the first Lotharingian hand suggest a Metz origin.[72]

The third codex (B_2) (Bamberg, Staatsbibliothek, Cod. Lit. 59), was written c. 1039–46 in an anonymous atelier which supplied several manuscripts used in the diocese of Verden (province of Mainz) in Saxony.[73] A version of the Romano-German pontifical, it includes a rite for the reconciliation of penitents on Maundy Thursday.[74] The fourth codex (C) (Cracow, Jagellonian Library, MS 2057), was written at Tyniec monastery near Cracow for Cracow cathedral c. 1075.[75] Its editor argued that it was based on a Lotharingian or Rhineland model on the grounds of the script type, and of the saints in the litany; this is likely because Tyniec had close links with Brauweiler near Cologne which provided abbots for the new Polish foundation. Further evidence for a Lotharingian model is that the prayers for the benediction of princes, arms and the banner in C are like those in the first Anglo-Saxon coronation *ordo*, the earliest evidence of which is from Arras.[76] Like B_2 it only includes a reconciliation rite for Maundy Thursday.[77]

The manuscript history therefore suggests that the distinctive north-central reconciliation rite was already in existence and being disseminated in the first quarter of the eleventh century. As table 5 of appendix 2 demonstrates the two earliest examples, B_1 and P, are very similar; it is there-

---

[68] 'Ce Pontifical semble intermédiaire entre le Gélasien du VIIIe siècle et le Pontifical Romano-Germanique': Martimort, *Documentation liturgique*, no. 53, 65–7.
[69] Hoffmann, *Buchkunst*, 254–5.
[70] Fos 43v–51r.
[71] Hoffmann, *Buchkunst*, 254–5.
[72] Leroquais, *Pontificaux*, ii. 175–9.
[73] On this manuscript see the description by Hoffmann in *Bamberger Handschriften*, 146–7. For a brief description of contents see also OR i. 79–84.
[74] Fos 1v–7v.
[75] CP, 14–16.
[76] On the *ordo* and its English origins see J. L. Nelson, 'The earliest surviving royal *ordo*: some liturgical and historical aspects', in B. Tierney and P. Linehan (eds), *Authority and power: studies in medieval law and government presented to Walter Ullmann*, Cambridge 1980, 29–48 (repr. in her *Politics and ritual*, 341–60).
[77] CP, nos 389–409, pp. 98–103.

fore probable that this rite was composed sometime in the tenth century. The manuscripts also show that this rite was associated with one area, the western Reich, whose heartland was Lotharingia; the exception to this conclusion is B_2. Mansfield's research demonstrated that the north-central rite continued in use in northern France in the period 1150–1350, but, as her research was limited to liturgical manuscripts in and from France, it is possible that the rite also persisted outside this area.

This rite therefore seems to have originated at about the same time, the tenth century, and in roughly the same area – the Rhineland/Lotharingia – as its more famous counterpart, the Romano-German pontifical. Mansfield argued that the north-central rite represented a combination of the Romano-German pontifical with older, local traditions, seeing it as an eleventh-century development from the Romano-German pontifical. The redating of the development of this rite to the tenth century makes it necessary to review this argument through a comparison of this rite with that in the Romano-German pontifical in terms of both structure and content in order to establish whether it represents instead a tradition independent from that recorded in the Romano-German pontifical.

Only two of the four codices (B_1 and P) include directions for the giving of penance at the beginning of Lent; these *ordines* are markedly different from each other. The rubric to the Ash Wednesday *ordo* in B_1 describes it as how penitents ought to present themselves to the bishop at the beginning of Lent, emphasising that public penance should at least appear to be voluntary.[78] It is followed by a description of the giving of penance taken from Regino of Prüm's early tenth-century canon law collection, composed for the archbishop of Trier, which was also cited by Burchard in his early eleventh-century *Decretum*.[79] B_1, however, includes an addition found in neither Regino nor Burchard, namely that after the penitents have been expelled from the doors of the church with the responsory, 'In the sweat of thy brow thou shall eat bread', the bishop is instructed to close the door of the church, and the clergy to follow with a responsory and verse; the text then continues as in the Regino and Burchard versions.[80]

B_1 is not the only eleventh-century pontifical to use Regino's description

---

[78] 'Ordo quomodo poenitentes in caput quadregesimae episcopo se debent repraesentare.' For historians who have seen public penance as involuntary and involving incarceration see Poschmann, *Penance*, 135–8, esp. p. 137, and, following him, Vogel, 'Pénitence publique', 141–3. De Jong in 'What was public' shows that public penance, even if involuntary in practice, had to be appear to be voluntary.

[79] Regino, *Libri duo* i.295, pp. 136–7; Burchard, *Decretum* xix.26, 984.

[80] 'Quo finito, claudat eis episcopus ecclesiae januam et clerus prosequatur R. *Ecce Adam quasi unus*. V. *Cherubim et flammeum* etc. ut videntes sanctam ecclesiam pro facinoribus suis tremefactam atque commotam, non parui pendant poenitentiam': Martène, *Ritibus*, i. 793. I have only been able to check this text against six copies of Burchard's *Decretum*, and none of Regino's *Libri duo*, although this text seemingly did not feature in the six manuscripts used by Wasserschleben for his edition of Regino.

of the entry into penance in place of a rite; an eleventh-century pontifical from Freising, compiled c. 1023–39, omits a ritual for penance but includes this description in Burchard's version,[81] together with other extracts from Burchard and the penitential attributed to Bede.[82] Whilst the inclusion of various texts from the canon law tradition may suggest a didactic rather than a practical use for the Freising manuscript, the textual addition in B_1, to allow for the closing of the door, suggests that this text was used in a practical context. This is confirmed by the omission of the false attribution of the text to a canon of the Council of Agde, given by both Regino and Burchard, which was included in the Freising codex; the text thus conforms to the norms of liturgical, as opposed to canon law, books which did not usually include a specific authority for each text.[83]

This text was followed – in Martène's edition – by an *ordo* for the absolution of penitents at the beginning of Lent.[84] In a communal service, the seven penitential psalms are followed by the Kyrie Eleison, the Lord's Prayer, several *preces* and five absolution prayers. A comparison of this *ordo* with its possible sources, namely the Romano-German pontifical, the Gelasian and the Gregorian sacramentaries, suggests it is a unique combination of existing elements.[85] Although it is ostensibly an absolution rite, the prayers are not absolution prayers as defined by the compilers of the Romano-German pontifical who used *absolutio* only to describe those prayers which appear in the Maundy Thursday reconciliation *ordo*, and which use a form of *absolutio* or *absolvere*.[86] B_1's compilers had a looser interpretation: in the Romano-German pontifical absolution only followed completion of the penance and the formal reconciliation of the penitent; in B_1 absolution occurs before the completion of the penance and reconciliation of the penitent. B_1's rite therefore appears to anticipate the change in penitential theory usually associated with twelfth-century scholastic theologians, that absolution could occur before the completion of satisfaction by the penitent. This change is also anticipated in other *ordines* of the period, for example that at the beginning of book xix of Burchard's *Decretum*. Liturgy may therefore have led to theological change rather than the process happening the other way around.[87]

B_1's two rites for entry into penance became a feature of the north-central

---

[81] Munich, Bayerische Staatsbibliothek, Clm 6425.
[82] For the text see OR v. 367–81. It includes the *ordo* for secret penance given in Burchard, *Decretum* xix.2–7, 949–78. This codex is also discussed in ch. 4 above.
[83] 'Ex concilio Agathensi', Regino, *Libri duo* i.295, p. 136; 'ex concilio Agathensi capite ix', Burchard, *Decretum* xix.26, 984.
[84] 'Absolutio poenitentium in caput jejunii': Martène, *Ritibus*, i. 793.
[85] See appendix 2, table 2.
[86] For example, 'ipse te absolvat per ministerium nostrum ab omnibus peccatis tuis', and 'absolvimus vos ab omni vinculo delictorum vestrorum': *PRG* xcix.249, 247, ii. 65–6.
[87] On this point, if in a later context, see Mansfield, *Humiliation*, 200.

family.[88] They were probably intended for two different audiences: Regino's penitential rite for the minority of public penitents who did penance during Lent and were not absolved until Maundy Thursday; the absolution rite for the majority of people who made their (annual) confession at the beginning of Lent and were immediately absolved. But such an explanation does not explain the absence of specific absolution prayers from the Maundy Thursday reconciliation rite in three out of the four eleventh-century copies of the north-central rite.

Turning to the P codex, although the main, early eleventh-century, text contains no *ordo* for giving penance, the late eleventh-century supplement contains two.[89] A comparison of both with their possible sources suggests that the first rite is similar, but not identical, to the Romano-German pontifical's Ash Wednesday rite for public penance; there is also no mention of the imposition of the ashes.[90] This omission is remedied in the second rite which cites the provision found in the Romano-German pontifical for the imposition of ashes and also for the ejection of the penitent from the church.[91] The second rite, described as 'item ordo ad dandam penitentiam', may be a continuation of the first, for a marginal sign indicates that the two are related, whilst the responsory, 'In the sweat of thy brow', is incomplete in the second *ordo*, but exists in a complete version in the first. The expulsion of the penitents is followed by two prayers; whilst both can be found in the Romano-German pontifical, one is used in the Ash Wednesday *ordo*, the other in the *ordo* for secret penance. So there are parallels between P and the Romano-German pontifical's *ordines* for both public and secret penance; but they also share a common source in the Gelasian and Gregorian sacramentaries, making it impossible to conclude that the *ordo* in P is a direct copy of that in the Romano-German pontifical. Instead they may both have been drawing upon common sources.

The supplement to the P codex has connections with the diocese of Cambrai. A mid eleventh-century pontifical of the bishop of Cambrai (K) contains a more elaborate version of P's *ordo*, under the rubric, 'the *ordo* for how penitents should do penance at the beginning of Lent'.[92] These similarities therefore probably represent a common Cambrai tradition. The K codex rectifies P's failing by including the imposition of ashes on the heads of the

---

[88] Mansfield saw the Beauvais two-stage rite for Ash Wednesday as a clumsy combination of antiquarian elements rather than as a unified composition: ibid. 196.
[89] *Ordo* i, BN, MS lat. 13313, fo. 135r; *Ordo* ii, fo. 136r, continued on fos 167v–8v.
[90] See appendix 2, table 3.
[91] PRG xcix.71, 73, ii. 21.
[92] 'Ordo in capite ieiunii quomodo paenitentes paeniteant': Cologne, Diözesan- und Dombibliothek, Cod. 141, fos 27r–30r, written c. 1050 at St Vaast, Arras, for the bishop of Cambrai. For a recent description of this manuscript see G. Gattermann (ed.), *Handschriftencensus Rheinland*, Wiesbaden 1993, no. 1105, pp. 654–5. Andrieu's assessment (OR i.108–14) is also useful. For details of the similarities between P and K see appendix 2, table 4.

clergy and people, but does not follow the Romano-German pontifical's version for this event.[93]

P and B_1 show a variety of provisions for the giving of penance on Ash Wednesday, and a variety of influences, including the Gelasian. These innovations anticipate characteristics of the later medieval north-central rite. But it is more difficult to establish from these rites whether they represent a tradition independent of the Romano-German pontifical or a development from it. The Maundy Thursday rite for the reconciliation of penitents provides more evidence to assess this question.

All four codices, B_1, P, B_2 and C, include a text for the reconciliation of the penitents on Maundy Thursday. Comparison of these *ordines* against each other suggests that, whilst not identical, they belong to the same textual family.[94] Mansfield suggested that the north-central family was 'thus invented at the moment of fusion of the new Rhenish influence with the older Gelasian tradition'.[95] It is therefore worth comparing the rite to the Romano-German pontifical to establish whether it is dependent on it.[96]

The principal elements of the north-central rite are very similar but the sequence, and therefore the structure, are different from that of the Romano-German pontifical.[97] Both begin in the same way, with the bishop sitting in front of the doors of the church, the penitents with the archdeacon at a distance in the atrium awaiting the bishop's command.[98] But in the north-central rite the bishop then intones the antiphon, 'venite, venite, venite filii, audite me, timorem domini docebo vos [come, come, come, my sons, hear me, I will teach you fear of the Lord]', and Psalm cxviii, 'Beati immaculati [Blessed are the undefiled in the way who walk in the law of the Lord]'.[99] The deacon then says on behalf of the penitents, 'flectamus genua [Let us bend our knees]', and all the penitents kneel. The deacon then says on behalf of the bishop, 'levate [rise]'. This sequence is repeated a second and third time, with the bishop summoning the penitents, 'venite, venite [come, come]'. And so the penitents come to the middle of the paved area. After the third time the penitents with the deacon immediately run to the feet of the

---

[93] They differ in both the choice of antiphon and the inclusion of blessed water as part of the service.
[94] See appendix 2, table 5.
[95] Mansfield, *Humiliation*, 192–3.
[96] See appendix 2, table 6.
[97] The following account is taken from C; only substantial differences with other manuscripts have been noted.
[98] 'Sedente enim prae foribus aecclesiae poenitentibus in atrio eminus cum archidiacono iussum illius praestolantibus, dicat pontifex antiphonam': CP, no. 389, p. 98. B^2 differs slightly: 'Sedente pontifice prae foribus aecclesiae penitentibus autem cum archidiacono iussum illius in atrio praestolantibus dicat pontifex antiphonam: Venite': fo. 1v. Cf. PRG xcix.224, ii. 59.
[99] CP, no. 390, p. 99. This is an exceptionally long psalm in which the psalmist alternately prays to God for his mercy and professes his obedience to God's law. It does not feature in the Romano-German reconciliation *ordo* for Maundy Thursday.

bishop and prostrate themselves before him, until the bishop nods to the other deacon as a signal that he should command the penitents to rise. The clergy then take up the antiphon, 'Venite, venite filii [Come, come my sons]', followed by another with a similar refrain.[100] This sequence comes much earlier than that in the Romano-German rite. After this the archdeacon presents a petition on the part of the penitents, 'Adest o venerabilis pontifex tempus acceptum [O venerable pontiff, the acceptable time is here]'.[101] This petition, which begins the Romano-German pontifical's rite, here comes after the penitents have prostrated themselves before the bishop. The north-central rite therefore reverses the order of events in the Romano-German pontifical's rite. In the north-central rite the archdeacon's petition is followed by the bishop getting up and making all the penitents prostrate themselves before him whilst Psalms lvi, lxvi and lxix are sung over them.[102] Again these psalms do not feature in the Romano-German pontifical. After the psalms are finished the Lord's Prayer is said, with three *preces* which acknowledge guilt and ask for mercy:

> Iniquitates meas ego cognosco et delictum meum (contra me est semper). Averte faciem tuam a peccatis meis. Redde mihi laetitiam. [I recognise my iniquities and my sin (is always before me). Turn Thy face away from my sins (and blot out all my iniquities). Give me back the joy (of Thy salvation and strengthen me with a strong spirit)].[103]

This text is a version of that recited in the Romano-German pontifical by the bishop when he prostrates himself in recognition of his own sinfulness and asks for God's help near the beginning of the service, after the archdeacon's petition; here the bishop remains upright and these verses are recited on behalf of the assembled company.[104] They are followed by two alternative prayers in which the minister requests the Lord's help in carrying out His work.[105] Versions of both prayers are found in the Gelasian sacramentary's

---

100 Ibid. no. 391, p. 99: 'Et diaconus ex parte poenitentium: Flectamus genua. Tunc omnes genua astantes flectant poenitentes. Quo facto dicit diaconus ex parte pontificis: Levate. Similiter agitur secundo et tertio repetente episcopo; Venite, venite, subsequente diacono: Flectamus genua ut antea. Et sic ad medium pavimentum solotenus veniat. Quando autem tertio domnus episcopus annuntiaverit antiphonam: Venite, venite, prosequatur diaconus: Flectamus genua. Mox cum diacono poenitentes corruunt ad pedes episcopi sicque prostrati iaceant, usque dum domnus episcopus innuat alteri diacono, ut dicat: Levate. Et tunc prosequatur clerus iterum antiphonam: Venite, venite, filii. Iterum sequitur antiphona: Venite.' This initial sequence is slightly different in P (fo. 43v) where Psalm cxviii is not said after the first rendition of the antiphon, but after the final rendition of the antiphon by the clergy.
101 CP, no. 392, p. 99.
102 Ibid. no. 393.
103 Ibid. no. 394.
104 PRG xcix.226, ii. 60.
105 CP, nos 395–6, pp. 100–1.

ordo for the reconciliation of penitents,[106] in the Supplement to the Gregorian *Hadrianum* amongst the prayers for the reconciliation of the penitent on Maundy Thursday,[107] and in the Romano-German pontifical's reconciliation *ordo* where they occur amongst the sixteen alternative prayers which follow the restoration of the penitents to the church.[108] The second prayer, 'O God most benign Creator', follows the version found in the Romano-German pontifical which is longer than that contained in either the Gelasian or Gregorian sacramentaries and includes an additional section which reiterates the request to God to offer salvation to the penitent through his priest:

> So then Lord be propitious to those who tremble and make supplication in expectation of Your condemnation and stretch out the right hand of salvation to raise up the humility of those who lie low. To us Your servants, whom You have established among the ministers of the apostolic keys and priestly office, not from worth of election but by the gift of Your grace, give confidence to perform what belongs to Your power. Recognise, most loving shepherd, the sheep of Your redemption and in answer to the prayers of Your church release those who are confined by the fetters of their sins.[109]

This is a prayer in which the bishop asks the Lord to accept the penitents' penance, that they may be reconciled with the Church. The inclusion of the section found in the Romano-German pontifical suggests that the version found in the C codex is dependent on either the Romano-German pontifical itself, or its source. After one or both of these prayers has been said, the penitents should get up and the deacon should request the bishop to restore in them what has been corrupted by the instigations of the devil and to reconcile them with God so that they may enjoy eternal life.[110] This prayer occurs much earlier in the Romano-German pontifical rite where it follows the bishop's acknowledgement of his own sinfulness, and comes before the *venite* sequence and the penitents' entry into the Church.[111] The north-central text is also written for many penitents whilst the Romano-German pontifical's is written for a single penitent. Then the bishop should indicate to the penitents that what has been washed away through penance should not be

---

106 *The Gelasian sacramentary*, 63–5.
107 SGR, nos 1383, 1384, i. 452–3.
108 PRG xcix.230, 245, ii. 61, 64.
109 'Propitiare ergo domine trementibus atque supplicibus sub sententiae tuae expectatione et ad humilitatem iacentium sublevandam dexteram salutis extende. Nobis quoque servis tuis quos apostolicae clavis sacerdotalisque officii ministros, non electione meriti, sed dono gratiae tuae constituisti, da fiduciam tanti muneris exequendi et ipse in nostro ministerio quod tuae potestatis est operare. Agnosce piissime pastor oves tuae redemptionis et constrictis vinculis peccatorum aecclesiae tuae precibus exoratus absolve': ibid. no. 245, ii. 65; CP, no. 396, p. 100.
110 Ibid. no. 397, p. 101.
111 PRG xcix.227, ii. 60.

repeated.[112] This is an injunction which does not occur until the very end of the Romano-German pontifical's *ordo* after the penitents have been anointed with holy water and censed and told to rise up.[113] Whilst in the Romano-German pontifical it marks the end of the penitential process and the restoration of the penitents to the church, here, in the north-central rite, the injunction merely marks a stage in the penitents' reconciliation with the Church. Then the bishop begins the antiphon, 'Venite, venite', and the clergy with bishop and psalmist say Psalm xxxiii, the verses of this psalm being always followed by 'venite, venite'.[114] Meanwhile, the penitents are returned by the hand from the archdeacon to the bishop, and the bishop returns them to the deacon who in turn assembles them in good order. And thus the penitents are restored to the church.[115] In the Romano-German pontifical the penitent's own priest is involved in this sequence, handing the penitent to the archdeacon who in turn hands the penitent to the bishop.[116] The absence of the penitent's priest from this process is significant, suggesting that the rite had become exclusive to the cathedral's clergy. Then the bishop begins the antiphon, 'Cor mundum [Create a clean heart in me, O God, and renew an upright spirit within me]', together with penitential Psalm l, 'Miserere mei Deus [Have mercy on me O God]'. At the end of this, the bishop should prostrate himself, one with the penitents, in prayer.[117] The clergy should then recite the litany, followed by the Kyrie Eleison, the Our Father, and then a series of *preces* which are identical to those in the Romano-German pontifical but which lack the responsories.[118] There then follow several intercessory prayers,[119] which all petition the Lord to be merciful to the penitents and to receive them back, and restore their chance of eternal life: thus one begs God to give the bounty of His pardon to His servants, weakened by the lengthy squalor of penance, so that they may put on again the wedding garment and enter the royal banquet from which they were excluded.[120] This is the end; with the exception of the C codex, no

---

[112] 'Et indicantur ab episcopo poenitentes, ut quod penitendo diluerint, iterando non revocent': CP, no. 398, p. 101.
[113] PRG xcix.251, ii.67.
[114] CP, no. 399, p. 101.
[115] 'Interim penitentes manuatim ab archidiacono reddantur episcopo, et episcopus reddat diacono qui ex parte eius est et ordinatim congregentur. Sicque restituantur aecclesiae': ibid. no. 400.
[116] PRG xcix.229, ii. 61.
[117] CP, no. 401, p. 101.
[118] They are identical except for the last one: ibid. no. 402; cf. PRG xcix.229, ii. 61.
[119] CP, nos 403–7, p. 102.
[120] 'Deus misericors, Deus clemens, qui secundum multitudinem miserationum tuarum paenitentium crimina deles et praeteritorium delictorum culpas venia remissionis evacuas, maiestatem tuam supplices deprecamur, ut his famulis tuis longo squalore poenitentiae maceratis miserationis veniam largiri digneris, ut nuptiali vestae recepta ad regalem mensam unde eiecti fuerant mereantur introire. Per.': ibid. no. 404, p. 102. A version of this prayer appears in PRG xcix.239, ii. 63.

provision is made for absolving the penitents and restoring them to the Church.[121] The rite therefore ends rather inconclusively: the Romano-German pontifical's rite ends with a little drama in which the penitents are sprinkled with water and censed and told to rise up, they have been restored to life and to the Church; the north-central rite with a prayer for the reconciliation of the penitent.[122]

The structure of the north-central rite is therefore different from that of the Romano-German pontifical. The first two parts are reversed: the penitents enter into the church before being presented to the bishop. The reconciliation prayers are then said. But in only one of the *ordines*, C, are the penitents absolved. The effect of this is to dilute the cumulative drama of the Romano-German pontifical's rite, which begins with the penitents outside the church, continues with their restoration to the human Church and culminates in a quasi-sacramental recognition of their reconciliation through the use of holy water; the penitents become part of the metaphysical Church. The north-central rite also does not make the link between the physical and spiritual Church made in the Romano-German rite: the restoration of the penitent comes *after* their entry into the physical church.

Although these four eleventh-century examples of the north-central rite share the same basic structure, albeit with minor variations, they vary in content, in particular in their choice of reconciliation prayers. Both the earlier manuscripts, B_1 and P, which date from the first quarter of the eleventh century, have simpler and shorter rites than those of the two later manuscripts; they omit four of the alternative reconciliation prayers found in both the later manuscripts.[123] The C rite includes two absolution prayers not found in the other three manuscripts and which have no obvious source. The second prayer is of especial interest because it is written in the first person singular indicative, for either singular or plural penitents. This early use of the indicative in an absolution prayer represents a contemporary change from absolution being said in the optative, and thus reflects the increased authority assumed by the bishop in this rite. He is no longer merely a channel for God's grace, petitioning Him to absolve the sinner, but is now able to speak for God and petition the absolution of the sinner himself.[124] There is some overlap in the content of the Romano-German pontifical's rite and the north-central rite: of the twenty-eight items in the Romano-German *ordo*, eleven are found in codex B_1 for example, ten in P, fourteen in B_2 and twelve in C. But the north-central rite also includes items not found in the Romano-German one: B_1 has three, for example, P has two, B_2 has eight and

---

[121] CP, nos 408–9, pp. 102–3.
[122] PRG xcix.251, ii. 67.
[123] CP, nos 404–7, p. 102.
[124] 'Vice inquam eiusdem beati Petri, cui licet merito longe sumus dissimiles, quomodo potestate a Deo concessa existimus consimiles, ego divinitus te <vos> absolve a vinculis peccatorum tuorum <<vestrorum>>. Per.': ibid. no. 409, p. 103.

C has five. The examples of the north-central rite are not therefore identical, nor is the north-central rite identical in terms of content with that in the Romano-German pontifical. But does the overlap indicate that the north-central rite was dependent upon that of the Romano-German pontifical, or do they owe their common features to earlier sources, namely the Gelasian and Gregorian sacramentaries? The Gelasian provided a significant proportion of the elements in the north-central *ordo*: twenty out of thirty-seven. The Romano-German pontifical provided eighteen, but only nine of these are Gelasian in origin. This would seem to suggest that both the Romano-German pontifical and the Gelasian should be seen as important and independent sources for the north-central rite.

There was, therefore, a different liturgical tradition in Lotharingia and northern France for the Maundy Thursday reconciliation of penitents. Whilst the internal textual evidence suggests, and earlier historians have argued, that the north-central rite was a combination of the Romano-German pontifical's *ordo* with earlier, local traditions based on the Gelasian, circumstantial evidence suggests that the north-central rite may, in fact, be independent of that recorded in the Romano-German pontifical. There is less evidence than was previously thought to suggest that the Romano-German pontifical was widely distributed. There is no evidence that it was used in the province of Trier or in north-eastern France, little evidence that it was used within the province of Cologne, and none that it was use in these places in the late tenth century. The earliest evidence for the north-central rite is from the first quarter of the eleventh century. Moreover, there is evidence in another pontifical, the K codex from Cambrai, that the elements from the north-central rite influenced a rite which followed in essence the structure of that in the Romano-German pontifical. In K's rite, amongst other things, for example, after the presentation of the penitents, which follows the Romano-German rite, the bishop then, in a formula taken from the north-central family, recites three psalms over the penitents who are prostrate before him; as in the north-central family these psalms are followed by the Lord's Prayer and certain *preces*, and four prayers, two found in the north-central C codex, two in the Romano-German pontifical.[125] The K text then returns to the Romano-German *ordo*. The K codex, written c. 1050, has another parallel with a manuscript containing the north-central penitential rite; it includes a coronation *ordo* which shares a common source with that in P, written c. 1025.[126] K is probably therefore an example of the Romano-German pontifical influencing a pre-existing rite. The common elements between the Romano-German pontifical and the north-central rite may therefore owe more to a common Carolingian inheritance than to each other. Regino of Prüm has left evidence for a liturgical tradition of public

---

[125] See appendix 2, tables 5, 6.
[126] *Ordines coronationis Franciae: texts and ordines for the coronation of Frankish and French kings and queens in the Middle Ages*, ed. R. A. Jackson, Philadephia 1995, 201–3.

penance in Lotharingia c. 906, over forty years before the Romano-German pontifical was compiled in Mainz. Regino concentrated mostly on Ash Wednesday, and the codex with the earliest example of the north-central reconciliation rite, B_1, drew upon Regino for its Ash Wednesday instructions. It is therefore at least possible that the north-central rite was compiled independently of that in the Romano-German pontifical, sometime in the tenth century, even if this cannot be demonstrated with certainty.

The reconciliation rite was one to which scribes, and presumably therefore their clients, were attached. Codex P contains other Lotharingian influences in addition to the north-central reconciliation rite. But it was (probably) compiled at a time when, and in a place where, the Romano-German pontifical should have been available, that is Mainz between 1000 and 1025, by a team of three Mainz and one Lotharingian (from Metz) scribes.[127] Comparison with manuscripts copied for Bishop Abraham of Freising (d. 993/4) suggests that the manuscript was copied in Mainz. Abraham, we know, also sent a scribe from Freising to Metz where he worked with local scribes on manuscripts for Freising's collections.[128] It is therefore possible that the sole Metz scribe of P was the client bishop's representative. The inclusion of the north-central rather than the Romano-German pontifical's reconciliation rite suggests that their Lotharingian client, either the bishopric of Metz or that of Cambrai, wished to record their own, local tradition; possible confirmation of this lies in the fact that it was the Lotharingian scribe who copied the north-central rite.

Local tradition explains the historical longevity of this rite but not its origins. Mansfield has sought these in theology. She suggested that a change in the Ash Wednesday rite, namely the immediate absolution of penitents, explained why the penitents were led into the church immediately in the Maundy Thursday rite, and why there were no absolution prayers included in it.[129] Whilst the centre and climax of the Romano-German pontifical's rite is the reintroduction of the penitents into the church, the north-central rite assumes that the penitents have already been restored to, or remained members of, the Church. This development, Mansfield suggested, preceded the changes in penitential doctrine made by the twelfth-century theologians who distinguished between the guilt, *culpa*, of the sinner and the penalty due, *poena*, for the sin.[130] If a sinner felt genuine contrition, s/he could redeem the

---

[127] It is unlikely but not impossible that the Lotharingian scribe (Hand B) was working separately. Hoffmann, *Buchkunst*, 254, identified the hands as follows: hand A, fos 2–35v line 8, fos 140r–68v line 14; hand B, fos 37r–81v, fos 83v lines 7–102v line 2; hand C, fos 106r–31v; hand D, fos 132r–9v line 8; fos 203v–4r; hand E, fo. 168v lines 15–170v.
[128] J. Vezin, 'Les Manuscrits en Lotharingie autour de l'an mil', in D. Iogna-Prat and J.-C. Picard (eds), *Religion et culture autour de l'an mil: royaume capétien et Lotharingie: actes du colloque: Hugues Capet 987–1987: la France de l'an mil: Auxerre, 26 et 27 juin 1987–Metz, 11 et 12 septembre 1987*, Paris 1990, 309–14.
[129] Mansfield, *Humiliation*, 208.
[130] 'Such a development even before Scholastic theology had fully worked out the justifi-

consequences of his (or her) guilt and thus ensure his (or her) own eternal salvation, although the sinner still needed to make satisfaction for the sin and thus remit the penalty due. Thus sinners could be absolved of their guilt and reconciled with the Church before making satisfaction through the performance of penance. These theological changes provided a retrospective justification for a liturgical change, documented in the north-central rite, which had already occurred, namely the immediate absolution of sinners on Ash Wednesday before they made satisfaction through the performance of penance. She also argued that a change in the twelfth-century Ash Wednesday rite, separating the Lenten benediction of the people from the imposition of penance, split the communal from the individual aspects of the rite, and was reflected in an increased emphasis on the individual in the Maundy Thursday rite. This became merely a public expiation of sins by an individual rather than a communal rite, as in the Romano-German pontifical, where the penitents were scapegoats who had offended the community but through their penance redeemed themselves and restored the purity of the entire Church.[131] However, in both the north-central and Romano-German rites for Maundy Thursday the archdeacon concludes his presentation of the penitents to the bishop, 'Penance is the favour which advantages them individually and aids them all in common.'[132] Whilst the focus was perhaps changing, penance was not yet confined to the individual. Mansfield's analysis therefore requires a little amendment, especially in the light of the evidence of earlier eleventh-century examples of the rite which, in at least one case, included an 'unreformed' Ash Wednesday *ordo*. Her analysis is a good description of the differences between the Romano-German and the north-central rites but fails to answer the question why the north-central reconciliation rite, which developed in Lotharingia at roughly the same time as the Romano-German pontifical in the Rhineland, took the form it did.

One of the more distinctive features of the north-central reconciliation rite is the way in which it highlights episcopal authority. This is not unexpected: public penance was, after all, an episcopal prerogative. As Frankish royal power diminished in the late ninth century, bishops resumed more or less sole responsibility for public penance, without the effective royal support they had enjoyed under Charlemagne and Louis the Pious. But the north-central rite's emphasis on episcopal authority is greater than that in the Romano-German pontifical, although they both originated at around the same time and inherited the same Carolingian legacy. It begins outside the

---

cation in the power of the keys for immediate absolution before the completion of the required satisfaction suggests that the theology may have been responding to the liturgy as much as the other way round': ibid. 200.
[131] Ibid. 209.
[132] 'Unicum itaque est poenitentiae suffragium quod et singulis prodest et omnibus in commune succurrit': *CP*, no. 392, p. 99; cf. *PRG* xcix.225, ii. 60.

doors of the church with a public command by the bishop to the penitents to come and hear him, not, as in the Romano-German and the Gelasian rites, with the archdeacon presenting the penitents to the bishop.[133] The penitents then approach the bishop and acknowledge his authority: they approach him in three stages, genuflecting and getting up each time at the command of the archdeacon, before prostrating themselves at the bishop's feet.[134] Only then are they presented to the bishop by the archdeacon. After the presentation, in the Romano-German and Gelasian traditions, the bishop prostrates himself and acknowledges his own sinfulness,[135] but in the north-central rite his speech is attributed to the archdeacon, speaking on behalf of the penitents, and the bishop remains upright.[136] The rite therefore preserves and reinforces his episcopal authority by making him distinct from the penitents; he remains upright until after the penitents have been restored to the Church, whilst they remain prostrate for most of the service; he does not acknowledge any similarity in status between himself and the penitents as sinners. This distinction is underlined by two prayers which in the north-central rite are placed after the presentation of the penitents rather than, as in the Romano-German pontifical, after the restoration of the penitents: both petition God to grant mercy to the penitents whilst emphasising the bishop's authority to act as God's minister.[137] By distinguishing between the minister and the penitents, they contain no hint that as a mortal man the bishop might also be sinful.[138]

A clue to this emphasis on episcopal authority may lie in the important role played by bishops in tenth-century Lotharingian society. They controlled both the economic power of the cities, and vast territories.[139] They inherited from the Carolingians certain judicial and administrative responsibilities; thus the bishops of Metz appear to have inherited comital rights, at least in the city, sometime in the early tenth century; by the 930s they had acquired the old royal palace and appointed their own count of the palace.[140] Research

---

[133] CP, nos 389–90, pp. 99–100.
[134] Ibid. no. 391, p. 100.
[135] 'Hic ergo dum ad poenitudinis actionem tantis excitatur exemplis, sub conspectu ingemiscentis ecclesiae, venerabilis pontifex, protestatur et dicit: "Iniquitates meas ego agnosco et delictum meum contra me est semper. Averte faciem tuam a peccatis meis, Domine et omnes iniquitates meas dele. Redde mihi laetitiam salutaris tui, et spiritu principali confirma me" ': *The Gelasian sacramentary*, 64. This text was taken up by the compilers of the Romano-German pontifical: PRG xcix.226, ii. 60.
[136] CP, no. 394, p. 100.
[137] Ibid. nos 395–6, pp. 100–1.
[138] The north French rite expands on that in the Romano-German pontifical for it allows the penitents to get up before they are handed by the deacon to the bishop and thus restored to the Church.
[139] M. Parisse, 'Les Hommes et le pouvoir dans la Lorraine en l'an mil', in Iogna-Prat and Picard, *Religion et culture*, 259–66.
[140] V. Chatelain, 'Le Comte de Metz et la vouerie épiscopale du VIIIe au XIIIe siècle', *Jahrbuch der Gesellschaft für lothringische Geschichte und Altertumskunde* x (1898), 72–119 at

on individual sees, those of Metz, Liège, Verdun and Toul, suggests that bishops were usually appointed from the local aristocracy.[141] Nevertheless, despite the seeming aggrandisement of these bishoprics, or rather perhaps because of it, there was considerable tension. Major local families competed for control of the bishopric and its resources; at Liège, for example, such competition led to the imposition of Balderic on the see of Liège by his uncles Regnier and Radolf and the ousting of Rather, sometime bishop of Verona at Christmas 953.[142] In 929 the inhabitants of Metz blinded then ejected Bishop Benno who had been imposed on them by Henry the Fowler, and appointed a local man in his place.[143] Tension thus often existed between the bishop and local aristocrats: the recurrent tension between the castellan and bishop in eleventh-century Cambrai is well-known.[144] Competition for resources also led to considerable tension between bishops and their own entourage: Gerard, bishop of Toul (963–94), for example, appears to have come into conflict not only with the local nobility, but also with his own *milites*, the local abbeys and his cathedral's community of canons.[145] Wideric, abbot of Saint Evre, who wrote the life of Gerard at the request of Bishop Bruno of Toul (1019–52), the future Pope Leo IX, described how after Gerard anathematised two nobles for usurping Toul's land, they then attacked the bishop, dragged him from the church's altar, and forced him at swordpoint to absolve them.[146] Wideric presented this incident as an example of Gerard's passivity and willingness to face martyrdom. It can also be read as an eleventh-century view of the tension which existed between Gerard and the local nobility. Nor was Gerard an innocent figure. John Nightingale has shown that he had a

---

pp. 103–8. Trier and Toul also appear to have acquired the revenues of the old Carolingian comté about this time (pp. 109–11).

141 Reuter, ' "Imperial church system" ', 347–74 at p. 353; M. Parisse, 'L'Évêque impérial dans son diocèse: l'exemple lorrain aux Xe et XIe siècles', in L. Fenske, W. Rösener and T. Zotz (eds), *Institutionen, Kultur und Gesellschaft im Mittelalter: Festschrift für Josef Fleckenstein zu seinem 65. Geburtstag*, Sigmaringen 1984, 179–93; J.-P. Evrard, 'Verdun au temps de l'évêque Haymon (988–1024)', in Iogna-Prat and Picard, *Religion et culture*, 273–8; J.-L. Kupper, *Liège et l'église impériale XIe–XIIe siècles*, Paris 1981; Chatelain, 'Comte de Metz'.

142 On this incident see Kupper, *Liège*, 113–14. In general see ibid. 109–45; T. Reuter, '*Filii matris nostrae pugnant adversum nos*: bonds and tensions between prelates and their *milites* in the German high Middle Ages', in *Chiesa e mondo feudale nei secoli X–XII: atti della dodecisma settimana internazionale di studio Mendola, 24–28 agosto 1992*, Milan 1995, 247–76.

143 M. Parisse, 'Princes laïque et/ou moines, les évêques du Xe siècle', in *Il secolo di ferro* (Settimane xxxviii, 1991), 449–513 at p. 454.

144 For example, in 1012: Reuter, '*Filii matris*', 262. For further discussion of the relations of the bishops of Cambrai with their castellans see ibid. 257, 270. See also the castle built outside Liège probably by the duke of Lotharingia during Notker's episcopate (972–1008): Kupper, *Liège*, 465.

145 J. Nightingale, 'Bishop Gerard of Toul (963–94) and attitudes to episcopal office', in T. Reuter (ed.), *Warriors and churchmen in the high Middle Ages: essays presented to Karl Leyser*, London–Rio Grande 1992, 41–62.

146 Widric, *Vita S. Gerardi episcopi tullensis*, ed. G. Waitz (MGH, SS iv), c. xx, pp. 501–2. See also *Ex miraculi S. Mansueti auctore Adsone*, ed. G. Waitz (MGH, SS iv), 509–14.

military retinue which he had to reward with land; this led him into conflict with the local monastery at whose expense grants were made.[147] There are other examples of similar tensions in other sees, including Liège and Trier, whilst Haymo, on becoming bishop of Verdun (988–1024), had to restore lands lost to the counts of Blois and of Troyes, and to the faithful men of Count Godefroid of Verdun.[148] Such local tensions were compounded because Lotharingia, especially lower Lotharingia, was an area of considerable political tension and fluctuating control in which one political authority seldom dominated: a situation exemplified institutionally, perhaps, by the bishopric of Cambrai, which was under the political control of the Ottonian ruler but part of the west Frankish province of Rheims.[149] As a result, Lotharingian bishops were frequently engaged in the power politics of the region. In the first half of the tenth century the bishops of Metz, for example, defended their city on at least two occasions against the forces of the east Frankish rulers.[150] Kupper has suggested that the east Frankish rulers were anxious to support and enlarge the powers of the bishop of Liège in the tenth and eleventh centuries in order to establish a strong bastion against the counts of Flanders and Frisia.[151]

The picture is rather confused but is one of widespread tension especially for resources and authority amongst the social elite. Indeed Reuter has suggested that this culminated in a widespread breakdown of an idea of community between bishops and their *milites* which began in the second half of the eleventh century.[152] Tensions had obviously been in existence for some time. Bishops had great authority, but were also vulnerable.[153] The early eleventh-century Saxon bishop, Thietmar of Merseburg, despised the Lotharingians for their contempt for episcopal excommunication; Gerard of Toul's experience at the hands of his nobles suggests that Thietmar's opinion

---

[147] Nightingale, 'Bishop Gerard'.
[148] Evrard, 'Verdun'. For other sees see Reuter, '*Filii matris*', 268–9. These tensions continued into the eleventh century: Conrad, bishop of Trier, was killed by his *milites* in 1066, which Reuter has suggested (p. 271) is a sign of 'some kind of breakdown in authority or community'.
[149] Reuter, *Germany*, 237. On the nobility's exploitation of east versus west Frankish involvement in Lotharingia see B. Schneidmüller, 'Französische Lothringenpolitik im 10. Jahrhundert', in *Jahrbuch für westdeutsche Landesgeschichte* v (1979), 1–31.
[150] Against Henry I in 923 and Otto I in 939 see Chatelain, 'Comte de Metz', 112. See also the archbishops of Trier who looked to west Frankia in the mid 980s in support of their claim to primacy over Mainz: Mayr-Harting, *Ottonian book illumination*, ii. 82–3. In the late tenth century Beatrice, the regent for the duchy of Trier and sister of Hugh Capet of Francia, helped the Empress Adelaide and the Empress Theophanu to defend Otto III against the ambitions of Henry of Bavaria. For a review of the relations, both familial and political, between the nobility and the episcopate in Lotharingia see Parisse, 'Hommes et le pouvoir'.
[151] Kupper, *Liège*, 421–47.
[152] Reuter, '*Filii matris*', 271.
[153] Platelle discusses the important role of the bishop and public penance in eleventh-century Flanders and shows how the bishops worked with civil justice using public penance as one instrument of their authority: 'Violence'.

had some grounding in fact.[154] In such an environment the bishop had to maintain his authority whilst administering a rite such as public penance, which might be imposed upon unwilling penitents; he could not afford to show himself as their equal by prostrating himself with them and acknowledging his own sinfulness.

The differences between the north-central and Romano-German rites are in part explicable in terms of differing assumptions about the role of the bishop: Lotharingian bishops needed to assert themselves in order to preserve and safeguard their authority. But this is not a complete explanation of the north-central rite's peculiarities, and, in particular, it does not explain (as Mansfield's emphasis on the underlying theological changes does), why the rite includes neither prayers nor a ceremony for the absolution of the penitents on Maundy Thursday. We must therefore see social and theological forces working in parallel to produce a very different *ordo* from that recorded in the Romano-German pontifical.

The manuscript evidence requires that the liturgical changes documented in the north-central rite, which Mansfield argued preceded those in scholastic theology, be backdated from the eleventh to the tenth century. The appearance of the north-central rite at this time suggests a new stress on the individual but again predates other evidence, from the eleventh and twelfth centuries, for a renewed emphasis on individual sensibilities. In any case, these are only partial explanations: they do not explain why this rite appeared when and where it did.[155] The decline of Carolingian power in Lotharingian and north-west Frankia in the tenth century may thus provide the best explanation for the context in which it evolved: penance, and public penance as an aspect of rulership, was part of the legacy the tenth-century bishops inherited from the ninth-century Carolingian rulers.

Some Italian evidence

Jungmann identified three *ordines* for secret penance found in three Italian codices as belonging to the same liturgical family and sharing two important and unusual traits. First, he noted that they depart from conventional *ordines* for secret penance by providing unambiguous evidence that the rite was administered to several penitents at one time, although he failed to describe this at any length. Second, he argued that one member of the Italian group, the Arezzo pontifical, was important and early evidence for the evolution of a one-stop penitential procedure, that is that confession and the imposition of

---

[154] 'Innumeras antistitum excommunicaciones spreverunt et propter hoc stare diu non poterunt': Thietmar, *Chronicon* iv.14, p. 148.
[155] Although this rite continued in use in northern France until at least the early fourteenth century, its long ritual life probably owes more to the inertia of local traditions than to the circumstances surrounding its original composition.

penance were followed by immediate absolution, rather than a period of time, usually Lent, intervening between the second and third procedures.[156] Jungmann dated the Arezzo pontifical, and therefore evidence of the change in penitential procedure, to c. 1000; later historians have therefore cited Jungmann's second conclusion as evidence for a change in penitential procedure c. 1000 but neglected the implications of his first conclusion about the public aspect of secret penance.[157]

The three codices in which this *ordo* is recorded are: A (Milan, Biblioteca Ambrosiana, Cod. T. 27); *Vl* (Rome, Biblioteca Vallicelliana, cod. B. 58); and *Va* (BAV, MS Vat. lat. 4772 – the Arezzo pontifical). A is recorded in a collection of pastoral rites, including those for scrutiny and baptism, anointing of the sick, funeral rites, and blessings for ashes and hair shirts, as well as the more usual water and salt. This collection, which lacks a provenance before 1830, was dated by its editor on grounds of its palaeography and content to eleventh-century northern Italy.[158] *Vl* is recorded in a composite codex of several penitentials written in different Italian hands; this *ordo* appears to have been written on a spare quire at the end and is followed by a collection of penitential canons concerning homicide.[159] It seems to have been composed in an eleventh-century Italian scriptorium but a more detailed provenance is not known.[160] *Va* is recorded in a pontifical written in Arezzo for use in the cathedral there.[161] Originally dated to the early eleventh century,[162] Garrison's research on Tuscan manuscript decoration suggests it was written in the late eleventh or early twelfth century.[163] The codex finishes with the penitential *ordo* followed by extracts from the penitential canons contained in Burchard of Worm's *Decretum*, and then by several penitential prayers.

These three examples therefore all survive in eleventh-century manuscripts, only one of which may be securely dated to the end of the eleventh century. Textual variants between the texts of the *ordines* suggests they are not directly related. In the absence of more detailed dates and provenances it is difficult to date the development of this *ordo* securely without further work on the other rites with which it is associated, especially those in A, which is unfortunately beyond the scope of this study. Although Jungmann's dating of

---

[156] Jungmann, *Bussriten*, 190–6.
[157] Poschmann, *Penance*, 145.
[158] *North Italian services of the eleventh century*, ed. C. Lambot (HBS lxvii, 1931). Unfortunately I have not been able either to examine this manuscript or to find a more recent consideration of its palaeography.
[159] Fos 184v–7r. For a partial edition see *Bussbücher I*, 774–9.
[160] Vogel, '*Libri paenitentiales*', 85.
[161] *Bussbücher II*, 403–7.
[162] Stated most recently by Salmon, *Manuscrits*, no. 44, ii. 28–9.
[163] E. B. Garrison, *Studies in the history of medieval Italian painting*, Florence 1960, 314, 372, and 'Random notes on early Italian manuscripts', *La bibliofilia* lxxx (1978), 197–214 at p. 212.

THE PRACTICE OF PENANCE

c. 1000 is based on an insecure premise, namely a premature date for Va, this textual family of *ordines* may have tenth-century origins. But without a more secure dating and more secure provenances for this family it is impossible even to begin to suggest a context for which this text might have been composed or in which it might have been used.

It is unnecessary to construct a genealogy of contents for these three texts because Jungmann's research has demonstrated that, whilst they are related, Va is different from both A and Vl and all three differ from other preceding *ordines*.[164] But Jungmann, and subsequent historians, have failed to consider how it was intended that the *ordo* should be used, and the implications of this for our knowledge of eleventh-century penitential practice. Consideration of this question will therefore be made using the only securely dated text, Va, as a case study.

The *ordo* begins conventionally with instructions to the priest that when a penitent wishes to confess he ought to prepare himself by saying the standard preparation prayer, either alone in his own *cubiculum* or silently before they both enter the church.[165] Versions of this rubric are found in private penitential *ordines* from the ninth century onwards;[166] it is amplified in the Vl text to allow for bishops to act as alternative ministers.[167] Both Va and Vl suggest that they are to be administered to a single penitent. But after this 'those who ought to confess their sins are introduced, and they being prostrate on their face' the priest recites the responsory followed by the seven penitential psalms and a litany; the response to which is given in the plural suggesting that these texts were all intended to be said as part of a communal service, involving priest, several penitents and, perhaps, an audience[168] (the Vl text adds the detail that this should take place in the middle of the church).[169] Then come four [alternative] intercessory prayers, which are still part of a communal service as they are followed by this rubric

---

164 Jungmann, *Bussriten*, 194–5.
165 'Presbyteri quando fidelium recipiunt confessiones humiliare se debent et cum tristitia gemitu lacrimisque debent orare non solum pro suis delictis, sed etiam pro fratrum causa. Ait enim Apostolus: Quis infirmatur et ego non infirmor? Cum ergo venerit aliquis ad sacerdotem confiteri peccata sua, mandet ei sacerdos, ut expectet modicum donec intret Ecclesiam aut in cubiculum suum ad orationem. Si autem locus non est aptus ad hoc, in corde suo dicat hanc orationem. Domine Deus omnipotens propitius esto mihi peccatori ut condigne': *Bussbücher II*, 403.
166 For a similar text see Regino, *Libri duo* i.301, pp. 139–40; Burchard, *Decretum* xix.ii, 949–50.
167 'Episcopi vel presbyteri quando fidelium recipiunt': *Bussbücher I*, 776. In this it follows the version given in Regino, *Libri duo* i.301, p. 139. The A text contains a briefer rubric and an alternative preparation sequence: *North Italian services*, 35.
168 'Tunc introducantur hi qui peccata sua confiteri debent; prostratis in faciem sacerdos dicat': *Bussbücher II*, 403.
169 'Tunc introducantur hi qui peccata sua confiteri debent; Quibus in medio Ecclesiae in faciem prostratis sacerdos dicat': *Bussbücher I*, 776.

these prayers having been said, those [people] who are with him should rise up. Then the priest, seating himself before the altar with the cross of the Lord next to him on the right hand side, each [penitent] coming to him individually, should stand supplicant before him, so that the observant priest questions him soothingly and pleasantly.[170]

There then follows an interrogation of the orthodoxy of the penitent's beliefs and intention to repent fully which is fairly standard for *ordines* of this type. The text of the rubrics and prayers which follow after this refer only to a single penitent.

These rubrics suggest that the ritual began as a communal service involving several penitents as well as the priest, before evolving into a one-to-one encounter between priest and penitent for confession and absolution. Even this confession was a public affair: the priest and penitent were situated before the altar, in full view of both the other penitents and anyone else present. It was not a private ceremony in twentieth-century terms. The audience might not be able to hear what was going on, but they would be able to watch the proceedings. After the priest has questioned the penitent about his behaviour, the rubric instructs both the priest and the penitent to prostrate themselves on the ground and sing the Kyrie and the Pater Noster and to recite various prayers; they should then both get up and the priest tell the penitent, now before him on bended knees, what his penance should be. Before the priest absolved the penitent the penitent should get up.[171] The *ordo* ends with the priest making the sign of the cross over the penitent.[172] These various changes of position would make clear to the other penitents, and any other audience, the progress of the *ordo*. The language of gesture was as important as that of the spoken word. The possible presence of an audience may explain the introduction of the imposition of hands, which Jungmann argued was a recent innovation, evidenced in the Arezzo text, and by the making of the sign of the cross after the absolution prayer.[173] The penitent had to be seen to be absolved, even if it was not a formal 'public' penance.

The *Va* and *Vl* texts are very similar but related only indirectly to the *A* text which shows more clearly that this *ordo* was a hybrid between public and secret penitential *ordines*. After the priest's preparation prayer, the rubric instructs him to go outside the doors of the church and ask the penitents

---

170 'His expletis et hi qui cum eo surgant. Tunc sacerdote ante altare sedente et juxta eum crux Domini in dextera parte, unusquisque pro se singuli veniens, humiliter flexis genibus stet ante eum, quia sacerdos intuitus blande ac suaviter interrogat eum dicens . . .': *Bussbücher II*, 404–5.
171 'Tunc dicat ei sacerdos surgere et statim per stolam qua indutus est in dextera manu poenitens faciat sibi remissionem dicens . . .': ibid. 406.
172 'Per hoc signum salutiferae crucis D. N. J. Xti et per intercessionem istorum et omnium sanctorum misereatur tibi omnipotens Deus et donet tibi humilitatem veram, perserverantiam bonam, et indulgeat tibi omnia peccata tua praeterita, praesentia et futura et liberet te a laqueo diaboli et perducat te in vitam aeternam, per.': ibid. 407.
173 Jungmann, *Bussriten*, 190–4.

whether they wish to come to penance; they should reply 'Volumus'.[174] The priest should then, taking his/her right hand, lead each penitent into the church saying, 'come because the Lord Jesus Christ calls you to penance'.[175] Although penitents are taken into the church singly, the use of the second person plural, 'vos', reinforces the communal nature of the ritual. But the rest of the service refers to only a single penitent and is similar, although not identical to, the other two texts. After the *interrogatio* of the penitent and his promise to amend his ways, the priest lays his hands on the penitent's head whilst he recites a prayer in which he asks that God accept the penitent's confession and delete what he has done.[176] The service concludes with various alternative absolution prayers and, as in the other two texts, ends with the priest making the sign of the cross.

The initial ceremony in the only penitential *ordo* in the A codex echoes the 'venite' ceremony of the Maundy Thursday reconciliation rite in both the Romano-German pontifical and the north-central family. But the codicological context of its related *ordines* in the Va and Vl texts suggests it was an *ordo* for secret penance. In the Vl text this *ordo* is associated with Ash Wednesday: it is preceded by an instruction to the priest to address his flock on the need for penance at the beginning of Lent which was originally found in Theodulf's capitulary. It is, however, distinguished from public penance; the Vl text also contains a version of Regino's description of public penance whilst the Va codex includes an *ordo* for the reconciliation of penitents on Maundy Thursday.[177]

Historians of the late medieval and early modern periods have argued for the ambivalence between public and private inherent in all forms of penitential practice in their periods.[178] These three Italian *ordines* are evidence for an apparent ambivalence in the eleventh and tenth centuries between public and secret penance: the one-stop penance, characteristic of secret penance, is administered to several penitents, in a manner reminiscent of public penance, by either a priest or a bishop, in a service which owes more to the rites for secret (or personal) penance than those for public (or communal) penance. But whilst it may be difficult for modern historians to establish the differences between public and secret penance in this period, contemporaries were able to distinguish between the two as is made clear by the inclusion in the Va codex of an explicit *ordo* for the reconciliation of penitents on Maundy Thursday.[179]

---

[174] *North Italian services*, 35–6.
[175] 'Venite quia vocat vos dominus Iesus Christus ad paenitentiam': ibid.
[176] 'Praesta et da ei spacium paenitentiae ut et quod factum est deleas et nunquam aliquando aliud fieri permittas': ibid. 40.
[177] *Bussbücher* I, 774–5; Vatican, BAV, MS Vat. lat. 4772, fos 42–4.
[178] Bossy, 'Social history of confession', and *Christianity*, 35–56; N. Bériou, 'Autour de Latran IV (1215): la naissance de la confession moderne et sa diffusion', in Groupe de la Bussière, *Pratiques de la confession*, 74–93.
[179] Vatican, BAV, MS Vat. lat. 4772, fos 42–4.

Parochial penance

Unfortunately, as with those *ordines* in the Romano-German pontifical, these three families of rites survive in manuscripts which can only be associated with the higher echelons of the clergy. The reasons for this are two-fold: firstly, the majority of these manuscripts contain rites for public penance, of interest only to the higher clergy; secondly, such manuscripts were likely, once they had become redundant, to be preserved only in monastic and cathedral libraries. Yet, as we saw earlier, the evidence of both penitentials and episcopal capitularies of synodal legislation suggests that the lower, rural clergy were expected to administer penance, raising the question of how they did so. What *ordines* did they use?

There is evidence from the ninth century that some such priests in Bavaria and northern France possessed the necessary books: a sacramentary and a penitential.[180] But few of these books have been preserved, perhaps because rural churches lacked the mechanisms for institutional continuity available to larger institutions: redundant books were presumably thrown away or lost. Nevertheless Rob Meens's analysis of 106 manuscripts containing one or more of the so-called tripartite penitentials (penitentials drawing upon the Irish, Anglo-Saxon and Frankish traditions) demonstrates that in the ninth century the majority of such penitentials were used in a pastoral setting as practical guides to confessors on the ground. Manuscripts used in a pastoral setting include those handbooks which contain episcopal capitularies, sermons and liturgical works with a penitential, those which consist of only one penitential, and those which combine a penitential with liturgical *ordines*.[181] However, Meens admits that there was a marked decline in the number of such pastoral manuscripts in the tenth century when compared to the ninth: only three compared to twenty-eight. As he suggests, this might reflect increasing episcopal control in the tenth century or perhaps a decline in the delivery of pastoral care. The large numbers of penitentials copied in the ninth century may also have, to some extent, satiated the demand for such books; those churches which wanted one had one. Nevertheless, manuscripts were copied in this period, such as those manuscripts with penitential *ordines* discussed earlier in chapter 1. *Libelli* or collections of pastoral rites, including not just penance but baptism and death rites, such as A, were also copied in this period, presumably for those with an interest in the *cura animarum*.[182] Several at least have a monastic provenance and, it has been

---

[180] Hammer, 'Country churches'. His analysis of clerical inventories demonstrates that all churches owned a sacramentary but that penitentials were fewer in number although this may be because penitential texts were bound in with other texts and classified under another heading: Meens, 'Priests and books'.

[181] Idem, 'Frequency', 35–45.

[182] Palazzo, *Liturgical books*, 187–94, provides an introduction to these collections, sometimes known as *rituales*. For a more detailed study of this genre see P.-M. Gy, 'Collectaire, rituel, processionnal', *Revue des sciences philosophiques et théologiques* xliv (1960), 441–69.

suggested, were used for pastoral work outside the monastery.[183] Whilst such liturgical works remain relatively few in number in this period, they would repay a more detailed study in their own right.[184]

For, despite the selective nature of the surviving material, the evidence of the penitential rites suggests that penitential practice was of continuing importance at all levels within the Church. These three different families of penitential *ordines* therefore show how the rites for both public and secret penance evolved in response to local circumstances in three different areas at roughly the same time as the Romano-German pontifical. The monastery of Fulda evolved its own rites for penance for use not only within the community but on its estates; one for secret, or personal, penance, and a communal rite which was administered by the abbot. The north-central rite evolved in Lotharingia and northern west Frankia as part of an attempt by local bishops to assert their authority in the face of declining royal power. And in northern and central Italy a semi-public rite for secret penance appeared. The variation within the rites belonging to each family shows the continuing importance which copyists attributed to penance. These rites were not static: as the differences in the Fulda rites for penance over fifty years, and the differences in the north-central rite for reconciliation on Maundy Thursday between that in the Beauvais pontifical (s. xi^{in}) and that exported to Poland (c. 1075), testify. Their continuing change and evolution demonstrates the importance which these rites had for the clergy who composed and used them, and therefore for the people upon whom they were imposed.

See, for example, the *rituales* preserved in: Paris, Bibliothèque Mazarine, MS 525 (provenance: Asti, Piemont, s. xi); Milan, Biblioteca Ambrosiana, Cod. T. 27, edited in *North Italian services*; Monza, Biblioteca capitolare, Cod. b-15/128, described by F. dell'Oro in 'Un rituale del secolo X proveniente dall'Italia settentrionale', in de Clerck and Palazzo, *Rituels*, 215–49. See also Vatican, BAV, MS Archiv. S. Pietro H. 58 (Rome, s. x–xii) which combines liturgical with other material (including a penitential) in a clerical handbook: Salmon, 'Un Témoin'.

[183] Palazzo, *Liturgical books*, 188. See, for example, *Ein Rituale in beneventanischer Schrift*.

[184] The social history of such *libelli* or *rituales* is a topic which I intend to consider in the future.

6

Penance and the Wider World

In April 999 Arduin, marquis of Ivrea, was called before a church council in Rome, presided over by the emperor and pope, excommunicated and sentenced to live as an itinerant pilgrim for his murder of Bishop Peter of Vercelli in 997.[1] In 1073 Count Theoderic went barefoot to Jerusalem to atone for his murder of Conrad, archbishop of Trier.[2] Although it is a moot point whether Arduin ever did penance, he and Theoderic are only two amongst many known (and probably many more unknown) penitential pilgrims.[3] Pilgrimage as a sentence for particularly heinous crimes, such as parricide or the murder of a cleric, had a long-established tradition: the sinner was made an outcast, exiled from the community to which he belonged, either for an indefinite period, as in the case of Arduin, or assigned a more precise objective, as in the case of Theoderic. Such a policy had its own dangers which were recognised by the authorities, who made repeated attempts throughout the ninth and tenth centuries to put an end to the practice, so that penitents could not escape from fulfilling the requirements of their penitential sentence by leaving the community, but must instead remain in one place to perform their penance under the supervision of their bishop.[4] Yet, as the sentences imposed on Arduin and Theoderic and the repeated references in other sources to the problems caused by penitential pilgrims wandering the countryside in their chains reveal, penitential pilgrimage continued as a practice. For the sight of such pilgrims, usually barefoot, often clad in iron, on the road would have instilled in those who

---

[1] MGH, Constitutiones I, no. xxv, p. 53. This case was discussed more fully in the introduction.
[2] Bernold of Constance, Chronicon, ed. G. Pertz (MGH, SS v), a. 1066, a. 1073, pp. 428–30; Vogel, 'Le Pèlerinage', 129.
[3] Ibid. 128–9. See also the penitential pilgrimage to Jerusalem of Robert II, duke of Normandy (1028–35), probably for his murder of his brother: Orderic Vitalis, Historia aecclesiastica, ed. M. Chibnall, Oxford 1968–80, ii. 10; D. C. Douglas, William the Conqueror: the Norman impact upon England, London 1964, 35–6. For other examples see Platelle, 'Violence', 145–61; Bull, Knightly piety, ch. v.
[4] See Vogel, 'Le Pèlerinage', on penitential pilgrimage in general, and (pp. 137–8) on the unsuccessful efforts of ninth-century rulers and churchmen to put a stop to the practice. A canon issued by the Council of Mainz (847) that parricides should stay in one place was taken up by Regino and Burchard (p. 138). But only one tenth-century insular penitential suggests pilgrimage as a penance for the murder of a cleric: Penitential of Pseudo-Egbert IV.vi, ed. B. Thorpe, in Ancient laws and institutions of England, London 1840, ii. 205.

saw them a healthy respect for the institution of penance, as well as satisfying the demands of the wider community for suitable punishment of criminals.[5]

But such penitential sentences were not the norm and were imposed on only a minority of sinners. This chapter investigates instead the effect which the practice of penance had upon the majority of Christians through studying its impact on certain key areas of the early medieval world – rulership, politics, warfare and sexual relations. It does not explore the relationship between penance and specific sins, such as homicide, incest, sexual relations outside marriage or the practice of magic, for example, but rather how far penitential practice influenced the way in which life was conducted by both the clergy and more especially the laity in this period, suggesting possible ways in which the historian can try to overcome the problems of the prescriptive bias of the bulk of material for penitential practice outlined in the previous chapters.

Let us begin by starting at the top, for the importance of kings in this period means that the impact made by penance on perceptions of kingship has implications for the role of penance in the wider world.

Royal penance

Royal penance is a constant, if minor, theme in medieval writings about kings and kingship.[6] The Old Testament provided the models of King David and Achab; the golden age of the 'happy Christian emperors' that of the Emperor Theodosius who did penance at the behest of St Ambrose for his role in the massacre by imperial troops at Thessalonika in 390,[7] and in the more recent past that of the Carolingian emperor, Louis the Pious, who performed public penance voluntarily at Attigny in 821 and under episcopal duress at Soissons in 833.[8] Perhaps most famously Henry IV performed a penitential act before

---

[5] For references to penitential pilgrims in chains see J. Sumption, *Pilgrimage: an image of mediaeval religion*, London 1975, ch. vii, esp. p. 102; E.-R. Labande, 'Recherches sur les pèlerins dans l'Europe des XIe et XIIe siècles', in *Cahiers de civilisation médiévale* i (1958), 159–69, 339–47; Platelle, 'Violence', 145–59. Whilst penitential pilgrimage was sanctioned by canon law, the imposition of iron chains was not, although it is frequently mentioned in *vitae* and seems to have been a response to popular demand for the chastisement and humiliation of notorious sinners: ibid. 153.

[6] The starting point for any scholar wishing to study royal penance is still R. Schieffer, 'Von Mailand nach Canossa: ein Beitrag zur Geschichte der christlichen Herrscherbusse von Theodosius der Grosse bis zu Heinrich IV', *DA* xxviii (1972), 333–70.

[7] 2 Reg. XII; 3 Reg. XXI.xxvii–xxix. The phrase is from Augustine, *De civitate dei* V.xxiv: *Saint Augustine: The city of God against the pagans*, ed. and trans. W. M. Green, London–Cambridge, Mass. 1963, ii. 261–3. For the example of Theodosius see ep. li, *Sancti Ambrosi opera pars X: epistulae et acta*, II/i: *Epistularum libri VII–VIII*, ed. M. Zelzer (CCEL lxxxii, 1990), ii. 60–7. The most recent analysis of these events is that of N. McLynn in *Ambrose of Milan: Church and court in a Christian capital*, Berkeley–London 1994, 317–30.

[8] For Louis the Pious see de Jong, 'Power and humility', and T. F. X. Noble, 'Louis the Pious and his piety reconsidered', *Revue belge de philologie et d'histoire* lviii (1980), 297–316.

Pope Gregory VII at Canossa in 1077.[9] Medieval writers were especially fond of the Davidic model, in which the ruler's penance was used by churchmen to assert the superiority of spiritual over secular authority, and to demonstrate the ruler's humility before God. By portraying kings as undergoing the same penitential rituals as other Christians, they were shown to be ordinary sinners, but by humiliating themselves before God kings also exalted themselves in the eyes of their subjects, advertising their relationship with the Almighty. Royal penance need not be in and of itself humiliating; rather, it could be empowering, as Thomas F. X. Noble has shown for Louis the Pious's penance at Attigny, when the emperor did public penance for his sins against his family.[10] The king acknowledged his sin, showing himself thus to be human but at the same time demonstrating his connection with God. On the other hand, penance was sometimes a submissive and humbling experience for the king, as it was for Louis the Pious at Soissons in 833, when, as part of a dispute between himself and a significant number of his magnates, led by his three eldest sons, the Carolingian emperor was forced to undergo public penance and was thus stripped of his office.[11] Whilst the penances of Louis the Pious and Henry IV are familiar to historians, those ascribed in the intervening period to Otto III (983–1002) and Henry III (1039–56) are less so, yet they provide evidence not only for the development and refinement of a Davidic model of royal penance in this period, but also for an alternative model for royal penance.[12]

Otto III's penance is known to us through two detailed accounts which follow the traditional model for royal penance, of sacerdotal superiority and royal humility.[13] They are found in the anonymous early eleventh-century *Life* of the south-Italian Greek monk, Nilus, and Peter Damian's mid eleventh-century *Life* of the Latin monk, Romuald; both agreed that Otto undertook a penitential pilgrimage to the shrine of St Michael at Monte Gargano for his involvement in the suppression of the Rome rebellion in 998 in which the anti-pope John Philagathos, who was also Otto's godfather, was mutilated – his ears, nose and tongue were cut off, and his eyes put out – and

---

[9] *Das Register Gregors VII*, ed. E. Caspar (MGH, Epistolae selectae, 2nd edn, Berlin, 1955), IV.xii, pp. 311–14. See Morrison, 'Canossa'; Schieffer, 'Von Mailand nach Canossa'; T. Reuter, 'Canossa: drama or stage-management?', unpubl. paper.
[10] Noble, 'Louis the Pious'.
[11] *Episcoporum de poenitentia, quam Hludovicus imperator professus est, relatio Compendiensis* (833), MGH, *Capitularia II*, no. cxcvii, pp. 51–5; *Agobardi cartula de poenitentia ab imperatore acta*, ibid. no. cxcviii, pp. 56–7. On Louis's penance at Soissons see de Jong, 'Power and humility'.
[12] Neither these two cases of royal penance nor that ascribed to the west Frankish king Robert the Pious (987–1031) by the author of his *vita*, Helgaud of Fleury, are mentioned by Schieffer, 'Von Mailand nach Canossa'. Koziol notices those of Robert the Pious and Henry III only briefly: *Begging*, 102. On the case of Robert the Pious see S. Hamilton, 'A new model for royal penance? Helgaud of Fleury's *Life of Robert the Pious*', EME vi (1997), 189–200.
[13] For a more detailed consideration of Otto III's penance, on which the following account is based, see Hamilton, 'Otto III's penance'.

the rebellion's leader, Crescentius, executed.[14] But they give different accounts of the specific circumstances behind Otto's penance.

According to the earlier Greek *Life* of Nilus, Otto III reneged on a promise he made to Nilus to give him custody of Philagathos. Instead Philagathos was led in a parade of humiliation around Rome, whereupon Nilus cursed the emperor and left Rome. But Otto subsequently 'proclaimed that he repented; he went on foot from Rome to the incorporeal commander-in-chief at Gargano'.[15] On Otto's return from the shrine of St Michael at Gargano he visited Nilus at his monastery at Serperi and offered him anything he wanted; Nilus refused, saying he only wanted the salvation of Otto's soul: 'Even if you happen to be emperor, you have to die as one of mankind and come to judgement, and give an account of the good and evil deeds you have done.'[16] The emperor, moved to tears, placed his crown in the hands of the saint and received his blessing. This was in line with the teachings of Basilian monasticism that forgiveness depends on obedience; Otto demonstrated such obedience by acknowledging his sin, through penance, and thus Nilus' authority over him.[17]

Peter Damian, writing c. 1042, gave a different account of Otto's penitential pilgrimage to Monte Gargano. He described how Crescentius was besieged by Otto's men in the Castel Sant'Angelo and was deceived into giving himself up through the promise of a safe conduct, whereupon he was executed. Afterwards, to compound his sin, Otto accepted Crescentius' wife as a concubine. But he then confessed the sin of perjury to the holy man Romuald and for the sake of penance went barefoot to Monte Gargano, and subsequently spent the whole of Lent with Romuald at his monastery of St Apollinaris at Classe where he undertook various penitential acts and promised to relinquish the empire and become a monk.[18]

Both *vitae* are historically inaccurate. Peter Damian seems to have fused the siege of Tivoli in 1001 with the Rome rebellion of 997–8 and omits any reference to John Philagathos; and Mathilde Uhrlirz has demonstrated that Otto must have visited Serperi before he went to Gargano, rather than on his return as recorded in the *Vita Nili*.[19] Both authors used this incident to demonstrate the superiority of their respective saints over secular authority. Indeed this is one of the main themes of both works: Nilus' encounter with the emperor is merely the culmination of a series of victorious encounters

---

14 VN, c. xci, p. 128. The *vita* is more widely available in a less accurate edition in PG cxx. 9–166; both editions follow the same chapter division. Peter Damian, *Vita Beati Romualdi*, ed. G. Tabacco (Fonti per la storia d'Italia xciv, Rome 1957), c. xxv, pp. 52–4.
15 VN, c. xci, p. 128.
16 Ibid. c. xciii, p. 129.
17 Basil the Great, *The shorter rules*, c. xv, PG xxxi. 1092.
18 Peter Damian, *Vita Romualdi*, c. xxv, pp. 52–4.
19 C. Phipps, 'Saint Peter Damian's *Vita Beati Romualdi*: introduction, translation and analysis', unpubl. PhD diss. London 1988, 200–3; M. Uhrlirz, *Jahrbücher des deutschen Reiches unter Otto II. und Otto III.*, II: *Otto III., 983–1002*, Berlin 1954, 291–2, 534–7.

with various lords, including the prefect of Calabria and the widow of the prince of Capua; Romuald's encounter is merely one of several in which he converted noblemen to the monastic life, including the doge of Venice, a Frankish count and a son of the Polish duke.[20]

These claims to ecclesiastical superiority over secular authority had become such a commonplace of both western and eastern Christianity that both of these authors, Latin and Greek, felt able to appropriate the same incident, Otto III's penitential pilgrimage, to assert their subject's authority over the king. They were following in a long and distinguished tradition which stretched back to Ambrose and Theodosius; more recently Hincmar of Rheims (845–82) had cited David's penance to argue that a king should be judged by the Church, as had his contemporary Sedulius Scottus (d. c. 884), to demonstrate the need for a pious ruler to show humility and submit to the admonitions of priests.[21] Both ninth-century writers also linked David's penance and humble submission to Nathan to the humility shown by Theodosius in his penance at the behest of Ambrose.[22] This association between a good king and penance was at least in part an extension of Carolingian ideas of rulership: kingship is an *officium* or *ministerium*, and the ruler must therefore demonstrate his humility before God.[23] David's penance was thus often used by Carolingian writers, especially episcopal writers, to assert the superiority of ecclesiastical authority over royal power.

The very popularity of this model of royal penance has, however, led some historians to misinterpret the penance of one eleventh-century king, Henry III of Germany (1039–56), who is reported to have done public penance at his mother's funeral in 1043.[24] This incident is known only through a letter written to the king by Bern, abbot of Reichenau, which survives in a fragment published by the Magdeburg Centuriators in their section on funeral practices in which he described how,

---

[20] VN, cc. liii, lxxix, pp. 95–6, 117–18; Peter Damian, *Vita Romualdi*, cc. v, xi, xxvi, pp. 21–5, 32–3, 54–6; Hamilton, 'Otto III's penance', 92–3.

[21] Hincmar of Rheims, *De divortio Lotharii regis et Theutbergae reginae*, ed. L. Böhringer (MGH, Concilia iv, supplementum i, Hanover 1992), 246–50. See also J. L. Nelson, 'Kingship, law and liturgy in the political thought of Hincmar of Rheims', EHR xcii (1977), 241–79 at p. 246 n. 4 (repr. in her *Politics and ritual*, 133–71). Sedulius Scottus, *Liber de rectoribus christianis*, ed. S. Hellmann, in *Sedulius Scottus*, Munich 1906, xii.53–7. For what follows see Hamilton, 'A new model for royal penance?', esp. pp. 197–9.

[22] Sedulius Scottus, *Liber de rectoribus Christianis* xii.53–7. For Hincmar see *De divortio*, 247.

[23] H. H. Anton, *Fürstenspiegel und Herrscherethos in der Karolingerzeit*, Bonn 1968, 404–30. For a review of the ideas associated with the rule of Louis the Pious see K. F. Werner, 'Hludovicus Augustus: gouverner l'empire chrétien – idées et réalités', in P. Godman and R. Collins (eds), *Charlemagne's heir: new perspectives on the reign of Louis the Pious (814–40)*, Oxford 1990, 3–123.

[24] For further detail on what follows see S. Hamilton, 'The practice of penance, c. 900–c. 1050', unpubl. PhD diss., London 1997, 218–35.

When recently you had to commend your mother Gisela of blessed memory to the earth in human fashion, you threw off the royal purple and assumed the mourning habit of penitence. With bare feet, with hands stretched out in the shape of the cross, you sank to the ground in the presence of all the people, you wet the pavement with tears, you did public penance, and you moved all those present to tears. Thus by weeping and by penance you satisfied the priests of the Lord, who will render account for you, and you appeased divine mercy.[25]

Both Franz Josef Schmale, who edited Bern's correspondence, and Carl Erdmann drew parallels between the final sentence, about how the king through his penance satisfied the priests, and the fifth-century Gelasian letter, written by Pope Gelasius I to the Emperor Anastastius, which argued that sacerdotal authority was superior to that of royal power:

There are two things, most august emperor, by which this world is chiefly ruled: the sacred authority of the priesthood and the royal power. Of these two, the priests carry the greater weight, because they will have to render account in the divine judgement even for the kings of men.[26]

Thus Bern's account has been interpreted as setting Henry's penance within the Davidic model. Yet the parallels with the Gelasian letter's ultimate source for this phrase, Paul's letter to the Hebrews xiii.17, are more convincing: 'Obey them that have the rule over you, and submit yourselves: for they watch for our souls, as they that must give account, that they may do so with joy, and not with grief: for that is unprofitable for you', especially as this phrase was widely used; Bern may have been familiar with it from the Benedictine rule where it is used to describe the duties of the abbot.[27] And

---

[25] 'Cum nuper uenerandae memoriae matrem uestram Giselam more humano terrae commendare debuissetis, abiecta regali purpura, assumptoque lugubri poenitentiae habitu, nudis pedibus, expansis in modum crucis manibus, coram omni populo in terram corruistis, lachrymis pauimentum rigastis, publicam poenitentiam egistis omnesque qui aderant ad lachrymas commouistis. Sic flendo, sic poenitendo Domini sacerdotibus, qui pro uobis rationem reddituri sunt, satisfecistis et misericordiam diuinam placastis': *Die Briefe des Abtes Bern von Reichenau*, ed. F. J. Schmale, Stuttgart 1961, no. xxiv, 54. See also Flacius Illyricus, *Historia ecclesiae: undecima centuria*, 298.

[26] 'Duo quippe sunt, imperator auguste, quibus principaliter mundus hic regitur: auctoritas sacrata pontificum, et regalis potestas. In quibus tanto gravius est pondus sacerdotum, quanto etiam pro ipsis regibus hominum in divino reddituri sunt examine rationem': *Epistolae Romanorum pontificum genuinae et quae ad eos scriptae sunt a S. Hilaro usque ad Pelagium II*, ed. A. Thiel, Brunsberg 1858, ep. xii.2, pp. 350–1; Erdmann, *Politischen Ideenwelt*, 112–19.

[27] 'Obedite praepositis vestris, et subjacete eis; ipsi enim pervigilant, quasi rationem pro animabus vestris reddituri, ut cum gaudio hoc faciant, et non gementes; hoc enim non expedit vobis': Hebrews xiii.17. See the Benedictine rule: 'Sciatque quia qui suscipit animas regendas paret se ad rationem reddendam et quantum sub cura sua fratrum se habere scierit numerum, agnoscat pro certo quia in die iudicii ipsarum omnium animarum est redditurus domino rationem, sine dubio addita et suae animae': *RB*, c. ii, vv. xxxvii–viii, ii. 450. A further argument against such a reading is that the Gelasian text was not widely known in

indeed Bern's description echoes the monastic punishment process for grave faults as much as that for liturgical penance: the Benedictine rule prescribes that the errant monk should prostrate himself outside the doors of the oratory during his penance, then when satisfaction has been done, he should appear prostrate at the feet of the abbot and the community, and then be accepted back into the community.[28]

Previous historians have placed Henry's penance in the context of royal ideology, specifically that of Christological kingship.[29] Henry is seen to be acting at Speyer as the representative of sinful man, being reconciled to the divine mercy of God through a penitential act, thus exemplifying the salvation of mankind by his imitation of Christ's humility on the cross. By his prostration he shows how sinful man would, like Christ, be raised up to reign in eternity. This ideological explanation connects Henry's action at Speyer in 1043 with the peace indulgences he promulgated later that year and with the penitential element in the victory celebrations after the defeat of the Hungarians at the battle of Menfö in 1044, for which Henry, fasting, barefoot and clad in wool, led a thanksgiving procession around the churches of Regensburg.[30] But Henry's actions after the battle were not unusual as victory celebrations nor is there an overt link between his actions at Speyer and his subsequent acts as peace-maker and victorious king, and attempts to establish one ignore the explicit link which Bern made between Henry's penance and his mother's death: 'When recently you had to [debuissetis] commend your mother to the earth in human fashion, you ... assumed the mournful habit of penance.'[31]

The funeral of the king's mother, who was also the only queen at court at this time, was an important state occasion: she was, according to the Altaich Annalist, buried at Speyer by her son and the bishops and princes of the realm, next to her husband, the Emperor Conrad.[32] A lead tablet placed in her tomb details the thirteen bishops and archbishops who participated in her funeral and suggests that the *sacerdotes* whom the king satisfied by his penance included all the most important prelates of his realm.[33] But why

---

the early Middle Ages: L. Knabe, *Die gelasianische Zweigewaltentheorie bis zum Ende des Investiturstreits*, Berlin 1936.

[28] *RB*, c. xliv, ii. 592–4.

[29] Erdmann, *Politischen Ideenwelt*, 112–19; K. Schnith, 'Recht und Friede: zum Königsgedanken im Umkreis Heinrichs III', *Historisches Jahrbuch* lxxxi (1962), 22–57.

[30] See Hamilton, 'The practice of penance', 224–5.

[31] See, however, L. Bornscheuer, *Miseriae regum: Untersuchungen zum Krisen- und Todesgedanken in den herrschaftstheologischen Vorstellungen der ottonish-salischen Zeit*, Berlin 1968, 206–7, who dismisses attempts to connect Speyer with another event and sees it as merely another manifestation of *humiliatio-exaltio*.

[32] *Annales Altahenses maiores*, a. 1043, ed. E. L. B. ab Oefele (MGH, SRG iv, 1891), 32.

[33] H. J. Rieckenberg, 'Das Geburtsdatum der Kaiserin Gisela', *DA* ix (1952), 535–8. The text of the tablet is given at pp. 535–6. For a plate of the tablet with accompanying commentary see H. E. Kubach and W. Haas, *Der Dom zu Speyer*, Munich 1972, ii, plate 1459, and now *Das Reich der Salier 1024–1125: Katalog zur Ausstellung des Landes Rheinland-Pfalz veranstaltet*

Henry had to undertake penance at his mother's funeral is something upon which Bern fails to enlighten us. Gisela's funeral was widely reported by her contemporaries, but none of them mention Henry's penance,[34] and this, together with the laudatory tone of Bern's letter, and of his other correspondence with Henry, suggests that Henry's penance was regarded as a personal, rather than a public matter;[35] Henry was fulfilling his filial duty – doing what he ought – to satisfy the priests on his mother's behalf; his actions were those of a son, rather than of a king.[36]

There is evidence that other children assumed direct responsibility for their parents' sins. About 160 years before Gisela's death Louis the German had a vision of his father, Louis the Pious, in the afterlife, in which the emperor asked him to free him from his torments so that he might have eternal life. Louis took prompt action and dispatched letters to the monasteries throughout his kingdom asking them to intervene on behalf of the soul

---

vom römisch-germanischen Zentralmuseum Mainz Forschunginstitut für Vor- und Frühgeschichte in Verbindung mit dem bischöflichen Dom- und Diözesanmuseum Mainz in Speyer 1992, Sigmaringen 1992, 290–2. To date this tablet has been primarily of interest to genealogists who are interested in whether the date of her birth, recorded on the tablet as 999, is accurate. Such tablets are not uncommon, although no others (to my knowledge) record in such detail those present at the funeral. A similar plaque was also found in the tomb of Gisela's husband, Conrad II, recording the date of his death and that he was buried in the presence of his son: Kubach and Haas, *Der Dom*, i. 932–3; ii, plate 1449; *Das Reich der Salier*, 289. It is unclear why such plaques were placed with the dead. However, in his *Constitutions*, Lanfranc, archbishop of Canterbury (1070–89), required that a written absolution of sins be placed on the chest of a dead monk in his tomb: *Decreta Lanfranci: the monastic constitutions of Lanfranc*, ed. D. Knowles, London 1951, 130. Professor Robert Bartlett suggests that inscribed lead crosses had a similar function for English bishops: *England under the Norman and Angevin kings*, Oxford 2000. I would like to thank Professor Bartlett for telling me about these Anglo-Norman examples. Other examples seem to have served the simple purpose of identifying the dead person. Thus two eleventh-century lead plaques record the deaths of two *reclusae* enclosed at Saint-Armand, Rouen: H. Platelle, 'Les Relations entre l'abbaye Saint-Amand de Rouen et l'abbaye Saint-Amand d'Elnone', in *La Normandie bénédictine au temps de Guillaume le Conquérant (XIe siècle)*, Lille 1967, 83–106 at pp. 84–6.

34 Lampert of Hersfeld, *Annales*, a. 1043, in *Lamperti monachi hersfeldensis opera*, ed. O. Holder Egger (MGH, SRG xxxviii, 1894), 58; *Annales altahenses maiores*, a. 1043, p. 32; Hermann of Reichenau, *Chronicon*, a. 1043, ed. G. H. Pertz (MGH, SS v, 1843), p. 124. *Annales Sangallenses maiores (St Gallerstiftsbibliothek cod. 915 u. 453)*, a. 1043, in *Die annalistischen Aufzeichnungen des Klosters St. Gallen*, ed. C. Henking, St Gallen 1884, 319–20.

35 On the tone of Bern's correspondence with Henry III see Hamilton, 'The practice of penance', 219–20.

36 It is of course possible that Henry was doing penance on his own behalf for reasons unspecified. He could also have fallen out with his mother, but there is no evidence to suggest this hypothesis: ibid. 224–35. If Henry were doing penance for an offence against his mother, one might expect more tangible evidence of his penance such as that of Duke Theoderic I, who established the monastery of Sainte-Maxe de Bar on the orders of the pope as a penance for placing his mother in prison: *Fundatio ecclesiae S. Maximi Barrensis*, ed. O. Holder Egger (MGH, SS xv/2), 981. The evidence for Theoderic's case is somewhat problematic: see the discussion in Parisse, 'Les Hommes et le pouvoir', 260.

in torment with prayers.³⁷ But Henry did not simply delegate the prayers to the clergy; instead he acted in the way recommended by the ninth-century Frankish noblewoman, Dhuoda. Writing c. 842, she advised her son William, who was with the court of Charles the Bald, to pray not only for himself but also for his father and godfather, and the dead, especially his father's parents, and also gave him specific instructions on the prayers he should say for her after her own death.³⁸ That this practice continued into the eleventh century is suggested by the inclusion of a prayer to be said on behalf of the father or mother of the orator in the eleventh-century prayerbook probably composed for Arnulf, archbishop of Milan (998–1018).³⁹ There was also a tradition in German noble families, especially those from Saxony, of surviving family members undertaking penitential actions on behalf of the dead.⁴⁰ Karl Leyser suggested that this task was the specific responsibility of women.⁴¹ But there were no obvious surviving women to perform this action for Gisela; she had no daughters and Henry was a widower. Henry's action was only unusual in that he was a man, but as he was a member of the Suabian nobility it fits into an overall pattern of personal supplication to God by the laity on behalf of their dead relations, in addition to the prayers of the clergy. The difference in the behaviour of Henry and of Louis probably reflects not so much a difference in their personalities as a change in lay piety over the course of the two centuries.

Previous historians have demonstrated how Henry's actions should be seen as part of a tradition of royal ritual; through making supplication to God, the ruler expressed the source of his power to his audience and also his own humanity. Such an interpretation should not be dismissed out of hand; most rituals are polysemic.⁴² But all royal rituals must have a catalyst in an event, and this ideological aspect should not obscure the other functions of the ritual, including the desire of the king to mourn and do penance on behalf of his mother.

---

37 *Annales fuldenses*, a. 874, ed. F. Kurze (MGH, SRG vii, 1891), 80. For evidence that these letters were sent see Flodoard, *Historia remensis ecclesiae* III.xx, 513.
38 Dhuoda, *Manuel pour mon fils*, ed. P. Riché, trans. B. de Vregille and C. Mondésert (SC ccxxv, Paris 1975), VIII.vii, xiv, xv; X.v, vi, pp. 310, 318–22, 354, 356. On this aspect see Hamilton, 'The practice of penance', 201–9.
39 'Oratio pro patre uel matre quomodo oratur', ed. O. Heiming, in 'Ein benediktinisch-ambrosianisches Gebetbuch des frühen 11. Jahrhunderts: Brit. Mus. Egerton 3763 (ehemals Dyson Perrins 48)', *Archiv für Liturgiewissenschaft* viii/2 (1964), 325–435, no. lvi, pp. 419–20. I follow here the attribution to Arnulf put forward by D. H. Turner in 'The prayerbook of Archbishop Arnulph II of Milan', *Rev. Bén.* lxx (1960), 360–92, rather than that of Heiming who argued for a monastic context for the prayerbook.
40 *VMP*, c. viii, pp. 158–61; Thietmar, *Chronicon* II.xl; VI.lxxxv, pp. 88–91, 376–7; Bruno of Querfurt, *Vita S. Adalberti episcopi*, ed. G. H. Pertz (MGH, SS iv), c. xii, p. 600.
41 K. Leyser, *Rule and conflict in an early medieval society: Ottonian Saxony*, Bloomington–London 1979, 72.
42 Turner, *Forest of symbols*, 50–1. On the significance of this for medieval rituals see Koziol, *Begging*, 307–11.

Bern's letter shows that the 'Davidic' paradigm did not exhaust the resonance of royal penance: kings could also be represented as acting in a 'private' (i.e. familiar) context, which was rendered, at least in this case, as more important than the public one.

Penance and lay piety

Henry III's behaviour also fits into the model of monastic piety which seems to have been a commonplace of descriptions of tenth-century Ottonian royalty; thus Otto I is recorded by Widukind of Corvey as attending Matins, mass and Vespers every day, and Thietmar described how Otto III kept nightly vigils and regular fasts in terms which recall Dhuoda's advice to her son to confess his sins in secret with sighs and tears.[43] It was a model which emphasised an awareness of personal sinfulness, and suggests one way in which the Church's attempts to promote penitential awareness found a response in the personal piety of certain princes and nobles in this period.

More tangible evidence than the models of good kingship presented by Widukind and Thietmar may be found in the prayerbook composed for Otto III, probably whilst he was a child, on the orders of his chancellor Willigis, archbishop of Mainz (975–1011).[44] Although prayers concerned with personal salvation are a commonplace of early medieval prayerbooks, one prayer in this collection headed, 'whoever prays this prayer daily shall not feel the torments of hell in eternity' stands out.[45] It requires the orator to make a long avowal of his sinfulness, requests God's mercy by recalling previous examples of His aid to Tobias and Sarah, a married couple, an indication amongst others suggesting a lay audience for the prayer. It asks God to give the orator virtue and to save him, requesting the Lord to dissolve all his sins before he dies: 'I pray to you St Peter who hold the keys of the kingdom of heaven to absolve me from my sins on this earth.'[46]

---

[43] Widukind of Corvey, *Rerum gestarum saxonicarum libri tres*, ed. H.-E. Lohmann and P. Hirsch (MGH, SRG lx, 1935), III.lxxv, pp. 126–7. 'Hic egregius cesar, quamvis exterius vultu semper hilari se simularet, tamen consciencie secreto plurima facinora ingemiscens, noctis silencio vigiliis oracionibusque intentus, lacrimarum quoque rivis abluere non desistit': Thietmar, *Chronicon* IV.xlviii, p. 187. Cf. 'Da illis, quod melius nosti, tuam occulte cum suspirio et lachrymis ueram confessionem': Dhuoda, *Manuel* III.xi, p. 196.

[44] Munich, Bayerische Staatsbibliothek, Clm 30111. The most recent study of this codex is K. Görich and E. Klemm, *Bayerische Staatsbibliothek: das Gebetbuch Ottos III. Clm 30111* (Patrimonia lxxxiv, Munich 1995).

[45] 'Quicumque hac oratione oraverit cottidie tormenta inferni in aeternum non sentiet' (fos 31–4). For the fullest description of the prayerbook's contents see J. A. Endres and A. Ebner, 'Ein Königsgebetbuch des elften Jahrhunderts', in S. Ehses (ed.), *Festschrift zum elfhundertjährigen Jubiläum des deutschen Campo Santo in Rom*, Freiburg-im-Breisgau 1897, 296–307 at pp. 303–4.

[46] 'Te deprecor, sancte Petre, qui tenes claues regni coelorum, ut mea peccata soluas super

Prayers such as this, which emphasise the importance attached to repentance, originated in a monastic setting.[47] Although more than sixty prayerbooks survive from the tenth and eleventh centuries, only a few of them seem to have been composed for non-ecclesiastics.[48] Yet not all the prayerbooks owned by laymen and women may have survived; the evidence of ninth-century wills suggests that the nobility owned *libelli precum*, whilst Dhuoda's manual suggests how one member of the ninth-century nobility thought one should pray personally and provides a pointer as to how the prayerbook associated with Otto III may have been used.[49] She advised her son to confess his sins in secret and through true amendment and satisfaction spend his time in penance in order to merit salvation.[50] The evidence from prayerbooks, especially, suggests that personal prayer was becoming more widespread amongst the laity from the ninth to eleventh centuries. Penitential concerns were an especial preoccupation of such books, and they provided one means whereby penitential interests entered the mainstream, as it were, of early medieval anxiety about salvation. Such anxiety was not always selfish: feminine piety was recorded in more altruistic terms; Mathilda, wife of Henry the Fowler, and founder of the convent of canonesses at Quedlinburg, is recorded in her *Vita posterior*, written c. 1002, as spending the night in prayer secretly in church asking for the pardon of sinners and eternal rest for souls.[51] The laity were aware of their own sinfulness and mortality and were making some efforts to deal with it; prayer was not something which they always delegated to the clergy. Rather the religious services which the clergy undertook were a necessary adjunct to their own efforts. Penance was an important element in both halves of this equation.

---

terram': ibid. 304. Mayr-Harting discusses the penitential import of this prayer in *Ottonian book illumination*, i. 173.

[47] K. Hughes, 'Some aspects of Irish influence on early English private prayer', *Studia Celtica* v (1970), 48–61; Frantzen, *Literature*, 84–91.

[48] P. Salmon, 'Livrets de prières de l'époque carolingienne', *Rev. Bén.* lxxxvi (1976), 218–34, and 'Livrets de prières de l'époque carolingienne: nouvelle liste de manuscrits', ibid. xc (1980), 147–9. For further detail see Hamilton, 'The practice of penance', 198–213.

[49] For example, Eberhard of Friuli (d. 867) left his daughter Heiliwich a prayerbook together with a passionary, a psalter and a missal; Eccard of Mâcon (d. 876) left his sister a psalter and a prayerbook containing some psalms: P. Riché, 'Les Bibliothèques de trois aristocrates laïcs carolingiens', *Le Moyen Âge* lxix (1963), 87–104 (repr. in his *Instruction et vie religieuse dans le haut moyen âge*, London 1981, no. viii); R. McKitterick, *The Carolingians and the written word*, Cambridge 1989, 246–8. On Dhuoda see M. A. Claussen, 'God and man in Dhuoda's *Liber manualis*', in W. J. Sheils and D. Wood (eds), *Women in the Church* (SCH xxvii, 1990), 43–52, who shows how Dhuoda had her own view of what constituted lay spirituality.

[50] Dhuoda, *Manuel* III.xi, p. 196.

[51] VMP, c. x, pp. 163–7; Widukind, *Rerum gestarum saxonicarum* III.lxxiv, p. 150. For her prayers and psalmody see also VMA, c. ix, pp. 129–30.

Penance and politics

Penance was an important element not only in ideas about kingship but in the political relationships of the period. The council of Hohenaltheim (916) ordained that as Erchanger and his allies had sinned, so a penance was enjoined on them to give up the world, put down their arms and enter a monastery.[52] Their offences were to have seized the bishop of Constance and plotted against the king. They were condemned for *infidelitas* and thus treated in a similar fashion to public penitents in earlier centuries.[53] Penance was a useful form of punishment for political enemies and as such public penance, especially monastic imprisonment, had a long pedigree stretching back via the Carolingians to Visigothic Spain. The canon of Hohenaltheim suggests that tenth-century ecclesiastical authorities still regarded penance as an appropriate punishment for rebellion but, acting outside the confines of a church council, the attitude of the secular authorities was more ambivalent: Erchanger was sentenced in his absence and seemingly never performed his penance for when King Conrad caught up with him a few months later he had him executed.

The secular authorities had their own distinct form of punishment for political crimes, *harmiscara*, which most often took the form of carrying either a dog or a saddle some considerable distance before prostrating oneself at the feet of one's lord; it was usually imposed for *scandala*, crimes which upset the social order severely, such as rebellion against one's superior.[54] Thus Widukind of Corvey describes how Eberhard, duke of the Franks, ravaged the town of Helmarshausen and massacred its inhabitants and was subsequently sentenced by King Otto I to pay a hundred talents' worth of horses and, with his leading men, to carry dogs all the way to the royal city of Magdeburg.[55] *Harmiscara* allowed the rebel to submit and return to royal authority by performing a humiliating task; it was thus a ritual of reconciliation. There were diverse political rituals of reconciliation in the early medieval world. Geoffrey Koziol's study of west Frankish rituals of supplication in this period suggests that begging for pardon was often best achieved through penitential actions, that is by appearing prostrate, barefoot and in plain clothes at one's lord's knee, whilst Gerd Althoff has identified a specific ritual of *deditio* in the Ottonian and Salian world; in this ritual rebels appeared as penitents, in

---

[52] c. xxi, MGH, *Concilia* VI, 28–9; Leyser, 'Early medieval canon law', 64.
[53] Ibid. On this case see also Reuter, *Germany*, 131, and for the most recent outline of the link between public penance and political rebellion see de Jong, 'What was public'.
[54] On this practice and also the etymology of the word see now J.-M. Moeglin, 'Harmiscara-harmschar-hachée: le dossier des rituels d'humiliation et de soumission au moyen âge', *Archivum Latinitatis Medii Aevi* liv (1996), 11–65; J. Hemming, 'Sellam gestare: saddle-bearing punishments and the case of Rhiannon', *Viator* xxviii (1997), 45–64. See also B. Schwenk, 'Das Hundetragen: ein Rechtsbrauch im Mittelalter', *Historisches Jahrbuch* cx (1990), 289–308.
[55] Widukind, *Rerum gestarum saxonicarum* II.vi, p. 40; Hemming, '*Sellam gestare*', 52.

sackcloth and barefoot, and performed an act of submission before the ruler.⁵⁶ Although a wholly secular ritual, *deditio* relied on its parallels with penance: the rebel assumed penitential dress whilst the ruler received the penitent in his role as *vicarius Christi*.⁵⁷ These secular rituals all had overt penitential overtones, and were undergone by those who had contested authority. *Harmiscara*'s popularity may, as de Jong has suggested, explain why the revised form of public penance quickly became so popular within the ninth-century Frankish world.⁵⁸ The co-existence of other forms of penitential reconciliatory ritual may explain the continued popularity of public penance in the tenth- and eleventh-century worlds. The popularity of these rituals owes something to the fact that the procedures allowed the restitution of the victim's honour; not all supplicants were restored but the process itself had the potential for reconciliation.⁵⁹

Although there is evidence from the late ninth century that *harmiscara* was used by the clergy, it was normally the perogative of secular lords.⁶⁰ Public penance was envisaged by the Church as a punishment, and whilst it relied on secular authority to enforce it against recalcitrant noblemen, it was the main weapon available to the Church to discipline its own errant clergy, and had been used as such since antiquity. Records and accounts of councils show that as well as seeking to inculcate the clergy with standards of good behav-

---

⁵⁶ Koziol, *Begging*, esp. ch. vi; Althoff, 'Das Privileg der "deditio" '.
⁵⁷ T. Reuter, 'Unruhestiftung, Fehde, Rebellion, Widerstand: Gewalt und Frieden in der Politik der Salierzeit', in S. Weinfurter (ed.), *Die Salier und das Reich*, Sigmaringen 1991, iii. 297–325 at pp. 320–5, and 'Canossa'; Althoff, 'Das Privileg der "deditio" '. For application of their views to the political rituals of the later Middles Ages (thirteenth and fourteenth centuries) see J.-M. Moeglin, 'Pénitence publique et amende honorable au moyen âge', *Revue historique* ccxcviii (1997), 225–69.
⁵⁸ de Jong, 'Power and humility', 46–9, and 'What was public', 887–93.
⁵⁹ Neither *deditio* nor *harmiscara* can have been spontaneous gestures; *deditio* involved the unconditional surrender of the rebel to the king, and as such the terms needed to be arranged by intermediaries in advance: Althoff, 'Das Privileg der "deditio" '. Perhaps the most famous example of a political penitent who was not restored is Tassilo, duke of Bavaria, who, six years after his defeat, capture and imprisonment in a monastery as a penitent by Charlemagne, appeared before the synod of Frankfurt in 794 to ask for forgiveness from Charlemagne for the sins he had committed against the Frankish kings and the *regnum Francorum*, which was granted. Charlemagne also accepted the duchy of Bavaria from Tassilo as alms: Council of Frankfurt (794), c. iii, *MGH, Conc. II*, i. 165–6; de Jong, 'What was public', 880–2; S. Airlie, 'Narratives of triumph and rituals of submission: Charlemagne's mastering of Bavaria', *TRHS* 6th ser. ix (1999), 93–119.
⁶⁰ Grivo, a vassal of Hincmar, bishop of Laon (858–71; d. 877) offered to undergo *harmiscara* in order to reconcile himself with the bishop: PL cxxiv. 1034A; Moeglin, 'Harmiscara-harmschar-hachée', 23. Rebels did sometimes perform a *deditio* before bishops, as the Margrave Bernhard did before Archbishop Gero of Magdeburg in 1017, although in this case Gero required imperial support: 'Gero archiepiscopus iussu imperatoris Bernhardum marchionem nudis pedibus emendationem sibi promittentem suscepit et aecclesiae presentavit, solutis omnibus bannis ab eo inpositis': Thietmar, *Chronicon* VII.1, pp. 458–60.

iour, they were occasions when the clergy were often disciplined. But the conciliar records which survive are mostly from the metropolitan tip of a much larger iceberg, dealing with errant bishops rather than more junior clergy; their cases were presumably dealt with at diocesan synods which left few records and in episcopal courts which left even fewer.[61] In 992 penance was demanded and obtained from Arnulf, archbishop of Reims, for his *infidelitas* to King Hugh and King Robert of west Frankia. Such occasions were seldom wholly clerical and issues concerning who held episcopal office were matters for the wider polity.[62] Nevertheless they were usually dealt with in an ecclesiastical forum: when Rudolf, bishop of Senlis, and his brother, Guy, another cleric, were implicated in the murder of Evrardus, subdean of Chartres in 1018x19, Fulbert, bishop of Chartres (1006–28), first offered them the choice of penance or trial before their fellow bishops, and later excommunicated Guy (Rudolf having died) for his *crimen manifestum* and refused the brothers' attempts to reach an agreement and compose for the murder.[63] For Fulbert the appropriate punishment for such a public crime committed by a cleric against another cleric was public penance; the case concerned the Church and should be dealt with in accordance with ecclesiastical procedures and, as the case dragged on, Fulbert became increasingly recalcitrant, refusing all alternatives.[64]

Descriptions of the penitential processes followed in such cases are, however, very rare; yet the account given by Peter Damian of how he imposed penance on the Milanese clergy explains why penance worked as a mechanism for both political punishment and reconciliation. Sent to Milan as one of two papal legates, probably in December 1059, in response to the sometimes violent disorder wrought by the Patarenes's challenge to the endemic simony and nicolaitism of the Church of Milan, Peter Damian's mission was to assert the Roman Church's authority over the Milanese Church and to deal with a married and simoniac clergy.[65] Damian gives a

---

[61] For Bishop Udalrich of Augsburg's use of episcopal courts to make admonitions and impose penalties for misconduct see Gerhard, *Vita sancti Oudalrici episcopi Augustani*, ed. G. Waitz (MGH, SS iv), c. vi, pp. 394–5.

[62] Koziol, *Begging*, 1–4, 9.

[63] *Fulbert of Chartres*, epp. xxix–xxxvi, pp. 52–66. This case has been studied by Peters in 'The death of the subdean'. In a letter to Rudolf, bishop of Senlis, Fulbert tells him that in choosing to stand trial he obviously prefers public condemnation to making secret satisfaction for his sins through confession: 'Verum enim vero satis admirari nequimus quidnam mali est quod tam audacter ad iudicium properatis nisi forte quod abhorrere humanum est publice dampnari eligitis, quam secreta satisfactione purgari': ibid. ep. xxxii, p. 58.

[64] Peters suggests that Fulbert's increasing obstinacy may have been because he was uncertain that he would win his case in a public trial: 'The death of the subdean'.

[65] *Briefe des Petrus Damiani*, no. lxv, ii. 228–47. On the problem of dating this visit more accurately than c. 1059x1061 see ibid. ii. 230 n. 10. The pope's intervention was requested by the Patarenes's opponents in Milan: H. E. J. Cowdrey, 'The papacy, the Patarenes and the Church of Milan', *TRHS* 5th ser. xviii (1968), 25–48 (repr. in his *Popes, monks and crusaders*, London 1984, no. v).

vivid account of how a meeting of the clergy of the Milanese Church was held after a large crowd assembled outside the episcopal palace to defend the Ambrosian Church's independence from Rome. At a public gathering attended by both the clergy and the people, Damian first preached a sermon justifying Rome's claims to superiority over Milan, and then investigated the clergy and discovered that simony was the norm for ordination to any rank from bishop downwards. He then, in the face of a mob which had the potential to turn murderous, and basing his decision on canon law, extracted from the clergy a 'solemn and irrevocable promise of free ordinations for now and hereafter, first in written documents, then by giving their hands and lastly by swearing an oath on the Gospels'.[66] At the end of this three-stage process, the archbishop of Milan prostrated himself on the floor and asked for a penance to be imposed on him for his failure to root out this crime. Damian imposed 'a penance of one hundred years, prescribing that it could be redeemed by the annual payment of a specific amount of money'.[67] After this, they went into the cathedral (*maior aecclesia*) and in the presence of a great gathering of the people and the clergy, the archbishop's chaplain, not the archbishop, swore by touching the Gospels that the archbishop would strive at all costs sincerely and faithfully to root out the two heresies of nicolaitism and simony. Then the majority of the people, reportedly more than 1,000, assembled from the suburbs as well as the city, took the same oath against the simoniacs and nicolaitans. The clerics were then given their penance followed by a reconciliation during mass: those who had paid their fee for office merely as part of the normal procedures, unaware that it was a sin, received a five-year penance, during which they should fast on bread and water two days a week, and during the forty days before Christmas and Easter, three days a week; those who paid more for their office received a seven-year penance to be observed in a similar way, but should fast on Fridays for the rest of their lives. They could, however, commute one day's fasting per week by reciting either one psalter, or by saying half a psalter with fifty prostrations, or by feeding a poor person, washing his feet and giving him a denarius. In addition, the archbishop promised to send them all on pilgrimage, to either Rome or Tours, and proposed himself to visit Compostella. Whilst all were reconciled, not all were allowed to return to office; only those who were well-educated, chaste and considered upright in their behaviour. The latter had each to take an oath before the altar condemning all heresies, especially those of nicolaitism and simony, afterwards receiving the symbols of their rank from the hands of the bishop in a symbolic reordination.

It was an insecure compromise because, by allowing most of the clergy to

---

[66] 'Exegimus igitur ex tunc et deinceps gratuitae promotionis inviolabilem sponsionem prius per monimenta litterarum deinde per manum postremo per evangelicum sacramentum': *Briefe des Petrus Damiani*, ii. 240.
[67] 'Centum itaque annorum sibi penitentiam inididi, redemptionemque eius taxata per unumquemque annum poecuniae quantitate praefixi': ibid. ii. 244.

retain their offices, it failed to meet the demands of the Patarini; the city continued to be plagued by unrest. Nevertheless Peter Damian was not the first churchman to recognise how vital it was to involve all the parties, including the lay audience; Rather of Verona, almost a century earlier, argued that the laity ignored the clergy's absolutions and excommunications because the clergy themselves did not take these sentences seriously when they were imposed upon them.[68] The imposition of penance on both the archbishop and the other clergy was the means by which they were seen by the lay public to have been publicly disciplined and to have atoned.[69] Penance justified the retention of what was substantially the old order in Milan; as such it was as much part of the machinery for the resolution of this political crisis as the oaths which Damian extracted from the Milanese clergy, whose apparent voluntary entry into penance was crucial to the success of his mission.

The role of penance seemingly extended beyond relations between the clergy and the laity, and amongst the clergy themselves, to include relations within the royal family, for relations between Mathilda, the wife of Henry the Fowler and her son Otto I were depicted in penitential terms on one occasion by the clerical authors of her earlier and later *vitae*. According to both accounts, after her husband's death the nobles inspired Otto I and his brother Henry to turn against their mother, because they felt she was wasting her dower in needless and profligate generosity to the Church; they forced her to leave her dower lands and to take the veil.[70] But according to her hagiographers Mathilda's sufferings had direct consequences for both her sons: Otto suffered defeat, whilst Henry was struck by serious illness. Consequently, Otto's wife Edith instigated his reconciliation with his mother.[71] This was described by the author of the later life in distinctly penitential terms; after Edith's exhortations, Otto was moved by penitence, and recalling the crime he had committed, by God's inspiration recognised the wrong he had done his mother. He therefore sent a delegation to recall his mother with a letter. Mathilda is described as Christ's handmaid, and the content of the letter, echoing the vocabulary used in the liturgies for the reconciliation of penitents, assumes that she is able to act as an intercessor with God, begging her 'for God's sake forgive us, and implore the pardon of remission from Christ'.[72]

---

68 *Die Briefe des Bischofs Rather von Verona*, ed. F. Weigle (MGH, Die Briefe der deutschen Kaiserzeit i, Weimar 1949), no. xvi, p. 97.
69 For a similar case in which a lay audience was also important see the Council of Rheims (1049): Southern, *Making of the Middle Ages*, 122–4. On the importance of the populace in the eleventh century see R. I. Moore, 'Family, community and cult on the eve of the Gregorian Reform', *TRHS* 5th ser. xxx (1980), 49–69.
70 VMA, c. v, pp. 122–4; VMP, c. xi, pp. 167–9.
71 VMA, c. vi, pp. 124–5. In the *VMP* (c. xii, p. 169) the bishops and *principes* of the kingdom requested Edith to approach Otto to become reconciled with his mother.
72 'Rex autem penitentia compunctus et commissi haut immemor reatus deo inspirante in sancta matre se deliquisse cognovit. Haut mora missis episcopis, ducibus ac comitibus et omnibus sapientissimis militum matrem cum honore revocandam praecepit Christi famule huiusmodi scripta deferri: "O venerabilis domina, dei iracundiam iam satis nimiumque

He acknowledged he had sinned, asked for pardon and her favour. Otto then went to meet his mother, asking her on bended knee to impose whatever punishment she desired, if only he might return to the grace of reconciliation. Mathilda immediately offered her son the kiss of peace, and in words very similar to the prayers in the reconciliation liturgy suggested that God might grant him forgiveness, as He forgives every penitent who completely regrets what he has done and does not commit the same sin again.[73] The kiss as a definitive sign of reconciliation was a widely known variant on the kiss of peace in both secular and monastic society. Otto was thus absolved by his mother in the presence of his bishops in a secular ritual depicted in penitential terms.

Both versions of this story were probably composed by women. The earlier *Life* was written shortly after Mathilda's death in 968, probably in 973/4 at Mathilda's foundation at Quedlinburg.[74] The later *Life* was composed at Nordhausen soon after Henry II became king in 1002 in order to legitimise his claim to the throne by portraying Henry's grandfather, Henry, duke of Bavaria, as Mathilda's favourite son, thus connecting Henry II directly to the family saint of the Ottonian dynasty.[75] The later *Life* therefore includes a separate reconciliation scene between Mathilda and Henry, but again in penitential terms: he confessed his sins to his mother, adding that he did not doubt that he would gain pardon and remission from Christ if she would whole-heartedly forgive him. And he wept, showing his contrition.

Although charter evidence suggests that a rupture may have taken place between Mathilda and Otto, the quarrel was not otherwise recorded.[76] The subject of the quarrel, the right of a widow to control her dower, may perhaps have had an especial appeal for the female aristocratic convent audiences of the *vitae*.[77] Its inclusion may also have been intended to defend Nordhausen's

---

exacerbavimus in nos persecutione vestra. Fatemur, quod peccavimus et iniuste contra vos egimus; propter deum nobis dimittite et a Christo veniam remissionis implorate. Quodlibet supplicium libenter patimur tantum, ut vestra gratia fruamur. Ad hec ut ad nos iter dirigatis, petimus; nos et omnia nostra ditioni vestre subdimus, insuper et restituemus, quicquid vobis iniuste abstraximus. Nil nobis iocundum erit, antequam vos videre contigerit" ': ibid. c. xii, pp. 169–70.

[73] 'Deus autem vobis tribuat indulgentiam per ineffabilem suam misericordiam, qui paratus est misereri cuique penitenti, si commissa perfecte defleverit et postmodum non admiserit', ibid., c. xiii, p. 171.

[74] VMA, 9–42. Schütte, the VMA's editor, thus refutes the argument of P. Corbet that the author was Abbess Richburga of Nordhausen: *Les Saints ottoniens: sainteté dynastique, sainteté royale et sainteté féminine autour de l'an mil*, Sigmaringen 1986, 153.

[75] VMP, 42–88; Bornscheuer, *Miseriae regum*, 60–2.

[76] K. Schmid, 'Neue Quellen zum Verständnis des Adels im 10. Jahrhundert', in E. Hlawitschka (ed.), *Königswahl und Thronfolge in ottonisch-frühdeutscher Zeit*, Darmstadt 1971, 389–416.

[77] As suggested by J. L. Nelson in 'Gender and genre in women historians of the early Middle Ages', in J.-P. Genet (ed.), *L'Historiographie médiévale en Europe: Paris 29 mars–1 avril 1989*, Paris 1991, 149–63 at p. 156 (repr. in her *Frankish world*, 183–97).

claims to the endowment it received from Mathilda. But both works also had an 'official' function, to show Mathilda as the protector of the Ottonian dynasty and as conduit of God's grace, and, in the case of the later *Life*, to legitimise Henry II, suggesting that the *vitae* may have been heard by members of the royal family on their visits to Nordhausen and Quedlinburg.[78] Although both *Lives* were composed by religious whose views of the ritual process may have been influenced unduly by the liturgy, especially in their choice of language, the importance of the message which they sought to communicate to the court suggests that their accounts must at some level have reflected the reality: the cross-over between liturgical and secular reconciliation was not only linguistic, but as we have seen, grounded in actual political behaviour.

Although the most detailed, this is not the only account of a secular ritual of reconciliation recorded in penitential terms; the ritual of *deditio* required the offender to appear as a penitent before the ruler. Thus Thietmar recorded how the rebel Henry of Schweinfurt, clothed as a penitent, submitted to Henry II.[79] Henry was a king, Mathilda both a saint and a queen; it is not therefore surprising to find each of them following the model of Christ and acting as reconciler. But these accounts of events at court suggest that, in the eyes of some clergy at least, penance was an accepted part of the process of political reconciliation, and as such essential to the working of the political community. The boundary between the rituals of ecclesiastical penance and secular *deditio* was a very fine one and perhaps not always appreciated by members of the clerical elite.

Penance and warfare

Homicide was not controversial; it was regarded as one of the most heinous of sins and the penitentials usually begin their lists of sins with various forms of homicide, of which the most scandalous, parricide, often took precedence.[80] The heinousness of such a sin merited especially harsh penances in practice.[81] But whilst it was universally agreed that penance should be done for murder,

[78] Corbet, *Les Saints ottoniens*, 148–73. On the importance of Quedlinburg and Nordhausen as royal residences in the itinerary of the Ottonians and Salians see Bernhardt, *Itinerant kingship*, 138–49, 176, 292–4.

[79] 'Heinricus vero se nimis in omnibus culpabilem lacrimabiliter professus more et habitu penitentis regi se tradidit eiusque iussione ab archipresule predicto in castellum Ivicansten detruditur diligenterque a suis militibus die noctuque servatur': Thietmar, *Chronicon* VI.ii, p. 276.

[80] For example Columbanus, *Paenitentiale*, in *Irish penitentials*, B.I. xiii, pp. 98, 102; Halitgar, *Poenitentiale* VI.xxii, in *Bussbücher II*, 295; Burchard, *Decretum* xix.v, 951–3. This is not a universal rule: see Theodore, *Poenitentiale* IV, in *Bussbücher II*, 548.

[81] For example, the case of Count Theoderic, who killed his son, went to Pope Alexander II (1061–73) who awarded him a penance which included fasting, exclusion from the Church for a year, and from communion for a further three years: ep. xxxvii, Mansi, *Concilia*, xix. 966. Another example is St Romuald who, as a young man, was present when his father

churchmen's attitude to warfare was more ambivalent, and, indeed, warfare was often sanctioned by the Church. It is thus worth exploring the role played by penance in what was one of the dominant activities of this world – the call to the host was usually the occasion for the holding of the annual assembly in the spring. War was a crucial mechanism for the ordering of the state. The clergy thus sought an ideological justification for war: it was acceptable, even admirable, if fought in defence of the Church and the Kingdom, which were seen as virtually co-terminous. Hincmar of Rheims (845–82) argued that those who died faithfully in war conducted for the peace of the kingdom deserved prayers, offerings and masses, whilst Archbishop Heriveus of Rheims, for example, as a large landowner, was only one of the west Frankish nobles who contributed a force to Charles III's campaign against the Magyars in 919.[82] Justifying civil wars was more difficult: the mid ninth-century Carolingian clerics responded to the civil wars within the empire between the sons of Louis the Pious with the Augustinian idea of *bellum deo auctore*; war was necessary to execute divine vengeance and seek a spiritual peace rather than be satisfied with temporal peace. None the less, clerics such as Agobard of Lyons, Hincmar of Rheims (d. 882) and Sedulius (d. c. 884) were seemingly opposed to internal war, whilst seeking various justifications for it and for their own involvement.[83]

The more simplistic evidence of the penitentials presents a similarly confused picture. Most eighth- and ninth-century penitentials awarded a forty-day penance to those who killed in battle.[84] However, two ninth-century penitentials, widely copied in the tenth century, analysed the motives of those involved more thoroughly. Hrabanus Maurus, following the civil war between Louis the Pious's sons, argued that a penance be imposed for killings committed in wars between kings.[85] He also considered the importance of motive behind a killing in battle: was it carried out through greed or a sense of duty; if the latter, it deserved a lesser penance. Halitgar of Cambrai, writing slightly earlier, in about 830, distinguished further: killing was wrong,

---

killed a kinsman as a result of a feud over the ownership of some property. Romuald consequently entered the monastery of St Apollinaris to do a penance of forty days for his involvement in the crime, although he did not wound anyone, during which time he discovered his monastic vocation with the help of St Apollinare himself who appeared to him in a vision: Peter Damian, *Vita Romualdi*, cc. i–ii, pp. 13–19. For further examples see Platelle who makes a case study of the penances imposed for parricide as part of his examination of the interaction between secular and ecclesiastical power in eleventh-century Flanders: 'Violence', 170–3.

82 Hincmar, *De regis persona et regio ministerio*, c. xv, PL cxxv. 844. For Heriveus see *Annales de Flodoard*, a. 920, pp. 2–3 (Flodoard began his *Annals* c. 920). On clerical participation in war in the ninth century in general see F. Prinz, *Klerus und Krieg im früheren Mittelalter*, Stuttgart 1971.
83 F. H. Russell, *The just war in the Middle Ages*, Cambridge 1975, 29–32.
84 Vogel, 'Le Pèlerinage', 145–6; Kottje, *Bussbücher*, 240.
85 Hrabanus Maurus, *Poenitentium liber ad Otgarium*, c. xv, PL cxii. 1411–13 (see also his *Paenitentiale ad Heribaldum*, c. iv, PL cx. 471–3); Kottje, *Bussbücher*, 240–4.

and he decreed a penance of twenty-one weeks' fasting for anyone who killed in a public military expedition, or of twenty-eight weeks for anyone who killed in battle out of hostility or covetousness, but killing in battle to defend oneself or one's close kin was not a sin meriting a penance.[86] Halitgar's innovation, that penance was unnecessary for killing in defence of one's kin, was not widely adopted. Regino viewed all killing as wrong, even if committed in the course of a just war, prescribing a forty-day penance for anyone who killed a man in public war.[87] Following Hrabanus he decreed that if a man killed through avarice or a desire to please his temporal lord he should be more heavily punished than if he fought in a public war.[88] A century later Burchard of Worms also followed Hrabanus but gave specific penances for homicide in war: for him who kills in defence of the peace at the orders of a legitimate prince, the penance is three Lents; if, however, he kills without the orders of a legitimate prince, the penance is one *carina* (forty days on bread and water) for seven sequential years.[89] Burchard suggests the continuing importance of the penitential tradition represented by Hrabanus: even a just war was seen as essentially sinful.[90]

But how did these teachings reach the wider community? At least three post-battle penitential ordinances are recorded for the early medieval period and suggest that some attempt was made to put the teachings of the penitentials into effect. The earliest was that issued after the battle of Fontenoy in 843. On the day after the battle, in which Kings Louis II and Charles the Bald defeated the Emperor Lothar in their fight for Louis the Pious's inheritance, the bishops of the victors' kingdoms held a council at which they decreed that because Charles and Louis and their men had fought for justice and through their victory demonstrated God's judgement, they had acted as God's ministers, and were thus immune from any blame for the battle.[91] The ordinance thus reflected Halitgar's minority argument that killing in defence of oneself or one's kin was not sinful. According to Nithard,

---

86 'Si quis aliquis expeditione publica occidit hominem sine causa, jejunet hebdomadas XXI, si autem forsitan se defendendo, aut parentes suos, aut familias suas, occidisset aliquem, ille non erit reus. Si voluerit jejunare, in illius potestate est, qui coactus hoc fecit. Si homicidium in pace fecerit, et non fuerit turba per potestatem aut inimicitiae causa, ut res ejus capiat, jejunet hebdomadas XXVIII et res ejus, quem occidit, reddat uxori vel filiis ejus': *Bussbücher I*, 485; discussed in Kottje, *Bussbücher*, 243–4.

87 Regino, *Libri duo* II.1, li, pp. 233–4.

88 Ibid. II.1, pp. 233–4 (from Hrabanus Maurus, *Paenitentiale ad Heribaldum*, c. iv, PL cx. 471–2. See also his *Liber ad Otgarium*, c. xv, PL cxii. 1411–12).

89 Burchard, *Decretum* VI.xxiii, 770–1.

90 Kottje, *Bussbücher*, 244. For further developments of the penance for war see the Penitential of Pseudo-Theodore (mid ninth-century) which imposed a penance of forty days for homicide in public war or on the orders of one's lord; in the latter case, the lord thereby also incurred a penance: *Bussbücher II*, 555, 559. The Penitential of Arundel (s. x/xi) imposed a penance of one year for homicide in royal battle and two years in a war of doubtful justice waged by a *princeps* not a king: *Bussbücher I*, 441.

91 Nithard, *Historiarum libri IIII*, ed. E. Müller (MGH, SRG lxiv, 1907), III.i, pp. 28–9.

our source for the Fontenoy ordinance, it was also ordained that any individual knowing himself to have been motivated by anger, hatred or pride was to confess secretly and be assigned a penance.[92]

Eighty years later, certain of the bishops of west Frankia issued an ordinance after the battle of Soissons fought between Robert I and Charles III (the Simple), rivals for the west Frankish crown, on 15 June 923.[93] The Soissons ordinance is a short text, recording that in the second year of Seulf's episcopate (27 August 923–26 August 924) a meeting of the holy fathers, that is Seulf, archbishop of Rheims (922–5), Abbo, bishop of Soissons (909–37), Adelelmus of Laon (921–30), Stephen of Cambrai (909–33/4), Adelelmus of Senlis (923–36) and Ariardus of Noyon (923/4–32), with legates from certain other bishops in the Rheims province, decreed that those who had taken part in the battle at Soissons between Robert and Charles should do penance for three years in three Lents.[94] The first Lent they should be excluded from the church and reconciled on Maundy Thursday. For all three Lents they should fast on bread, salt and water every Monday, Wednesday and Friday, or else redeem this fast. Similarly they should fast for fifteen days before both the nativity of St John the Baptist and Christmas and every Friday throughout the whole year, unless they redeem the penance, except when a feast falls on this day, or they are prevented by illness or military service from observing the fast.

Unlike the Fontenoy ordinance, that of Soissons therefore reflects the mainstream penitential tradition: the imposition of a penance for three years is analogous to the penance of three Lents imposed by Burchard for killing in a just war on the orders of a legitimate prince for the defence of the peace. But whilst the canonists usually ordained that no one should return to the military world after he had performed penance, and certainly not whilst he was performing penance, the Soissons ordinance excused men from their penance if they were obliged to perform military service.[95] The ordinance appears,

---

[92] J. L. Nelson, 'Ninth-century knighthood: the evidence of Nithard', in C. Harper-Bill, C. Holdsworth and J. L. Nelson (eds), *Studies in medieval history presented to R. Allen Brown*, Woodbridge 1989, 255–66 at p. 262 (repr. in her *Frankish world*, 75–87), and her 'Violence in the Carolingian world and the ritualisation of ninth-century warfare', in G. Halsall (ed.), *Violence and society in the early medieval west*, Woodbridge 1998, 90–107.

[93] Mansi, *Concilia* xviiiA. 345–6. For a review of the work on this text up until 1980 see Schröder, *Westfränkische Synoden*, 212–16.

[94] The Soissons ordinance cannot be dated more precisely but it is probable that it was issued after Rodulf's coronation on 13 July 923, and after Charles's capture in the late summer of that year, as part of an episcopal effort to restore the peace under a new king.

[95] For example, 'Ut nullus post poenitentiae actionem ad militiam saecularem redire debeat': Burchard, *Decretum* xix.lxvi, 999 (derived from Regino, *Libri duo* i. cccxviii). Cf. 'Similiter quindecim diebus ante nativitatem S. Joannis Baptistae, et quindecim diebus ante nativitatem Domini Salvatoris, omni quoque sexta feria per totum annum, nisi redemerint, aut festivitas celebris ipsa die acciderit, vel eum infirmitate sive militia detentum esse contigerit': Mansi, *Concilia* xviiiA. 346.

therefore, to reflect both the reality and the ambiguity of contemporary attitudes to war: it was sinful, it was also inevitable.

The best known ordinance, however, was that issued by the Norman bishops after William the Conqueror's victory at Hastings in 1066.[96] It was confirmed by the papal legate Erminfrid, although its precise date remains uncertain.[97] The text is aimed only at members of William's army.[98] As its manuscript distribution is entirely English, this suggests that it was targeted at a Norman audience within England, and, as many of the Norman army returned across the Channel after the battle, it also suggests an earlier, rather than a later, date for the ordinance.[99] It was more sophisticated than the Soissons ordinance, taking into account both the intentions and motives of the participants, distinguishing between those who were willing to, but did not, kill anyone, and those who did, and giving the equivalent to a penance for homicide, commonly seven years, to those who fought for gain, and one of only three years to those who fought as in public war, with justice as their motive. It also included behaviour after the battle including penance for attacks on the Church. It therefore reflects the traditional canonical distinction for motives in war, and also, like Soissons, the standard canonical three-year penance for killing in a just war.

War was a commonplace of the whole of this period. Yet the Soissons and Hastings ordinances appear to be unique: both seem to have survived entirely by chance. The Soissons ordinance was entered into two tenth-century codices, both forms of episcopal handbook, in Rheims, whilst the Hastings ordinance is recorded in association with records of the council of Winchester (1070) in three English manuscripts from Exeter, Sherborne and Winchester.[100] There is no external evidence that either ordinance was put

---

96 *Councils and synods*, no. lxxxviii, pp. 581–4.
97 Ibid. H. E. J. Cowdrey argues for a date of 1067 for the ordinance on the grounds of proximity to the battle: 'Bishop Ermenfrid of Sion and the penitential ordinance following the battle of Hastings', *JEH* xx (1969), 225–42 at p. 233 n. 6. C. Morton argues for a date of 1070: 'Pope Alexander II and the Norman conquest', *Latomus* xxxiv (1975), 362–82.
98 'Hic est paenitentiae institutio secundum decreta Normannorum presulum, auctoritate summi pontificis confirmata per legatum suum Ermenfredum episcopum Sedunensem, imponenda illis hominibus quos W. Normmanorum dux suo iussu, et qui ante hunc iussu sui erant, et ex debito ei militiam debebant': *Councils and synods*, no. lxxxviii, p. 583.
99 Ibid. 582. The ordinance is recorded only in association with the canons of the Council of Winchester and survives in manuscripts from Exeter, Sherborne and Winchester: Morton, 'Pope Alexander II', 381 n. 55. For the view that the ordinance was instigated by English bishops and only circulated in England see ibid. 377.
100 The Soissons ordinance is recorded in two manuscripts, both from Rheims: Vatican, BAV, MS Reg. lat. 418, fo. 2r, and Berlin, Staatsbibliothek, MS Phillips 1765, fos 95v–6r. The Vatican manuscript is from the early tenth century and the other texts deal with the actions of Seulf's predecessor as archbishop of Rheims, Heriveus; the ordinance was added in a later hand. Bautier suggested that the Vatican codex was compiled by Flodoard, but Michel Sot has recently argued that it was already in existence when Flodoard compiled his *Historia remensis ecclesiae* and that he intended the codex to be consulted alongside his history as an account of Heriveus' episcopate: R.-H. Bautier, 'Un Recueil de textes pour

into effect; they may have remained merely as episcopal statements of intent. Whilst the Soissons manuscript tradition was limited to Rheims, that for Hastings, together with the papal legate's confirmation, suggests that an attempt was made to publicise the ordinance within England but not Normandy: it survives only in manuscripts from three English sees. Ordinances may have been issued after other battles but left no trace; the similarities between the Hastings and Soissons ordinances may thus be due to a common tradition in synodal practice or, as seems more likely, because they share a common debt to the penitential material.

But both ordinances may have been preserved not by accident but because they were unusual. Both battles saw the death of a consecrated king; indeed this was the fact which later chroniclers, who knew nothing else about Soissons, remembered.[101] Kings were, however, seldom killed in battle in this period.[102] The Soissons ordinance may be an attempt to restore the spiritual peace of the kingdom which had been upset by the killing of an anointed king; in more normal internecine wars such a penance could be left to local bishops and priests. Unlike the Hastings ordinance it was directed at all those

---

servir à la biographie de l'archevêque de Reims, Hervé (xe siècle): son attribution à Flodoard', in *Mélanges Louis Halphen*, Paris 1951, 1–6; Sot, *Un Historien et son église*, 233–6. The Berlin manuscript also preserves various documents associated with the history of the see of Rheims and has been variously dated to the early tenth century (H. Mordek, *Kirchenrecht und Reform im Frankenreich: die 'Collectio vetus Gallica', die älteste systematische Kanonessammlung des Fränkischen Gallen*, Berlin 1975, 261) and to the eleventh century (Schröder, *Westfränkischen Synoden*, 212). For further detail see Hamilton, 'The practice of penance', 248–50. For a general history of Rheims in the tenth century see R. McKitterick, 'The Carolingian kings and the see of Rheims, 882–987', in P. Wormald, D. Bullough and R. Collins (eds), *Ideal and reality in Frankish and Anglo-Saxon society*, Oxford 1983, 228–49. The Hastings ordinance is recorded in Cambridge, Corpus Christi College, MS 190, pp. 293–4 (provenance, Exeter), described in M. R. James, *A descriptive catalogue of the manuscripts in the library of Corpus Christi College Cambridge*, Cambridge 1912, i. 453–63; BL, MS Cotton Tib. C.i, fos 111v–12v (s. xi^2, Sherborne), described in N. R. Ker, *Catalogue of manuscripts containing Anglo-Saxon*, Oxford 1957, no. 197, pp. 260–1; Oxford, Bodleian Library, MS Junius 121, fos 3–4 (s. xi$^{3/4}$, Worcester), described ibid. no. 338, 412–18.

101 *Annales de Flodoard*, a. 923, pp. 13–14; Adalbert of St Maximin of Trier, *Continuatio Reginonis*, ed. F. Kurze in *Reginonis abbatis prumiensis chronicon cum continuatio Treverensi* (MGH, SRG I, 1890; repr. 1978), a. 922, pp. 156–7; Widukind, *Rerum gestarum saxonicarum* I.xxx, p. 25; Richer, *Historiarum libri quatuor*, ed. R. Latouche, *Histoire de France (888–995)*, Paris 1930–7, cc. xliiii–vi, i. 88–94; Folcuin, *Gesta abbatum S. Bertini Sithiensium*, ed. O. Holder-Egger (MGH, SS xiii), 625; *Annales Lobienses*, a. 923, ed. G. Waitz (MGH, SS xiii), 233; Adémar of Chabannes, *Chronique*, ed. J. Chavanon, Paris 1897, III.xxii, pp. 141–3; Rodulf Glaber, *Historiarum* III.ix.(39), pp. 162–4. See P. Lauer, *Robert Ier et Raoul de Bourgogne rois de France*, 10–13. For an analysis of how the report of Robert's death was mythologised by later chroniclers see C. von Kalckstein, *Geschichte des französischen Königtums unter den ersten Capetingern*, I: *Der Kamp der Robertiner und Karolinger*, Leipzig 1877, 482–3.

102 The martyr Edmund of East Anglia who died in battle against the Vikings was very much the exception, hence his cult: Abbo of Fleury, *Passio sancti Edmundi*, in *Three lives of English saints*, ed. M. Winterbottom, Toronto 1972, 67–87.

involved, probably because the civil war had been a traumatic one; the ordinance was an attempt by the bishops to heal the scars of a divided polity. This suggestion is based on the premise that the significance of the coronation rite was recognised, even if the right of the individual to be crowned was disputed. The killing of a king was therefore an offence against the divine order, and all those who had contributed to his death by participating in the battle must be punished. But the texts of the ordinances both fail to mention the death of the king. At most, it was merely a contributing factor to the decision to set and record a post-battle ordinance.

The Soissons ordinance reflects the clergy's view that warfare was a necessary fact of life. Its pragmatic attitude – all participants must do penance for their involvement but they are excused if on military service – was at odds with the canonical attitude which regarded public penance as incompatible with the profession of arms. The Soissons ordinance shows not only the continuance of the 'public' penitential tradition – the penitent is excluded from the Church for the course of the first Lent – but it also shows how it was adapted and diluted by pragmatic bishops anxious to preserve the dual principles of involvement in just war as good, and homicide in any circumstances as bad. But unlike the Fontenoy ordinance, which was published on the day after the battle, and whose provisions were, as Nithard's account demonstrates, made known to those involved, there is no evidence that the Soissons ordinance was made known to any of the participating warriors. But the pragmatic attitude taken by the bishops at Soissons suggests that they at least tried to make their penance a real possibility for lay people: it was not surrounded by impossible conditions, and could always be commuted through alms. They thus acknowledged the reality of warfare.

Penance and sexual relations

Sex was another area of lay behaviour which the Church sought to regulate through penance and where, consequently, the laity were likely to fall foul of ecclesiastical rules. The Church's views on sexual intercourse were ambivalent. One strand, embodied by Jerome, argued that it was better to remain a virgin than to marry.[103] Thus Odo of Cluny in his life of Gerald, count of Aurillac, praised him as a model of secular chastity: his horror of sex led him to hide himself behind closed doors to wash away from himself the stains of his wet dreams, both literally and by shedding tears.[104] The other strand,

---

[103] Jerome, *Adversus Iovinianum*, ep. xxii in *Santi Eusebii Hieronymi epistolae*, ed. I. Hilberg (CSEL liv, Vienna 1910), 143–211; P. J. Payer, 'Early medieval regulations concerning marital sexual relations', *Journal of Medieval History* vi (1980), 353–76 at p. 354. Jerome's views were based on 1. Cor. vii.7–39.

[104] Odo of Cluny, *Vita sancti Geraldi Auriliacensis comitis* i.34, PL cxxxiii. 662–3; Airlie, 'Anxiety of sanctity', 391–2; J. M. H. Smith, 'Religion and lay society', in McKitterick, *New*

embodied by Augustine, held that sexual intercourse was allowed but only between married couples when undertaken for the sake of procreation.[105] Augustine's view inevitably generated complications entailing further regulation, principally over who could marry whom, and exactly when in the Christian year sexual relations were permissible, in addition to the prohibition of adulterous and homosexual acts and certain sexual positions. Much of the evidence for the Church's attitude in this period is contained in the penitentials; indeed, recent work has argued that penitentials were important to the development of a sexual code in early medieval Europe, although this argument is not yet proven.[106] But the evidence from the narrative and conciliar sources for the period provides some clues as to how the penitential canons on sexual relations were interpreted by the laity at this time.

The Church regarded sexuality as polluting, both physically and spiritually (thus Odo portrayed Gerald as washing himself both physically and mentally) and therefore incompatible with the major events of the Christian year. This view had its basis in Scripture, but was elaborated first by the Fathers, notably Caesarius of Arles, and further by the penitentials, being further refined and developed until Burchard's *Decretum*, reaching the point where it has been calculated that a devout married couple could licitly have had sexual relations on fewer than forty-four days of the year, once the periods of abstinence required by both the woman's own physiological cycle, and those for major Church festivals, such as Lent and Advent, had been taken into account.[107]

It is impossible to determine how far these injunctions were followed but there is evidence that the clergy attempted to impose this agenda on the laity.[108] In his mid eleventh-century account Ekkehard of St Gall described how a previous member of his community, Iso (d. 877), was conceived on Holy Saturday, the last day in Lent.[109] Iso's parents were devout people, according to Ekkehard, who kept the Lenten fast and also remained chaste for

---

Cambridge medieval history, ii. 654–78 at p. 668; Nelson, 'Monks, secular men and masculinity'.
[105] Augustine, *De bono coniugali*, cc. vi–vii, ed. J. Zycha (CSEL xli, Vienna 1900), 194–6; Payer, 'Early medieval regulations', 353.
[106] Payer, *Sex and the penitentials*; Brundage, *Law, sex and Christian society*, 152–69.
[107] J.-L. Flandrin, *Un Temps pour embrasser: aux origines de la morale sexuelle occidentale (VIe–XIe siècle)*, Paris 1983, 41–71.
[108] On this problem for the ninth century see Smith, 'Religion and lay society', 667–8. See also the material assembled by Flandrin in *Un Temps pour embrasser*.
[109] *Ekkehardi IV, Casus Sancti Galli*, ed. H. F. Haefele, Darmstadt 1980, 70–2; on this text see the study by de Jong, 'Pollution, penance and sanctity'. Kottje cites it as a case of 'mixed' public and private penance in 'Busspraxis', 393–4. The implications of this 'mixed' practice are explored in Meens, 'Frequency', 48–50. On Iso himself see J. Duft, 'Iso monachus – doctor nominatissimus', in H. Maurer (ed.), *Churrätisches und st. gallisches Mittelalter: Festschrift für Otto P. Clavadetscher zu seinem funfundsechzigsten Geburtstag*, Sigmaringen 1984, 146–55. This may be a case of a double sin. Iso's father came on his mother after she had bathed; Burchard prescribed a minor penance, a three-day fast, for taking a bath with one's wife: *Decretum* xix.cxxxviii, 1010.

the whole of Lent. But on Easter Saturday his mother was resting, having taken a bath in preparation for her change from her Lenten garments to ones more appropriate for the Easter celebration, when her husband came upon her and they had intercourse. Although Burchard regarded sexual relations in Lent as a relatively minor sin on a par with breaking the Lenten fast, suitable for a secret penance of forty days or twenty-six *solidi* if sober, or twenty days if drunk, Iso's parents took it very seriously.[110] Immediately upon realising their sin, yelling and lamenting, thus attracting the attention of the servants, they rushed to the church, barefoot, and spinkled with ashes, confessed their sin in public to the priest before the whole community and were given a penance, that is to stand by the church doors for a day and a night, and were ordered not to take communion. They were, however, very anxious to communicate on Easter Sunday and hurried to the nearest village where they again confessed and asked the priest's permission to communicate the next day, Easter day, but were refused. They therefore spent the Easter night fasting and crying, dressed in sackcloth and ashes, and so attended the Easter vigil standing at the back of the church, excluded from the service. However, as the mass of Easter was ending a man whom they took to be the priest from the nearby village but who subsequently turned out to be an angel appeared and led them to the pyx, and thus they were given communion after all and ordered to dress in their festive clothes and given the kiss of peace.

This account was written c. 1050 about events which supposedly occurred more than two hundred years before. But the point of the story, that out of bad behaviour can come good, if suitably atoned for, would be lost on Ekkehard's audience if the details about the penance were hopelessly unrealistic and out of date.[111] It did not therefore seem unlikely to Ekkehard's audience that a lay couple should instigate the penitential process and thereby prescribe their own severe and public penance. Ekkehard's text was apparently written for his fellow monks at St Gall, although it is possible that it was also heard by lay visitors. Although the couple's punishment, being excluded and made to stand at the back of the church as obvious penitents, echoes the process for public penance it also bears a close resemblance to monastic public penance, in which the penitent had to stand by the door and was not allowed to participate in the service.[112] Perhaps Ekkehard distorted his representation of lay behaviour, viewing it through his monastic lens.

---

110 Ibid. xix.v, 960A (prohibition of sexual relations in Lent), 962D (on breaking the Lenten fast). For over-indulgence in food and drink ten days' fasting but for drunkenness through vainglory, thirty days', ibid. 963A.
111 de Jong, 'Pollution, penance and sanctity'.
112 The ninth-century bishop, Isaac of Langres (d. 880) maintained the late antique idea that the penitent 'audientes' should be present during services at the back of the church, although excluded from communion: 'c. xvii: Ut, qui poenitentiam publicae gerunt, uno anno cum cilitio sint inter audientes': Isaac de Langres, *Capitula de poenitentibus*, MGH, Capit. Ep. II, 192–3 (cited by de Jong, 'Pollution, penance and sanctity', 151 n. 15). On monastic public penance see ch. 3 above.

Yet we also need to ask why public penance was imposed for what was essentially a private sin.[113] The answer seems to be twofold: Iso's parents through publicly declaring their sin made it a matter for public penance but they had also upset the decreed norms for behaviour on this the most sacred of days, when Jesus Christ was officially dead, and offended the whole community by breaking what was a collective rite, the Lenten fast. Ekkehard's tale thus fits into another ecclesiastical tradition: in his chronicle, Thietmar, the early eleventh-century bishop of Merseburg, included two accounts of children conceived at prohibited times who were thus the work of the devil but were saved through baptism.[114] Penance is often referred to as a second baptism, and thus Iso's parents saved not only themselves but their unborn child. Such stories obviously circulated in ecclesiastical circles, and were, presumably, intended ultimately to encourage the laity to obey the Church's regulations, but they are not evidence that the laity did so.[115]

Rather more is known about the laity's attitudes to the Church's rulings on incest, that is marriage or intercourse within the prohibited degrees of relationship, because evidence survives from councils and *vitae* of the Church's efforts to enforce them.[116] The Church sought to enforce its rulings through the penitentials, which dealt with incest in the varying degrees, defined as seven in this period,[117] and through penitential *ordines*: several for penance 'in the usual way' included incest in the priest's preliminary assessment of the penitents' willingness to confess and do penance – if s/he had committed incest the process might not continue – as well as asking them questions on their sexual relations in the *interrogatio*.[118] But how far did the laity follow the Church's rulings?

---

[113] Kottje, 'Busspraxis', 393–4, argues that this is a form of mixed penance. De Jong argues that this story demonstrates that mixed penance – that is a penitential procedure which follows the ritual norms of public penance but is administered by the local priest – had become acceptable practice in the eleventh century; she also emphasises the importance attached in the story to the intensity of penitential action by Iso's parents which helped to speed up a process which normally took the whole of Lent, and how it was their voluntary confession which led to their forgiveness rather than their humiliation before the community: 'Pollution, penance and sanctity'.
[114] Thietmar, *Chronicon* I.xxiv, xxv, pp. 30, 32.
[115] Flandrin, *Un Temps pour embrasser*, 143–8.
[116] M. de Jong, 'To the limits of kinship: anti-incest legislation in the early medieval west (500–900)', in J. Bremmer (ed.), *From Sappho to de Sade: moments in the history of sexuality*, London–New York 1989, 36–59. Although incest usually refers to intercourse with blood relations it also applied to spiritual relations made through baptism. On the latter see J. H. Lynch, 'Spiritual kinship and sexual prohibitions in early medieval Europe', in S. Kuttner and K. Pennington (eds), *Proceedings of the sixth international congress of medieval canon law*, Vatican 1985, 271–88.
[117] Payer, *Sex and the penitentials*, 30–2, 125–6. On relationships forbidden for marriage see Regino, *Libri duo*, II. cc, pp. 291–2; Burchard, *Decretum VII: De incestu*, also XVII.viii; XIX.v, 779–86, 920, 929, 965–7.
[118] For example, 'Et require ab eo diligenter, si est incestuosus aut suo seniori infidelis; et si non vult incestum dimittere, non potes ei dare poenitentiam; si autem vult, potes': Regino,

The Church condemned the marriages of certain couples as incestuous at several councils. The most famous case is that of Count Otto of Hammerstein and Irmgard of Gottfried, who were both excommunicated at the Council of Nijmegen in 1018 for their maintenance of their unlawful marriage.[119] In this case the Church was acting in conjunction with the ruler: the emperor Henry II justified his objection to the marriage union of two powerful families on the grounds of their consanguinity. Otto appealed to the emperor unsuccessfully for, in the face of their obstinacy, Henry besieged the castle of Hammerstein in the autumn of 1020.[120] The couple then appealed to the papacy, an action which was implicitly condemned at the Council of Seligenstadt in 1023.[121] The marriage continued; Conrad II gave up the case in 1027, perhaps because he encountered challenges from the Church about the lawfulness of his own marriage.[122] Both Conrad II and his son Henry III appear to have ignored the Church's rulings for their own marriages and succeeded in doing so without encountering major trouble. Conrad II was related to his wife Gisela within five degrees of consanguinity since both were descendants of Henry the Fowler. This may be the reason why Aribo, archbishop of Mainz, refused to crown Gisela queen after Conrad's election and coronation on 8 September 1024; Gisela was crowned three weeks later by the archbishop of Cologne.[123] Henry III married Agnes of Poitou to whom he was probably related within the fourth degree but managed to ignore the objections of Poppo, abbot of Stablo.[124] For incest legislation to be enforced it seems that there often had to be a political dimension.[125] Constance Bouchard's study of marriages amongst

---

Libri duo I.ccciv, p. 141. For a similar injunction see the *ordines* in Burchard, *Decretum* XIX.iv, 950–1. See also that in the Romano-German pontifical, *PRG* cxxxvi.9 (certain manuscripts only), ii. 236, and the Fulda sacramentary, *SF*, no. 437 (2375), p. 281. Another avenue for such teachings were conciliar proceedings. For example the Council of Reims (1049) ordained excommunication on all those guilty of incest: Mansi, *Concilia*, xix. 737–8.
[119] Thietmar, *Chronicon* VIII.vii, xviii, pp. 500, 514–15. S. Reicke, 'Der Hammersteinische Ehehandel im Lichte der mittelalterlichen Herrschaftsordnung', *Rheinische Vierteljahrsblätter* xxxviii (1974), 203–24; A. Gerlich, 'Hammersteiner Ehe', in *LMA* iv. 1892. They appear to have been related in the fourth degree of consanguinity.
[120] Thietmar, *Chronicon* VIII.xviii, pp. 514–15; Gerlich, 'Hammersteiner Ehe'.
[121] See ch. 2.
[122] Reicke, 'Der Hammersteinische Ehehandel', 222.
[123] On Gisela's ancestry see Wipo, *Gesta Chuonradi II. imperatoris*, c. iv, in *Die Werke Wipos*, ed. H. Bresslau (MGH, SRG lxi, 1915, repr. 1956), 25–6. For the account of her coronation see Hermann of Reichenau, *Chronicon*, a. 1024, p. 120. N. Bischoff, 'Über die Chronologie der Kaiserin Gisela und über die Verweigerung ihrer Krönung durch Aribo von Mainz', in *Mitteilungen des Instituts für Österreichische Geschichtsforschung* lviii (1950), 285–309.
[124] H. Thomas, 'Zur Kritik an der Ehe Heinrichs III. mit Agnes von Poitou', in K. U. Jäschke and R. Wenskus (eds), *Festschrift für Helmut Beumann zum 65. Geburtstag*, Sigmaringen 1977, 224–35.
[125] The Council of Rome (997) held by Otto III and Pope Gregory V condemned Robert II of France's second marriage as being within the prohibited degrees of both actual and spiritual kinship: Mansi, *Concilia*, xix. 225. Otto was asserting his authority as emperor and ruler of Germany over Robert as king of west Frankia but Robert ignored his prohibition for at

the west Frankish nobility in the tenth and eleventh centuries suggests that they usually sought to refrain from marrying their relations; similar work needs to be done on the east Frankish nobility before coming to any conclusions about lay attitudes to incest legislation.[126] But the three cases discussed above suggest that incest was not an issue which particularly bothered east Frankish nobles and that it was possible to evade ecclesiastical censure if one were sufficiently powerful and could invoke episcopal aid. A case in point is that of Thiefried, *Burggraf* of Trier, who invoked the aid of Poppo, archbishop of Trier (1016–47) in order to remain married to his wife in the face of a charge of consanguinity.[127] The clergy undoubtedly sought to promote their views by portraying laymen, even kings, as filled with guilt for the crime of incest, and only too keen to do penance, but the laity appear to have been willing to continue to marry within the remoter degrees of relationship and certain members of the clergy were willing to assist them in doing so.[128]

But penance, and the doctrine of sin for which it stood, was a powerful tool in the Church's armoury in enforcing its own sexual code. At the Council of Trosly (927) Count Herluin came to do penance for remarrying during the lifetime of his wife.[129] A century later Count Dodicho 'ruined himself' through his association with an apostate nun and in *c*. 1015–20 he made over his whole *predium* to St Liborius and the church at Paderborn for the benefit of his soul and its future commemoration.[130] We do not know the full political and personal reasons which led up to this grant, or whether he made it willingly. But taken at face value it suggests that for one man the Church's view of sin equalled his own and that he was sufficiently worried about his future salvation to take practical steps to help ensure it, and undo the consequences of his past behaviour.

Penance and the lower orders

Penance was meant to be universal, yet in the absence of surviving *litterae poenitentiales*, historians who wish to study the practice of penance outside the circle of the higher orders, the clerics, nobles and kings with whom this

---

least another five years: G. Duby, *The knight, the lady and the priest: the making of modern marriage in medieval France*, trans. B. Bray, Harmondsworth 1983, 75–85.
126 C. Bouchard, 'Consanguinity and noble marriages in the tenth and eleventh centuries', *Speculum* lvi (1981), 268–87.
127 This case is discussed in greater detail in Reuter, 'Filii matris', 263.
128 On the case of Robert the Pious's reported penance for his incest see Hamilton, 'A new model for royal penance?'.
129 'Herluinus comes ad poenitentiam venit pro uxore quam duxerat alia vivente': Flodoard, *Annales*, a. 927.
130 *Vita Meinwerci episcopi Patherbrunnensis*, ed. F. Tenckhoff (MGH, SRG lix, 1921), c. xlix, pp. 41–2; *Regesta historiae Westfaliae accedit codex diplomaticus*, I: *Mit den ältesten geschichtlichen Nachrichten bis zum Jahre 1125*, ed. H. A. Erhard, Münster 1847, nos xcv, xcvi, ii. 76. The case is cited by Leyser in *Rule and conflict*, 59–60.

chapter has been mainly concerned, have to overcome the prescriptive and idealistic bias of the material to establish whether there is any evidence that the lower orders experienced penance.

According to both the legislation and the liturgy the rural clergy were to summon everyone from the smallest to the grandest to confess at the beginning of Lent.[131] These references seem to be no more than formulaic lip service to Christianity's universal message: the Church should include everyone. This theme also underlies the earliest depiction of the giving of penance, found in the Göttingen codex of the Fulda sacramentary, showing penance being administered to laymen and women, and accompanying a vernacular confession prayer: penance was meant to be administered to those who could not speak Latin.[132] The Romano-German pontifical made a similar provision.[133] This use of the vernacular need not imply that the *ordo* was targeted at the lower orders: there is currently insufficient evidence to assess how far the tenth-century Lotharingian, German and Italian aristocracy, as opposed to their ninth-century counterparts, were literate in Latin.[134]

But the performance of a penitential sentence was a physical rather than a verbal process; it was not confined to the donation of land or payment of alms or saying of prayers or fasting. Peter Damian wrote to the monks of Monte Cassino praising the way in which they had been so successful in promoting the practice of weekly flagellation on a Friday not only in their monastery but also amongst the multitudes living in the surrounding towns and villages.[135]

---

[131] 'Monemus fratres et consacerdotes omnes parrochiae nostrae, ut studiose provideant, quatinus nullus sit in parrochiis suis a minimo usque ad maximum, cuius confessionem non suscipiant. De his vero, qui in multis parrochiis possessiones habent et secundum suam voluntatem aliquando in una, aliquando in altera parrochia commorantur et incertum manet, cui confessi sint, ut nullus sine confessione remanere possit. Et si ad nullam confessi fuerint, cogantur venire ad confessionem. Si autem venire noluerint, excommunicetur': Ruotger of Trier, *Capit.* c. xxvi, MGH, *Capit. Ep. I*, 70. Cf. Burchard, *Decretum* XIX.i–ii, 949; *Poenitentiale Valicellianum (sic) III* (Biblioteca Vallicelliana, Cod. B. 58), in *Bussbücher* I, 775; Council of Trier (927), c. xiv, MGH, *Concilia VI*, 83; Council of Mainz (950x954), ibid. 176–7. See also the text beginning 'Feria quarta ante quadragesimam plebem ad confessionem inuitate' found in both Rather's *Synodica*, 133, and the *Admonitio synodalis*, no. lxiii, p. 58. Mention is also made in various *ordines*, for example PRG xcix.44, ii. 14; SF lv, p. 42. For further details see chs 1, 2 and 4 above.

[132] See ch. 5 above.

[133] 'Deinde fiat confessio peccatorum rusticis verbis': PRG cxxxvi.23, ii. 242.

[134] For this view of the ninth-century aristocracy see McKitterick, *Carolingians and the written word*.

[135] 'Observatio sextae feriae, dilectissimi, cui sancta vestra devotio dedicavit, et ieiunii salutaris inediam, et apostolicorum verberum, disciplinam, quot hominum multitudines ad exemplum salutis attraxerit, et tanquam novella divinae plantationis 'oliva' in exuberantium germinum propagines pullulaverit, testes sunt non modo monasteria, que vestra, hoc est suorum gaudent imitari vestigia magistrorum, set et multitudine urbium atque villarum, que se communiter ingerentes atque letantes idipsum plausibiliter arripiunt institutum': *Die Briefe des Petrus Damiani*, no. clxi, iv. 135–6. I would like to thank Dr Diana Webb of King's College London for this reference.

Before dismissing this comment as mere hopeful rhetoric by one of the most vocal promoters of the monastic life in his lifetime, we should remember that flagellation was not only an established element of internal monastic discipline but also an officially recognised method for commuting penance.[136] Damian's comment thus provides both a possible, if tantalising, glimpse of the spread of one of the more accessible forms of penitential devotion amongst the villagers living around Monte Cassino, and at the same time demonstrates the difficulty facing historians who wish to study the practice of penance amongst the lower orders.

Other evidence, however, suggests that the poor were marginalised into a supporting role. Penance could be commuted by feeding or giving alms to the poor, an option available only to the rich.[137] The sources themselves categorised society more strictly: thus the Romano-German pontifical's *ordo* for penance 'in the usual way' classifies the penitent by his office – *comes, castaldius, ministerialis, negociator, massarius, monetarius, escarius, iudex* or *notarius* – before advising him on his future conduct; for example a penitent judge should not accept bribes.[138] The practice of penance seems here to be reserved for the well-off. But other sources contain hints that penance extended a little further down the scale. Regino began his book ii on the laity with instructions that the bishop on his visitation of the diocese should examine the plebs of each *parochia* to discover what sins, especially of a serious nature, had been committed.[139] He outlined how a bishop might check up on his priests, who were, as other capitularies suggest, expected to investigate the behaviour of all members of their flock, and bring to public penance anyone guilty of serious or public sins.[140] Regino's *inquisitio* is followed by a set of penitential canons which, like other sets, appear to provide occasional insights into the lives of the lower orders. In his section on penances for homicide, he suggested that if a man went with another man into a wood to fell a tree, and one was killed by a falling tree, then the other was not guilty of murder; it was an accidental death.[141] But Alfred's laws in ninth-century Wessex include a similar provision, suggesting it was a topos of *leges*.[142] Similarly there are numerous canons in the penitential tradition

---

136 See ch. 1.
137 Regino, *Libri duo* II.ccccxlvi, ccccxlix, ccccli-iv, pp. 389–92; Burchard, *Decretum* XIX. xii, xiii, xvi, xx, xxiii, 981–3. For ninth-century practice see Smith, 'Religion and lay society', 668–9.
138 *PRG* cxxxvi.14, ii. 240.
139 Regino, *Libri duo* II.i, pp. 206–7.
140 For example, Atto of Vercelli, c. xc, MGH, *Capit. Ep. III*, 296–7. See ch. 2 above for a fuller discussion of this issue.
141 'Si duo fratres in silua arbores succiderint et appropinquante casura unius arboris frater fratri *cave* dixent, et ille fugiens in pressuram arboris inciderit et mortuus fuerit, vivens frater innocens de sanguine germani diiudicetur': Regino, *Libri duo* II.xviii, p. 221. It was taken up by Burchard in his *Decretum* XIX.v, 954B.
142 Alfred, *Leges*, c. xiii, in *English historical documents, I: 500–1042*, ed. and trans.

which deal with childcare and infanticide, such as the penance for a mother who places her child in an oven or on the roof to cure it of fever.[143] This particular canon appears to be less concerned with the child's safety than with the 'superstitious' belief underpinning such practice; it entered the tradition in the eighth century and continued into the eleventh. Yet Burchard also included questions about superstitions in the priest's interrogation of the penitent in book xix of the *Decretum* which appear to be original to his text and to deal with contemporary rural superstitions and fertility rites, using vernacular words. He thus prescribes a penance for those who believe in what the Germans call 'werewolves' (incidentally the earliest reference to this belief), and for those who participate in a ritual undertaken by women to bring rain which involves a naked girl having a henbane plant, the German word for which is, according to Burchard, 'belisa', tied to the little toe of her right foot before being sprinkled with water from the river.[144] Such legislation may suggest that penance would be administered at a level beneath that of the elite. Legislation is, however, prescriptive: it is evidence of intent rather than of practice.

The Council of Trier (c. 927) described the reconciliation of penitents on Maundy Thursday in terms which suggested an attempt to address contemporary problems: priests should ensure that the penitents appear before the doors of the church on Maundy Thursday in order to be reconciled with a downcast face, and that they pray there rather than recount funny stories (*fabula ioca*) to each other.[145] This prohibition may mean that the penitents no longer took the process seriously. But it could also mean that the penitents reassured themselves with popular tales, perhaps about saints, for *fabula* usually refer to made-up stories, and, according to Bernard of Angers's early eleventh-century account of the miracles worked by Sainte Foy, the laity, particularly the *vulgus*, referred to her miracles as her *ioca*.[146] This passing reference suggests in any case an attempt to obviate problems generated in an existing penitential system by its popularity and general application.

This is the impression also given by Ekkehard's throw-away description of how the entire community of Iso's parents' village observed Lent collectively, dressed in penitential clothes, before changing their clothes in order to celebrate Easter equally collectively. Perhaps more telling are Thietmar's refer-

---

D. Whitelock, 2nd edn, London 1979, 411. See also Rothair's Edict (643), no. cxxxviii, *Edictus Rothari*, ed. F. Blühme (MGH, Legum IV, Hanover 1868), 31.
[143] Burchard, *Decretum* XIX.cxlix, 1012. On this canon's early history, going back to the Theodorian tradition, see Meens, 'Children and confession', 60.
[144] '[Q]uod vulgaris stultitia weruwolff vocat': Burchard, *Decretum* XIX.v, 971B; 'quae Teutonicae belisa vocatur', XIX.v, 976C–D; Vogel, 'Pratiques superstitieuses'.
[145] 'Quando vero veniunt ad fores aecclesiae, vultu diecto orent ibi nec ullis fabulis iocisve se occupent': c. xv, MGH, *Concilia* VI, 84. This council is discussed in more detail in ch. 2. *Fabula* usually refer to a made-up or fabulous story and in Gregory of Tours's *Histories* to a rumour: Du Cange, *Glossarium mediae*, iii. 176.
[146] *Liber miraculorum sanctae Fidis*, ed. L. Robertini, Spoleto 1994, I.xxviii, pp. 132–3.

ences to penitents: he describes how the funeral procession for Otto III, bringing the body back from Italy to be interned at Aachen on Easter Sunday 1002 made a circuit of the churches in Cologne and passed the penitents waiting outside the cathedral to be reconciled on Maundy Thursday.[147] Elsewhere he refers to a man being buried in Cologne in 'the southern part of the church at the place where penitents appear on Maundy Thursday'.[148] Both references suggest that public penance was to Thietmar normative and supports the impression given by the liturgical evidence of the widespread imposition of public penance.

Penitential *ordines* are prescriptive, but as chapters 4 and 5 suggest, many were put into practice, perhaps explaining why, despite some overlaps of material, they prove a richer source of information for penitential practice than legislation and sermons. The overlaps suggest that certain injunctions in the *ordines* had become formulaic: the priest should not only match the penance to the sin, but award the penance appropriate to the penitent's circumstances.[149] Commutations were often required to be means-tested: the poor should pay less than the rich.[150] These broadbrush generalisations may be no more than manifestations of the universal pastoral message: penance for all. But more specific injunctions in certain of the *ordines* suggest that an attempt was made to realise these generalisations: servants, for example, should not be given lengthy fasts as penances because they have no control over their own diet or work.[151] Another instruction, common to several *ordines*, is that laymen should put down their sticks before entering into (public) penance on Ash Wednesday.[152] This gesture signifies their transition from lay to penitential status: according to the canons a penitent might not carry a weapon or go to war.[153] Evidence from Charlemagne's reign suggests that sticks or staffs were regarded as weapons, if too ineffectual for battle, and were associated with men of low status.[154] This reference is therefore implic-

---

[147] 'In cena Domini ad sanctum Petrum portatur, ubi, penitentibus more aecclesiastico introductis et indulgentia resolutis, animae presentis corporis ab archipresule remissio datur, a consacerdotibus autem memoria eposcitur, lacrimabiliter, autem a populo supplici impenditur': Thietmar, *Chronicon* IV.liii, p. 192.

[148] 'Sepultus in Colonia in eodem loco, ubi ipse prius rogavit, in australi parte templi, quo in cena Domini penitentes introducuntur': ibid. VI.lxxxvi, p. 376.

[149] Atto, c. xc, *MGH, Capit. Ep. III*, 296–7; *PRG* xcix.46–8, ii. 15.

[150] For example, Burchard, *Decretum* XIX.xv, xxii, xxiii, 982–3.

[151] 'Sed et hoc sciendum est, ut, cum venerint servi vel ancillae ad penitentiam, non eos cogatis ieiunare tantum quantum divites, quia non sunt in sua potestate. Ideoque medietatem penitentiae eis imponite': *PRG* xcix.55, ii. 18. See also Biblioteca Vallicelliana, Cod. E. 15, *Bussbücher I*, 243.

[152] 'Denique cum sacerdos susceperit penitentem si laicus est dimisso baculo, quisque vero ille est sive laicus sive clericus seu monachus suppliciter inclinet se ante sacerdotem': *PRG* xcix.44, ii. 14.

[153] For example, Burchard, *Decretum* XIX.lxvi, 999.

[154] Charlemagne, Capit. no. lxxvii, cc. xvi–xvii, *Capitularia regum francorum I*, ed. A. Boretius (MGH, Legum ii/1, Hanover 1883), 172. The changes in status upon entry into

itly universalising: penance was available to all and a stick symbolised lay status, both low and high. But penance was not restricted to men either: many of the prayers in the *ordines* refer to the penitents as *famuli* and *famulae*.[155]

The inclusion of such incidental details in otherwise prescriptive sources suggests that penance was not only intended to reach the lower orders, as the great injunctions of episcopal legislation imply, but actually did so. It must be acknowledged that the tenth-century non-prescriptive sources seem largely unconcerned with the issue of popular penance. This is because contemporary chronicles and *vitae* written in the area under consideration largely ignore the lower orders, whilst miracle collections are more concerned with the saint's protective power for his community than with extending his protection to the sinful lower orders.[156] The eleventh century suggests a reversal of this picture: Platelle's work on *vitae* demonstrated that confession and the consequent penance were not unknown amongst the laity in late eleventh-century Flanders, although he conceded that there are not enough examples to consider the practice as widespread.[157] Moreover, most of his penitents had sufficient wealth to found monasteries, or at least give them donations of land.[158] But the evidence outlined above for penitential practice by the lower orders suggests that further research in this area may produce dividends. Scattered though the references over two centuries and throughout and beyond the area covered by this study, the evidence suggests that throughout this period the Church's universal call to penance was answered by the lower orders.

---

penance are discussed by Leyser, 'Early medieval canon law', esp. at pp. 57–60; de Jong, 'Power and humility', 33–4.

[155] For example, SF, no. 437 (2375), p. 281; PRG cxxxvi.2, ii. 234; xcix.45, ii. 15.

[156] B. Ward, *Miracles and the medieval mind: theory, record and event, 1000–1215*, Aldershot 1982, esp. ch. iii; P. R. Morison, 'The miraculous and French society, c. 950–1100', unpubl. DPhil. diss. Oxford 1983.

[157] Platelle, 'Violence', 143.

[158] For example, the six founders of Affligem (1083) confessed their sins to the archbishop of Cologne who urged them to return to their own lands and do penance for their faults: *Chronicon affligemense*, ed. G. Pertz (MGH, SS ix), c. ii, p. 408; Platelle, 'Violence', 141–2. See also the case of a wife murderer who, overcome by guilt, gave all his holdings to his daughter, who founded a monastery, whilst he went to the Holy Land as penance; returning to Flanders, he became a monk and died in penance: *Vita Godeliph*, ed. M. Coens, in 'La Vie ancienne de sainte Godelive de Ghistelles par Drogon de Bergues', *Analecta Bollandiana* xliv (1926), 102–37 (written c. 1084). This case is also discussed in Platelle, 'Violence', 105–8.

Afterword

This study of the practice of penance in the *Reich* in the period 900–1050 has revealed a much greater diversity than had hitherto been suspected by historians. Diversity in the liturgical rites available for penance, which could vary considerably as, for example, between those followed in the archdiocese of Trier and in the archdiocese of Mainz; or even within the archdiocese of Mainz, between the episcopal rites first codified in the Romano-German pontifical in the monastery of St Alban, Mainz, in the mid tenth century and those collected by the monks of Fulda. Diversity in the types of penance available, which did not follow the simple 'Carolingian dichotomy' identified by Cyrille Vogel between public penance for public sins and secret penance for secret sins, but instead combined elements usually identified as peculiar to either public or secret penance to form a mixed penance, as in the Fulda rite for private or annual penance, which took many of its elements from public penance but was not administered by a bishop, or the public nature of the rites for secret penance administered in northern Italy. The confused nature of the reality of penitential practice is typified by the case of Arduin of Ivrea, who was condemned to a penance which contained all the disadvantages of public penance but was nevertheless classified as a secret penance. Diversity too in the contexts in which penance was practised, ranging from the episcopal politics of Lotharingia to monastic discipline, from a royal funeral to the clerical reforming politics of Milan, from the court to the village. A level of diversity is to be expected from any detailed study, and it must also be in part a reflection of the variety of sources used; the penitential practices recorded in the narrative sources often seem to be more varied than those detailed in sources belonging to more prescriptive genres. The descriptions found in canon law, or episcopal capitularies, for example, often follow the precedents of that particular genre. But this variety also suggests that penance, far from being a relatively rare practice, confined to members of the elite, may have been more widely practised, not only by the clergy, but by the laity, than is often supposed.

It would, however, be misleading to take too simple a view of a complicated religious idea and practice. Of course, on a religious level the practice of penance answered the problem of how Christians could overcome the sinfulness inherent in their earthly life and attain eternal salvation; while, viewed in terms of power structures, its administration was a clerical prerogative and an especially powerful tool with which the clergy sought to both control and educate the laity. But the laity was not always so easily controlled: certain sinners such as Arduin of Ivrea, or Otto and Irmingard of Hammerstein were willing to ignore the penitential sentences imposed on them. Penance was not a universal system and clerical authority was not always recognised as superior.[1] But individual cases also suggest that, whilst penance may have been valued as a political and educational institution by the clergy, it was also one which the laity themselves were usually willing to embrace. Henry III, albeit a king, is reported to have done penance at his mother's funeral. Archbishop Ruotger of Trier described penitents as engaged in nervous story-telling as they queued up for reconciliation on Maundy Thursday. These cases suggest the importance which penitential practice had for some laity as well as clergy in this period. But penance was also used by bishops both to ensure the obedience of their clergy, and as a mechanism through which they might communicate with their mostly rural priests. Monastic lords apparently made use of penance to educate and prepare their tenants for Easter. Consideration of material from a number of different genres, and in particular the use of other types of source to reflect back on the penitential liturgies, has made it possible to recognise the diverse ways in which penance was regarded and used by all involved.

The practice of penance thus took different forms. This study has sought not only to show the important regional differences which existed between liturgies, but to argue for the local influences which lie behind these differences. It has also presented evidence for the continued importance and development of public penance in this period, though without undertaking similar studies of other regions it is impossible to say how far the changes noted are wholly the result of local factors. One question in particular arises from the Italian evidence. Both the *ordines* examined in chapter 5 and the case of Arduin of Ivrea, with which this study began, suggest that public penance as defined both legally and liturgically in northern France, Lotharingia and the Rhineland, was not widely practised in Italy. Owing to the scattered nature of Italian manuscript holdings, distributed in local libraries throughout Italy, which I have not been able to consult, it is possible that there is evidence, outside Italian copies of the Romano-German pontifical, for rites of public penance, but the omission of this rite from the twelfth-century Roman pontifical suggests that it had effectively disappeared from Italy sometime before.[2] But if so, why? It was not because of antipathy towards penance in general: Frankish penitentials and *ordines* for secret penance were, as we have seen, widely copied in tenth- and eleventh-century Italy. It may rather be the result of the continued existence of a successful local secular judicial system; bishops had less opportunity to use penance to assert their authority over the clergy and laity within their dioceses.[3] If this is

---

[1] For the argument for lay scepticism in the later period of 1100–1500 see S. Reynolds, 'Social mentalities and the case of medieval scepticism', *TRHS* 6th ser. i (1991), 21–41.
[2] *Le Pontifical du moyen âge*, ed. M. Andrieu (SeT lxxxvii, 1940).
[3] C. Wickham, 'Lawyers' time: history and memory in tenth- and eleventh-century Italy', in his *Land and power: studies in Italian and European social history, 400–1200*, London 1994, 275–93.

the case, then the attempts of Bishop Atto of Vercelli to use public penance as a means of maintaining his control over his clergy appear old-fashioned. That Italy was different is a commonplace of medieval historiography; quite why it was different in this particular instance is an area which requires further investigation.

The continued importance of public penance in the period supports the conclusions reached by Mary Mansfield from her work on thirteenth- and fourteenth-century northern France, namely that the introduction in 1215 of the requirement that all Christians should make an annual confession, was not accompanied by a decline in public penance. My own researches help to undermine the view put forward by the Catholic historians of the mid twentieth century who saw the period 900–1200 as one of transition from a system of tariff or secret penance, to one of confession and only very occasional public penance. It is clear that there was no such switch to confession in this period: 'public' penance, 'secret' penance, and forms of mixed, of not so formal nor so secret, penance continued to be important. It is also clear that penitential practice was widespread in the period 900–1050; the apparent sudden popularity of penance in the long twelfth century, as proposed by Alexander Murray, seems to be more a trick of the evidential light than reality.[4]

It was, however, a period which saw some specific liturgical changes. In Lotharingia and north-east France, for example, the rite for the reconciliation of penitents on Maundy Thursday differed from that in the Rhineland; rather than expecting the penitents to wait outside the church before they were reconciled by the bishop, and to witness the bishop's own humble behaviour, they were invited into the church before they were reconciled and the bishop refrained from humiliating himself in front of them. I have sought to explain this change in local terms, as a response to clerical needs, but it is, of course, also possible that other changes, such as the gradual transition to one-stage penance, the granting of absolution at the same time as the awarding of penance, were the result of lay concern; that lay demands for a process which guaranteed the effectiveness of personal penance and future salvation led to the the new practice. Only further study of other local liturgies will provide the context necessary to put such changes in a fuller perspective.

Just as penance seems to have been used for several purposes, so the distinctions beloved of modern historians, especially those between public and private penance, were far less distinct in the terminology of the time. Although contemporary writers sometimes distinguished between the practices of secret and public penance, many writers chose to refer to penance in an unadorned fashion, merely as *poenitentia*. Thus the composers of the

---

[4] Murray, 'Confession'. Murray's apparent discovery of the popular practice of confession, as distinct from penance, seems also to be a reflection of the pastoral concerns of the authors of the *miracula* in his sample, rather than a reflection of a greater reality.

Romano-German pontifical did not identify the rite administered by the bishop for entry into penance on Ash Wednesday and reconciliation on Maundy Thursday as public penance, merely as penance, whilst the monks of Fulda, for example, referred to a version of the service used for the public ejection of penitents on Ash Wednesday as 'ordo priuatae seu annualis poenitentiae'.[5] Conversely, in Italy rites for 'secret' penance were conducted in public. Historians should thus be wary of imposing twentieth-century views of what constituted the practices of public or secret penance onto the early medieval period. Indeed the ambiguity of the language often adopted by contemporaries may have been deliberate. Previous research has attempted to distinguish between the practices for secret and public penance, between the concerns of individual conscience and those of the community. In doing so, modern historians have read back from the codification embarked on by theologians and canonists in the twelfth century to the earlier period. But whilst contemporaries could distinguish between the practices now known to historians as *paenitentia secreta* and *paenitentia publica*, in the majority of cases some form of secret penance was applied, with public penance being reserved for *scandala*. However, even in the case of public penance, there were no hard and fast rules. Individuals appeared as sinners, shamed before the whole community, and were exiled for a time from it, but they were also prayed for by, and remained a part of, that community: in the words of the archdeacon when presenting the penitents to the bishop on Maundy Thursday: 'Unique therefore is the favour of penance which advantages them individually and aids them all in common.'[6]

---

[5] SF lv. 42.
[6] 'Unicum itaque est poenitentiae suffragium, quod et singulis prodest et omnibus in commune succurrit': PRG xcix.225, ii. 60.

APPENDIX 1

The Distribution of the Romano-German Pontifical

The Romano-German pontifical survives in thirty-nine manuscripts and in four main recensions (A, B, C and D), and was copied in Germany, north and south Italy, France and England. Michel Andrieu, writing in the 1920s, and Cyrille Vogel, writing in the 1950s, therefore argued that the Romano-German pontifical was widely disseminated and had considerable influence on the development of the liturgy. Yet the more detailed analysis of its manuscript dissemination presented in this appendix suggests that the case for the significance of the Romano-German pontifical has been overstated.

Table 2 contains brief details of all the surviving Romano-German pontifical manuscripts, analysed by date, scriptorium and provenance.[1] Drawing upon the researches of Andrieu, Vogel and Reinhard Elze, supplemented where necessary from more recent work, it provides the basis for a study of the manuscript dissemination of the Romano-German pontifical within four distinct geographic areas over the course of the tenth and eleventh centuries: Germany, Italy, France and England.

Germany

The majority of the manuscripts (twenty-six out of a total of thirty-nine) were written in Germany, and of these sixteen were copied in the eleventh century. Most of these are from churches within the provinces of Mainz and Salzburg (see table 1).

The eleventh-century distribution pattern suggests that the Romano-German pontifical was as successful in Mainz as in Salzburg. A higher proportion of twelfth-century manuscripts are from Mainz, and this may reflect the eleventh-century distribution comprising, to some extent, replacement copies of earlier manuscripts which have disappeared; this is certainly the case for the only twelfth-century codex from the Salzburg province, the Passau pontifical, which is a copy of an early eleventh-century Passau pontifical.[2]

---

[1] Both Andrieu and Vogel argued that the Cracow pontifical (Jagiellonian Library, MS 2057) also belonged to the Romano-German family but, on the basis of its penitential rite, I consider this manuscript to be part of the north-central family and thus it is discussed in ch. 5.
[2] Vienna, Nationalbibliothek, Cod. lat. 1817. For evidence that this is a copy see the discussion in OR i. 388.

APPENDIX 1

Table 1
Number of German Romano-German pontifical manuscripts analysed
by province (for fuller details see table 2)

	s. xi	s. xii	s. xiii	s. xiv	Total
Mainz	7	7	–	–	14
Salzburg	6	1	–	–	7
Trier	–	–	–	–	–
Cologne	2	–	–	–	2
Unknown	1	–	–	1	2
Total	16	8	–	1	25

In the provinces of both Mainz and Salzburg the success of the Romano-German pontifical was due to the patronage of the archbishop and his suffragan bishops: copies were made for the bishops of Eichstätt, Freising and Regensburg.[3] Bishops may also be behind those examples which were made for monastic communities; Bamberg, Staatsbibliothek, Cod. Lit. 55, was made on the orders of Bishop Otto (1102–39) for the nearby community of St Michael in Bamberg.[4] Another copy, Bamberg, Staatsbibliothek, Cod. Lit. 53, was commissioned for and donated to Bamberg cathedral by Henry II after its foundation in 1007.[5] This evidence confirms the thesis of Andrieu and Vogel that the Romano-German pontifical was promoted by the German rulers in conjunction with their bishops.

But the distribution of the Romano-German pontifical within Germany is almost wholly confined to the provinces of Mainz and Salzburg. No copies survive from the Trier province, despite the fact that Archbishop Egbert (977–93) was a great patron of book production, especially for his own see;[6] the pontificals which have survived from Trier do not belong to the orthodox Romano-German pontifical tradition.[7] And only two Romano-German pontifical codices have been attributed to the province of Cologne: BL, MS Add. 17004, and MS Cotton Vitellius, E. xii.[8] The attribution of MS Add. 17004 to Cologne is by no means certain.[9] It includes mention of a Bishop

---

[3] For Gondekar II, bishop of Eichstätt (1057–75), see ibid. i. 117–34; that for Bishop Egilbert of Freising (1006–39) is now Munich, Bayerische Staatsbibliothek, Clm 6425 (with its companion volume Clm 21587) on which see ibid. i. 220–32, and Hoffmann, *Buchkunst*, i. 211; that for Regensburg is BN, MS lat. 1231, on which see Leroquais, *Pontificaux*, ii. 138–44.
[4] OR i. 73–8.
[5] Described by Hoffmann in *Buchkunst*, i. 406–7, and OR i. 41–63.
[6] Mayr-Harting, *Ottonian book illumination*, ii. 60–81.
[7] For example, BN, MS lat. 13313.
[8] M. Lapidge, 'Ealdred of York and MS Cotton Vitellius E. XII', *Yorkshire Archaeological Journal* lv (1983), 11–25 (repr. in his *Anglo-Latin literature, 900–1066*, London–Rio Grande 1993, 453–67).
[9] Although written in a German hand it was in use in Picardy by the early twelfth century and soon entered the collection of the cathedral of Amiens, coming to England after the

Herimann which may refer to either the bishop of Bamberg (1065–75) or the archbishop of Cologne (1036–56). Michael Lapidge has recently argued for a Cologne origin as the bishop of Bamberg was unpopular with his chapter, making him an unlikely owner of a pontifical, and because the litany includes SS Gorgonius and Walburg who are often associated, albeit not exclusively, with Cologne.[10] But Andrieu, whilst aware of the Cologne possibility, opted for Bamberg because it had a tradition, dating from its foundation in 1007, of using the Romano-German pontifical.[11] The Cotton manuscript has been attributed to Cologne on different grounds. Written in a German script from the first half of the eleventh century, it was badly damaged in the 1731 fire. Lapidge has argued that it was probably the exemplar of an English copy of the Romano-German pontifical, Cambridge, Corpus Christi College, MS 163, which contains an *ordo* for the dedication of a church which invokes three bishops of Cologne amongst the list of confessors: Eberigisil, Cunibert and Heribert. Using the Corpus Christi manuscript to fill in the *lacunae* of the Cotton manuscript, he suggested a Cologne provenance for the Cotton manuscript.[12] It is surprising that more copies have not survived from this province, especially when pontificals belonging to other traditions have been preserved there.[13] This pattern, when compared to the twenty-one Romano-German pontifical manuscripts surviving from Mainz and Salzburg, suggests that the Romano-German pontifical was probably not widely adopted in these two provinces.

Italy

Of copies of the Romano-German pontifical made in Italy, seven now survive. There are no surviving German exemplars with an Italian provenance, but at least three such codices must have existed for the Italian manuscripts belong to three different recensions.[14]

It is less clear when the Romano-German pontifical arrived in Italy. Andrieu and Vogel suggested that it was known in Rome in the second half of the tenth century. They postulated that it was introduced by Otto I and his entourage in 960, soon after its composition, arguing that the description in the *Liber pontificalis* of the process used to ordain Pope Leo VIII and

---

medieval period: J. Brückmann, 'Latin manuscript pontificals and benedictionals in England and Wales', *Traditio* xxix (1973), 391–458 at pp. 421–3.
[10] Lapidge, 'Ealdred', 464 n. 57.
[11] OR i. 144.
[12] Lapidge, 'Ealdred', 463: 'In other words, CCCC 163 is either a copy of Vitellius E. xii or both manuscripts are copies of a common exemplar.'
[13] For example, Cologne, Dom- und Diözesanbibliothek, Cod. 141. For a description see P. Jaffé and W. Wattenbach, *Ecclesiae metropolitanae coloniensis codices manuscripti*, Berlin 1874, 59–60; Gattermann, *Handschriftencensus Rheinland*, no. 1105, i. 654–5.
[14] PRG iii. 56.

Pope John XIII in 963 and 965 respectively, through several grades of holy orders, reflected the sequence of grades in the ordination liturgy of the Romano-German pontifical.[15] But Roger Reynolds has recently demonstrated that the description in the *Liber pontificalis* reflects more accurately the sequence in the *ordo* in the eighth- century Frankish ordination rite, which survives in two tenth-century south Italian pontificals.[16] He therefore suggests an alternative liturgy to the Romano-German rite for the papal ordinations in the 960s, and so undermines the evidence that the pontifical was known and used in Rome as early as 963. Other evidence put forward by Andrieu and Vogel for the Romano- German pontifical being known in late tenth-century Rome is equally tenuous. Both the Monte Cassino and Vallicelliana mid eleventh-century copies of the pontifical include an interpolation made in the reign of Otto III (996–1002), the 'Carmen in Assumptione sanctae Mariae' sung on the feast of the Assumption, for it ends 'Gaudeat omnis homo quia regnat tertius Otto Illius imperio', which, it is suggested, relates to Assumption Day 999 which Otto III spent in Rome.[17] But, as Vogel acknowledged, the interpolation could also have been made in Mainz and subsequently copied in Italy. Andrieu furthermore suggested that the monastery of Reichenau supplied the late tenth-century papacy with copies of the Romano-German pontifical, on the basis of the famous privilege of Pope Gregory V (996–9) in which he granted the abbey of Reichenau several privileges, on condition that they provide the Holy See with books and white horses: 'statuens ut monasterium debeat pensionis nomine in sui consecratione codicem sacramentorum I, epistolarium I, evangeliorum I, equos albos II'.[18] Andrieu suggested that liturgical manuscripts sent by Reichenau must have conformed to the Romano-Germanic rite as it was practised throughout Germany.[19] But none of the surviving Romano-German pontifical manuscripts listed in table 2 was produced in a Reichenau scriptorium, although several eleventh-century sacramentaries have been attributed to Reichenau.[20] Thus the evidence adduced by previous scholars that the Romano-German pontifical was known in tenth- and early eleventh-century Rome is somewhat inconclusive. It is further undermined by the comment made by Bern, abbot of Reichenau (d. 1048), in his *libellus*

---

[15] OR i. 511–13; PRG iii. 46–51; Vogel, 'Le Pontifical romano-germanique du Xe siècle', 44–5, and *Medieval liturgy*, 237–9.
[16] Reynolds, 'Ritual of clerical ordination', 437–45.
[17] PRG xcix.457, ii. 138–40; OR i. 516–18; Vogel, *Medieval liturgy*, 243 n. 241.
[18] A. Brackmann, *Germania pontificia sive repertorium privilegiorum et litterarum a Romanis pontificibus ante annum MCLXXXXVIII Germaniae ecclesiis monasteriis civitatibus singulisque personis concessorum*, Berlin 1923, ii/1, 152, no. xii.
[19] 'Il va de soi que les exemplaires envoyés à Rome par les moines de Reichenau étaient conformes au rite romano-germanique, tel qu'on le pratiquait dans les pays alémaniques et rhénans': OR i. 515–16.
[20] Hoffmann, *Buchkunst*.

on the mass suggesting that the Roman liturgy had not been adapted to German norms by the time of Henry II's imperial coronation (1014) as the Roman clergy omitted the *filioque* clause.[21]

The evidence suggests that texts belonging to three different recensions arrived and circulated independently in the north, centre and south of eleventh-century Italy. Probably the earliest Italian manuscript is the Alessandrina codex which belongs to the latest recension (C), written for Salzburg.[22] It was copied in the early eleventh century, possibly in Rome.[23] Unfortunately, nothing is known of its medieval provenance but it demonstrates that this exemplar was present in Italy in the first half of the eleventh century.

The earliest certain evidence that the Romano-German pontifical was known in Italy is Tuscan not Roman; the earliest surviving copy of the Romano-German pontifical being Lucca, Biblioteca capitolare, Cod. 607. Probably copied in Lucca from a Mainz model at the earliest in the late tenth century, or more probably the early eleventh century,[24] it was almost certainly the model for the copy made in the neighbouring diocese of Pistoia in the course of the eleventh century.[25] Both manuscripts belong to the B recension.

The two south Italian Romano-German pontifical codices belong to the earlier A recension but were copied after the Lucca codex. Both are written in a Beneventan hand; that of the Monte Cassino codex (Cod. 451) dates, on palaeographical grounds, to the second quarter of the mid eleventh century.[26] The Vallicellian codex (Cod. D. 5) may be a copy of that from Monte Cassino;[27] written later, it is in a hand which is very similar, if not identical, to that used at Monte Cassino.[28] The manuscript tradition of the Romano-German pontifical therefore appears limited in southern Italy to two codices which both originated at Monte Cassino.

Only two examples survive from northern Italy: Milan, Biblioteca Ambrosiana, Cod. Z. 52. sup, and Milan, Biblioteca capitolare, Cod. 53. Both follow a Mainz exemplar, but unfortunately nothing is known of their provenance, nor is it known whether the texts are related.[29]

---

[21] Bern of Reichenau, *Libellus de quibusdam rebus ad missae officium pertinentibus*, PL cxlii. 1055–80 at cols 1060–1.
[22] Rome, Biblioteca Alessandrina, Cod. 173; OR i. 282–7.
[23] Ibid. i. 282.
[24] Andrieu dated the Lucca codex to the late tenth century: ibid. i. 157. Reynolds has argued for the later date on palaeographical grounds: 'Ritual of clerical ordination', 439.
[25] Pistoia, Biblioteca capitolare, Cod. 141.
[26] E. A. Loew, *The Beneventan script: a history of south Italian minuscule*, 2nd edn, rev. V. Brown, Rome 1980, ii. 203; OR i. 177–204.
[27] Loew, *Beneventan script*, ii. 128.
[28] On the characteristics of this hand and traits found in Vallicelliana, Cod. D. 5 see ibid. i. 214–15.
[29] OR i. 170–1, 175–6.

APPENDIX 1

France

At least five Romano-German pontifical manuscripts are known to have been written or used in France in the eleventh century.[30] The first three are related. The Vendôme codex is a German manuscript written in the second third of the eleventh century for use in the province of Salzburg, with a provenance from the abbey of the Trinity, Vendôme.[31] It must have been in France by the mid eleventh century, for it appears to have been the model for both the Paris and Vitry codices.[32] The Paris manuscript was written in mid eleventh-century France for the church of Angers, in the west of France.[33] By the end of the eleventh century, however, it had been adapted for use in the diocese of Sées.[34] The Vitry manuscript was made for use in the eastern diocese of Châlons-sur-Marne, a suffragan of Rheims, at the end of the eleventh century. The pontifical's known provenance is the abbey of Trois-Fontaines in the diocese of Châlons, but Leroquais argued that the text suggests that it had originally been copied for a house of canons regular in the diocese of Châlons.[35] Without more detailed work on all three codices, it is impossible to establish their exact relationship to one another. But their close relationship suggests a pattern akin to that we shall see was the English experience, where the copying of the Romano-German pontifical can be attributed to one man and his circle. Without further evidence, however, the role of Vendôme in the promotion of the Romano-German pontifical within France must remain a hypothesis.

The London codex was written, as suggested above, for either Cologne or possibly Bamberg sometime in the second half of the eleventh century; the script and text do not suggest a closer dating.[36] By the twelfth century the manuscript was in Picardy, possibly at the abbey of St Riquier, and was subsequently used and owned by the cathedral of Amiens.[37] It is uncertain quite when it reached northern France.

The Wolfenbüttel codex is in two parts.[38] The first part is a copy of the

---

[30] Vendôme, Bibliothèque municipale, MS 14; BN, MS lat. 820; Vitry-le-François, Bibliothèque municipale, MS 36; BL, MS Add. 17004; Wolfenbüttel, Herzog-August-Bibliothek, Cod. Guelf 15 Weissenburg.
[31] Leroquais, *Pontificaux*, ii. 404–13. For the script's date and its attribution to a Lorsch scribe see Hoffmann, *Buchkunst*, 220.
[32] Leroquais, *Pontificaux*, i. 427, argued that the Paris and Vitry manuscripts were probably copied from and certainly corrected after the Vendôme manuscript.
[33] Ibid. i. 292–304.
[34] It includes, in another hand, supplements at both the beginning and the end for use in Sées: ibid. See also OR i. 352–5. J. Vezin has discussed the problems of this manuscript more recently, but despite his hesitancy, he appears to support the conclusions of Andrieu and Leroquais: *Les Scriptoria d'Angers au XIe siècle*, Paris 1974, 100–2.
[35] Leroquais, *Pontificaux*, ii. 421–8.
[36] Lapidge, 'Ealdred', 463–4.
[37] Brückmann, 'Latin manuscript pontificals', 421.
[38] Wolfenbüttel, Herzog-August-Bibliothek, Cod. Guelf. 15 Weissenburg.

Romano-German pontifical which was written for the church of Besançon in the eleventh century;[39] the second part appears to be a partial copy of the Romano-German pontifical made in Germany, possibly in Weissenburg, in the eleventh century.[40] The two copies were bound together by the thirteenth century as the whole codex was then owned by the monastery of SS Peter and Paul at Weissenburg. The Besançon codex is not an exact copy of the Vendôme model, though its French half includes a text found only in the Vitry and Paris codices,[41] but without further research it is impossible to conclude that there is a close relationship between the Wolfenbüttel codex and the Vendôme group.

There were, therefore, at least five Romano-German pontifical manuscripts in use in France in the eleventh and twelfth centuries; other examples may not have survived. But Leroquais identified seventeen pontificals from the tenth and eleventh centuries which still survive in French libraries; and he identified a further fourteen for the twelfth century.[42] The Romano-German pontifical again appears as merely one of the players in the liturgical market of the tenth and eleventh centuries, accounting for at most around 30 per cent of it, and possibly under 24 per cent if we we assume that the London codex did not reach France until the twelfth century. Nor was the Romano-German pontifical the only pontifical imported into France: Leroquais's total includes three examples from England,[43] and at least two from Germany.[44] When assessing the impact of the Romano-German pontifical we should also take into account the fact that of these five, only three copies were made in France, two (possibly three) from the same exemplar. It was not, therefore, widely copied; neither the London nor the Wolfenbüttel codices appear to have spawned any further copies.

All five manuscripts are eleventh-century. For the four for which we have a precise dating, the earliest, the Vendôme codex, a German manuscript, is dated to the second third of the eleventh century, whilst the Paris, Vitry and London codices are dated to the second half of the eleventh century. It is therefore highly possible that the Romano-German pontifical did not reach

---

[39] H. Butzmann (ed.), *Kataloge der Herzog-August-Bibliothek Wolfenbüttel: die Weissenburger Handschriften*, Frankfurt 1964, 117–25; OR i. 441–52.
[40] Ibid.
[41] Ibid. i. 356, 445: 'Dum qui iuvenis cupit se in primis accingi gladio.' For a discussion of these rituals see J. Flori, 'A Propos de l'adoubement des chevaliers au XIe siècle: le prétendu *pontifical de Reims* et l'*ordo ad armandum* de Cambrai', *Frühmittelalterliche Studien* xix (1985), 330–49, and 'Du Nouveau sur l'adoubement des chevaliers (XIe–XIIIe siècles)', *Le Moyen Âge* ii (1985), 201–26.
[42] Leroquais, *Pontificaux*, i, p. xxv.
[43] BN, MS lat. 943 (the Sherborne pontifical); Rouen, Bibliothèque municipale, MS 368 (the pontifical from Saint-Germans in Cornwall); Rouen, Bibliothèque municipale, MS 369 (the pontifical of Winchester).
[44] Troyes, Bibliothèque municipale, MS 2141 (a pontifical from Worms), s. x^{ex}; and Metz, Bibliothèque municipale, MS 334, which has been attributed to both Metz and Constance.

France until, at the earliest, some eighty years after it first emerged from the scriptorium of St Alban in Mainz. And when it did so, it was merely one liturgical text amongst several others competing for clerical attention.

England

Five Romano-German pontifical manuscripts are known to have been written or used in England. As in the Italian and French experience, three and possibly four of these manuscripts are related: Lapidge has shown that the German manuscript, BL, Cotton Vitellius E. xii (c. 1000–50) was exported to England where it probably became the model for three English copies.[45] Various liturgical texts were added by an English scribe in the second half of the eleventh century; these can be associated with Ealdred, bishop of Worcester (1046–60) and archbishop of York (1060–9). Lapidge therefore suggested that Ealdred acquired the German part of this manuscript in Cologne as the head of an embassy to the imperial court in 1054. He argued that the Vitellius manuscript was the model for Cambridge, Corpus Christi College, MS 163 which was written by two Anglo-Saxon scribes in the second half of the eleventh century, whilst cautioning that damage to the Vitellius manuscript means that it is uncertain whether the two codices belong to the same recension of the Romano-German pontifical.[46] CCCC 163 seems not to have been much used.[47] The Vitellius model also seems to have been the model for the Romano-German elements of the complex combination of sacramentary, pontifical and benedictional known as the Leofric Missal; several additions, including part of the Romano-German pontifical, were made to this codex under Leofric, bishop of Devon and Cornwall (1046–72). Evidence of a link between the Vitellius and the Leofric Missal is found in the English supplement to the Vitellius manuscript which was written by a scribe identified as the copier of some of the liturgical materials in the Leofric Missal. Lapidge thus argued that this scribe was a member of Ealdred's household who joined Leofric's household on the archbishop's death and took Cotton Vitellius E. xii to Exeter with him where it served as a model for the excerpts of the Romano-German pontifical included in the Leofric Missal.[48] Ealdred, and the Vitellius codex, appear, therefore, to be behind three of the manuscripts of the Romano-German pontifical in England.

Two manuscripts appear to be independent of the Ealdred group. Cambridge, Corpus Christi College, MS 265, is a compilation of texts made

---

[45] Lapidge, 'Ealdred'.
[46] The script is dateable to the mid eleventh century at the earliest but is probably later: Dumville, *Liturgy*, 73; Lapidge, 'Origin of CCCC 163', 18–28.
[47] Dumville, *Liturgy*, 73.
[48] These are *PRG* xcix.300, 276–87, 304–10, 328–30, ii. 75–91; Lapidge, 'Ealdred', 465–6.

at Worcester in the third quarter of the eleventh century, which seems to be based upon a compilation made under Wulfstan I, bishop of Worcester (1002–16x23). Amongst these texts is a copy of the Romano-German pontifical. It is possible that CCCC 265 is also based on Ealdred's exemplar, but Vogel and Elze suggested that it belonged to a Mainz family, and is therefore independent of Cotton Vitellius E. xii. It may therefore be based on a German model copied in England as early as c. 1010, but without further work its origins remain uncertain. BL, Cotton Tiberius C. i includes a Romano-German pontifical written in mid eleventh-century Germany to which Old English confession forms were added, demonstrating that it was used. This codex is associated with the bishopric and monastery of Sherborne.[49] These manuscripts suggest that Ealdred did not have a monopoly on the entry of the Romano-German pontifical into England.

The Romano-German pontifical thus did not dominate liturgical production in England: David Dumville has identified twenty-one pontificals written in Anglo-Saxon England in the tenth and eleventh centuries, two of which are copies of the Romano-German pontifical.[50] As in France, one copy seems to be the model for most of the copies made in England and, as in France, there is no evidence that the Romano-German pontifical was known in England until possibly the early and more probably the mid eleventh century.

Conclusions

The Romano-German pontifical was popular in the eleventh-century German archdioceses of Mainz and Salzburg, but its impact outside this area was limited in scope, and delayed in time until the mid eleventh century. It was merely one of several collections circulating in eleventh-century Europe, and despite its impact on late medieval Roman liturgy, should not be assigned a retrospective significance.

---

[49] Dumville, *Liturgy*, 134; N. R. Ker, 'Three Old English texts in a Salisbury pontifical, Cotton Tiberius C. i', in P. Clemoes (ed.), *The Anglo-Saxons: studies in some aspects of their history and culture presented to Bruce Dickins*, London 1959, 262–79.
[50] Dumville, *Liturgy*, 67–8.

Table 2
Existing manuscripts of the Romano-German pontifical

	Date	Scriptorium	Provenance	PRG Family	Comments
Manuscripts written in Germany					
Eleventh century					
1 Bamberg, Staatsbibliothek, Cod. Lit. 50	s. xi	?	monastery of Michelsberg, Bamberg	Mainz	Mutilated with *lacunae*.
2 Bamberg, Staatsbibliothek, Cod. Lit. 53	1007–24	monastery of Seeon	Bamberg cathedral	Mainz	Includes a miniature of Henry II supported by two bishops. Written for Bamberg cathedral.
3 Bamberg, Staatsbibliothek, Cod. Lit. 54	1067	?	Hildesheim	Mainz	Based on a model made under Otto III.
4 Bamberg, Staatsbibliothek, Cod. Lit. 59	1039–49	Benedictine monastery	Verden cathedral	Mainz	Written for Verden cathedral library?
5 Eichstätt, Diözesanarchiv, MS B. 4	1071–3	Tegernsee school	Eichstätt cathedral	Mainz	Written for Bishop Gundekar II of Eichstätt (1057–75).
6 London, BL, MS Add. 17004	s. xi	Germany Cologne? Bamberg?	Amiens cathedral from s. xiii^{in}	?	There is some dispute as to where it was written.
7 London, BL, MS Cotton Tiberius C. i	s. xi^2	Germany	monastery of Sherbourne	?	Part copy of the *PRG* included with other English texts.
8 London, BL, MS Cotton Vitellius E. xii, fos 116–60	s. xi^1	Cologne?	archdiocese of York	?	Badly damaged in the Cotton fire.
9 Munich, Bayerische Staatsbibliothek, Clm 14690	s. xi	?	Saint Emmeran, Regensburg	Salzburg	Fragments only.

No.	Shelfmark	Date	Origin	Location	Region	Notes
10	Munich, Bayerische Staatsbibliothek, Clm 6425 and Clm 21587	c. 1023–39	Lorsch 'School'	Freising cathedral	Salzburg	Written under Egilbert, bishop of Freising and imperial chancellor in hand associated with other Freising manuscripts.
11	Paris, BN, MS lat. 1231	1069–89	?	Regensburg cathedral	Salzburg	Written for Otto of Riedenburg, bishop of Regensburg (1069–89)
12	Vendôme, Bibliothèque municipale, MS 14	s. xi[1]	Lorsch?	abbey of the Trinity, Vendôme	Salzburg	
13	Vienna, Österreichische Nationalbibliothek, Cod. Lat. 701	1025–50	Mainz	St Alban's abbey, Mainz	Mainz	For use in the abbey itself.
14	Vienna, Österreichische Nationalbibliothek, Cod. Lat. 1830	s. xi[2]	?	Salzburg	Salzburg	
15	Vienna, Österreichische Nationalbibliothek, Cod. Lat. 1832	1042–71	?	St Maria monastery, near Gurk, Carinthia.	Salzburg	Dated on grounds of charter on fo. 1[a].
16	Wolfenbüttel, Herzog-August-Bibliothek, Cod. Guelf 15 Weissenburg	s. xi	Besançon? & Weissenburg	Besançon cathedral	Mainz	Two part copies of PRG – one German, one French.

Twelfth century

No.	Shelfmark	Date	Origin	Location	Region	Notes
17	Bamberg, Staatsbibliothek, Cod. Lit. 51	s. xii	?	Bamberg cathedral	Mainz	German.
18	Bamberg, Staatsbibliothek, Cod. Lit. 52	s. xii	?	Bamberg cathedral	Mainz	German.
19	Bamberg, Staatsbibliothek, Cod. Lit. 55	c. 1124–39	?	monastery of St Michael's, Bamberg	Mainz	Made on the orders of Bishop Otto of Bamberg (1102–39).
20	Munich, Bayerische Staatsbibliothek, Clm 3909	1138–43	Augsburg	Augsburg cathedral	Mainz	Part I of pontifical.
21	Munich, Bayerische Staatsbibliothek, Clm 3917	s. xi[ex]–xii[in]	?	Augsburg cathedral	Mainz	Part II of pontifical.
22	Saint Gall, Stiftsbibliothek, Cod. 399	s. xii	Bavarian abbey	St Gall	Mainz	
23	Vienna, Österreichische Nationalbibliothek, Cod. lat. 1817	s. xii[2]	?	Passau	Salzburg	Based on a model of c. 1002/3.

	Date	Scriptorium	Provenance	PRG Family	Comments
24 Wolfenbüttel, Herzog-August-Bibliothek, Cod. Guelf 141 Helmstadt	s. xii^{in}	?	St Michael's monastery, Luneburg, Verden by s. xiii^m	Mainz	Maundy Thursday reconcilation *ordo* adapted for monastic use.
25 Wolfenbüttel, Herzog-August-Bibliothek, Cod. Guelf 493 Helmstadt	s. xii^{in}		St Gombert d'Anspach, Franconia by s. xiv	Mainz	

Fourteenth century

	Date	Scriptorium	Provenance	PRG Family	Comments
26 Bamberg, Staatsbibliothek, Cod. Lit. 56	s. xiv		Bamberg cathedral	?	

Manuscripts written in Italy

Eleventh century

	Date	Scriptorium	Provenance	PRG Family	Comments
27 Lucca, Biblioteca capitolare, Cod. 607	s. x^{ex}–s. xi^{in}	Lucca	Lucca cathedral	Mainz	The earliest copy of the PRG.
28 Milan, Biblioteca Ambrosiana, Cod. Z. 52. sup.	s. xi	N. Italy	?	Mainz	
29 Milan, Biblioteca capitolare, Cod. 53	s. xi	N. Italy	?	Mainz	
30 Monte Cassino, Abbey Library, Cod. 451	c. 1050	Benevento	Monte Cassino	Mainz	Copied, possibly for the monastery, from a Rhineland manuscript which was interpolated in Rome c. 996–1002
31 Pistoia, Biblioteca capitolare, Cod. 141	s. xi	?	Pistoia cathedral	Mainz	
32 Rome, Biblioteca Alessandrina, Cod. 173	s. xi^{in}	Rome?	?	Salzburg	
33 Rome, Biblioteca Vallicelliana, Cod. D. 5	post 1050	Benevento	?	Mainz	Copied possibly from the same model as Monte Cassino 451.

Manuscripts written in France

Eleventh century

34 Paris, BN, MS lat. 820	s. xi^mid	Angers	Sées cathedral	Written before death of Henry I (1031–60); adapted for Sées use at end of s. xi.
35 Vitry-le-François, Bibliothèque municipale, MS 36	s. xi^ex	Châlons?	abbey of Trois-Fontaines, diocese of Châlons	Probably written for an abbey of canons regular in diocese of Châlons.
36 Wolfenbüttel, Herzog-August-Bibliothek, Cod. Guelf 15 Weissenburg	s. xi	Weissenburg	monastery of SS Peter & Paul, Weissenburg	Part-French, part-German (see no. 15).

Manuscripts written in England

Eleventh century

37 Cambridge, Corpus Christi College, MS 163	s. xi^mid	?	a nunnery	Manuscript suggests not much used.
38 Cambridge, Corpus Christi College, MS 265	s. xi²	Worcester	Worcester cathedral	?
39 Oxford, Bodleian Library, MS Bodley 579	s. xi²	Exeter	Exeter	Part of the Leofric Missal.

APPENDIX 2

Penitential Rites Outside the Romano-German Pontifical Tradition

Table 1
A comparison of the *ordines* for entry into penance in *ordo* xcix of the PRG and the Fulda sacramentaries

PRG *ordo* xcic		Fulda *ordo* **A**		*ordo* **B**	*ordo* **C**
44	Instructions to priest on receipt of penitents	1	In part only	–	–
45	Priest says preparation prayer: 'Domine deus esto mihi peccatori'	6i	In part only (347)	1	1
46	Priest instructs penitent on the vices		–	–	–
47 & 48	Priest should take into account the penitent's status in determining the appropriate penance		–	–	–
49	Priest should take into account the quality of both the sin and of the man and the degree of contrition expressed before assigning penance		–	–	–
50	Interrogation of belief: 'Credis in patrem'	2	Wording same	2	2 Wording different but contains a similar interrogation of belief
50a	Confession prayer by the penitent acknowledging sins: 'Confiteor tibi domine caeli et terrae'			5	5
51	Priest request God's mercy: 'Misereatur tui omnipotens Deus'		–	–	–
52	Priest to remind penitent of need to avoid vices and hidden sin		–	–	–
53	Penitent acknowleges his sinfulness: 'Multa quidem et innumerabilia sunt alia peccata mea'	4	Prayer acknowledging sinfulness: 'Multa quidem et innumerabilia sunt alia peccata mea' (no. 346)	–	–
54	Priests indicates to penitent his penance	4	Indicate to penitent his penance (rubric v. similar) (no. 346)	–	–

OUTSIDE THE ROMANO-GERMAN PONTIFICAL TRADITION

PRG *ordo* xcic		Fulda *ordo* A		*ordo* B	*ordo* C
55	Servants are not to fast as much as the rich	–		–	–
56	7 penitential psalms followed by *preces*	7	7 penitential psalms with prayers and *preces* (nos 353–9)	7	7
57	Prayers requesting remission of sins: 'Exaudi domine preces nostras'	6ii	'Exaudi domines preces nostras' (no. 347)	8i)	9i)
58	'Da quaesumus domine huic'	6iv	'Da quaesumus domine huic famulo' (no. 350)	–	–
59	'Preueniat hunc famulum tuum'	6v	'Preueniat hunc famulum tuum' (no. 351)	8ii)	9iii)
60	'Adesto domine supplicationibus nostris'	6vi	'Adesto domine supplicationibus nostris' (no. 352)	8iii)	9iv)
61	'Domine deus noster qui peccatis nostris offenderis'	6vii	'Domine deus noster qui peccatis nostris offenderis' (no. 353)	8iv)	9v)
62	'Exaudi quaesumus omnipotens Deus'	–	–	–	–
63	'Adesto domine supplicationibus nostris'	6vi	'Adesto domine supplicationibus nostris'	8iii)	9iv)
64	'Precor domine clementiae tuae'	–	–	–	–
65	Take penitent to the church and say Psalm xxxvii, Psalm cii and Psalm l and Psalm liii, then *Kyrie*, *Pater Noster* and *preces*	–	–	–	–
66	'Deus cuius indulgentia cuncti indigent'	–	–	–	–
67	Missa post confessionem		√ (Text different)		–	–

Table 2

The possible sources for the Ash Wednesday *ordo* and absolution *ordines* in the Beauvais Pontifical (B_1)

Beauvais Pontifical Ordo I	PRG/other	Possible sources — Gelasian (H. A. Wilson)	c. 8th Gelasian (St Gall 348)	Gregorian (Supplemented *Hadrianum*)
Ordo quomodo poenitentes in caput quadragesimae episcopo se debent repraesentare				
In capite quadragesimae omnes poenitentes qui publicam suscipiunt aut susceperunt poenitentiam ante fores ecclesiae se repraesentent episcopo civitatis. . . .	Regino, *Libri duo*, 136–7			
In sacra autem Domini Coena rursus ab eorum decanis et eorum presbyteris ecclesiae liminibus repraesententur.	Burchard, *Decretum* xix. 26			
Absolutio poenitentium in caput ieiunii				
1 7 penitential psalms.	PRG xcix, no. 65			
2 Kyrie Eleison.	PRG xcix, no. 65			
3 Lord's Prayer.	PRG xcix, no. 65			
4 Capitula: Salvos fac servos tuos domine Deus meus sperantes in te Mitte eis Domine auxilium de sancto Et de Sion	PRG xcix, no. 65 (not as complete)			

	Nihil proficiat inimicus in eis			
	Et filius iniquitatis			
	Esto illis Domine turris fortitudinis			
	A facie			
	Domine exaudi orationem meam			
	Et clamor meus			
	Dominus vobiscum			
	Et cum spiritu tuo			
5	Exaudi preces nostras	PRG xcix, nos 57, 231	√ (p. 14, no. 1)	√ (no. 246)	√ (nos 3951, 1379)
6	Omnipotens sempiterne Deus confitentibus	PRG xcix, nos 67, 233		√ (no. 493)	√ (nos 3966, 2719, 102*, 112*)
7	Omnipotens et misericors Deus qui peccatorum indulgentiam	PRG xcix, no. 237		√ (no. 491)	√ (nos 3967, 2722, 102*, 113*)
8	Praeveniat hos famulos tuos	PRG xcix, nos 59, 232	√ (p. 14, no. 2)	√ (no. 247)	√ (nos 3952, 1380)
9	Adesto Domine supplicationibus nostri nec sit	PRG xcix, no. 60	√ (p. 14, no. 3))	√ (no. 248)	√ (nos 3953, 1381)
	Absolutio poenitentiam in coena Domini				
1	Adesto domine supplicationibus nostris et me qui maxime misericordia primus indigeo	PRG xcix, no. 230		√ (no. 490)	√ (nos 3963, 1383)
2	Praeste (sic) Deus aurem supplicationibus				
3	Placatum redde Deus nostrorum				
4	Suscipe Domine nostrorum				
5	Absolve nos Deus et alieno et nostro delicto				

Table 3
The possible sources for the *ordines ad dandam paenitentiam* in Paris, BN, MS lat. 13313 (P)

Paris BN, MS lat. 13313 Ordo I	PRG	Gelasian	Possible sources c. 8th Gelasian (St Gall 348)	Gregorian (Supplemented *Hadrianum*)
Ordo ad dandam paenitentem				
1 Psalm xxxvii	Order of psalms same as PRG xcix, no. 65			
2 Deus cuius indulgentia nemo non indiget	Similar to PRG xcix, no. 66 PRG cxxxvi, no. 10			√ ((no. 3969)
3 Psalm cii	See above.			
4 Deus sub cuius oculis	PRG xcix, no. 234 PRG cxxxvi, no. 11	√ (p. 252)		√ ((no. 3959)
5 Psalm l				
6 Deus infinitae misericordiae	PRG xcix, no. 233	√ (p. 252)		√ ((no. 3958)
7 Psalm li				
8 Precor clementiae et misericordiae tuae maiestatem	PRG xcix, no. 64 PRG cxxxvi, no. 12	√ (p. 14, no. 5)	√ (no. 250)	√ ((no. 3960)
9 Response: In sudore uultis tui	PRG xcix, no. 73			
10 Versus: Pro eo quia obedisti	PRG xcix, no. 73			
Ordo II				
Item ordo ad dandam poenitentiam				
1 Exaudi domine peccatis nostris				

Ordo II continued

Orationes et preces super penitentem confitentem peccata sua more solito feria iiii infra linia.

1	Exaudi domine preces nostras et confitentium tibi parce peccatis	PRG xcix, no. 57 PRG cxxxvi, no. 29	√ (p. 14, no. 1)	√ (no. 246)	√ (no. 1379) (no. 3951)
2	*Imposition of ashes:* Hic mittendus est cinis super caput penitentis et dicendum: Memento homo quia pulvis es et ita pulverem reverteris. *Statimque ponendum cilicium et dicendum:* Converte cor tuum et humilia animam tuam in cinere et cilicio. Cor enim contritum et humiliatum deus non despicit.	PRG xcix, no. 71			
3	Preveniat hunc famulum tuum	PRG xcix, no. 59	√ (p. 14, no. 2)	√ (no. 247)	√ (no. 1380) (no. 3952)
4	*Ejection of the penitent from the Church* Post hanc eiciendus est ab aecclesia et tali modo increpandus. Ecce eiceris hodie a sinu matris tuae sancte aecclesiae propter peccatum tuum sicut Adam primus homo etectus est a paradiso propter transgressionem suam. Et in sudore.	PRG xcix, no. 73.			
5	Adesto supplicationibus nostris domine ne sit ab hoc famulo tuo	PRG xcix, no. 60 PRG cxxxvi, no. 32	√ (p. 14, no. 3)	√ (no. 247)	√ (no. 1381) (no. 3953)
6	Domine deus noster qui offensione nostra non vinceris	PRG cxxxvi, no. 33	√ (p. 14, no. 4)	√ (no. 249)	√ (no. 1382) (no. 3954)

Table 4

The possible sources for the Ash Wednesday *ordo* in Cologne, MS 141 (K) and a comparison with the Paris codex (P)

Cologne, MS 141 (K)	Paris, MS lat. 13313 (P)	Possible sources			PRG
		Gelasian	c. 8th Gelasian (St Gall 348)	Gregorian (Supplemented Hadrianum)	
Ordo in capite ieiunii quomodo paenitentes paeniteant.					
1 In primis prosternant se in oratorio et dicat cleru psalmum *Domine ne in furore II.* (xxxvii)	I.1				Order of psalms the the same as PRG xcix, no. 65
2 Et dicat episcopus *Deus cuius indulgentia nemo non indiget*	I.2			√ (no. 3969)	PRG xcix, no. 66 PRG xcccvi, no. 10
3 Et dicant circumstantes clerici psalmu *Benedic anima mea (usque renovabitur ut aquilae iuventus tua)* (ciii)	I.3				PRG xcix, no. 65 (see above)
4 *Deus sub cuius oculis omne cor trepidat*	I.4	√ (p. 252)		√ (no. 3959)	PRG xcix, no. 234 PRG cxxxvi, no. 11
5 *Psalmus. Miserere mei deus (usque omnes iniquitates meas dele)* (l)	I.5				see above
6 *Deus infinitae misericordiae veritatisque*	I.6	√ (p. 252)		√ (no. 3958)	PRG xcix, no. 233

7	Psalmus. Quid gloriaris usque videbunt iusti et timebunt. (li)	I.7		see above
8	Precor domine Ihesus clementiae et misericordiae tuae.	I.8	√ (p. 14, no. 5)	√ (no. 250)	*PRG* xcix, no. 64
9	Exaudi domini preces nostras et confitentium tibi	II.1	√ (p. 14, no. 1)	√ (no. 246)	*PRG* cxxxvi, no. 12 *PRG* xcix, no. 57
10	Imposition of ashes Hic mittendus est pulvis super capita eorum cum acqua benedicata et dicat memento . . . Statimque imponendum cilicium.	II.2			*PRG* cxxxvi, no. 29 *PRG* xcix, no. 71
11	Praeveniat hos famulos tuos et famulas tuas quaesumus domine	II.3	√ (p. 14, no. 2)	√ (no. 247)	*PRG* xcix, no. 59
12	Ejection of penitents from the church Post haec eicendi sunt ab ecclesia	II.4			*PRG* xcix, no. 73
13	Adesto supplicationibus nostris domine ne sit ab his famulis tuis	II.5	√ (p. 14, no. 3)	√ (no. 247)	*PRG* xcix, no. 60 *PRG* cxxxvi, no. 32
14	Domine deus noster qui offensione nostra non vinceris sed satisfactione placaris	II.6	√ (p. 14, no. 4)	√ (no. 249)	*PRG* xcix, no. 33
15	Tunc moneat domnus praesul eos ne in(de)precatione eadant	—			
16	Omnipotens sempiterne deus parce metuentibus ignosce peccantibus	—			*PRG* xcix, no. 74
17	Deus qui humiliatione flecteris et satisfactione placaris	—			*PRG* xcix, no. 76
18	Omnipotens deus qui niniuitis	—			*PRG* xcix, no. 77

Cologne, MS 141 (K)	Paris, MS lat. 13313 (P)	Possible sources		PRG
		c. 8th Gelasian (St Gall 348)	Gregorian (Supplemented *Hadrianum*)	
19 Tunc de super mittat aquam benedictam et choris incipit antiphon *Exaudi nos* Ps. *Salvum ne fac cum Gloria*	–	Gelasian		*PRG* xcix, no. 78
20 Antiphon. *Immutemur* Interim dum canuntur antiphon ponendi sunt cineres super capita cleri et populi cum acqua benedicta et preces	–			*PRG* xcix, no. 78
21 *Concede nobis*				*PRG* xcix, no. 79

Table 5

A comparison between the contents of the members of the 'north-central family' of *ordines* for Maundy Thursday and their possible sources

Cracow pontifical (C)	Beavais (B$_1$)	BN, MS lat. 13313 (P)	Bamberg Cod. 59 (B$_2$)	Köln, Cod. 141 (K)	Gelasian	Gregorian (Supplemented *Hadriánum*)	PRG	c. 8th Gelasian (St Gall 348)
389	1	1	1	1	—	—	√	—
390	2	2	2	—	—	—	√	—
391	3	3	3	—	—	—	√	—
392	4	4	4	2	√ (p. 63)	√ (no. 110*)	√	√
393	5	5	5	5	—	—	—	—
394	6	6	6	6, 3	√ (p. 64)	— (no. 110*)	√	—
395	7	7	7	7	√ (p. 64)	√ (nos 1383, 100*)	√	√
396	8	8	8	8	√ (p. 65)	√ (no. 1385)	√	√
397	9	9	10	4, 10(?)	√ (p. 64)	—	√	—
398	10	10	11	11	√ (p. 64)	—	√	—
399	11	11	12	12	—	—	√	—
400	12	12	13	13	—	—	√	—
401	13	13	14	14	—	—	√	—
402	14	14	15	15	—	—	√	—
403	15	15	16	16	√ (p. 102)	√ (nos 102*, 112*)	√	√
404	—	—	18	—	√ (p. 66)	—	√	—
405	—	—	24	—	—	—	—	—
407	—	—	27	—	—	—	√	—
408	—	—	—	—	—	—	—	—

Cracow pontifical (C)	Beavais (B₁)	BN, MS lat. 13313 (P)	Bamberg Cod. 59 (B₂)	Köln, Cod. 141 (K)	Gelasian	Gregorian (Supplemented *Hadrianum*)	PRG	c. 8th Gelasian (St Gall)
409	—	—	—	—	—	—	—	—
—	16 (PRG 237)	16	—	17	√ (p. 65)	√ (nos 103*, 113*)	√	—
—	17 (PRG 238)	17	17	18	√ (pp. 65–6)	—	√	—
—	18	—	—	—	√ (p. 66)	—	—	—
—	—	—	9 (PRG 235)	—	√ (pp. 64–5)	√ (no. 1384)	√	—
—	—	—	18 (PRG 231)	—	√ (pp. 14, 325)	√ (no. 1379)	√	—
—	—	—	19 (PRG 232)	—	√ (pp. 14, 325)	√ (no. 1380)	√	—
—	—	—	20	—	√ (pp. 14, 325)	√ (no. 1381)	—	—
—	—	—	21	—	√ (pp. 14, 325)	√ (no. 1382)	—	—
—	—	—	22	—	√ (pp. 14, 325)	—	—	—
—	—	—	23	—	—	—	—	—
—	—	—	26	3 (PRG 226)	√ (p. 64)	—	√	—
—	—	—	—	4 (PRG 227)	√ (p. 64)	—	√	—
—	—	—	—	9 (PRG 247)	—	—	√	—
—	—	—	—	10 (PRG 227)	—	—	√	—
—	—	—	—	19 (PRG 251)	—	—	√	—

Table 6

A comparison between the contents of the Romano-German and the 'north-central family' of *ordines* for Maundy Thursday

PRG, *ordo xcix*		C	B₁	P	B₂	K
224	*Tunc egreditur penitens*	389	–	1	1	1
225	*Adesto o venerabilis pontifex*	392	4	4	–	2
226	*Hic ergo dum ad poenitudinis . . .*	–		5		3
	Iniquitates meas ego	394	6	8	3	6
227	*Quo ita supplicante...*	–	–	6	–	4
	Redintegra in eo	397	9	11	7	4, 10
228	*Tunc dicit pontifex antiphonam Venite.*	389	–	–	–	11
		390	3	2	–	
	Et diaconus ex parte penitentiam. Flectamus genua . . .	391	2	3	–	11
		399	11	12	8	
229	*Quandiu vero psalmus. Venite filii*	391	–	–	–	11
	Semper manuatim	400	12	12	9	
	Cor mundum crea	401	12	12	10	
		402	12	12	11	
230	*Adesto domine supplicationibus nostris*	395	7	9	4	7
231	*Exaudi domine preces*	–	–	–	15	
232	*Praeveniat hos famulos tuos*	–	–	–	16	
233	*Deus infinitae misericordiae*	–	–	–	–	
234	*Deus, sub cuis oculis*	–	–	–	–	

PRG, ordo xcix		C	B₁	P	B₂	K
235	Praesta quaesumus domine	–	–	–	6	
236	Omnipotens sempiterne Deus confitentibus tibi	403	13	13	12	12
237	Omnipotens et misericors Deus qui peccatorum	–	14	–	–	13
238	Domine sancte pater omnipotens aeterne Deus respice	–	15	14	13	14
239	Deus misericors deus clemens	404	–	–	14	
240	Maiestatem tuam	406	–	–	22	
241	Famulos tuos quaesumus	407	–	–	24	
242	Deus qui confitentium tibi corda purificas	–	–	–	–	
243	Deus qui mundum in peccati fovea iacentem	–	–	–	–	
244	Domine sancte pater omnipotens rex regum	–	–	–	–	
245	Deus humani generis benignissime conditor	396	8	10	5	8
246	*Absolutio pluralis.* Dominus Iesus Christus qui dignatus	–	–	–	–	
247	Praesta quaesumus domine his famulis	–	–	–	–	9

248	*Absolutio singularis.* Sicut principali sententia constat	—	—	—	—	—	—	—
249	Frater N. dominus noster Iesus Christus	—	—	—	—	—	—	—
250	Frater N. absolutionem et	—	—	—	—	—	—	—
251	*Hic aspergat eos aqua*	398	10	—	—	—	15	
		393	5	—	—	—	5	
		405	—	—	—	2	—	
		408	—	—	—	21	—	
		409	—	—	—	—	—	
		—	—	—	7	—	—	
		—	—	—	—	17	—	
		—	—	—	—	18	—	
		—	—	—	—	19	—	
		—	—	—	—	20	—	
		—	—	16	—	23	—	
		—	—	—	—	—	—	

Bibliography

Unpublished primary sources

ENGLAND

Cambridge, Corpus Christi College
MSS 163, 265

London, British Library
MS Add. 17004
MS Cotton Tiberius C. i
MS Cotton Vitellius E. xii
MS Egerton 3763

Oxford, Bodleian Library
MS Bodley 579

FRANCE

Paris, Bibliothèque nationale
Fonds latin
MSS lat. 820, 1231, 3878, 10575, 13313, 17333, 17334, 18005, 18220

GERMANY

Bamberg, Staatsbibliothek
MS Can. 6
Cods Lit. 1, 2, 3, 50, 53, 54, 59

Berlin, Staatsbibliothek
MS Hamilton 290
MS theol. lat. fo. 2

Cologne, Diözesan- und Dombibliothek
Cods 88, 118, 123, 141

Munich, Bayerische Staatsbibliothek
Clm 3851, 3853, 3909, 3917, 4456, 6421, 6425, 6426, 12673, 21587

Wolfenbüttel, Herzog-August-Bibliothek
Cod. Guelf. 15 Weissenburg
Cod. Guelf. 141 Helmstadt
Cod. Guelf. 493 Helmstadt
Cod. Guelf. 555 Helmstadt
Cod. Guelf. 1151 Helmstadt

ITALY

Rome, Biblioteca Vallicelliana
Cods B. 8, B. 58, C. 6, C. 32, C. 36, E. 15, E. 62, F. 29

Vatican, Biblioteca Apostolica Vaticana
MSS Archivio S. Pietro F. 12, H. 58
MSS Barb. lat. 631, 1450
MSS Palat. lat. 485, 494
MSS Regin. lat. 191, 207
MS Ross. lat. 204
MSS Vat. lat. 1339, 1355, 3548, 3806, 4772, 4880, 4928, 5768, 7790

Primary printed sources

Abbo of Fleury, *Collectio canonum*, PL cxxxix. 473–508
―――― *Passio sancti Edmundi*, in *Three lives of English saints*, ed. M. Winterbottom, Toronto 1972
Adalbert of St Maximin of Trier, *Continuatio Reginonis*, ed. F. Kurze, in *Reginonis abbatis Prumiensis chronicon cum continuatio Treverensi* (MGH, SRG l, 1890, repr. 1978)
Adémar of Chabannes, *Chronique*, ed. J. Chavanon, Paris 1897
Admonitio synodalis, ed. R. Amiet, in 'Une "Admonitio synodalis" de l'époque carolingienne: étude critique et édition', *Mediaeval Studies* xxvi (1964), 12–82
Agobardi cartula de poenitentia ab imperatore acta, in MGH, *Capitularia* II, no. cxcviii, 56–7
Ambrose, *Sancti Ambrosi opera pars X: epistulae et acta*, II/i: *Epistularum libri VII–VIII*, ed. M. Zelzer (CCEL lxxxii, 1990)
Annales altahenses maiores, ed. E. L. B. ab Oefele (MGH, SRG iv, 1891)
Annales fuldenses, ed. F. Kurze (MGH, SRG vii, 1891)
Annales hildesheimenses, ed. G. Waitz (MGH, SRG viii, 1878, repr. 1947)
Annales lobienses, ed. G. Waitz (MGH, SS xiii), 224–35
Annales de Saint-Bertin, ed. F. Grat, J. Vielliard and S. Clémencet, intro. L. Levillain, Paris 1964
Annales sangallenses maiores (St Gallerstiftsbibliothek cod. 915 u. 453), ed. C. Henking, in *Die annalistischen Aufzeichnungen des Klosters St. Gallen*, St Gallen 1884
Anselm of Lucca, *Collectio canonum una cum collectione minore*, ed. F. Thaner, Innsbruck 1906, 1915
Astronomer, *Vita Hludowici imperatoris*, ed. E. Tremp (MGH, SRG lxiv, 1995)
Augustine, *De bono coniugali*, ed. J. Zycha (CSEL xli, 1900), 187–231
―――― *De civitate dei: Saint Augustine, The city of God against the pagans*, ed. and trans. W. M. Green, London–Cambridge, Mass. 1963
Basil the Great, *The shorter rules*, PG xxxi. 1051–306
Benedict of Aniane, *Excerptus diversarum modus paenitentiarum*, PL ciii. 1417–20
―――― 'Modus penitentiarum Benedicti abbatis Anianensis (ante 821)', ed. J. Semmler, in K. Hallinger (ed.), *Initia consuetudines Benedictinae: consuetudines saeculi octavi et noni* (CCM i, 1963), 565–82

Bern of Reichenau, *Die Briefe des Abtes Bern von Reichenau*, ed. F. J. Schmale, Stuttgart 1961
—— *Libellus de quibusdam rebus ad missae officium pertinentibus*, PL cxlii. 1055–80
—— 'Sermo de poenitentia', ed. C. Erdmann, in *Forschungen zur politischen Ideenwelt des Frühmittelalters*, Berlin 1951, 116–17
Bernold of Constance, *Chronicon*, ed. G. Pertz (MGH, SS v), 400–67
βιοσ και πολιτεια του 'οσιου πατρος 'ημων Νειλου του Νεου, ed. G. Giovanelli, Grottaferrata 1972
Bonizo, *Liber de vita Christiana*, ed. E. Perels, Berlin 1930
Brackmann, A., *Germania pontificia sive repertorium privilegiorum et litterarum a Romanis pontificibus ante annum MCLXXXXVIII Germaniae ecclesiis monasteriis civitatibus singulisque personis concessorum*, Berlin 1923
Bruno of Querfurt, *Vita quinque fratrum* (MGH, SS xv/2), 709–38
—— *Vita S. Adalberti episcopi*, ed. G. H. Pertz (MGH, SS iv), 596–612
Burchard of Worms, *Decretum*, PL cxl. 537–1058
—— *Lex familiae ecclesiae wormatiensis*, ed. L. Weiland, in MGH, *Constitutiones* I, 639–44
Bussbücher und die Bussdisciplin der Kirche, ed. H. J. Schmitz, Mainz 1883
Bussbücher und das kanonische Bussverfahren, ed. H. J. Schmitz, Düsseldorf 1898
Bussordnungen der abendländischen Kirche, ed. F. W. H. Wasserschleben, Halle 1851
Canones Theodori Cantuariensis und ihre Überlieferungsformen, ed. P. Finsterwalder, Weimar 1929
Chrodegang of Metz, *Regula canonicorum*, PL lxxxix. 1057–95
—— *S. Chrodegangi Metensis episcopi (742–66): regula canonicorum aus dem Leidener Codex Vossianus Latinus 94 mit Umschrift der Tironischen Noten*, ed. W. Schmitz, Hanover 1889
—— *The Old English version of the enlarged rule of Chrodegang together with the Latin original: an Old English version of the capitula of Theodulf together with the Latin original: an interlinear Old English rendering of the epitome of Benedict of Aniane*, ed. A. S. Napier (Early English Text Society cl, 1916)
Chronicon affligemense, ed. G. Pertz (MGH, SS ix), 407–17
Collectio Anselmo dedicata, in J.-C. Besse, *Histoire des textes du droit de l'église au moyen âge de Denys à Gratien: collectio Anselmo dedicata: étude et texte: extraits*, Paris 1960
Collectio capitularium Ansegisi, ed. G. Schmitz (MGH, Capitularia regum Francorum n.s. i, Hanover 1996)
Consuetudines floriacenses antiquiores, ed. A. Davril and L. Donnat with M. Wegener, C. Elvert and K. Hallinger (CCM vii/3, 1984), 7–60
Cosiddetto pontificale di Poitiers (Paris, Bibliothèque de l'Arsenal, cod. 227), ed. A. Martini, Rome 1979
Councils and synods with other documents relating to the English Church, i/2: *1066–1204*, ed. D. Whitelock, M. Brett and C. N. L. Brooke, Oxford 1981
Councils of Urban II, ed. R. Somerville, Amsterdam 1972
Cracow pontifical (Pontificale Cracoviense saeculi xi): Cracow, Jagellionian Library, MS. 2057, ed. Z. Obertynski (HBS c, 1967–71)
De vera et falsa poenitentia, PL xl. 1113–30

Decrees of the ecumenical councils, I: *Nicea to Lateran V*, ed. N. P. Tanner, London–Washington, DC 1990

Decreta Lanfranci: the monastic constitutions of Lanfranc, ed. D. Knowles, London 1951

Dhuoda, *Manuel pour mon fils*, ed. P. Riché, trans. B. de Vregille and C. Mondésert (SC ccxxv, Paris 1975)

Edictus Rothari, ed. F. Blühme (MGH, Legum iv, Hanover 1868), 3–90

Ekkehardi IV, Casus Sancti Galli, ed. H. F. Haefele, Darmstadt 1980

English historical documents, I: *500–1042*, ed. and trans. D. Whitelock, 2nd edn, London 1979

Episcoporum de poenitentia, quam Hludovicus imperator professus est, relatio Compendiensis (833), in MGH, *Capitularia II*, no. cxcvii, 51–5

Epistolae Romanorum pontificum genuinae et quae ad eos scriptae sunt a S. Hilaro usque ad Pelagium II, ed. A. Thiel, Brunsberg 1858

Ex miraculi S. Mansueti auctore Adsone, ed. G. Waitz (MGH, SS iv), 509–14

Flodoard, *Les Annales de Flodoard*, ed. P. Lauer, Paris 1905

—— *Historia remensis ecclesiae*, ed. J. Heller and G. Waitz (MGH, SS xiii), 405–599

Folcuin, *Gesta abbatum S. Bertini Sithiensium*, ed. O. Holder-Egger (MGH, SS xiii), 607–35

Fränkishe Sacramentarium Gelasianum in alamannischer Ueberlieferung, ed. L. C. Mohlberg, Münster, Westfalia 1918

Fulbert of Chartres, *The letters and poems of Fulbert of Chartres*, ed. F. Behrends, Oxford 1976

Fundatio ecclesiae S. Maximi Barrensis, ed. O. Holder Egger (MGH, SS xv/2), 980–1

Gelasian sacramentary: liber sacramentorum romanae ecclesiae, ed. H. A. Wilson, Oxford 1894

Gerard of Cambrai, *Acti synodi Atrebatensis in Manichaeos*, PL cxlii. 1271–312

Gerbert of Rheims, *Die Briefsammlung Gerbert von Reims*, ed. F. Weigle (MGH, Die Briefe der deutschen Kaiserzeit ii, Berlin 1966)

Gerhard, *Vita sancti Oudalrici episcopi Augustani*, ed. G. Waitz (MGH, SS iv), 377–425

Gesta abbatum Gemblaciensium auctore Sigeberto, ed. G. Pertz (MGH, SS viii), 523–42

Gesta Trevorum, ed. G. Waitz (MGH, SS viii), 111–260

Gregory I, *Moralia in Iob*, ed. M. Adriaen (CCSL cxliii.B, 1985)

—— *Registrum epistolarum*, ed. P. Ewald and L. M. Hartmann (MGH, Epistolarum i, 2nd edn, Berlin 1957)

Gregory VII, *Das Register Gregors VII*, ed. E. Caspar (MGH, Epistolae selectae, 2nd edn, Berlin 1955)

Halitgar of Cambrai, *Collectio libri vi*, partially edited in Schmitz, *Die Bussbücher und das kanonische Bussverfahren*, 274–300; full text in PL cv. 649–710

Hariulf, *Chronique de l'abbaye de Saint-Riquier*, ed. F. Lot, Paris 1894

Heiming, O., 'Ein benediktinisch-ambrosianisches Gebetbuch des frühen 11. Jahrhunderts: Brit. Mus. Egerton 3763 (ehemals Dyson Perrins 48)', *Archiv für Liturgiewissenschaft* viii/2 (1964), 325–435

Helgaud of Fleury, *Vie de Robert le Pieux: epitoma vitae regis Rotberti Pii*, ed. with French trans. by R. H. Bautier and G. Labory, Paris 1965

Hermann of Reichenau, *Chronicon*, ed. G. H. Pertz (MGH, SS v), 67–133
Hildemar, *Expositio regulae ab Hildemaro tradita*, ed. R. Mittermüller, Regensburg 1880
Hincmar of Rheims, *De divortio Lotharii regis et Theutbergae reginae*, ed. L. Böhringer (MGH, Concilia iv, supplementum i, Hanover 1992)
—— *De regis persona et regio ministerio*, PL cxxv. 833–56
Historia custodum aretinorum (MGH, SS xxx/2), 1471–82
Hrabanus Maurus, *Paenitentiale ad Heribaldum episcopum Antissiodorensem*, PL cx. 467–94
—— *Poenitentium liber ad Otgarium*, PL cxii. 1397–424
Institutes of Justinian: text, translation and commentary, ed. J. A. C. Thomas, Leiden–Amsterdam–Oxford 1975
Irish penitentials, ed. L. Bieler with D. A. Binchy, Dublin 1975
Jerome, *Adversus Iovinianum*, ep. xxii, in *Sancti Eusebii Hieronymi epistolae*, ed. I. Hilberg (CSEL liv, 1910), 143–211
John Cassian, *De institutes coenobiorum et de octo principalium vitiorum remediis libri XII*, ed. J.-C. Guy, in *Jean Cassien: institutiones cénobitiques* (SC cix, 1965)
Lampert of Hersfeld, *Annales*, in *Lamperti monachi Hersfeldensis opera*, ed. O. Holder Egger (MGH, SRG xxxviii, 1894), 1–304
Liber miraculorum sanctae Fidis, ed. L. Robertini, Spoleto 1994
Liber precationum quas Carolus Calvus imperator Hludovici pii caesaris filius sibi adolescenti pro quotidiano usuante annos vigintiquinque supra septigentos in unum colligi et literis scribri aureis mandavit, ed. F. Ninguarda, Ingolstadt 1583
Liber tramitis aevi Odilonis abbatis, ed. P. Dinter (CCM x, 1980)
McNeill, J. T. and H. M. Gamer, *Medieval handbooks of penance: a translation of the principal 'libri poenitentiales'*, New York 1938
Mansi, J. D., *Sacrorum conciliorum nova et amplissima collectio*, Venice 1759–98, repr. Graz 1960
Martène, E., *De antiquis ecclesiae ritibus libri*, 2nd edn, Antwerp 1736–8
MGH, *Capitula episcoporum*, I, ed. P. Brommer, Hanover 1984
MGH, *Capitula episcoporum*, II, ed. R. Pokorny and M. Stratmann, Hanover 1995
MGH, *Capitula episcoporum*, III, ed. R. Pokorny, Hanover 1995
MGH, *Capitularia*, I: *Capitularia regum francorum*, I, ed. A. Boretius (MGH, Legum ii/1, Hanover 1883)
MGH, *Capitualaria*, II: *Capitularia regum francorum*, II, ed. A. Boretius and V. Krause (MGH, Legum ii/2, Hanover 1897)
MGH, *Concilia*, II: *Concilia aevi Karolini*, I, ed. A. Werminghoff (MGH, Legum iii, Hanover–Leipzig 1906)
MGH, *Concilia*, III: *Concilia aevi Karolini*, II: 843–59, ed. W. Hartmann (MGH, Hanover 1984)
MGH, *Concilia* VI: *Concilia aevi Saxonici*, I: 916–60, ed. E.-D. Hehl and H. Fuhrmann (MGH, Hanover 1987)
MGH, *Constitutiones et acta publica imperatorum et regum*, I: *911–1197*, ed. L. Weiland (MGH, Legum iv/1, Hanover 1893)
MGH, *Diplomatum regum et imperatorum Germaniae*, II/i: *Ottonis III. Diplomata*, ed. T. Sickel, Hanover 1893
MGH, *Diplomatum regum et imperatorum Germaniae*, III: *Heinrici II et Arduini Diplomata*, ed. H. Bresslau and H. Bloch with M. Meyer and R. Holtzmann, Hanover 1900–3

MGH, *Diplomatum regum et imperatorum Germaniae*, V: *Heinrici III. Diplomata*, ed. H. Bresslau and P. Kehr, Berlin 1931

MGH, *Ordines de celebrando concilio*, ed. H. Schneider, Hanover 1996

Nithard, *Historiarum libri IIII*, ed. E. Müller (MGH, SRG lxiv, 1907)

North Italian services of the eleventh century, ed. C. Lambot (HBS lxvii, 1931)

Odo of Cluny, *Vita sancti Geraldi Auriliacensis comitis*, PL cxxxiii. 639–704

Officium ecclesiasticum abbatum secundum usum Eveshamensis monasterii, ed. H. A. Wilson (HBS vi, 1893)

Orderic Vitalis, *Historia aecclesiastica*, ed. M. Chibnall, Oxford 1968–80

Ordines coronationis Franciae: texts and ordines for the coronation of Frankish and French kings and queens in the Middle Ages, ed. R. A. Jackson, Philadephia 1995

Ordines romani du haut moyen âge, ed. M. Andrieu, Louvain 1931–61

Paenitentialia Franciae, Italiae et Hispaniae saeculi VIII–XI, I: *Paenitentialia minora Franciae et Italiae saeculi VIII–IX*, ed. R. Kottje with L. Körntgen and U. Spengler-Reffgen (CCSL clvi, 1994)

Paenitentialia Franciae, Italiae et Hispaniae saeculi VIII–XI, II: *Paenitentialia Hispaniae*, ed. F. Bezler with L. Körntgen (CCSL clviA, 1998)

Pauli Warnefridi diaconi casinensis commentarium in regulam Benedicti, Monte Cassino 1880

Penitential of Pseudo-Egbert, ed. B. Thorpe, in *Ancient laws and institutions of England*, London 1840, ii. 170–239

Peter Damian, *Die Briefe des Petrus Damiani*, ed. K. Reindel (MGH, Die Briefe des deutschen Kaiserzeit iv, Munich 1983–93)

—— *Vita beati Romualdi*, ed. G. Tabacco (Fonti per la storia d'Italia xciv, 1957)

Poenitentiale Remense und der sogen: excarpsus Cummeani: Überlieferung, Quellen und Entwicklung zweier kontinentaler Bussbücher aus der 1. Hälfte des 8. Jahrhunderts, ed. F. Asbach, Regensburg 1975

Pontifical du moyen âge, ed. M. Andrieu (SeT lxxxvii, 1940)

Pontifical romano-germanique du Xe siècle, ed. C. Vogel and R. Elze (SeT ccvi, ccvii, cclxix, 1963, 1972)

Precum libelli quattuor aevi Karolini, ed. A. Wilmart, Rome 1940

Pseudo-Augustine, *Sermo cxvii*, PL xxxix. 1977

—— *Sermo III: ad monachos: de poenitentia*, PL lviii. 875–6

Rather of Verona, *Die Briefe des Bischofs Rather von Verona*, ed. F. Weigle (MGH, Die Briefe der deutschen Kaiserzeit i, Weimar 1949)

—— *Ratherii Veronensis opera minora*, ed. P. L. D. Reid (CCCM xlvi, 1976)

—— *The complete works of Rather of Verona*, trans. P. L. D. Reid, Binghamton, NY 1991

Redactio fuldensis-trevirensis, ed. M. Wegener, C. Elvert and K. Hallinger (CCM, vii/3, 1984), 257–322

Redactio Sancti Emmerammi dicta Einsidelensis, ed. M. Wegener, C. Elvert and K. Hallinger (CCM vii/3, 1984), 187–256

Regesta historiae Westfaliae accedit codex diplomaticus: die Quellen der Geschichte Westfalens in chronologisch geordneten Nachweisungen und Auszügen begleitet von einem Urkundenbuch I: mit den ältesten geschichtlichen Nachrichten bis zum Jahre 1125, ed. H. A. Erhard, Münster 1847

Regino of Prüm, *Libri duo de synodalibus causis et disciplinis ecclesiasticis*, ed. F. Wasserschleben, Leipzig 1840

—— *Libri duo de synodalibus causis et disciplinis ecclesiasticis*, PL cxxxii. 185–400

―――― *Reginonis abbatis Prumiensis Chronicon cum continuatio Treverensi*, ed. F. Kurze (MGH, SRG l, 1890, repr. 1978)
Règle de Saint Benoît, ed. A. de Vogüe with J. Neufville (SC clxxxi–lxxxvi, 1972)
Regularis concordia Angliae nationis monachorum sanctimonialumque, ed. T. Symons, London 1953
Richer, *Historiarum libri quatuor*, ed. R. Latouche, in *Histoire de France (888–995)*, Paris 1930–7
Rituale in beneventanischer Schrift: Roma, Biblioteca Vallicelliana, Cod. 32. Ende des 11. Jahrhunderts, ed. A. Odermatt (Spicilegium Friburgense xxvi, 1980)
Rodolfi Glabri historiarum libri quinque, ed. J. France, Oxford 1989
Sacramentaire Grégorien: ses principales formes d'après les plus anciens manuscrits, ed. J. Deshusses (Spicilegium Friburgense xvi, xxiv, xxxviii, 1971, 1979, 1982)
Sacramentarium Fuldense saeculi X: Cod. theol. 231 der K. Universitätsbibliothek zu Göttingen, ed. G. Richter and A. Schönfelder, Fulda 1912 (repr. HBS ci, 1972–7)
Schneider, H., 'Eine Freisinger Synodalpredigt aus der Zeit der Ungarneinfälle (Clm 6245)', in H. Mordek (ed.), *Papsttum, Kirche und Recht im Mittelalter: Festschrift für Horst Fuhrmann zum 65. Geburtstag*, Tübingen 1991, 95–115 (text edited at pp. 107–15)
Sedulius Scottus, *Liber de rectoribus christianis*, ed. S. Hellmann, in *Sedulius Scottus*, Munich 1906
Sermo synodalis, PL cxxxv. 1069–74
Smaragdus, *Diadema monachorum*, PL cii. 593–690
―――― *Expositio in regulam s. Benedicti*, ed. A. Spannagel and P. Engelbert (CCM viii, 1974)
Somerville, R. and B. C. Brasington, *Prefaces to canon law books in Latin Christianity: selected translations, 500–1245*, New Haven–London 1998
Sylvester II (Gerbert of Rheims), *Epistolae et decreta pontificia*, PL cxxxix. 269–86
Thegan, *Gesta Hludowici imperatoris*, ed. E. Tremp (MGH, SRG lxiv, 1995)
Thietmar of Merseburg, *Chronicon*, ed. R. Holtzmann (MGH, SRG n.s. ix, Berlin 1955)
Ulrich, *Antiquiores consuetudines cluniacensis monasterii*, PL cxlix. 643–778
Vita Burchardi episcopi wormatiensis, ed. G. H. Waitz (MGH, SS iv), 829–46
'Vita Godeliph', ed. M. Coens, in 'La Vie ancienne de sainte Godelive de Ghistelles par Drogon de Bergues', *Analecta Bollandiana* xliv (1926), 102–37
'Vita Mathildis reginae antiquior', in *Die Lebensbeschreibungen der Königin Mathilde*, ed. B. Schütte (MGH, SRG lxvi, 1994)
'Vita Mathildis reginae posterior', in *Die Lebensbeschreibungen der Königin Mathilde*, ed. B. Schütte (MGH, SRG lxvi, 1994)
Vita Meinwerci episcopi Patherbrunnensis, ed. F. Tenckhoff (MGH, SRG lix, 1921)
Widric, *Vita S. Gerardi episcopi tullensis*, ed. G. Waitz (MGH, SS iv), 490–505
Widukind of Corvey, *Rerum gestarum saxonicarum libri tres*, ed. H.-E. Lohmann and P. Hirsch (MGH, SRG lx, 1935)
Wipo, *Gesta Chuonradi II. imperatoris*, in *Die Werke Wipos*, ed. H. Bresslau (MGH, SRG lxi, 1915, repr. 1956), 1–62
―――― *Tetralogus*, in *Die Werke Wipos*, 475–86

Secondary sources

Academia caesarea Vindobonensis (ed.), *Tabulae codicum manuscriptorum praeter graecos et orientales in Bibliotheca Palatina Vindobonensi asservatorum*, Vienna 1864–1912
Addleshaw, G. W. O., *The development of the parochial system from Charlemagne (768–814) to Urban II (1088–1099)*, London 1954
Airlie, S., 'The anxiety of sanctity: St Gerald of Aurillac and his maker', *JEH* xliii (1992), 372–95
―――― 'Narratives of triumph and rituals of submission: Charlemagne's mastering of Bavaria', *TRHS* 6th ser. ix (1999), 93–119
Althoff, G., *Adels- und Königsfamilien im Spiegel ihrer Memorialüberlieferung: Studien zum Totengedenken der Billunger und Ottonen*, Munich 1984
―――― *Verwandte, Freunde und Getreue: zum politischen Stellenwert der Gruppenbindungen im früheren Mittelalter*, Darmstadt 1990
―――― *Amicitiae und pacta: Bündnis, Einung, Politik und Gebetsgedenken im beginnenden 10. Jahrhundert* (MGH, Schriften xxxvii, Hanover 1992)
―――― 'Das Privileg der "deditio": Formen gütlicher Konfliktbeendigung in der mittelalterlichen Adelsgesellschaft', in his *Spielregeln der Politik im Mittelalter*, 99–125
―――― *Spielregeln der Politik im Mittelalter*, Darmstadt 1997
Amann, É., 'Pénitence–repentir', in *DTC* xii/1, 722–48
―――― 'Pénitence–sacrement: la pénitence primitive', in *DTC* xii/1, 749–845
―――― 'Pénitence–sacrement: la pénitence privée: son organisation, premières spéculations à son sujet', in *DTC* xii/1, 845–948
Amiet, R., 'Inventaire des manuscrits liturgiques conservés dans les bibliothèques et les archives de Rome', *Scriptorium* xxxix (1985), 109–18
Amos, T. L., 'Monks and pastoral care in the early Middle Ages', in T. F. X. Noble and J. J. Contreni (eds), *Religion, culture and society in the early Middle Ages: studies in honour of Richard E. Sullivan*, Kalamazoo 1987, 165–80
Anciaux, P., *La Théologie du sacrement de pénitence au XIIe siècle*, Louvain 1949
Anton, H. H., *Fürstenspiegel und Herrscherethos in der Karolingerzeit*, Bonn 1968
―――― *Trier im frühen Mittelalter*, Paderborn–Munich–Vienna–Zurich 1987
Autenrieth, J., 'Die kanonistischen Handschriften der Dombibliothek Konstantz', in Autenrieth and Kottje, *Kirchenrechtliche Texte*, 7–21
―――― and R. Kottje, *Kirchenrechtliche Texte im Bodenseegebiet: mittelalterliche Überlieferung in Konstanz, auf der Reichenau und in St Gallen*, Sigmaringen 1975
Avitabile, L., M. C. di Franco, V. Jemolo and A. Petrucci, 'Censimento dei codici dei secoli XI–XII', *SM* 3rd ser. ix (1968), 1115–94
Avril, J., 'Recherches sur la politique paroissiale des établissements monastiques et canoniaux (XIe et XIIIe s.)', *Revue Mabillon* lix (1980), 453–517
―――― 'Paroisses et dépendances monastiques au moyen âge', in *Sous la règle de Saint Benoît: structures monastiques et sociétés en France du moyen âge à l'époque moderne: abbaye bénédictine Sainte-Marie de Paris 23–25 octobre 1980*, Geneva–Paris 1982, 95–105
―――― 'Remarques sur un aspect de la vie paroissale: la pratique de la confession et de la communion du Xe au XIVe siècle', in *L'Encadrement religieux des fidèles*, i. 345–63
―――― 'L'Évolution du synode diocésain principalement dans la France du nord

du Xe au XIII siécle', in P. A. Linehan (ed.), *Proceedings of the seventh international congress of medieval canon law*, Vatican City 1988, 305–25
────── 'La Paroisse médiévale: bilan et perspectives d'après quelques travaux récents', *Revue d'histoire de l'église de France* liv (1988), 91–113
Baker, D. (ed.), *The materials, sources and methods of ecclesiastical history* (SCH xi, 1975)
Baldwin, J., 'From the ordeal to confession', in Biller and Minnis, *Handling sin*, 191–209
Bartlett, R., *England under the Norman and Angevin kings*, Oxford 2000
Bautier, R.-H., 'Un Recueil de textes pour servir à la biographie de l'archevêque de Reims, Hervé (xe siècle): son attribution à Flodoard', in *Mélanges Louis Halphen*, Paris 1951, 1–6
Benton, J. F., 'Consciousness of self and perceptions of individuality', in G. Constable and R. L. Benson (eds), *Renaissance and renewal in the twelfth century*, Oxford 1982, 263–95
Berggren, E., *The psychology of confession*, Leiden 1975
Bériou, N., 'Autour de Latran IV (1215): la naissance de la confession moderne et sa diffusion', in Groupe de la Bussière, *Pratiques de la confession*, 74–93.
Berlière, U., 'L'Exercice du ministère paroissial par les moines du XIIe au XVIIIe siècle', *Rev. Bén.* xxxix (1927), 340–64
Bernhardt, J. W., *Itinerant kingship and royal monasteries in early medieval Germany c. 936–1075*, Cambridge 1993
Berschin, W., *Bonizo von Sutri: Leben und Werk*, Berlin–New York 1972
Beumann, H., 'Die Bedeutung Lotharingiens für die ottonische Missionspolitik im Osten', in his *Wissenschaft vom Mittelalter: Ausgewählte Aufsätze*, Vienna 1972, 377–409
Bibliothèque nationale: catalogue général des manuscrits latins, Paris 1938–88
Biller, P., 'Confession in the Middle Ages: introduction', in Biller and Minnis, *Handling sin*, 1–35
────── and A. J. Minnis (eds), *Handling sin: confession in the Middle Ages*, Woodbridge 1998
Bischoff, N., 'Über die Chronologie der Kaiserin Gisela und über die Verweigerung ihrer Krönung durch Aribo von Mainz', in *Mitteilungen des Instituts für Österreichische Geschichtsforschung* lviii (1950), 285–309
Bishop, E., *Liturgica historica: papers on the liturgy and religious life of the western Church*, Oxford 1918
Blair, J., 'Introduction: from minster to parish church', in his *Minsters and parish churches*, 1–19
────── 'Debate: ecclesiastical organisation and pastoral care in Anglo-Saxon England', *EME* iv (1995), 193–212
────── (ed.), *Minsters and parish churches: the local church in transition, 950–1200*, Oxford 1988
────── and R. Sharpe (eds), *Pastoral care before the parish*, Leicester 1992
Bo, V., *Storia della parrocchia: i secoli dell'infanzia (sec. VI–XI)*, Rome 1990
Boese, H., *Die lateinischen Handschriften der Sammlung Hamilton zu Berlin Staatsbibliothek zu Berlin-Preussischer Kulturbesitz*, Weisbaden 1966
Bolton, B., *The medieval reformation*, London 1983
Bornscheuer, L., *Miseriae regum: Untersuchungen zum Krisen- und Todesgedanken*

in den herrschaftstheologischen Vorstellungen der ottonish-salischen Zeit, Berlin 1968

Bossy, J., 'The social history of confession in the age of Reformation', TRHS 5th ser. xxv (1975), 21–38

—— Christianity in the west, 1400–1700, Oxford 1985

—— 'Christian life in the late Middle Ages: prayers', TRHS 6th ser. i (1991), 137–50

Bouchard, C., 'Consanguinity and noble marriages in the tenth and eleventh centuries', Speculum lvi (1981), 268–87

—— Sword, miter and cloister: nobility and the Church in Burgundy, 980–1198, Ithaca–London 1987

Bougard, F., La Justice dans le royaume d'Italie de la fin du VIIIe siècle au début du XIe siècle, Rome 1995

Boyd, C., Tithes and parishes in medieval Italy: the historical roots of a modern problem, Ithaca 1952

Boye, M., 'Quellenkatalog der Synoden Deutschlands und Reichsitaliens von 922–1059', Neues Archiv für sächsische Geschichte und Alterhumskunde xlviii (1930), 45–96

Bradley, E. S., Henry Charles Lea: a biography, Philadelphia 1931

Braeckmans, L., Confession et communion au moyen âge et au concile de Trente, Gembloux 1971

Brandenburg, E., 'Probleme um die Kaiserin Gisela', Berichte über die Verhandlungen der Sächsischen Akademie der Wissenschaften zu Leipzig: philogisch-historische Klasse lxxx (1928), 1–38

Brasington, B. C., 'Prologues to canonical collections as a source for jurisprudential change to the eve of the Investiture Contest', Frühmittelalterliche Studien xxviii (1994), 226–42

Brommer, P., 'Die bischöfliche Gesetzgebung Theodulfs von Orléans', ZRG Kan. Abt. lx (1974), 1–120

—— 'Capitula episcoporum: Bemerkungen zu den bischöflichen Kapitularien', Zeitschrift für Kirchengeschichte xci (1980), 207–36

—— Capitula episcoporum: die bischöflichen Kapitularien des 9. und 10. Jahrhunderts (Typologie xliii, 1985)

Brückmann, J., 'Latin manuscript pontificals and benedictionals in England and Wales', Traditio xxix (1973), 391–458

Brundage, J., Law, sex and Christian society in medieval Europe, Chicago–London 1987

Bührer-Thierry, G., Évêques et pouvoir dans le royaume de Germanie: les églises de Bavière et de Souabe, 876–973, Paris 1997

Bull, M., Knightly piety and the lay response to the First Crusade: the Limousin and Gascony, c. 970–1130, Oxford 1993

Bullough, D. A., Carolingian renewal: sources and heritage, Manchester 1991

Bulst, N., Untersuchungen zu den Klosterreformen Wilhelms von Dijon (962–1031), Bonn 1973

Büttner, H., Zur frühmittelalterlichen Reichsgeschichte an Rhein, Main und Neckar, ed. A. Gerlich, Darmstadt 1975

Butzmann, H. (ed.), Kataloge der Herzog-August-Bibliothek Wolfenbüttel: die Weissenburger Handschriften, Frankfurt 1964

Bynum, C. Walker, 'Did the twelfth century discover the individual?', in her Jesus as mother: studies in the spirituality of the high Middle Ages, Berkeley 1982, 85–109

Cambridge, E. and D. Rollason, 'Debate: the pastoral organisation of the Anglo-Saxon Church: a review of the "minster hypothesis" ', EME iv (1995), 87–104

Cattaneo, E., 'La partecipazione dei laici alla liturgia', in *I laici nella "societas cristiana" dei secoli XI e XII: atti della terza settimana internazionale di studio Mendola 21–27 agosto 1965* (Miscellanea v, 1965), 396–427

Charles-Edwards, T., 'The penitential of Theodore and the *Iudicia Theodori*', in M. Lapidge (ed.), *Archbishop Theodore: commemorative studies on his life and influence*, Cambridge 1995, 141–74

Chatelain, V., 'Le Comte de Metz et la vouerie épiscopale du VIIIe au XIIIe siècle', *Jahrbuch der Gesellschaft für lothringische Geschichte und Altertumskunde* x (1898), 72–119

Chauvet, L-M., '*Nova et vetera*: quelques leçons tirées de la tradition relative au sacrement de la reconciliation', in de Clerk and Palazzo, *Rituels*, 99–124

Chavasse, A., *Le Sacramentaire gélasien (Vaticanus Reginensis 316): sacramentaire presbytéral en usage dans les titres Romains au VIIe siècle*, Tournai–Rome 1958

Chelini, J., *L'Aube du moyen âge: naissance de la chrétienté occidentale: la vie religieuse des laïcs dans l'Europe carolingienne (750–900)*, Paris 1991

Chenu, M.-D., *Nature, man and society in the twelfth century: essays on new theological perspectives in the Latin west*, trans. J. Taylor and L. K. Little, Chicago–London 1968

Clark, I. D. L., 'Patriarch Poppo (1019–42) and the rebuilding of the basilica of Aquileia: the politics of conspicuous expenditure', in Sheils and Wood, *The Church and wealth*, 37–46

Claussen, M. A., 'God and man in Dhuoda's *Liber manualis*', in W. J. Sheils and D. Wood (eds), *Women in the Church* (SCH xxvii, 1990), 43–52

Constable, G., *Monastic tithes: from their origins to the twelfth century*, Cambridge 1964

—— 'Monastic possessions of churches and "spiritualia" in the age of reform', in *Il monachesimo e la riforma ecclesiastica (1049–1112): atti della quarta settimana internazionale di studio Mendola, 23–29 agosto 1968* (Miscellanea vi, 1971), 304–31

—— 'The treatise "Hortatur nos" and accompanying canonical works on the performance of pastoral works by monks', in his *Religious life and thought (11th–12th centuries)*, London 1979, no. ix

—— 'Monasteries, rural churches and the *cura animarum* in the early Middle Ages', in *Cristianizzazione ed organizzazione*, 349–89

—— 'The ceremonies and symbolism of entering religious life and taking the monastic habit, from the fourth to the twelfth centuries', in *Segni e riti*, 771–834

—— 'Cluny in the monastic world of the tenth century', in *Il secolo di ferro* (Settimane xxxviii, 1991), 391–437

Corbet, P., *Les Saints ottoniens: sainteté dynastique, sainteté royale et sainteté féminine autour de l'an mil*, Sigmaringen 1986

Coué, S., *Hagiographie im Kontext: Schreibanlass und Funktion von Bischofsviten aus dem 11. und vom Anfang des 12. Jahrhunderts*, Berlin–New York 1997

Coulet, N., *Les Visites pastorales* (Typologie xxiii, 1977)

Cowdrey, H. E. J., 'The papacy, the Patarenes and the Church of Milan', *TRHS* 5th ser. xviii (1968), 25–48 (repr. in his *Popes, monks and crusaders*, London 1984, no. v)
—— 'Bishop Ermenfrid of Sion and the penitential ordinance following the battle of Hastings', *JEH* xx (1969), 225–42
—— *The Cluniacs and the Gregorian reform*, Oxford 1970
Cramer, P., *Baptism and change in the early Middle Ages, c. 200–c. 1150*, Cambridge 1993
Cristianizzazione ed organizzazione ecclesiastica delle campagne nell'alto medioevo: espansione e resistenze (Settimane xxviii, 1982)
Cubitt, C., *Anglo-Saxon church councils, c. 650–c. 850*, London–New York 1995
Dalla Mutta, R., 'Un Rituel de l'onction des malades du IXe siècle en Flandre, chaînon important entre le rituel "carolingien" et les rituels des Xe–XIe siècles', in *Mens concordet*, 608–18
Dallen, J., 'The absence of a ritual of reconciliation in Celtic penance', in A. W. Sadler (ed.), *The journey of western spirituality*, Chico 1981, 79–106
—— *The reconciling community: the rite of penance*, New York 1986
Daniel, N., *Handschriften des zehnten Jahrhunderts aus der Freisinger Dombibliothek: Studien über Schriftcharakter und Herkunft der nachkarolingischen und ottonischen Handschriften einer bayerischen Bibliothek*, Munich 1973
Das Reich der Salier, 1024–1125: Katalog zur Ausstellung des Landes Rheinland-Pfalz veranstaltet vom römisch-germanischen Zentralmuseum Mainz Forschunginstitut für Vor- und Frühgeschichte in Verbindung mit dem bischöflichen Dom- und Diözesanmuseum Mainz in Speyer 1992, Sigmaringen 1992
Davril, A., 'Un Moine de Fleury aux environs de l'an mil: Thierry d'Amorbach', in Louis, *Études Ligériennes*, 97–104
—— 'Points de contact entre la *Vita Iohannis abbatis Gorziensis* et les *Consuetudines Floriacenses antiquiores*', in M. Parisse and O. G. Oexle (eds), *L'Abbaye de Gorze au Xe siècle*, Nancy 1993, 183–92
de Clerck, P. and É. Palazzo (eds), *Rituels: mélanges offerts à Pierre-Marie Gy*, Paris 1990
de Jong, M., 'Growing up in a Carolingian monastery: Magister Hildemar and his oblates', *Journal of Medieval History* ix (1983), 99–128
—— 'To the limits of kinship: anti-incest legislation in the early medieval west (500–900)', in J. Bremmer (ed.), *From Sappho to de Sade: moments in the history of sexuality*, London–New York 1989, 36–59
—— 'Power and humility in Carolingian society: the public penance of Louis the Pious', *EME* i (1992), 29–52
—— 'Carolingian monasticism: the power of prayer', in McKitterick, *New Cambridge medieval history*, 622–53
—— *In Samuel's image: child oblation in the early medieval west*, Leiden–New York–Cologne 1996
—— 'What was public about public penance? *paenitentia publica* and justice in the Carolingian world', in *La Giustizia nel'alto medioevo*, ii (Settimane xliii, 1996), 863–902
—— 'Pollution, penance and sanctity: Ekkehard's *Life* of Iso of St Gall', in J. Hill and M. Swan (eds), *The community, the family, and the saint: patterns of power in early medieval Europe*, Turnhout 1998, 145–58

de Valous, G., *Le Monachisme Clunisien des origines au XVe siècle: vie intérieure des monastères et organisation de l'ordre*, Paris 1935

Delisle, L., *Inventaire des manuscrits latins de Notre-Dames et d'autres fonds conservés à la Bibliothèque nationale sous les numéros 16719–18613*, Paris 1874

dell'Oro, F., 'Un rituale del secolo X proveniente dall'Italia settentrionale', in de Clerck and Palazzo, *Rituels*, 215–49

Dereine, C., 'Vie commune, règle de S. Augustin et chanoines réguliers au XIe siècle', *Revue d'histoire ecclésiastique* xli (1946), 356–406

Devailly, G., 'Le Clergé régulier de la ministère paroissal', *Cahiers d'histoire* xx (1975), 259–77

Dickinson, J. C., *The origins of the Austin canons and their introduction into England*, London 1950

Dictionnaire de droit canonique, ed. R. Naz, Paris 1935–65

Dictionnaire d'histoire et de géographie ecclésiastiques, Paris 1912–

Dictionnaire de théologie catholique, Paris 1930–46

Dooley, K., 'From penance to confession: the Celtic contribution', *Bijdragen: Tijdschrift voor filosofie en theologie* xliii (1982), 390–411

Douglas, D. C., *William the Conqueror: the Norman impact upon England*, London 1964

Du Cange, M. (suppl. D. P. Carpenterius and G. A. L. Henschel), *Glossarium mediae et infirmae latinitatis*, Paris 1840–50

Duby, G., *The knight, the lady and the priest: the making of modern marriage in medieval France*, trans. B. Bray, Harmondsworth 1983

―――― 'Introduction: private power, public power', in P. Ariès and G. Duby (eds), *A history of private life*, II: *Revelations of the medieval world*, Cambridge, Mass.–London 1988 (trans. by A. Goldhammer of *Histoire de la vie privée*, II: *De l'Europe féodale à la renaissance*, Paris 1985), 3–31

Duft, J., 'Iso monachus–doctor nominatissimus', in H. Maurer (ed.), *Churrätisches und st. gallisches Mittelalter: Festschrift für Otto P. Clavadetscher zu seinem funfundsechzigsten Geburtstag*, Sigmaringen 1984, 146–55

Dumville, D., *Liturgy and the ecclesiastical history of late Anglo-Saxon England: four studies*, Woodbridge 1992

Ebner, A., *Quellen und Forschungen zur Geschichte und Kunstgeschichte des Missale Romanum im Mittelalter: Iter Italicum*, Freiburg-im-Breisgau 1896

Eckel, A., *Charles le Simple*, Paris 1899

Edwards, C., 'German vernacular literature: a survey', in McKitterick, *Carolingian culture*, 141–70

Egbert: Erzbischoff von Trier, ed. R. J. Ronig, Trier 1993

Egger, C., 'La regole seguite dai canonici regolari nei secoli XI e XII', in *La vita comune del clero nei secoli xi e xii: atti della settimana di studio, Mendola, settembre 1959* (Miscellanea iii, 1962), ii. 9–12

L'Encadrement religieux des fidèles au moyen-âge et jusqu'au Concile de Trente: la paroisse – le clergé – la pastorale – la dévotion: actes du 109e congrès national des sociétés savantes, Dijon 1984: section d'histoire médiévale et de philologie, i, Paris 1985

Endres, J. A. and A. Ebner, 'Ein Königsgebetbuch des elften Jahrhunderts', in S. Ehses (ed.), *Festschrift zum elfhundertjährigen Jubiläum des deutschen Campo Santo in Rom*, Freiburg-im-Breisgau 1897, 296–307

Erdmann, C., *Forschungen zur politischen Ideenwelt des Frühmittelalters*, Berlin 1951

Evrard, J.-P., 'Verdun au temps de l'évêque Haymon (988–1024)', in Iogna-Prat and Picard, *Religion et culture*, 273–8

Falck, L., *Mainz im frühen und hohen Mittelalter*, Dusseldorf 1972

Fasola, L., 'Arduin von Ivrea', in *LMA* i. 915–16

Fazzalaro, F. J., *The place for the hearing of confessions: a historical synopsis and a commentary*, Washington, DC 1950

Fenske, L., W. Rösener and T. Zotz (eds), *Institutionen, Kultur und Gesellschaft im Mittelalter: Festschrift für Josef Fleckenstein zu seinem 65. Geburtstag*, Sigmaringen 1984

Fichtenau, H., *Lebensordnung des 10. Jahrhunderts: Studien über Denkart und Existenz im einstigen Karolingerreich*, Stuttgart 1984

—— *Living in the tenth century: mentalities and social orders*, Chicago–London 1991 (trans. by P. J. Geary of *Lebensordnung des 10. Jahrhunderts*)

Flacius Illyricus, M. and others, *Historia integram ecclesiae Christi: decima centuria*, Basle 1567

—— *Historia integram ecclesiae Christi: undecima centuria*, Basle 1567

Flandrin, J.-L., *Un Temps pour embrasser: aux origines de la morale sexuelle occidentale (VIe–XIe siècle)*, Paris 1983

Flori, J., 'A Propos de l'adoubement des chevaliers au XIe siècle: le prétendu *pontifical de Reims* et l'*ordo ad armandum* de Cambrai', *Frühmittelalterliche Studien* xix (1985), 330–49

—— 'Du Nouveau sur l'adoubement des chevaliers (XIe–XIIIe siècles)', *Le Moyen Âge* ii (1985), 201–26

Folz, R., 'La Pénitence publique aux IXe siècle d'après les canons de l'évêque Isaac de Langres', in *L'Encadrement religieux des fidèles*, i. 331–43

Fournier, P., 'Études critiques sur le Décret de Burchard de Worms', *Nouvelle Revue historique de droit français et étranger* 3rd ser. xxxiv (1910), 41–112, 213–21, 289–331, 564–84

—— 'Le Décret de Burchard de Worms', *Revue d'histoire ecclésiastique* xii/1 (1911), 451–73, 670–701

—— 'L'Oeuvre canonique de Réginon de Prüm', *Bibliothèque de l'École des Chartes* lxxxi (1920), 5–44

—— and G. Le Bras, *Histoire des collections canoniques en occident*, Paris 1931

Fransen, G., 'La Tradition manuscrite du Décret de Burchard de Worms: une premiére orientation', in A. Scheuermann and G. May (eds), *Ius sacrum: Klaus Mörsdorf zum 60. Geburtstag*, Vienna 1969, 111–18

—— *Les Collections canoniques* (Typologie x, 1973)

—— 'Les Sources de la Préface du Décret de Burchard de Worms', *Bulletin of Medieval Canon Law* n.s. iii (1973), 1–9

—— 'Le Décret de Burchard de Worms: valeur du texte de l'édition: essai du classement des manuscrits', *ZRG Kan. Abt.* lxiii (1977), 1–19

Frantzen, A. J., 'The significance of the Frankish penitentials', *JEH* xxx (1979), 409–21

—— *The literature of penance in Ango-Saxon England*, New Brunswick, NJ 1983

—— 'The penitentials attributed to Bede', *Speculum* lviii (1983), 573–97

—— 'The tradition of penitentials in Anglo-Saxon England', *Anglo-Saxon England* xi (1983), 23–56

Fuhrmann, H., *Einfluss und Verbreitung der pseudoisidorischen Fälschungen von ihrem Auftauchen bis in die neuere Zeit* (MGH, Schriften xxiv, Stuttgart 1972–4)

——— 'Die Synode von Hohenaltheim (916) – Quellenkundlichbetrachtet', DA xliii (1987), 440–68

Fürst, C. G., 'Kardinal', in *LMA* v. 950–2

Gamber, K., *Codices liturgici latini antiquiores*, 2nd edn, Oxford 1968

——— 'Liturgiegeschichte von Regensburg bis ins 16 Jahrhundert anhand der ehaltern Liturgiebücher', in *Liturgie im Bistum Regensburg von den Anfängen bis zur Gegenwart*, Munich–Zurich 1989, 13–37

——— with B. Baroffio, F. dell'Oro, A. Häriggi, J. Janini and A. M. Triacca, *Codices liturgici latini antiquiores: supplementum*, Freiburg 1988

Garrison, E. B., *Studies in the history of medieval Italian painting*, Florence 1960

——— 'Random notes on early Italian manuscripts', *La bibliofilia* lxxx (1978), 197–214

Gattermann, G. (ed.), *Handschriftencensus Rheinland*, Wiesbaden 1993

Gerlich, A., 'Hammersteiner Ehe', in *LMA* iv. 1892

Gilchrist, J. T., 'The reception of Pope Gregory VII into the canon law (1073–1141)', ZRG Kan. Abt. lix (1973), 35–82 (repr. in his *Canon law in the age of reform, c. 11th–c. 12th*, Aldershot 1993, no. viii)

Görich, K. and E. Klemm, *Bayerische Staatsbibliothek: das Gebetbuch Ottos III. Clm 30111* (Patrimonia lxxxiv, Munich 1995)

Gorre, R., *Die ersten Ketzer im 11. Jahrhundert: religiöse Eiferer –soziale Rebellen? Zum Wandel der Bedeutung religiöser Weltbilder* (Konstanzer Dissertationen iv, Constance 1982)

Grégoire, R., 'Repertorium liturgicum Italicum', SM 3rd ser. ix (1968), 465–592

——— 'Repertorium liturgicum Italicum: addenda I', SM 3rd ser. xi (1970), 537–56

Groupe de la Bussière (ed.), *Pratiques de la confession: des pères du désert à Vatican II: quinze études d'histoire*, Paris 1983

Gy, P.-M., 'Histoire liturgique du sacrement de pénitence', *La Maison Dieu* lvi (1958), 5–21

——— 'Collectaire, rituel, processionnal', *Revue des sciences philosophiques et théologiques* xliv (1960), 441–69

——— 'Les Bases de la pénitence moderne', *La Maison Dieu* cxvii (1974), 63–85

——— 'Typologie et ecclésiologie des livres liturgiques médiévaux', *La Maison Dieu* cxxi (1975), 7–21

Hafner, W., *Der Basiliuskommentar zur Regula S. Benedicti: ein Beitrag zur Autorenfrage karolingischer Regelkommentare*, Münster 1959

Hägele, G., *Das Paenitentiale Vallicellianum, I: Ein oberitalienischer Zweig der frühmittelalterlichen kontinentalen Bussbücher: Überlieferung, Verbreitung und Quellen*, Sigmaringen 1984

Hallinger, K., *Gorze–Kluny: Studien zu den monastischen Lebensformen und Gegensätzen im Hochmittelalter*, Rome 1950

——— (ed.), *Consuetudines saeculi X/XI/XII monumenta: introductiones* (CCM vii/1, 1984)

Halm, C. and G. Laubmann, *Catalogus codicum latinorum Bibliothecae regiae monacensis*, Munich 1868–81

Hamilton, B., 'Monastic revival in tenth-century Rome', *Studia Monastica* iv

(1962), 35–68 (repr. in his *Monastic reform, Catharism and the crusades (900–1300)*, London 1979, no. ii)

Hamilton, S., 'Otto III's penance: a case study of unity and diversity in the eleventh-century Church', in Swanson, *Unity and diversity*, 83–94

—— 'A new model for royal penance? Helgaud of Fleury's *Life of Robert the Pious*', *EME* vi (1997), 189–200

Hammer, Jr, C. I., 'Country churches, clerical inventories and the Carolingian Renaissance in Bavaria', *Church History* xlix (1980), 5–17

Hartmann, W., 'I vescovo com giudice', *Rivista di storia della chiesa in Italia* xl (1986), 320–41

—— *Die Synoden der karolingerzeit im Frankenreich und in Italien*, Paderborn–Munich–Vienna–Zurich 1989

—— and K. Pennington, *History of medieval canon law* (forthcoming)

Hay, D., *Annalists and historians: western historiography from the VIIIth to the XVIIIth century*, London 1977

Hefele, C. J., *Histoire des conciles d'après les documents originaux*, Paris 1907–52

Hellmann, M., 'Die Synode von Hohenaltheim (916): Bemerkungen über das Verhältnis von Königtum und Kirche im ostfränkischen Reich zu Beginn des 10. Jahrhunderts', *Historisches Jahrbuch* lxxiii (1953), 127–42

Hemming, J., '*Sellam gestare*: saddle-bearing punishments and the case of Rhiannon', *Viator* xxviii (1997), 45–64

Hildebrandt, M., *The external school in Carolingian society*, Leiden–New York–Cologne 1992

Hirsch, S. and H. Bresslau, *Jahrbücher des deutschen Reichs unter Heinrichs II.*, Leipzig 1862, 1875

Hocquard, C., 'La Règle de saint Chrodegang: état de quelques questions', in *Saint Chrodegang: communications présentées au colloque tenu à Metz à l'occasion du douzième centenaire de sa mort*, Metz 1967, 55–89

Hoffmann, H., *Buchkunst und Königtum im ottonisch und frühsalischen Reich* (MGH, Schriften xxx, Stuttgart 1986)

—— *Bamberger Handschriften des 10. und 11. Jahrhunderts* (MGH, Schriften xxxix, Hanover 1995)

—— and R. Pokorny, *Das Dekret des Bischofs Burchard von Worms: Textstufen–frühe Verbreitung–Vorlagen* (MGH, Hilfsmittel xii, 1991)

Hourlier, J., 'La Spiritualité à Saint-Riquier d'après Hariulf', *Revue Mabillon* l (1960), 1–20

Hughes, K., 'Some aspects of Irish influence on early English private prayer', *Studia Celtica* v (1970), 48–61

Hunt, N. (ed.), *Cluniac monasticism in the central Middle Ages*, London 1971

Iogna-Prat, D. and J.-C. Picard (eds), *Religion et culture autour de l'an mil: royaume capétien et Lotharingie: actes du colloque: Hugues Capet 987–1987: la France de l'an mil: Auxerre, 26 et 27 juin 1987–Metz, 11 et 12 septembre 1987*, Paris 1990

Irtenkauf, W., 'Die Litanei des Pommersfelder Königsgebetbuches (für Otto III)', in F. Dettweiler, H. Köllner and P. A. Riedl (eds), *Festschrift für K. H. Usener*, Marburg 1967, 129–36

Istituzioni ecclesiastiche della 'Societas christiana' dei secoli 11–12: diocesi, pievi e parrocchie: atti della 6a settimana internazionale di studio, Milano, 1–7 settembre 1974 (Miscellanea viii, 1977)

Istituzioni monastiche e istituzioni canonicali in occidente (1123–1215): atti della settima settimana internazionale di studio Mendola, 28 agosto–3 settembre 1977 (Miscellanea ix, 1980)

Jaffé, P. and W. Wattenbach, *Ecclesiae metropolitanae coloniensis codices manuscripti*, Berlin 1874

—— with W. Wattenbach, S. Loewenfeld, F. Kaltenbrunner and P. Ewald (eds), *Regesta pontificum romanorum ab condita ecclesia ad annum post Christum natum MCXCVIII*, 2nd edn, Leipzig 1885

Jakobs, H., 'Zu neuen Thesen über die Fuldaer Papsturkunden', *DA* xxxvii (1981), 792–5

—— (ed.), *Regesta pontificium Romanorum: Germania pontificia*, iv, Gottingen 1973

James, M. R., *A descriptive catalogue of the manuscripts in the library of Corpus Christi College Cambridge*, Cambridge 1912

Jäschke, K. U. and R. Wenskus (eds), *Festschrift für Helmut Beumann zum 65. Geburtstag*, Sigmaringen 1977

Jestice, P. G., 'The Gorzian reform and the light under the bushel', *Viator* xxiv (1993), 51–78

—— *Wayward monks and the religious revolution of the eleventh century*, Leiden 1997

Jungmann, J. A., *Die lateinischen Bussriten in ihrer geschichtlichen Entwicklung*, Innsbruck 1932

—— *The mass of the Roman rite: its origins and development*, trans. F. A. Brunner, New York 1950

Kalckstein, C. von, *Geschichte des französischen Königtums unter den ersten Capetingern*, I: *Der Kamp der Robertiner und Karolinger*, Leipzig 1877

Kentenich, G., *Beschreibendes Verzeichnis der Handschriften der Stadtbibliothek zu Trier*, IX: *Die juristischen Handschriften der Stadtbibliothek zu Trier*, Trier 1919

Ker, N. R., *Catalogue of manuscripts containing Anglo-Saxon*, Oxford 1957

—— 'Three Old English texts in a Salisbury pontifical, Cotton Tiberius C. i', in P. Clemoes (ed.), *The Anglo-Saxons: studies in some aspects of their history and culture presented to Bruce Dickins*, London 1959

Kerff, F., 'Mittelalterliche Quellen und mittelalterliche Wirklichkeit: zu den Konsequenzen einer jüngst erschienenen Edition für unser Bild kirchlicher Reformbemühungen', *Rheinische Vierteljarhrsblätter* li (1987), 275–86

—— '*Libri paenitentiales* und kirchliche Strafgerichtsbarkeit bis zum Decretum Gratiani: ein Diskussionsverschlag', *ZRG Kan. Abt.* lxxv (1989), 23–57

Kerner, M., 'Burchard, Bischof von Worms: kirchenrechtliche Sammlung und Hofrecht', in *LMA* ii. 947–51

Knabe, L., *Die gelasianische Zweigewaltentheorie bis zum Ende des Investiturstreits*, Berlin 1936

Körntgen, L., 'Ein italienisches Bussbuch und seine fränkischen Quellen: das anonyme Paenitentiale der Handschrift Vatikan Archiv. S. Pietro H. 58', in H. Mordek (ed.), *Aus Archiven und Bibliotheken: Festschrift für Raymund Kottje zum 65. Geburtstag*, Frankfurt 1992, 189–205

—— *Studien zu den Quellen der frühmittelalterlichen Bussbücher*, Sigmaringen 1993

Kottje, R., 'Kirchenrechtliche Interessen im Bodenseeraum vom 9. bis 12. Jahrhundert', in Autenrieth and Kottje, *Kirchenrechtliche Texte*, 23–41

―――― *Die Bussbücher Halitgars von Cambrai und des Hrabanus Maurus*, Berlin–New York 1980
―――― 'Bussbücher', in *LMA* ii. 1118–22
―――― 'Erfassung und Untersuchung der frühmittelalterlichen kontinentalen Bussbücher: Probleme, Ergebnisse, Aufgaben eines Forschungsprojektes an der Universität Bonn', *SM* 3rd ser. xxvi (1985), 941–50
―――― 'Busspraxis und Bussritus', in *Segni e riti*, 369–95
―――― 'Einleitung: monastische Reform oder Reformen?', in Kottje and Maurer, *Monastische Reformen*, 9–13
―――― and H. Maurer (eds), *Monastische Reformen im 9. und 10. Jahrhundert*, Sigmaringen 1989
Koziol, G., *Begging, pardon and favor: ritual and political order in early medieval France*, Ithaca 1992
Krause, V., 'Die Akten der Triburer Synode 895', *Neues Archiv der Gesellschaft für ältere deutsche Geschichtskunde* xvii (1892), 51–82, 283–326
Kristeller, P. O., *Latin manuscript books before 1600: a list of the printed catalogues and unpublished inventories of extant collections*, 4th enlarged edn by S. Krämer (MGH, Hilfsmittel, Munich 1993)
Kubach, H. E. and W. Haas, *Der Dom zu Speyer*, Munich 1972
Kupper, J.-L., *Liège et l'église impériale XIe–XIIe siècles*, Paris 1981
Labande, E.-R., 'Recherches sur les pèlerins dans l'Europe des XIe et XIIe siècles', in *Cahiers de civilisation médiévale* i (1958), 159–69, 339–47
Lambert, M., *Medieval heresy: popular movements from the Gregorian reform to the Reformation*, 2nd edn, Oxford 1992
Lapidge, M., 'The origin of CCCC 163', *Transactions of the Cambridge Bibliographical Society* viii (1981), 18–28
―――― 'Ealdred of York and Ms. Cotton Vitellius E. XII', *Yorkshire Archaeological Journal* lv (1983), 11–25 (repr. in his *Anglo-Latin literature*, 453–67)
―――― *Anglo-Latin literature, 900–1066*, London–Rio Grande 1993
Lauer, P., *Robert Ier et Raoul de Bourgogne rois de France*, Paris 1910
Lauer, R. F., *Studien zur ottonischen Mainzer Buchmalerei*, Bonn 1987
Lawrence, C. H., *Medieval monasticism: forms of religious life in western Europe in the Middle Ages*, 2nd edn, London 1989
Le Bras, G., 'Penitentials', in *DTC* xii. 1175–8
Le Goff, J., *The birth of purgatory*, London 1984 (trans. by A. Goldhammer of *La Naissance du purgatoire*, Paris 1981)
Lea, H. C., *A history of auricular confession and indulgences in the Latin Church*, London 1896
Leitschuh, F. and H. Fischer, *Katalog der Handschriften der Königlichen Bibliothek zu Bamberg*, Bamberg 1887–1912
Lemarignier, J. F., 'Encadrement religieux des campagnes et conjoncture politique dans les régions du royaume de France situées au nord de la Loire, de Charles le Chauve aux derniers Carolingiens (840–987)', in *Cristianizzazione ed organizzazione ecclesiastica*, 765–800
Leroquais, V., *Les Pontificaux manuscrits des bibliothèques publiques de France*, Paris 1938
Lexikon der christlichen Ikonographie, ed. E. Kirschbaum, W. Braunfels and others, Rome 1968–76
Lexikon des Mittelalters, Munich–Zurich, 1980–99

Leyser, K., *Rule and conflict in an early medieval society: Ottonian Saxony*, Bloomington–London 1979
—— 'Ottonian government', *EHR* xcvi (1981), 721–53 (repr. in his *Medieval Germany and its neighbours, 900–1250*, London 1982, 69–101)
—— review of H. Fichtenau, *Lebensordnung des 10. Jahrhunderts*, in *Francia* xiv (1986), 708–10
—— 'Early medieval canon law and the beginnings of knighthood', in Fenske, Rösener and Zotz, *Institutionen, Kultur und Gesellschaft im Mittelalter*, 549–66 (repr. in his *Communications and power*, i. 57–71)
—— *Communications and power in medieval Europe*, I: *The Carolingian and Ottonian centuries*, ed. T. Reuter, London 1994
—— *Communications and power in medieval Europe*, II: *The Gregorian revolution and beyond*, ed. T. Reuter, London 1994
Little, L. K., 'Les Techniques de la confession et la confession comme technique', in *Faire croire: modalités de la diffusion et de la reception des messages religieux du X au XIIe siècle* (Collection de l'École française de Rome li, 1981), 87–99
Locatelli, R., 'Les Chanoines et la reforme dans le diocèse de Besançon (vers 1050–1150)', in *Istituzioni monastiche e istituzioni canonicali*, 704–18
Loew, E. A., *The Beneventan script: a history of south Italian minuscule*, 2nd edn, rev. V. Brown, Rome 1980
Longère, J., 'Prière et pénitence', in N. Bériou, J. Berlioz and J. Longère, *Prier au moyen âge: pratiques et expériences (Ve–XVe siècles)*, Turnhout 1991
Lotter, F., 'Ein kanonistisches Handbuch über die Amtspflichten des Pfarrklerus als gemeinsame Vorlage für den Sermo synodalis "Fratres presbyteri" und Reginos Werk "De synodalibus causis" ', *ZRG Kan. Abt.* lxii (1976), 1–57
Louis, R. (ed.), *Études ligériennes d'histoire et d'archéologie médiévales: mémoires et exposés présentés à la semaine d'études médiévales de Saint-Benoit-sur-Loire de 3 au 10 juillet 1969*, Auxerre 1975
Lutterbach, H., 'Intentions – oder Tathaftung? Zum Bussverständnis in den frühmittelalterlichen Bussbüchern', *Frühmittelalterliche Studien* xxix (1995), 120–43
Lynch, J. H., 'Spiritual kinship and sexual prohibitions in early medieval Europe', in S. Kuttner and K. Pennington (eds), *Proceedings of the sixth international congress of medieval canon law*, Vatican City 1985, 271–88
McKitterick [Pierce], R., 'The "Frankish" penitentials', in Baker, *Materials, sources and methods*, 31–9
—— *The Frankish Church and the Carolingian reforms, 789–895*, London 1977
—— 'The Carolingian kings and the see of Rheims, 882–987', in P. Wormald, D. Bullough and R. Collins (eds), *Ideal and reality in Frankish and Anglo-Saxon society*, Oxford 1983, 228–49
—— *The Frankish kingdoms under the Carolingians, 751–987*, London 1983
—— *The Carolingians and the written word*, Cambridge 1989
—— 'Manuscripts and scriptoria in the reign of Charles the Bald, 840–877', in *Giovanni Scoto nel suo tempo: l'organizzazione del sapere in età Carolingia: atti del XXIV convegno storio internazionale: Accademia Tudertina, Centro di studi sulla spiritualità medievale*, Spoleto 1989, 201–34
—— 'Carolingian book production: some problems', *The Library* 6th ser. xii (1990), 1–33

―― 'Unity and diversity in the Carolingian Church', in Swanson, *Unity and diversity*, 59–82
―― (ed.), *Carolingian culture: emulation and innovation*, Cambridge 1994
―― (ed.), *The uses of literacy in early medieval Europe*, Cambridge 1990
―― (ed.), *New Cambridge medieval history*, II: c. 700–900, Cambridge 1995
McLaughlin, M., *Consorting with saints: prayer for the dead in early medieval France*, Ithaca–London 1994
McLynn, N., *Ambrose of Milan: Church and court in a Christian capital*, Berkeley–London 1994
Mahadevan, L., 'Überlieferung und Verbreitung des Bussbuchs *Capitula iudiciorum*', *ZRG Kan. Abt.* lxxii (1986), 17–75
Mansfield, M. C., *The humiliation of sinners: public penance in thirteenth-century France*, Ithaca–London 1995
Martimort, A.-G., *La Documentation liturgique de Dom Edmond Martène: études codicologiques* (SeT cclxxix, 1978)
Martini, A., 'L'*ordo paenitentiae in feria quarta quinquagesimae* del cosiddetto pontificale di Poitiers', in *Mens concordet*, 629–38
Maurer, H., 'St Margarethen in Waldkirch und St Alban in Mainz: zur Rolle der Liturgie bei der Eingliederung eines Klosters in die ottonischen Reichskirche', in Jäschke and Wenskus, *Festschrift für Helmut Beumann*, 215–23
Mayr-Harting, H., *Ottonian book illumination: an historical study*, London 1991
Meens, R., 'Children and confession in the early Middle Ages', in D. Wood (ed.), *The Church and childhood* (SCH xxxi, 1994), 53–65
―― *Het tripartite boeteboek: overlevering en betekenis van vroegmiddeleeuwse biechtvoorschriften (met editie en vertaling van vier tripartita)*, Hilversum 1994
―― 'The frequency and nature of early medieval penance', in Biller and Minnis, *Handling sin*, 35–61
Meersseman, G. G., 'I penitenti nei secoli XI e XII', in *I laici nella societas Christiana dei secoli XI e XII: atti della terza settimane internazionale di studio Mendola 21–27 agosto 1965* (Miscellanea v, Milan 1968)
Mens concordet voci: pour Mgr. A. Martimort à l'occasion de ses quarante années d'enseignement et des vingt ans de la Constitution 'Sacrosanctum Concilium', Paris 1983
Meyer, O., 'Überlieferung und Verberitung des Dekrets des Bischofs Burhard von Worms', *ZRG Kan. Abt.* xxiv (1935), 141–83
Michel, A., 'Pénitence–sacrement: pénitence du IVe concile du Latran à la réforme', in *DTC* xii. 948–1050
―― 'Pénitence–sacrement: la pénitence de la réforme à nos jours', in *DTC* xii. 1050–1127
Miller, M. C., *The formation of a medieval church: ecclesiastical change in Verona, 950–1150*, Ithaca–London 1993
Moeglin, J.-M., 'Harmiscara-harmschar-hachée: le dossier des rituels d'humiliation et de soumission au moyen âge', *Archivum Latinitatis Medii Aevi* liv (1996), 11–65
―― 'Pénitence publique et amende honorable au moyen âge', *Revue historique* ccxcviii (1997), 225–69
Mohrmann, C., *Liturgical Latin: its origin and character*, London 1957
Monticelli, G., *Raterio vescovo di Verona (890–974)*, Milan 1938

Moore, R. I., 'Family, community and cult on the eve of the Gregorian Reform', *TRHS* 5th ser. xxx (1980), 49–69
—— *The origins of European dissent*, 2nd edn, Oxford 1985
Mor, C. G., 'La reazione al "Decretum Burchardi" in Italia avanti la riforma Gregoriana', *Studi Gregoriani* i (1947), 197–206
Mordek, H., 'Handschriftenforschungen in Italien 1: zur Überlieferung des Dekrets Bischof Burchards von Worms', in *Quellen und Forschungen aus italienischen Archiven und Bibliotheken* li (1971), 626–51
—— *Kirchenrecht und Reform im Frankenreich: die 'Collectio vetus Gallica', die älteste systematische Kanonessammlung des Fränkischen Gallen*, Berlin 1975
Morin, D. G., 'Règlements inédits du Pape S. Grégoire VII pour les chanoines réguliers', *Rev. Bén.* xviii (1901), 177–83
Morin, J., *Commentarius historicus de disciplina in administratione sacramenti poenitentiae tredecim primis seculis in ecclesia occidentali, et hucusque in orientali observata, in decem libros distinctus*, Paris 1651
Morris, C., *The discovery of the individual, 1050–1200*, London 1972
—— *The papal monarchy: the western Church from 1050 to 1250*, Oxford 1989
Morrison, K. F., 'Canossa: a revision', *Traditio* xviii (1962), 121–48
—— 'Cardinal', in *New Catholic encyclopedia*, iii. 104–5
Mortimer, R., *The origins of private penance in the western Church*, Oxford 1939
Morton, C., 'Pope Alexander II and the Norman conquest', *Latomus* xxxiv (1975), 362–82
Mostert, M., *The political theology of Abbo of Fleury: a study of the ideas about society and law of the tenth-century monastic reform movement*, Hilversum 1987
Müller, J., *Untersuchungen zur Collectio duodecim partium*, Ebelsbach 1989
Müller, K., 'Der Umschwung in der Lehre von der Busse während des 12. Jahrhunderts', in *Theologische Abhandlungen: Carol von Weizsäcker zu seinem siebsigsten Geburtstage 11 December 1892*, Freiburg 1892, 289–320
Murray, A., 'Confession as a historical source in the thirteenth century', in R. H. C. Davis and J. M. Wallace-Hadrill (eds), *The writing of history in the Middle Ages: essays presented to R. W. Southern*, Oxford 1981, 275–322
—— 'Confession before 1215', *TRHS* 6th ser. iii (1993), 51–81
—— 'Counselling in medieval confession', in Biller and Minnis, *Handling sin*, 63–77
Mütherich, F., L. Grodecki, J. Taralon, and F. Wormald, *Le Siècle de l'an mil*, Paris 1973
Nelson, J. L., 'Ritual and reality', in Baker, *Materials, sources and methods*, 41–51 (repr. in her *Politics and ritual*, 329–39)
—— 'Kingship, law and liturgy in the political thought of Hincmar of Rheims', *EHR* xcii (1977), 241–79 (repr. in her *Politics and ritual*, 133–71)
—— 'The earliest surviving royal *ordo*: some liturgical and historical aspects', in B. Tierney and P. Linehan (eds), *Authority and power: studies in medieval law and government presented to Walter Ullmann*, Cambridge 1980, 29–48 (repr. in her *Politics and ritual*, 341–60)
—— 'The rites of the Conqueror', *Proceedings of the fourth Battle conference on Anglo-Norman studies*, Woodbridge 1982, 117–32, 210–21 (repr. in her *Politics and ritual*, 375–401)
—— 'Public histories and private history in the work of Nithard', *Speculum* lx (1985), 251–93 (repr. in her *Politics and ritual*, 195–237)

—— *Politics and ritual in medieval Europe*, London 1986
—— 'The second English *ordo*', in her *Politics and ritual*, 361–74
—— 'Making ends meet: wealth and poverty in the Carolingian Church', in Sheils and Wood, *The Church and wealth*, 25–36 (repr. in her *Frankish world*, 145–53)
—— 'Ninth-century knighthood: the evidence of Nithard', in C. Harper-Bill, C. Holdsworth and J. L. Nelson (eds), *Studies in medieval history presented to R. Allen Brown*, Woodbridge 1989, 255–66 (repr. in her *Frankish world*, 75–87)
—— 'The problematic in the private', *Social History* xv (1990), 355–64
—— 'Gender and genre in women historians of the early Middle Ages', in J.-P. Genet (ed.), *L'Historiographie médiévale en Europe: Paris 29 mars–1 avril 1989*, Paris 1991, 149–63 (repr. in her *Frankish world*, 183–97)
—— *The Frankish world, c. 750–c. 900*, London 1996
—— 'Violence in the Carolingian world and the ritualisation of ninth-century warfare', in G. Halsall (ed.), *Violence and society in the early medieval west*, Woodbridge 1998, 90–107
—— 'Monks, secular men and masculinity, c. 900', in D. M. Hadley (ed.), *Masculinity in medieval Europe*, London–New York 1999, 121–42
Neunheuser, B., 'Les Gestes de la prière à genoux et de la génuflexion dans les églises de rite romain', in *Gestes et paroles dans les diverses familles liturgiques: Conférence Saint-Serge XXIVe semaine d'études liturgiques, Paris, 28 Juin–1er Juillet 1977* (Bibliotheca 'Ephemerides Liturgicae' subsidia xiv, 1978), 153–65
Niermeyer, J. F., *Mediae latinitatis lexicon minus*, Leiden 1976
Nightingale, J., 'Bishop Gerard of Toul (963–94) and attitudes to episcopal office', in T. Reuter (ed.), *Warriors and churchmen in the high Middle Ages: essays presented to Karl Leyser*, London–Rio Grande 1992, 41–62
—— 'Oswald, Fleury and continental reform', in N. Brooks and C. Cubitt (eds), *St Oswald of Worcester: life and influence*, London–New York 1996, 23–45
Noble, T. F. X., 'Louis the Pious and his piety reconsidered', *Revue belge de philologie et d'histoire* lviii (1980), 297–316
Nocent, A., 'La Pénitence dans les *ordines* locaux transcrits dans le *De antiquis ecclesiae ritibus* d'Édmond Martène', *Studia Anselmiana* xci/*Analecta Liturgica* x (1986), 115–38
Oakley, T. P., *English penitential discipline and Anglo-Saxon law in their joint influence*, New York 1923
—— 'Some neglected aspects in the history of penance', *Catholic Historical Review* xxiv (1938–9), 293–309
—— 'The penitentials as a source for medieval history', *Speculum* xv (1940), 210–23
Palazzo, É., 'Les deux Rituels d'un *libellus* de Saint-Amand (Paris, BN lat. 13764)', in de Clerck and Palazzo, *Rituels*, 423–36
—— *Histoire des livres liturgiques: le moyen âge: des origines au XIIIème siècle*, Paris 1993
—— *Les Sacramentaires de Fulda: étude sur l'iconographie et la liturgie à l'époque ottonienne*, Münster 1994
—— *A history of liturgical books from the beginning to the thirteenth century*, Collegeville 1998 (trans. by M. Beaumont of *Histoire des livres liturgiques: le moyen âge: des origines au XIIIème siècle*, Paris 1993)

Parisse, M., *La Nécrologie de Gorze: contribution à l'histoire monastique* (Annales de l'est. Memoire xl), Nancy 1971

—— 'Les Chanoinesses dans l'empire germanique (IXe–XIe siècles)', *Francia: Forschungen zur westeuropäischen Geschichte* vi (1978), 107–26

—— 'L'Évêque impérial dans son diocèse: l'exemple lorrain aux Xe et XIe siècles', in Fenske, Rösener and Zotz, *Institutionen, Kultur und Gesellschaft im Mittelalter*, 179–93

—— 'Les Hommes et le pouvoir dans la Lorraine en l'an mil', in Iogna-Prat and Picard, *Religion et culture autour de l'an mil*, 259–66

—— 'Princes laïques et/ou moines, les évêques du Xe siècle', in *Il secolo di ferro* (Settimane xxxviii, 1991), 449–513

Parsons, D. (ed.), *Tenth-century studies: essays in commemoration of the millenium of the Council of Winchester and Regularis concordia*, London 1975

Paul, J., *L'Église et la culture en occident IXe–XIIe siècles*, Paris 1986

Paxton, F., *Christianizing death: the creation of a ritual process in early medieval Europe*, Ithaca–London 1990

Payen, J.-C., *Le Motif du repentir dans la littérature française médiévale: des origines à 1230*, Geneva 1967

Payer, P. J., 'Early medieval regulations concerning marital sexual relations', *Journal of Medieval History* vi (1980), 353–76

—— 'The humanity of the penitentials and the continuity of the penitential tradition', *Mediaeval Studies* xlvi (1984), 340–54

—— *Sex and the penitentials: the development of a sexual code, 550–1150*, Toronto 1984

Pelster, F., 'Das Dekret Bischof Burkhards von Worms (1000–1025) in vatikanischen Handschriften', in *Miscellanea Giovanni Mercati II* (SeT cxxii, 1946), 114–57

—— 'Das Dekret Burkhards von Worms in einer Redaktion aus dem Beginn der Gregorianischen Reform', *Studi Gregoriani* i (1947), 321–51

Peters, E., 'The death of the subdean: ecclesiastical order and disorder in eleventh-century Francia', in B. S. Bachrach and D. Nicholas (eds), *Law, custom and the social fabric in medieval Europe: essays in honour of Bryce Lyon*, Kalamazoo, Michigan 1992, 51–71

Pétrau-Gay, J., 'Burchard de Worms', in *Dictionnaire de droit canonique*, ii. 1141–57

Pfaff, R. W., *Medieval latin liturgy: a select bibliography*, Toronto 1982

Pierce [McKitterick], R., 'The "Frankish" penitentials', in Baker, *Materials, sources and methods*, 31–9

Platelle, H., 'Les Relations entre l'abbaye Saint-Amand de Rouen et l'abbaye Saint-Amand d'Elnone', in *La Normandie bénédictine au temps de Guillaume le Conquérant (XIe siècle)*, Lille 1967, 83–106

—— 'La Violence et ses remèdes en Flandre au XIe siècle', *Sacris Erudiri: Jaarboek voor Godsdienstwetenschappen* xx (1971), 101–73

—— 'La Paroisse et son curé jusqu'à la fin du XIIIe siècle: orientations de la recherche actuelle', in *L'Encadrement religieux des fidèles*, i. 11–26

Plotzek, J. M., K. Winnekes, S. Kraus (eds), *Biblioteca Apostolica Vaticana: Liturgie und Andacht im Mittelalter*, Stuttgart–Zurich 1992

Poggiaspalla, F., *La vita comuna del clero dalle origino alla riforma gregoriana*, Rome 1968

Pokorny, R., 'Die Kanones der Trierer synode des Jahres 927(?): ein Textfund zu den Capitula Ruotgers von Trier', *DA* xxxviii (1982), 1–25
—— 'Nochmals zur Admonitio Synodalis', *ZRG Kan. Abt.* lxxi (1985), 20–51
Pontal, O., *Les Statuts synodaux* (Typologie xi, 1975)
Poschmann, B., *Die abendländische Kirchenbusse in Ausgang des christlichen Altertums*, Munich 1928
—— *Die abendländische Kirchenbusse im frühen Mittelalter*, Breslau 1930
—— *Penance and the anointing of the sick*, Freiburg–London 1964 (trans. by F. Courtney of *Busse und letzte Ölung*, Freiburg-im-Breisgau 1951)
Prinz, F., *Klerus und Krieg im früheren Mittelalter*, Stuttgart 1971
Rädle, F., 'Smaragdus von St Mihiel', in *LMA* vii. 2011–12
Rasmussen, N. K., 'Le "Pontifical" de Beauvais (IXe–Xe siècle)', in *Studia Patristica, X: Texte und Untersuchungen zur Geschichte der altchristen Literatur*, cvii, Berlin 1970, 410–18
—— 'Unité et diversité des pontificaux latins au VIIIe, IXe et Xe siècles', in *Liturgie de l'église particulière et liturgie de l'église universelle: conférences Saint-Serge XXIIe semaine d'études liturgiques, Paris, 30 juin–3 juillet 1975* (Bibliotheca 'Ephemerides Liturgicae' subsidia vii, 1976), 393–410
—— 'Célébration épiscopale et célébration presbytérale: un essai de typologie', in *Segni e riti*, 581–603
—— *Les Pontificaux de haut moyen âge: genèse du livre liturgique de l'évêque*, Louvain 1998
Reicke, S., 'Der Hammersteinische Ehehandel im Lichte der mittelalterlichen Herrschaftsordnung', *Rheinische Vierteljahrsblätter* xxxviii (1974), 203–24
Reuter, T., 'The "imperial church system" of the Ottonian and Salian rulers: a reconsideration', *JEH* xxxiii (1982), 347–74
—— *Germany in the early Middle Ages, c. 800–c. 1050*, London 1991
—— 'Unruhestiftung, Fehde, Rebellion, Widerstand: Gewalt und Frieden in der Politik der Salierzeit', in S. Weinfurter (ed.), *Die Salier und das Reich*, Sigmaringen 1991, iii. 297–325
—— '*Filii matris nostrae pugnant adversum nos*: bonds and tensions between prelates and their *milites* in the German high Middle Ages', in *Chiesa e mondo feudale nei secoli X–XII: atti della dodecisma settimana internazionale di studio Mendola, 24–28 agosto 1992*, Milan 1995, 247–76
Reynolds, R. E., 'Rites of separation and reconciliation in the early Middle Ages', in *Segni e riti*, 405–33
—— 'The ritual of clerical ordination of the sacramentarium gelasianum saec. VIII: early evidence from southern Italy', in de Clerck and Palazzo, *Rituels*, 437–45
—— 'The organisation, law and liturgy of the western Church, 700–900', in McKitterick, *New Cambridge medieval history*, ii. 587–621
Reynolds, S., *Kingdoms and communities in western Europe, 900–1300*, Oxford 1984
—— 'Social mentalities and the case of medieval scepticism', *TRHS* 6th ser. i (1991), 21–41
—— *Fiefs and vassals: the medieval evidence reinterpreted*, Oxford 1994
Riché, P., 'Les Bibliothèques de trois aristocrates laïcs carolingiens', *Le Moyen Âge* lxix (1963), 87–104 (repr. in his *Instruction et vie religieuse dans le haut moyen âge*, London 1981, no. viii)

Richter, M., *The formation of the medieval west: studies in the oral culture of the barbarians*, Dublin 1994
Rieckenberg, H. J., 'Das Geburtsdatum der Kaiserin Gisela', *DA* ix (1952), 535–8
Robert Edwards, G., 'Purgatory: "birth" or evolution?', *JEH* xxxvi (1985), 634–46
Rose, V., *Verzeichniss der lateinischen Handschriften der königlichen Bibliothek zu Berlin*, I: *Die Meerman-Handschriften des Sir Thomas Phillips*, Berlin 1893
Rosenwein, B., 'Feudal war and monastic peace: Cluniac liturgy as ritual aggression', *Viator* ii (1971), 129–57
—— *Rhinoceros bound: Cluny in the tenth century*, Philadelphia 1982
—— *To be the neighbour of Saint Peter: the social meaning of Cluny's property, 909–1049*, Ithaca–London 1989
Rubellin, M., 'Vision de la société chrétienne à travers la confession et la pénitence au IXe siécle', in Groupe de la Bussière, *Pratiques de la confession*, 53–70
Russell, F. H., *The just war in the Middle Ages*, Cambridge, 1975
Ryan, J. J., 'Observations on the pre-Gratian canonical collections: some recent work and present problems', in *Collections de droit canonique médiéval: Louvain et Bruxelles 22–26 juillet 1958* (Bibliothèque de la Revue d'histoire ecclésiastique xxxiii, 1959), 88–103
Salmon, P., *Les Manuscrits liturgiques latins de la Bibliothèque Vaticane* (SeT ccli, ccliii, cclxi, cclxvii, cclxx, 1968–72)
—— 'Livrets de prières de l'époque carolingienne', *Rev. Bén.* lxxxvi (1976), 218–34
—— 'Un *Libellus officialis* du XIe siècle', *Rev. Bén.* lxxxvii (1977), 257–88
—— 'Un Témoin de la vie chrétienne dans une église de Rome au XIe siècle: le "liber officialis" de la Basilique des Saints-Apôtres', *Rivista di storia della chiesa in Italia* xxxiii (1979), 65–73
—— 'Livrets de prières de l'époque carolingienne: nouvelle liste de manuscrits', *Rev. Bén.* xc (1980), 147–9
Sandmann, M., 'Die Folge der Äbte', in Schmid, *Klostergemeinschaft*, i. 178–204
—— 'Wirkungsbereiche fuldischer Mönche', in Schmid, *Klostergemeinschaft*, ii. 743–4
—— 'Fulda: Kloster, "Schule" und Bibliothek', in *LMA* iv. 1020–2
Schieffer, R., 'Von Mailand nach Canossa: ein Beitrag zur Geschichte der christlichen Herrscherbusse von Theodosius der Grosse bis zu Heinrich IV', *DA* xxviii (1972), 333–70
—— 'Kanoniker', in *LMA* v. 903–4.
Schmid, K., 'Neue Quellen zum Verständnis des Adels im 10. Jahrhundert', in E. Hlawitschka (ed.), *Königswahl und Thronfolge in ottonisch-frühdeutscher Zeit*, Darmstadt 1971, 389–416
—— (ed.), *Die Klostergemeinschaft von Fulda in früheren Mittelalter*, Münster 1978
Schmitz, G., 'Das Konzil von Trosly (909): Überlieferung und Quellen', *DA* xxxiii (1977), 341–434
Schneidmüller, B., 'Französische Lothringenpolitik im 10. Jahrhundert', *Jahrbuch für westdeutsche Landesgeschichte* v (1979), 1–31
Schnith, K., 'Recht und Friede: zum Königsgedanken im Umkreis Heinrichs III.', *Historisches Jahrbuch* lxxxi (1962), 22–57

Schröder, I., *Die westfränkischen Synoden von 888 bis 987 und ihre Überlieferung* (MGH, Hilfsmittel iii, 1980)

Schroll, A., *Benedictine monasticism as reflected in the Warnefrid-Hildemar commentaries on the rule*, New York 1941

Schwark, B., *Bischof Rather von Verona als Theologe: ein Beitrag zur Geschichte der Theologie im Zeitalter der Ottonen*, Königsberg 1916

Schwenk, B., 'Das Hundetragen: ein Rechtsbrauch im Mittelalter', *Historisches Jahrbuch* cx (1990), 289–308

Il secolo di ferro (Settimane xxxviii, 1991)

Segni e riti nella chiesa altomedievale occidentale (Settimane xxxiii, 1987)

Semmler, J., 'Das Erbe der karolingischen Klosterreform im 10. Jahrhundert', in Kottje and Maurer, *Monastische Reformen*, 29–77

—— 'Institutiones Aquisgranenses', in LMA v. 451–2

Sergi, G., 'Movimento signorile e affermazione ecclesiastica nel contesto distrettuale di Pombia e Novara fra X e XI secolo', SM 3rd ser. xvi (1975), 153–206

Sheils, W. J. and D. Wood (eds), *The Church and wealth* (SCH xxiv, 1987)

Siegwart, J., *Die Chorherren- und Chorfrauengemeinschaften in der deutschsprachigen Schweiz von 6. Jahrhundert bis 1160 mit einem Überblick über die deutsche Kanonikerreform des 10. und 11. Jahrhundert*, Freiburg 1962

Smith, J. M. H., 'Religion and lay society', in McKitterick, *New Cambridge medieval history*, ii. 654–78

Sot, M., *Un Historien et son église au XIe siècle: Flodoard de Reims*, Paris 1993

Southern, R. W., *The making of the Middle Ages*, London 1953, repr. London 1987

Stafford, P., *Queens, concubines and dowagers: the king's wife in the early Middle Ages*, London–Washington, DC 1998

Steindorff, E., *Jahrbücher des deutschen Reichs unter Heinrich III.*, Leipzig 1874–81

Sumption, J., *Pilgrimage: an image of mediaeval religion*, London 1975

Swanson, R. (ed.), *Unity and diversity in the Church* (SCH xxxii, 1996)

Symons, T., 'Regularis concordia: history and derivation', in Parsons, *Tenth-century studies*, 37–59

Tellenbach, G., *Church, state and Christian society at the time of the Investiture Controversy*, Oxford 1940

—— *The Church in western Europe from the tenth to the early twelfth century*, Cambridge 1993 (trans. by T. Reuter of *Die westliche Kirche vom 10. bis zum frühen 12. Jahrhunderts*, 1988)

Tentler, T., *Sin and confession on the eve of the Reformation*, Princeton, NJ 1977

Thacker, A., 'Monks, preaching and pastoral care in early Anglo-Saxon England', in Blair and Sharpe, *Pastoral care before the parish*, 137–70

Theuerkauf, G., *Lex, speculum, compendium iuris: Rechtsaufzeichnung und Rechtsbewusstsein in Norddeutschland vom 8. bis zum 16. Jahrhundert*, Cologne–Graz 1968

Thomas, H., 'Zur Kritik an der Ehe Heinrichs III. mit Agnes von Poitou', in Jäschke and Wenskus, *Festschrift für Helmut Beumann*, 224–35

Timmers, J., 'Busse, Buss-Sakrament', in *Lexikon der christlichen Ikonographie*, i. 344

Török, J., 'Influence lotharingiennes sur la liturgie d'Europe centrale autour de l'an mil', in Iogna-Prat and Picard, *Religion et culture*, 285–89

Turner, D. H., 'The prayerbook of Archbishop Arnulph II of Milan', *Rev. Bén.* lxx (1960), 360–92

Turner, V., *The forest of symbols: aspects of Ndembu ritual*, Ithaca–London 1967

—— *From ritual to theatre: the human seriousness of play*, New York 1982

Tyrer, J. W., *Historical survey of Holy Week: its services and ceremonial* (Alcuin Club Collections xxix, 1932)

Uhlirz, M., *Jahrbücher des deutschen Reiches unter Otto II. und Otto III.*, II: *Otto III., 983–1002*, Berlin 1954

Vacandard, E., 'Confession du Ier au XIIIe siècle', in *DTC* iii/1, 838–94

Vezin, J., *Les Scriptoria d'Angers au XIe siècle*, Paris 1974

—— 'Les Manuscrits en Lotharingie autour de l'an mil', in Iogna-Prat and Picard, *Religion et culture*, 309–14

Vodola, E., *Excommunication in the Middle Ages*, Berkeley–Los Angeles–London 1986

Vogel, C., 'La Discipline pénitentielle en Gaule des origines au IXe siècle: le dossier hagiographique', *Revue des sciences religieuses* xxx (1956), 1–26, 157–86 (repr. in his *En Rémission*, no. vi)

—— 'L'Oeuvre liturgique de Mgr. M. Andrieu: un bilan provisoire', *Revue des sciences religieuses* xxxi (1957), 7–19

—— 'Composition légale et commutations dans le système de la pénitence tarifée', *Revue du droit canonique* viii, ix (1958, 1959), 289–318, 1–38, 341–59 (repr. in his *En Rémission*, no. v)

—— 'Précisions sur la date et l'ordonnance primitive du pontifical romano-germanique', *Ephemerides Liturgicae* lxxiv (1960), 145–62

—— 'Le Pontifical romano-germanique du Xe siècle: nature, date et importance du document', *Cahiers de civilisation médiévale* vi (1963), 27–48

—— 'Le Pèlerinage pénitentiel', *Revue des sciences religieuses* xxxviii (1964), 113–53 (repr. in his *En Rémission*, no. vii)

—— *Le Pécheur et la pénitence dans l'église ancienne*, Paris 1966

—— 'Les Rites de la pénitence publique aux Xe et XI siècles', in P. Gallais and Y.-J. Riou (eds), *Mélanges René Crozet*, Poitiers 1966, i. 137–44 (repr. in his *En Rémission*, no. viii)

—— *Le Pécheur et la pénitence au moyen âge*, Paris 1969

—— 'Pratiques superstitieuses au début du XIe siècle d'après le *Corrector sive medicus* de Burchard, évêque de Worms (965–1025)', in *Mélanges E.-R. Labande: études de civilisation médiévale (IXe–XIIe siècles)*, Poitiers 1974, 751–61 (repr. in his *En rémission*, no. x)

—— 'Les Rituels de la pénitence tarifée', in *Liturgia opera divina et umana: studi offerti à S. E. Mons. A. Bugnini*, Rome 1982, 419–27 (repr. in his *En Rémission*, no. xi)

—— Les '*Libri paenitentiales*' (Typologie xxvi, 1978), rev. A. J. Frantzen 1985

—— *Medieval liturgy: an introduction to the sources*, Washington, DC 1986 (trans. and rev. by W. Storey and N. Rasmussen with J. K. Brooks-Leonard of *Introduction aux sources de l'histoire du culte chrétien au moyen âge*, Spoleto 1966, rev. 1975)

—— *En Rémission des péchés: recherches sur les systèmes pénitentiels dans l'église latine*, ed. A. Faivre, Aldershot 1994

von Heinemann, O. (ed.), *Die Handschriften des Herzoglichen Bibliothek zu Wolfenbüttel*, Wolfenbüttel 1900–13

Vor dem Jahr 1000: abendländische Buchkunst zur Zeit der Kaiserin Theophanu: eine Ausstellung des Schnütgen-Museums zum Gedenken an den 1000. Todestag der Kaiserin Theophanu am 15. Juni 991 undiht Begräbnis in St. Pantaleon zu Köln, Cologne 1991

Wallace-Hadrill, J. M., *The Frankish Church*, Oxford 1983

Ward, B., *Miracles and the medieval mind: theory, record and event, 1000–1215*, Aldershot 1982

Warner, D., 'Henry II at Magdeburg: kingship, ritual and the cult of the saints', EME iii (1994), 135–66

—— 'Thietmar of Merseburg on rituals of kingship', *Viator* xxvi (1995), 53–76

Warner, G. F., *Descriptive catalogue of the illuminated manuscripts in the library of C. W. Dyson-Perrins*, Oxford 1920

Wasserschleben, F., *Beitraege zur Geschichte der vorgratianischen Kirchenrechtsquellen*, Leipzig 1839

Watkins, O. D., *A history of penance*, London 1920

Weigle, F., 'Ratherius von Verona im Kampf um das Kirchengut 961–68', *Quellen und Forschungen aus italienischen Archiven und Bibliotheken* xxviii (1937–8), 1–35

—— 'Il processo di Raterio di Verona', *Studi storici veronesi* iv (1953), 29–44

Wemple, S., 'The canonical resources of Atto of Vercelli (926–960)', *Traditio* xxvi (1970), 335–50

—— *Atto of Vercelli: Church, State and Christian society in tenth-century Italy*, Rome 1979

Werminghoff, A., 'Die Beschlüsse des Aachener Concils im Jahre 816', *Neues Archiv der Gesellschaft für ältere deutsche Geschichtskunde* xxvii (1902), 607–75

Werner, K. F., '*Hludovicus Augustus*: gouverner l'empire chrétien – idées et réalités', in P. Godman and R. Collins (eds), *Charlemagne's heir: new perspectives on the reign of Louis the Pious (814–40)*, Oxford 1990, 3–123

White, S. D., *Custom, kinship and gifts to saints: the 'laudatio parentum' in western France, 1050–1150*, Chapel Hill–London 1988

Wickham, C., 'Land disputes and their social framework in Lombard-Carolingian Italy, 700–900', in W. Davies and P. Fouracre (eds), *The settlement of disputes in early medieval Europe*, Cambridge 1986, 105–24

—— 'Lawyers' time: history and memory in tenth- and eleventh-century Italy', in his *Land and power: studies in Italian and European social history, 400–1200*, London 1994, 275–93

Wilmart, A., *Codices reginenses latini*, Vatican 1937–45

Witters, W., 'Smaragde au moyen âge: la diffusion de ses écrits d'après la tradition manuscrite', in Louis, *Études Ligériennes*, 361–76

Wolf, G., 'Der sogenannte "Gegenkönig" Arduin von Ivrea (ca. 955–1015)', *Archiv für Diplomatik: Schriftsgeschichte Siegel- und Wappenkunde* xxxix (1993), 19–34

Wollasch, J., 'Gerard de Brogne und seine Klostergründung', *Rev. Bén.* lxx (1960), 62–82, 224–31

—— *Mönchtum des Mittelalters zwischen Kirche und Welt*, Munich 1973

Wolter, H., *Die Synoden im Reichsgebiet und in Reichsitalien von 916 bis 1056*, Paderborn–Munich–Vienna–Zurich 1988

Wood, I., 'The *Vita Columbani* and Merovingian hagiography', *Peritia* i (1982), 63–80

Zelzer, K., 'Überlegungen zu einer Gesamtedition des frühnachkarolingischen Kommentars zur Regula S. Benedicti aus der Tradition des Hildemar von Corbie', *Rev. Bén.* xci (1981), 373–82

Unpublished material

Forshaw, H. P., 'The pastoral ministry of the priest-confessor in the early Middle Ages, 600–1100: a study of the origins and development of the role of the priest-confessor in the administration of private ecclesiastical penance in the west', unpubl. PhD diss. London 1975

Hamilton, S., 'The practice of penance, c. 900 – c. 1050', unpubl. PhD diss. London 1997

Meens, R., 'Priests and books in the Carolingian era', unpubl. paper delivered at the International Medieval Congress, University of Leeds, 15 July 1998

Morison, P. R., 'The miraculous and French society, c. 950–1100', unpubl. DPhil. diss. Oxford 1983

Nightingale, J., 'Monasteries and their patrons in the dioceses of Trier, Metz and Toul, *circa* 850–1000', unpubl. DPhil. diss. Oxford 1988

Phipps, C., 'Saint Peter Damian's *Vita beati Romualdi*: introduction, translation and analysis', unpubl. PhD diss. London 1988

Reuter, T., 'Canossa: drama or stage-management?', unpubl. paper

Index

Aachen, decrees of (816–17), 81, 98–100
Abbo, abbot of Fleury, 26 n. 6
absolution of penitents, 111, 120–1, 153, 159–60
Admonitio synodalis, 33, 63–7, 71–2
alms, 42, 64, 110, 203
Andrieu, Michel, 131–3, 211, 214
Ansegis, capitulary collection of, 47, 71
Anselm of Lucca, 27, 63
archdeacon, 119, 156, 158, 162
Arduin of Ivrea, penance of, 1–2, 7–8, 13, 173, 207–8
Arezzo, pontifical of, *see* Vatican City, BAV, MS Vat. lat. 4772
Arnulf, archbishop of Rheims, penance of, 186
Arnulph II, archbishop of Milan, prayerbook of, *see* London, BL, MS Egerton 3763
Arras, synod of (1025), 61–2
ashes, imposition of, 59, 92–3, 114–17
Ash Wednesday: entry into penance on, 34–6, 59–60, 73–4, 100, 104, 108–18, 138–40, 152–4, 162; confession on, 38–9, 59–60, 144; monastic service on, 92–3. *See also* ejection of penitents
Atto of Vercelli, *capitula* of, 72–6, 209
audience: for canon law, 27, 29–33, 43–4, 50; for conciliar records, 62–3; for episcopal *capitula*, 67–8; for liturgical books, 128–31, 149, 171–2; for mixed penance, 144; for penitentials, 45–50, 51; for 'public' penance, 115–17, 119–21, 162–3; for 'secret' penance, 148–9, 168–70; for synodal sermons, 66–7
Augsburg: pontifical of, *see* Munich, Bayerische Staatsbibliothek, Clm 3909; sermon by chorepiscopus at, 66–7. *See also* Udalrich
Augustine, 37, 191, 197; rule of, 100
authority: abbatial, 88; episcopal, 1–2, 29, 36–8, 53, 60–1, 65, 69, 72, 162–6; royal, 184–5, 188–90; sacerdotal, 39

baculum, significance of, 110, 139, 205–6

Bamberg, Staatsbibliothek:
MS Can. 6, 35 n. 49
Cod. Lit. 1, 137 n. 3
Cod. Lit. 50, 135 n. 164
Cod. Lit. 53, 127, 135 n. 163, 212
Cod. Lit. 54, 112 n. 39, 117 n. 70, 121, 135 n. 165
Cod. Lit. 55, 129–30, 212
Cod. Lit. 59, 151–2, 155
Beauvais, pontifical of, 150, 152–3, 155
Benedict of Aniane, 81, 84, 99; *Excerptus diversarum modus paenitentiarum*, 85–7; supplement to the *Hadrianum*, 104, 140, 156
Benedict, rule of: on confession, 88; on faults, 81–3, 179. *See also* Hildemar of Civate, Smaragdus
Berlin, Staatsbibliothek, Cod. Hamilton 290, 50, 51 n. 1, 62 n. 70
Bern, abbot of Reichenau, 177–80, 182, 214–15
Besançon pontifical, *see* Wolfenbüttel, Herzog-August-Bibliothek, Cod. Guelf. 15 Weissenburg
bishop: control of penitential process, 36–7; episcopal prerogative, 39, 61, 65, 74–5, 88; laying on of hands, 36, 56, 75, 117; role in Lotharingian world, 163–6. *See also* authority, episcopal
bribes, prohibition of payments to clergy, 60, 63–4, 69
Brunicho, *praepositus* of Worms, 31–2
Burchard, bishop of Worms: government of Worms, 38; *vita*, 31–2. *See also Decretum*

Cambrai, pontifical of, *see* Cologne, Diözesan und Dombibliothek, Cod. 141
Cambridge, Corpus Christi College, MS 163, 129, 213, 218; MS 265, 218–19
canon law collections, 25–44. *See also* audience for canon law
canons, regular, 78–9, 98–103; confession of, 100–2; public penance of, 101–2; 'secret' penance of, 101. *See also* Chrodegang of Metz

269

capitula, episcopal, 67–76; *capitula Antwerpensia*, 70; *capitula Bavarica*, 5; *capitula Cottoniana*, 70–1; of Mainz, 71–2; *Sangallensis*, 70–1, 74; *Trosleiana*, 70. *See also* Atto of Vercelli, Gerbald of Liège, Radulf of Bourges, Ruotger of Trier, Theodulf of Orléans
cardinal priests, 73–4
Carolingian dichotomy, 3, 4–5, 11, 43–4, 82, 127, 207
Carolingians: and church reform, 4, 67–8; and monastic reform, 81, 84; on penance, 4–7, 11–13, 20, 44, 46
Centuriators of Magdeburg, 9–10, 177
Châlons, Council of (813), 5, 38, 42, 56, 60
chrism, collection of, 17, 54, 59, 69; consecration of, 118
Chrodegang of Metz, rule for canons of, 98–102; and interpolated rule, 99–102. *See also* Aachen, decrees of
cilicium, 34, 101, 114
clergy, secular: behaviour expected of, 29; education of, 32, 43–4, 52–76; ownership of books, 51–2; penance of, 38, 186
Cluny, 79–80, 89. *See also* Odo of Cluny, Ulrich of Cluny
Collectio Anselmo dedicata, 32–3, 72, 126 n. 6
Collectio XII partium, 31 n. 27
Collection in Four Books, *see* Cologne, Diözesan und Dombibliothek, MS 124
Collection in LXXIV titles, 47
Collection in 98 Chapters, 30 n. 26
collective penance, 115–17, 204–5
Cologne, Diözesan und Dombibliothek, MS 124, 30 n. 26; Cod. 141, 154–5, 160–1, 213 n. 13
Cologne, penance at, 205; province of, 131–2; Romano-German pontificals of, copies made for, *see* London, BL, MS Add. 17004, MS Cotton Vitellius E.xii
commentaries on the rule of Benedict, *see* Hildemar of Civate, Smaragdus
communal entry into penance, 115–16, 130, 168–70. *See also* collective penance
communion, regular, 5, 58, 60–1, 64, 71
commutation of penance, 41–3, 64, 187, 193, 203, 205
confession, 15; annual, 5, 7, 10, 38–9, 58–9, 60–1, 64, 69–71, 108; devotional, 49; monastic, 88, 91; secrecy of, 122–3. *See also* Ash Wednesday, vernacular
Conrad I, 56, 57, 184
Conrad II, king and emperor, 179, 200
contrition, 7, 11, 15, 59, 75, 112, 119
councils, church, 53–63. *See also* Châlons, Dortmund, Erfurt, Hohenaltheim, Koblenz, Lateran IV, Mainz (847), Mainz (852) Nijmegen, Paris, Pavia, Rheims, Rome, Seligenstadt, Tribur, Trier, Trosly
Cracow, Jagellonian Library, MS 2057, 151, 155–62
Cracow pontifical, *see* Cracow, Jagellonian Library, MS 2057
cura animarum, *see* pastoral care
customaries, monastic, 89–94. *See also* Farfa, Fulda–Trier, Saint Emmeram of Regensburg

deacon, 39, 109, 155
deans, role in public penance, 35–6
Decretum (of Burchard of Worms): audience for, 29, 31–3, 41, 43–4; Book XIX, *De poenitentia*, 25, 27–9, 41, 43–4, 95, 128, 152–3, 192, 204; compilation of, 31–3; dependence on Regino of Prüm, 28, 34–6, 38–41; influence, 128; manuscript diffusion of, 19–20, 33; on public penance, 34–8, 152–3; on 'secret' penance, 18, 27, 38–44, 124; originality, 35, 40, 41–3; sources of, 25, 27–8, 32, 34–6, 38–41, 63
deditio, 184–5, 190
De Jong, Mayke, 7, 12–13, 18, 20, 185
De vera et falsa poenitentia, 15
Dhuoda, *Liber manualis*, 181–3
Dionysiana, 57, 72
Dortmund, Council of (1005), 32

Ealdred, bishop of Worcester and archbishop of York, pontifical of, *see* London, BL, MS Cotton Vitellius E. xii
education, *see* clergy, education of
Egbert, archbishop of Trier, 131–2
Egilbert, bishop of Freising, *see* Freising, pontifical of
Eigenkirchen, 52–3
ejection of penitents, 18, 27, 34, 36, 114, 152, 154
Ekkehard IV of St Gall, 8, 197–9, 204
episcopal capitularies, *see capitula*, episcopal

episcopal handbooks, 29, 30, 45–7, 51–2, 62, 171
Erchanger of Suabia, 57–8, 184
Erfurt, Council of (932), 62
excommunication, 1, 69–70; monastic, 82–3, 86, 90–1
exemption, monastic from episcopal jurisdiction, 142–3

fabula ioca, 204
Farfa, *Liber tramitis*, 80, 88–90, 92
fasting, 42–3, 110, 187, 193, 205
flagellation, *see* flogging
Fleury, 79–80, 89–90, 93
flogging, 90, 100, 202–3
Fontenoy, penitential ordinance of, 192–3, 196
fornication, *see* sexual, sins
Frantzen, Allen, 12, 16, 20, 26, 49
Freising, 51; pontifical of, *see* Munich, Bayerische Staatsbibliothek, Clm 6425
Fulbert, bishop of Chartres, 186
Fulda: abbey of, 79, 137; abbots of, 137, 142–3; liturgy of, 19; miracle book of, 14–15; pastoral tradition of, 97, 146–9; penitential liturgy of, 138–42, 143–50; sacramentary of, 19 n. 86, 122, 134, 136–50, 202 (*see also* Bamberg, Staatsbibliothek, Cod. Lit. 1; Göttingen, Niedersächsische Staats-Universitätsbibliothek, Cod. theol. 231; Vatican City, BAV, MS Vat. lat. 3548; Vercelli, Biblioteca capitolare, Cod. 181; Udine, Biblioteca capitolare, MS 1. *See also* schools, external
Fulda–Trier, monastic customary of, 89–90, 94, 102

Gelasian letter, 178
Gelasian sacramentary, 140, 155; Old Gelasian, 104; eighth-century or Frankish Gelasian, 104, 108, 118, 151, 156, 160
Gerald of Aurillac, 95, 196–7
Gerard, bishop of Cambrai, 61–2
Gerard, bishop of Toul, 164–5
Gerbald of Liège, *capitula* of, 64
Gervinus, abbot of St Riquier, 97–8
gesture, significance of, 112–13, 116, 119
Gisela, empress, 179–81, 200
Gorzian monasticism, 79–80, 89, 93–5
Göttingen, Niedersächsische Staats-Universitätsbibliothek, Cod. theol. 231, 137 n. 3, 138–44, 146–50, 202
Gregory the Great, 56–8, 92, 95, 98

Hadrianum, 104, 140, 156
hairshirt, *see cilicium*
Halitgar of Cambrai, penitential of, 25, 37, 39–40, 44, 46–7, 128, 191–2
Hammerstein, Irmengard of, marriage of, *see* incest
Hammerstein, Otto of, marriage of, *see* incest
harmiscara, 184–5
Hastings, penitential ordinance of, 87–8, 194–6
Hatto, abbot of Fulda and archbishop of Mainz, 27, 137
Henry II, king and emperor, 61, 189–91
Henry III, king and emperor, 175, 177–82, 200
Henry of Bavaria, 132, 188–9
heresy, 61–2
Heriveus, archbishop of Rheims, 55, 191
Hildemar of Civate, *Expostio regulae*, 83–9, 94, 102
Hildersheim, pontifical of, *see* Bamberg, Staatsbibliothek, Cod. Lit. 54
Hincmar, archbishop of Rheims, 177, 191; *capitula* of, 37, 60, 64, 71
Hohenaltheim, Council of (916), 56–8, 62, 184
homicide, 1, 42, 56–7, 147, 173, 190, 203–4
Hrabanus Maurus, 47, 62, 191–2

imprisonment, 118; in a monastery, 1–2, 57, 95
incest, 41, 61, 124, 199–201, 208
infanticide, 204
inquisitio, episcopal, 29, 53
Institutio canonicorum, *see* Aachen, decrees of
Institutio sanctimonialum, *see* Aachen, decrees of
interrogatio, 40, 43, 110–11, 124, 139, 144–5, 169–70
Irmengard of Hammerstein, *see* incest
Iso of St Gall: parents' penance, 197–9. *See also* Ekkehard IV of St Gall
Italy, penance in, 75–6, 166–70, 208–9

Jerome, St, on marriage, 196
John Philagathos, 175–6
Jungmann, Josef, 10, 16, 18, 150, 166–8

Kerff, F., 45
kingship, ideas of, 174–9
Koblenz, Council of (922), 62, 95

laity: Christian duties of, 5, 7, 10, 38–9, 58, 60–1, 64–5, 69–71, 76, 108; voluntary penance of, 197–9
Lateran IV Council (1215), see *omnes utriusque*
Lea, H. C., 10
Lent, duties in, 65, 70, 100. See also confession, annual
Leofric Missal, see Oxford, Bod. Lib., MS Bodley 579
Leyser, Karl, 21–2
Liège, diocese of, 164–5
liturgical books, see pontificals; prayerbooks; *rituale*; sacramentary
liturgy, 105; penitential, 16–17; for public penance, 104, and for Ash Wednesday, 104, 108–18, 127, and for Maundy Thursday, 118–21, 127, 130, and for 'secret' penance, 122–8; manuscripts of, 105–8, 136; monastic, 101, 129–30; of Rome, 16, 106. See also Arezzo, Augsburg, Beauvais, Besançon, Cambrai, Cracow, Freising, Fulda, Hildersheim, Metz, 'Poitiers', Romano-German and Salzburg pontificals
London, BL:
 MS Add. 17004, 135 n. 164, 212–13, 216 n. 30
 MS Cotton Claudius C. vi, 35 n. 49
 MS Cotton Tiberius C. i, 135 n. 164, 219
 MS Cotton Vitellius E. xii, 212–13, 218–19
 MS Egerton 3763, 181 n. 39
Louis the German, 7, 180–1, 192
Louis the Pious, penance of, 6–7, 21, 174–5, 180
Lucca, Biblioteca capitolare, Cod. 607, 133, 215

Magdeburg, diocese of, 132
Mainz: province of, 34, 135, 137, 211–12; Council of (847), 43, 65; Council of (852), 47; primacy dispute, 132; Synod of (950x4), 60–2. See also *capitula*, episcopal
Mansfield, Mary, 7 n. 32, 13, 16–20, 105–7, 116, 143, 150, 152, 155, 161, 166, 209

marriage, 200–1. See also incest
Martène, Edmond, 150
mass, 126–7. See also *missa post confessionem*
Mathilda, queen, 183, 188–90
Maundy Thursday, 16–17, 59, 64, 74; monastic, 93, 130. See also chrism, liturgy, public penance and reconciliation of penitents
Meens, Rob, 14–15, 45, 47, 171
Metz, bishops of, 163–4; pontifical attributed to, see Paris, BN, MS lat. 13313
Michelsberg, Bamberg, pontifical of the monastery of, see Bamberg, Staatsbibliothek Cod. Lit. 55
Milan, Biblioteca Ambrosiana:
 Cod. T. 27, 167–70, 172
 Cod. Z. 52 sup, 134 n. 158, 215
Milan, Biblioteca capitolare, Cod. 53, 134 n. 158, 215
Milan, clergy of, 186–8
miracula, 14–15
missa post confessionem, 113–14, 116, 126
mixed Gregorian-Gelasian sacramentaries, 104, 140, 157
monasticism, tenth-century reform of, 79–80. See also Gorzian monasticism, Cluny, Benedict, rule of
monks, pastoral ministry of, 94–8, 146–50; penitential discipline of, 81–8, 90–1. See also Fulda
Monte Cassino, 202–3
Monte Cassino, Abbey Library, Cod. 451, 134 n. 157, 215. See also Rome, Biblioteca Vallicelliana Cod. D. 5
Monte Gargano, 175–6
Morin, Jean, 10
Munich, Bayerische Staatsbibliothek:
 Clm 3909, 128, 135 n. 164
 Clm 6425, 63 n. 71, 128–9, 135 n. 164, 153, 212 n. 3
 Clm 27246, 62 n. 69
 Clm 30111, 182–3
murder, see homicide
Murray, Alexander, 14–16, 209
mutilation, 175–6

Nijmegen, Council of (1018), 61
Nilus, 98, 175–7
Nithard, 192–3, 196
north-central family of rites for public penance, 150–63, 166; Ash Wednesday, 152–4; comparison with

the Romano-German pontifical, 152, 155–62; reconciliation of penitents, 155–62

Odo of Cluny, 80, 89, 196. *See also* Gerald of Aurillac
omnes utriusque (Lateran IV [1215], c. 21), 7, 10, 13, 19
Otto I, king and emperor, 131, 133, 182, 184, 188–90
Otto III, king and emperor, 98, 175–7, 182–3. *See also* prayerbooks
Otto, count of Hammerstein, *see* incest
Oxford, Bodl. Lib., MS Bodley 579, 218

paenitentia occulta, *see* penance, secret
paenitentia publica, *see* penance, public
pagan practices, *see* superstitions
Paris, Bibliothèque nationale:
  MS lat. 820, 216
  MS lat. 1207 (I), 51–2
  MS lat. 1231, 135 n. 165
  MS lat. 13313, 151–5, 161
Paris, Council of (829), 6
parish, 52–3
parricide, 190. *See also* homicide
pastoral care, 11; monastic delivery of, 96–8, 146–50
Patarini, 186–7
Pavia, Council of (850), 75
peace-making, 39, 69–70
penance: as baptism, 38, 59, 70, 77, 119, 199; on behalf of the dead, 180–1; canonical (late antique), 3–4; Carolingian, 4–7; conduct of, 61; depiction of, 148–9; historiography of, 9–17; 'in the usual way', 122–8; language of, 209–10; as medicine, 25, 38, 82 n. 33; mixed, 8–9, 13, 138–50, 197–9, 207, 209; monastic, 84, 86–7, 125, 138–50, 179; one-stop procedure for, 11, 18–19, 27, 144, 153, 166–7; parochial, 171–2; personal, 14–15; public, 6–7, 13, 18, 21, 36–8, 57–61, 63, 73–5, 108–22, 140, 143–4, 150–63, 204–5; purpose of, 21–2; sacerdotal administration of, 73–5; secret (including tariff), 3–4, 7, 12–13, 18, 21, 38–44, 48–9, 101–2, 166–70; solemn penance, 7, 13; tripartite periodisation of, 2–8, 13. *See also* Carolingian dichotomy, collective penance, communal entry into penance, commutation, liturgy

penances: according to status, 110, 124, 203; examples of, 42, 56, 73, 124, 187, 193–4, 197–8, 200–1. *See also cicilicium*, commutation of penance, fasting, flogging, pilgrimage
penitential: attributed to Bede, 28, 128; Bede–Egbert double, 40, 47; 'Roman', 28; tripartite, 45, 171. *See also* Halitgar, Theodore
penitential ordinance, *see* Fontenoy, Hastings, Soissons
penitentials, 16, 44–50, 208; Anglo-Saxon, 12, 16, 26, 44; Frankish, 6, 44, 46–8; Italian, 48–50; judicial purpose of, 45–7, 64, 74; manuscripts of, 25–6, 44, 46–9; ownership of, 47–8, 51–2; pastoral purpose of, 45, 47–50. *See also* audience, penitentials for
penitents: behaviour of, 3, 6, 21, 57–8, 61, 75; detection of, 59–60, 69; recording of, 70–1, 74; supervision of, 61, 173. *See also* ejection, excommunication, imprisonment
Pentecost, 23; octave of, 73
perjury, 56–8, 147
Peter Damian, 98, 122, 175–7, 186–8, 202
pilgrimage, penitential, 7, 13, 42–3, 173–4, 187
Pistoia, Biblioteca capitolare, Cod. 141, 133, 215
'Poitiers' pontifical, 105, 112, 118, 141
pontificals, 104. *See also* Arezzo, Augsburg, Beauvais, Besancon, Cambrai, Cracow, Freising, Hildersheim, Metz, 'Poitiers', Romano-German
Poschmann, Bernhard, 10, 11, 18, 118
prayerbooks, 182–3. *See also* London, BL, MS Egerton 3763; Munich, Bayerische Staatsbibliothek, Clm 30111
preparation for penance by priest, 111
priest, behaviour expected of, 60, 63
psalms, penitential, 91, 113, 124, 144
Pseudo-Augustine, 56 n. 32, 77 n. 2
Pseudo-Isidore, 72
public and private, 7–8
publicity of penance, 4, 7, 74, 117, 122–3
punishment, political, 1–2, 57, 95, 184–99, 190

Radulf of Bourges, *capitula*, 59, 65, 70
Rathbod, archbishop of Trier, 27
Rather, bishop of Verona, 63–6, 98
reconciliation of penitents, 37, 65, 73–5, 118–21, 126–7, 138–9, 140–1, 143–4,

155–63, 184–90, 204; monastic, 83, 91, 93–4. *See also* bishop, episcopal prerogative and Maundy Thursday
Reformation, 9
Regensburg, *see* Saint Emmeram
Regino of Prüm, *Libri duo de synodalibus causis et disciplinis ecclesiasticis*: audience for, 27–9, 43–4; bishop's relations with clergy, 29, 203; compilation of, 27–8, 39–40; *inquisitio*, 53, 64–5, 203; manuscripts of, 30; *Nachleben*, 29–31, 58, 65, 71–2, 160–1; on public penance, 18–19, 34–8, 59–60, 75, 110, 116; on 'secret' penance, 38–44; on war, 192
regular clergy, *see* monks, canons
Regularis concordia (c. 970), 80, 93, 130
Reichenau, 79, 214. *See also* Bern
Rheims: episcopal *capitula*, 70–1; provincial councils of, 54, 55–6
rituale, 48, 171–2
Romano-German pontifical, 18–19, 104, 106–38; dissemination of, 131–5, 211–19; manuscripts of, 106–7, 121, 133–5, 211–19; monastic users of, 129–30; on penance 'in the usual way', 122–8, 203; on public penance, 16–17, 34, 36, 92–3, 108–21, 139–41, 150; recensions of, 131; users of, 128–31. *See also* Bamberg, Staatsbibliothek, Cods Lit 50, 53, 54, 55, 59; Cambridge, Corpus Christi College, MSS 163, 265; London, BL, MS Add. 17004, MS Cotton Tiberius C. i; MS Cotton Vitellius E. xii; Lucca, Biblioteca capitolare, Cod. 607; Monte Cassino, Abbey Library, Cod. 451; Munich, Bayerische Staatsbibliothek, Clms 3909, 6425; Oxford, Bodl. Lib., MS Bodley 579; Paris, Bibliotheque nationale, MSS lat. 820, 1231; Pistoia, Biblioteca capitolare, Cod. 141; Rome, Biblioteca Vallicelliana Cod. D. 5; Wolfenbüttel, Herzog-August-Bibliothek, Cod. Guelf. 15 Weissenburg, 141 Helmstadt, 493
Rome: appeal for papal pardon of penitents, 61; Council of (999), 1, 8
Rome, Biblioteca Vallicelliana:
Cod. B. 58, 49, 51 n. 1, 167–70
Cod. C. 6, 49
Cod. D. 5, 134 n. 157, 214–15
Cod. E. 62, 48 n. 119
Cod. F. 92, 49

Romuald, St, 98, 175–7, 190 n. 81
royal penance, 6–7, 174–82
Rudolf, bishop of Senlis, trial of, 186
rule of Augustine, *see* Augustine, rule of
rule of Benedict, *see* Benedict, rule of
rule of Chrodegang, *see* Chrodegang of Metz, rule
Ruotger, archbishop of Trier, 58–60, 63; *capitula* of, 59, 68–70, 208
rural churches, 51–3

sacramentary, *see* Gelasian, mixed Gregorian-Gelasian, Fulda, Saint-Amand, Saint Emmeram
Saint Alban, Mainz, 129–30
Saint-Amand, sacramentaries, 137
Saint Emmeram, Regensburg: customary of, 89; sacramentary of, 134
Saint Michael's monastery, Luneburg, 130
Sainte Foy, miracles of, 204
Salzburg, liturgy in the province of, 128–9, 131, 135, 211–12. *See also* Munich, Bayerische Staatsbibliothek, Clm 6425 (Freising pontifical)
satisfaction, 15, 56, 83–4, 90, 161–2
scandala, 7, 9
schools, 66; cathedral, 32, 43–4, 50; external, 78 n. 10, 98, 147
Sedulius Scottus, 177, 191
Seligenstadt, Council of (1023), 42 n. 91, 61–2
sermons, synodal, 63–7. See also *Admonitio synodalis*
sexual sins, 147, 196–201. *See also* incest
Smaragdus, 83–4, 88, 92
Soissons, penitential ordinance of, 71 n. 125, 193–4
staff, see *baculum*
superstitions, 40, 204
synods: diocesan, 69, 115; *ordines* for holding of, 55, 66. *See also* councils, sermons, synodal

Theodore, archbishop of Canterbury, penitential of, 28, 39
Theodosius, emperor, penance of, 174, 177
Theodulf of Orleans, *capitula*, 5, 39, 47, 64, 71–2
theology, of penance, 15, 161–2, 166
Thietmar of Merseburg, 165, 182, 190, 199, 204–5
Tribur, Council of (895), 30
Trier, Council of (927x8), 5, 58–60, 62–3,

# INDEX

69, 204; penitential practice in, 19, 35–6, 60, 70, 131; province of, 131–2, 212. *See also* Fulda–Trier monastic customary, Ruotger of Trier
Trosly, Council of (909), 55–6, 58, 62, 71

Udalrich, bishop of Augsburg, 66
Udine, Biblioteca capitolare, MS 1, 19 n. 86, 134 n. 159, 137 n. 3, 138 n. 8, 149
Ulrich of Cluny, *Antiquiores consuetudines Cluniacensis monasterii*, 89–91

Vatican City, BAV:
    Archivio S. Pietro, H. 58, 49, 52 n. 4, 172 n. 182
    MS Reg. lat. 418, 62 n. 68, 71 n. 126
    MS Vat. lat. 1355, 35 n. 49, 41 n. 83
    MS Vat. lat. 3548, 137 n. 3, 138, 143–6
    MS Vat. lat. 4772, 133 n. 156, 166–70
    MS Vat. lat. 4880, 35 n. 49
    MS Vat. lat. 7790, 35 n. 49
'Venite, venite', 119, 155
Vercelli, Biblioteca capitolare, Cod. 181, 137 n. 3, 138 n. 8, 149
Vercelli, bishops of, 1; sacramentary of, 134. *See also* Atto of Vercelli
Verden, diocese of, 151; pontifical of, *see* Wolfenbüttel, Herzog-August-Bibliothek, Cod. Guelf. 141 Helmstadt

Verdun, diocese of, 165
vernacular, use of for confession, 126, 144–5, 147–8, 202
Verona, Synod of (966), 63–5. *See also* Rather of Verona
vices and virtues, 41, 70, 110–12
Vogel, Cyrille, 5, 11–12, 16, 18, 34, 112, 115–16, 131, 133, 211, 214

war, 190–6
weeping, 40, 59, 110, 139
William, archbishop of Mainz, 131, 137
Willigis, archbishop of Mainz, 132, 137
Wolfenbüttel, Herzog-August-Bibliothek, Cod. Guelf.:
    15 Weissenburg, 116–17, 135 n. 164, 216 nn. 30, 38
    141 Helmstadt, 93 n. 96, 114 n. 54, 130 n. 137, 135 n. 164
    451 Helmstadt, 30 n. 26
    493 Helmstadt, 111 n. 36, 126 n. 123, 135 n. 163
Worms, *see* Burchard of Worms, schools
Wulfstan I, bishop of Worcester, *see* Cambridge, Corpus Christi College, MS 265

www.ingramcontent.com/pod-product-compliance
Lightning Source LLC
Chambersburg PA
CBHW071241230426
43668CB00011B/1528